Empirical Models and Policy-Making: Interaction and Institutions

- How are scientific models used in the policy domain?
- What factors determine the successful interaction between scientists and policy makers?
- How does the process of interaction work?

Empirical Models and Policy-Making: Interaction and Institutions challenges the usual assumption that when economic policy makers use economic models there is a one-way flow of information from the models to the policy analysis. In practice, as we learn from this book, the requirements and questions of policy makers play an important role in the development and revision of those very models. These articles, written by highly-placed practitioners and academic economists, explore how the interaction between modellers and policy makers and their institutional arrangements all contribute to the potential successful use of economic models in policy making. The range of cases and detail of circumstances covered, and the depth of insight from these analyses, combine to provide a convincing portrait of this hitherto hidden realm.

Professionals and students of economics, econometrics, policy-making and science studies will benefit greatly from this revealing, ground-breaking book.

Frank A. G. den Butter is Professor of Economics at the Free University, Amsterdam and Member of the Scientific Council for Government Policy, The Hague. **Mary S. Morgan** is Professor of History of Economics at the London School of Economics and Professor of History and Philosophy of Economics at the University of Amsterdam.

Empirical Models and Policy-Making: Interaction and Institutions

Edited by
Frank A. G. den Butter and
Mary S. Morgan

London and New York

First published 2000
by Routledge
11 New Fetter Lane, London EC4P 4EE

Simultaneously published in the USA and Canada
by Routledge
29 West 35th Street, New York, NY 10001

Routledge is an imprint of the Taylor & Francis Group

© 2000 selection and editorial matter Frank A. G. den Butter and
Mary S. Morgan; individual chapters © 2000 the contributors

Typeset in Garamond by Wearset, Boldon, Tyne and Wear
Printed and bound in Great Britain by Biddles Ltd, Guildford and
King's Lynn

British Library Cataloguing in Publication Data
A catalogue record for this book is available from the British
Library

Library of Congress Cataloging in Publication Data
Empirical models and policy-making: interaction and
institutions/[edited by] Frank A. G. den Butter & Mary S. Morgan.
   p. cm.
   1. Economic policy – Empirical models. I. Butter, F. A. G. den.
II. Morgan, Mary S.
HD87 .E47 2000
338.9–dc21

00–024810

ISBN 0-415-23217-1 (hbk)
ISBN 0-415-23605-3 (pbk)

Contents

List of illustrations   viii
Notes on contributors   ix
Preface   xiv
Acknowledgements   xvii

PART I
The Tinbergen tradition   I

1   The relevance of economic modelling for policy decisions   3
    G. ZALM

2   CPB models and employment policy in the Netherlands   10
    J. H. M. DONDERS AND J. J. GRAAFLAND

3   Models and macroeconomic policy in the Netherlands   26
    P. A. G. VAN BERGEIJK AND J. VAN SINDEREN

4   The IMF monetary model at 40   39
    J. J. POLAK

PART II
The variety of experience   55

5   Macroeconomic models and policy-making at the Bank of Canada   57
    P. DUGUAY AND D. LONGWORTH

6   Policy-making and model development: the case of the
    Nederlandsche Bank's model MORKMON   76
    P. J. A. VAN ELS

7   Transparency and accountability: empirical models and policy-
    making at the Reserve Bank of New Zealand   93
    D. G. MAYES AND W. A. RAZZAK

PART III
Model products and model usage   III

8   Modeling the World Economic Outlook at the IMF: a historical review   113
    J. M. BOUGHTON

9   Policy design and evaluation: EU structural funds and cohesion in the
    European periphery   129
    J. BRADLEY

10 Interaction between model builders and policy makers in the Norwegian
    tradition   146
    O. BJERKHOLT

11 Conflicts between macroeconomic forecasting and policy analysis   169
    S. WREN-LEWIS

PART IV
The interaction process and institutional
arrangements   185

12 US monetary policy and econometric modeling: tales from the FOMC
    transcripts 1984–1991   187
    H. J. EDISON AND J. MARQUEZ

13 Economic models and economic policy: what economic forecasters
    can do for government   206
    R. J. EVANS

14 The Troika process, economic models and macroeconomic policy
    in the USA   229
    M. R. DONIHUE AND J. KITCHEN

15 Emergent policy-making with macroeconometric models   244
    R. SMITH

PART V
Empirical models and policy-making   **257**

16 The relevance of economic modelling for policy-making: a panel
    discussion   259
    Edited by M. S. MORGAN
    Chairman: R. F. M. Lubbers
    Members: L. M. Lynch; E. Malinvaud; F. J. H. Don

17 What makes the models–policy interaction successful? 279
    F. A. G. DEN BUTTER AND M. S. MORGAN

    Index   313

List of illustrations

3.1	Value chain	28
3.2	Dutch empirical studies on the functioning of markets (1987–97)	33
6.1	Interest rate transmission to MORKMON	78
7.1	Developments in MCI thinking	100
9.1	CSF impacts of investment in basic infrastructure	134
9.2	CSF long-term benefits: exogenous process	135
9.3	CSF long-term benefits: endogenous process	135
9.4	Model-based CSF evaluation: main causal links	137
12.1	Material from the FOMC, December 1989	194
12.2	Material from the FOMC, February 1991	198
12.3	Material from the FOMC, July 1991	200
13.1	Members of Panel of Forecasters and their Relationship to Government	210

Notes on contributors

Peter A. G. van Bergeijk
Peter A. G. van Bergeijk is presently at UBS Group Economic Research in Zurich, Switzerland. He is Professor of Economic Policy at the Research Centre for Economic Policy (OCFEB) at Erasmus University Rotterdam, The Netherlands. Van Bergeijk's hands-on experience as a model builder and model user derives from his work at the Netherlands Economic Policy Directorate and De Nederlandsche Bank (the Dutch Central Bank).

Olav Bjerkholt
Olav Bjerkholt is Professor of Economics at the University of Oslo, Department of Economics. He was formerly Head of the Research Department of Statistics Norway from 1984 to 1996. He edited a two-volume edition of Ragnar Frisch's essays in 1995 and is now working on a biography of Ragnar Frisch.

John Bradley
John Bradley is a Research Professor at the Economic and Social Research Institute (ESRI) in Ireland. He specializes in analysis of the implications of EU Structural Funds, the Single Market and EMU for the smaller economies of the European periphery.

James M. Boughton
James M. Boughton, historian of the IMF, is the author of *Silent Revolution: The International Monetary Fund, 1979–1989*. He has a PhD from Duke University and was formerly an economist at the OECD and Professor of Economics at Indiana University.

Frank A. G. den Butter
Frank den Butter is Professor of Economics at the Free University, Amsterdam and Member of the Scientific Council for Government Policy, The Hague; founder and head of the Applied Labour Economics Research Team (ALERT) at the Free University; former director of the Tinbergen Institute and Chairman of the Royal Netherlands Economic Association.

F. J. H. Don

Henk Don (born 1954) studied econometrics at the University of Amsterdam. In 1994 he was appointed as Director of CPB Netherlands Bureau of Economic Policy Analysis. In that capacity, he is a member of the Dutch Social and Economic Council, of the Central Economic Committee, and of the cabinet Council for Economic Affairs. From 1991–99 he held a part-time chair in applied economics at the University of Amsterdam.

Jan H. M. Donders

Jan Donders (born 1955) is head of the Cyclical Analysis Division of the CPB Netherlands Bureau for Economic Policy Analysis. His PhD thesis (1993) discusses what possible government measures and/or changes in pay-determining institutions could help to improve the working of the labour market.

Michael R. Donihue

Michael Donihue is an Associate Professor of Economics at Colby College. His research specializes in macroeconomic modelling and the use of structural models in the analysis of policy issues. He served as Senior Economist for Macroeconomics and Forecasting at the Council of Economic Advisers during 1994 and 1995.

Pierre Duguay

Pierre Duguay is adviser to the Governing Council of the Bank of Canada. He started at the Bank in 1973, where he was an early user of the RDX2 model. He has successively headed the Department of Monetary and Financial Analysis and the Research Department.

Hali J. Edison

Hali Edison is senior economist in the Division of International Finance at the Board of Governors of the Federal Reserve System. She previously served as special adviser to Undersecretary of International Affairs at the US Treasury Department and consultant to the research department at the Norwegian Central Bank.

Peter J. A. van Els

Peter J. A. van Els graduated from Tilburg University in 1986 and received his PhD from the University of Amsterdam in 1995. He joined De Nederlandsche Bank (the Dutch Central Bank) in 1986, and has been closely involved in model-building and model use activities. As from 1992, Van Els is an assistant manager in the Bank's Econometric Research and Special Studies Department. He has published various articles on macroeconomic and monetary modelling in international journals.

Robert Evans

Robert Evans is lecturer in the sociology of science and technology at the Cardiff School of Social Sciences, Cardiff University. His research focuses on the use of science and other forms of expertise in economic and environmental policy-making. He has published in journals such as *Social Studies of Science, Science, Technology and Human Values* and *Science in Context*. A monograph based on his PhD thesis, *Macroeconomic Forecasting: A Sociological Appraisal* was published by Routledge in 1999.

Johan J. Graafland

Johan Graafland (born 1960) is with the CPB Netherlands Bureau for Economic Policy Analysis. His PhD thesis (1990) discusses the relevance of hysteresis in unemployment in the Netherlands. At present he is Head of CPB's AGE Models Division which investigates the impact of tax and social security policies on the Dutch labour market.

John Kitchen

John Kitchen is an economist in the Office of Economic Policy, US Department of the Treasury. He was Senior Economist for Macroeconomics and Forecasting at the Council of Economic Advisers from 1991–93. He currently represents the Department of Treasury as a T-3 member of the Troika.

David Longworth

David Longworth is Chief of the Research Department of the Bank of Canada. He started at the Bank in 1974, where he worked on the properties of the RDX2 model. He has held senior positions in the International Department and the Department of Monetary and Financial Analysis.

Ruud F. M. Lubbers

Prof. Ruud F. M. Lubbers, former Dutch Prime Minister, is currently professor of 'Globalization', and chair of Globus, the expert-centre for globalization and sustainable development at Tilburg University, The Netherlands. He is also visiting professor at the John F. Kennedy School of Government at Harvard University, USA and has recently been appointed as international chairman of the World Wildlife Fund.

Born in Rotterdam and a graduate of the Netherlands School of Economics, Lubbers' political career began in 1973 when he became Minister for Economic Affairs. In 1977 he continued in Parliament as Senior Deputy Leader, and later Parliamentary Leader, of the Christian Democratic Alliance. In November 1982 Lubbers was elected Prime Minister for the first time. During that period he was the key figure in introducing the 'Dutch Model' which led to the successful turn-around of the Dutch economy. Prof. Lubbers led three successive governments through to August 1994.

Lisa M. Lynch

Lisa M. Lynch is the William L. Clayton Professor of International Economic Affairs at the Fletcher School of Law and Diplomacy at Tufts University, Co-Editor of the *Journal of Labor Economics* and former Chief Economist, US Department of Labor.

Edmond Malinvaud

Edmond Malinvaud, born in 1923, had his main career at INSEE, but served as Directeur de la Prévision of the Finance Ministry in 1972 to 1974. He was a member of various committees in charge of policy advice. His academic research has become geared more and more exclusively to macroeconomics.

Jaime Marquez

Jaime Marquez is senior economist in the Division of International Finance at the Board of Governors of the Federal Reserve System.

David G. Mayes

David G. Mayes is Adviser to the Board of the Bank of Finland and Professor of Economics at South Bank University in London. He was previously Chief Economist and a member of the Monetary Policy Committee at the Reserve Bank of New Zealand.

Mary S. Morgan

Mary Morgan is Professor of the History of Economics at the London School of Economics and Professor of the History and Methodology of Economics at the University of Amsterdam. She maintains a long-standing research interest in the history of econometrics; more recent work focuses on the use of econometric and mathematical models in modern economics.

Jacques J. Polak

Jacques J. Polak (PhD Econ, University of Amsterdam, 1937) assisted Tinbergen's building of an econometric model of the US economy at the League of Nations (1937–39). He worked at the IMF from 1947–86, as the Director of the Research Department from 1958 to 1979 and as a member of the Executive Board thereafter.

Weshah A. Razzak

Weshah Razzak is Economic Adviser at the Reserve Bank of New Zealand. Previously at the University of North Carolina, he has published widely on macroeconomics, monetary policy and international finance.

Jarig van Sinderen

Jarig van Sinderen is Director General Policy Co-ordination of Industry and Services at the Netherlands Ministry of Economic Affairs in The Hague and Professor of Economics at Erasmus University, Rotterdam. Van Sinderen is an expert on economic modelling and on policy issues such as taxation and environmental policy. His supply side oriented MESEM model, which was built at the Ministry of

Economic Affairs, was used in the 1980s and 1990s for policy preparation. This model is still one of the cornerstones of the economic and scientific underpinning of the Dutch 'Polder-model'.

Ron Smith

Ron Smith is Professor of Applied Economics at Birkbeck College, London University and was a member of the Economic and Social Research Council's Macroeconomic Modelling Consortium, which funded UK macro-modelling until 1999.

Simon Wren-Lewis

Simon Wren-Lewis is currently Professor of Economics at the University of Exeter, UK. As well as earlier academic posts, he has also worked for many years in HM Treasury in the UK, and as head of macroeconomic research at the National Institute of Economic and Social Research in London.

Gerrit Zalm

Gerrit Zalm has been Minister of Finance in the Netherlands since 1994 and was former Director of CPB Netherlands Bureau for Economic Policy Analysis and Professor of Economic Policy at the Free University, Amsterdam; previously he held various positions at the Ministry of Economic Affairs and at the Ministry of Finance.

Preface

It is generally assumed that, when economic policy makers use economic models, the information flow is only one way: outputs flow from the models into the policy analysis. Yet, in practice, the requirements and questions of policy makers play an important role in the development and revision of economic models. How does this interaction between modellers and policy makers work? This research question can most easily be understood by re-interpreting it as a series of more specific questions along the following lines. How does the interaction work? What factors does successful interaction depend upon? What problems does interaction cause? What roles do different professional groups play in the interaction? How do the institutional or contractual arrangements of modellers and policy makers affect the process? What are the trade-offs between models designed for a specific purpose and models held to answer several questions in a general policy field? Do the arguments of model exercises really contribute to a consensus on the policy measures or are they just used as an alibi? Do the policy makers try to 'change' the calculations from the models? How is the plausibility of the policy advice from the models judged? What strategies do the modellers follow to make their work relevant for policy makers? What insights can social scientists offer on the process of interaction between modellers and policy makers? Exploring such questions as these, and a desire to seek answers to them, provided the motivation for the research and analyses of this volume.

This two-way interaction between economic models and policy-making, between modellers and policy makers, is almost certainly widespread and recognized by those participating in empirical modelling for policy work, but has been subject to very little systematic research and analysis. There is a paucity of published material on the topic, no doubt because research into the interaction faces an obvious problem, namely one of evidence. There is both a lack of evidence in the public domain and the nature of the evidence needed to provide material for analysis is inherently non-systematic. Although we can recognize the importance of institutional arrangements and can categorize these, this only takes us so far. The interaction process is a human one of day-to-day contacts, as much as being one of documents, so that much of the exchange of information we seek to understand is tied up in experience and embedded in the tacit knowledge of the participants. This being the case, we believed the most effective way to gain access to this experience was to invite contributions on the research topic from those practitioners involved in interactions. By encouraging participants in the interaction process to write detailed case studies especially focused on their own experience, we could hope to make explicit some of their tacit knowledge, and from this, to begin to understand and even outline an analysis of the elements involved in the process of interaction. Thus the authors of the articles in this book are mainly practitioner economists inside government and international agencies and 'academic' economists and statisticians with experience in the field; we include also a few contributions from those with a professional 'outside' interest in these questions, namely from the history and sociology of economics.

This book represents, also, the outcome of the 10th Anniversary Conference of the Tinbergen Institute, a highly appropriate venue for the examination of our research themes. The 'Tinbergen legacy' to Dutch economics involves a commitment to economic expertise instantiated in empirical models and put to use in the public service. Tinbergen himself was both the originator of empirical macroeconometric modelling and founder of the Dutch Central Planning Bureau, while the Dutch use of macroeconometric modelling is known internationally, not only for its historical precedence, but also as paradigmatic for the use of empirical models in the policy process. The conference involved a two-day workshop of intensive discussion of the research issues followed by an open conference day culminating in a panel discussion. Paper givers had written their contributions especially to address the research questions, and panel members, like paper givers, drew on their experience of the model-policy interaction to help us understand the interaction process.

Most of the essays in this book are detailed case studies of particular interactions between empirical models and policy-making and they cover a considerable range of experience. One example is given by the simple monetary and balance of payments model that has been instrumental during a period of 40 years in the design of the structural adjustment programmes of the IMF. The various ways that modellers and policy makers interact inside central banks provides a series of further examples. The definition of 'empirical models' is broad. The guiding principle is that the models give a quantitative assessment of policy measures in the form of impulse-response effects or scenario analysis and that they have been 'used' in some way in policy-making. It is part of the strength of these essays that they provide detailed information about particular instances. But none are mere descriptions – all the authors analyse their material to seek answers to the research questions. Taken together, the materials of this book help us to build up a picture of how such interactions work and contribute to a more general appreciation and understanding of the process involved.

One of the features of the research material available here is the richness of the discussion of each case. Each case study essay touches on many different aspects of the models-policy interaction and the nature of institutional arrangements, addressing several questions during their close examination of a chosen experience. This made it difficult to organize an order for the volume, as the essays could have been arranged in many different ways, and the content and interest of each chapter goes beyond that indicated in its section heading. We begin with some chapters especially defined as part of the Tinbergen legacy; the next set of chapters gives a feeling for the range of experience of institutions and interaction. Essays in the third section of the book deal more particularly with model products and how they are used, while the fourth section includes specific cases where institutional arrangements are discussed in terms of their outcomes for interaction. The final section brings together the general research themes both in the panel discussion and in the editors' attempts to understand the implications of all the case material and draw some conclusions about the nature and process of the empirical models – policy-making interaction. A selection of the chapters were previously published in a special issue of the journal *Economic Modelling*. Here we are able to publish together the full set of papers and the panel discussion.

Acknowledgements

We gratefully acknowledge the help of many people and organizations in helping us to realize our ambition to explore how empirical models and policy-making interact in practice.

First, we thank those who made the Tinbergen Institute 10th Year Anniversary Conference possible. We are grateful to the Ministry of Economic Affairs and the Ministry of Social Affairs and Employment in the Netherlands, the CPB Netherlands Bureau for Economic Policy Analysis and De Nederlandsche Bank NV for their financial support. We thank the Tinbergen Institute and its directors for providing intellectual and financial backing for the initiative. A more personal thanks go to Elfie Bonke, Irene Kluin, Edwin van Gameren and Udo Kock for help in arranging the conference and for organizing and transcribing the tapes of the panel discussion and to Philip Epstein for helping with this volume.

Second, we thank all the participants at the Tinbergen Institute Conference. We are aware our research questions were somewhat unusual and that we needed the participation of practitioner modellers from the policy domain to make the conference and this volume viable. We are most grateful that authors were prepared to write papers especially on the conference topic and we appreciate their continued commitment to the research questions in their willingness to revise and improve their chapters to take advantage of insights gained from the conference. (In this respect, we appreciate the contribution that participants, particularly Eilev Jansen, Anton Barten, Edmond Malinvaud and Piet Rietveld, made in refereeing the original papers for publication.) The conference discussions were most stimulating and critical to us as editors in understanding the general issues involved in the interaction of empirical models and policy-making. They were particularly important because most aspects of the use of models or interaction with policy-making are not normally subject to public discussion and open analysis: the nature of interactions is usually largely tacit and unreported. We are grateful to all participants at the conference in sharing their experience with us. We wish to mention expressly the contributions of Ralph Bryant and Kenneth Wallis who took part in the workshop and contributed substantially to the public day. Their perceptive questions helped the group to extend their thinking and their commentaries were insightful and fruitful for all our thinking about the topic.

Finally, we thank Elsevier for permission to reprint (with some minor revisions) those of the chapters in this volume which first appeared in a special issue of *Economic Modelling*, Volume 15:3 in 1998.

Part I

The Tinbergen tradition

Chapter 1

The relevance of economic modelling for policy decisions*

G. Zalm

The development of macroeconometric models is influenced by policy makers and vice versa. In this chapter the situation in this field in the Netherlands is sketched. The CPB National Bureau for Economic Policy Analysis plays a special role. While in other countries various institutes and ministries evaluate economic policy and prepare forecasts, in the Netherlands these functions are concentrated within the CPB. This approach holds some (scale) advantages, which should be used to make progress in the evaluation of new problems with which policy makers are confronted.

JEL classifications: A11, C5

1. Introduction

The information flow between economic policy makers and economic model builders is not a one-way flow. The requirements and questions of policy makers play an important role in the development of economic models. It is not only the information that flows, but also people who flow. I have crossed the bridge between empirical modelling and policy-making several times, so I can touch upon my own experience with respect to the interaction between macroeconometric modelling and policy-making.

First, I will sketch briefly the major economic problems of the twentieth century and their influence on macroeconomic modelling. It is interesting to notice that economic problems, such as the oil crises, the deterioration of public finance and long-term unemployment have led to fundamental changes in macroeconometric models. Second, I describe the use of macroeconometric models for policy evaluation. In the Netherlands, policy makers have relied heavily upon macroeconometric models. Third, I will talk about the influence of forecasts in the process of policy-making and fiscal policy. Finally, I give some suggestions for future research.

Reprinted from Economic Modelling, 15, G. Zalm, 'The relevance of economic modelling for policy decisions', pp. 309–16, Copyright (1998), with permission from Elsevier Science.

2. The importance of modelling for policy evaluation

2.1. Using models for policy evaluation

The most well-known disruptive economic problem in the twentieth century was the Great Depression. In the 1930s Western economies experienced massive unemployment and greatly reduced incomes. In the year 1935, in the Netherlands more than 10 per cent of the working population was unemployed, and real GDP was 25 per cent below its 1930 level. From the start of the Depression a theory, a model or a structure was needed, to offer possibilities that could reduce the economic hardship so many people faced. Confronted with the question of developing policy instruments to reduce these economic problems, Tinbergen (1936) developed the first macroeconometric model of the Dutch economy in 1936. Later he also prepared macroeconometric models for the US and UK economies. The efforts of Klein (1950) and Stone and Stone (1939) followed Tinbergen's model. After the Second World War, these Keynesian models increased in scale. The advances made in computer technology and better economic statistics improved the scope for developing models in this tradition.

However, in the 1970s, the inadequacy of these Keynesian models to deal with the large structural changes linked to the oil crises shook the trust of policy makers in these models. The increase in oil prices lead to double-digit inflation and rising unemployment and that clearly shook the confidence of the belief in the traditional Keynesian trade-off between inflation and unemployment. In a critical evaluation of the existing type of modelling, Lucas (1976) argued that conventional macroeconometric large-scale models were fatally flawed and were not useful for the policy debate. Economists and policy makers turned their heads to the supply side. It was realized that structures that were developed were far from ideal and blocked a continuation of a high growth path. Gradually, also by model builders, more emphasis was put on endogenizing the supply side of the economy. For example, it was demonstrated that a rise in real wages exceeding the rate of technical progress would increase unemployment. In the Netherlands this model extension has been very important for the acceptance of the policy of wage restraint (e.g. Den Butter, 1991).

In the 1980s, the structural problems had been worsened by the deterioration of public finance. In Western Europe this had been caused by the inability to trim the welfare state. In the Netherlands the deficit rose from almost zero in the beginning of the 1970s to almost 9 per cent of GDP in 1983. In the United States the combination of a policy of cutting taxes and increasing public spending was responsible for the rise in the budget deficit in the beginning of the 1980s. Moreover, this combination of a loose fiscal policy with a tight monetary policy to fight inflation led to a rise in the interest rate and the dollar. To deal with these problems, new macroeconometric models with a fully-fledged description of monetary sectors with an endogenous portfolio behaviour of the private and banking sectors were developed. These so-called monetary blocks have not always been successful. Although Ministers of Finance in a lot of countries were quite successful in bringing budget deficits down, they got little support from model builders. Nevertheless, almost all economists will agree that the future of the Dutch economy is better off with the present budget deficit than with the deficit of 1983.

Currently, the economy is in a better shape than in the 1980s. However, we still face some serious economic problems. One of the most severe problems is the duration of long-term unemployment, especially amongst low-skilled workers. As is typically the case in Europe today, the Dutch unemployment rate in this area is more than double the overall rate. The functioning of the labour market in its connection with the social security system is held responsible for this large share. Therefore a model with a detailed description of the tax system and the various labour-market institutions was required and the applied general equilibrium framework seemed appropriate.

Despite its incapability to predict large economic shocks or to deduce the structural flaws of the economy, the use of macroeconometric models in policy design is quite common and largely undisputed. Especially in the Netherlands, we have a very long tradition of relying upon technical expertise from macroeconometric models as a guide in macroeconomic policy formation. In 1936 the publication of the first macroeconometric model by Tinbergen (1936) was accompanied by the simulation of several policies and the effect on employment and the current account. In the post-war period different generations of this model have played a role in policy evaluation.

By experience, the idea that there should be one model for all problems has been abandoned. Instead, a large variety of economic models has been developed to cope with the broad range of different policy questions. This is a very natural development that Tinbergen certainly would have appreciated. A physicist by origin, in his early days nuclear scientists were looking for one model for the atomic nucleus. Nowadays, there are many models describing different aspects of the atomic nucleus. Economic science shows a similar development. At the CPB National Bureau for Economic Policy Analysis different models are used for different purposes. Donders and Graafland (1998, Chapter 2 in this volume) give a historical overview of (macroeconometric) model development at the CPB.

2.2. Fiscal policy and policy evaluation

In the use of macroeconometric models for policy evaluation, simulations to assess the effect of fiscal policy have been very important. Keynesian models have been focusing on the level of government expenditures and taxation. The so-called conjunctural–structural models have been used to investigate the impact of different tax rates on wages and, nowadays, detailed tax proposals are discussed with the help of a model.

At several points in time, macroeconometric models have been used intensively to investigate the effect of a particular policy under consideration. There are many examples to give. In 1992, the report of the committee for green taxes, the so-called

Wolfson committee, was guided by a thorough investigation of the employment effects of a shift between labour and green taxes and the impact on the competitive structure of industries. Similar efforts have been made with the Quest-model of the European Commission and the Green-model of the OECD.

Sometimes an outcome of a model creates its own policy rhetoric. In 1992, the CPB published an applied general equilibrium model, called MIMIC (Gelauff and Graafland, 1994). One of the doubtful outcomes was that a progressive tax system encourages employment. It even led to suggestions for a 'Robin-Hood' policy of raising the tax rate of the last bracket and lowering the tax rate of the first bracket. However, in these applied general equilibrium models, it is very hard to model the consequences of a more progressive tax system on training, work intensity and the desire for promotion and, therefore, the adverse effects of a progressive tax system can be underestimated. The model does not seem adequate for analysing such questions. Fortunately, policy makers base their judgements on more than the outcome of a single model.

2.3. The Dutch case of models and policy analysis

The institutional setting in the Netherlands differs from that in other countries. A central role has been laid down by law for the CPB, which is an independent organization within the Ministry of Economic Affairs. The CPB has the obligation to prepare every year a Spring forecast, the so-called Central Economic Plan. Since its founding, the CPB has expanded its tasks and nowadays it also puts a lot of time into policy analysis.

In the Netherlands, models, especially those from the CPB, have played an important role in policy analysis. As I have worked both with the Ministry of Economic Affairs and the CPB, I will shortly comment on the special relationship between the two as far as model-based policy analysis is concerned. At some Ministries, and at the Ministry of Economic Affairs in particular, own models were developed in reaction to the view that adjustments in CPB models to new circumstances were, in certain cases, slower than policy makers would like. This has not much to do with laziness or the monopoly position but with the high standards of the CPB. Models developed at Ministries, I know from experience, can be quickly fixed if and when it serves the policy objectives of the ministry. So, at the Ministry of Economic Affairs a number of model exercises have been conducted, and as a director of the department doing those exercises I have always supported it. However, I have never seen results published from the research at the Ministry of Economic Affairs which gave ammunition to the Ministry of Social Affairs or the Ministry of Finance in case of conflicting interest.

Besides, if the Ministry of Social Affairs or Finance were to develop their own models, the Ministry of Economic Affairs would rather rely on the CPB than on the models of the other ministries. This does not mean that the CPB work is beyond criticism and the government policies should only be based on it. The CPB has been criticized by independent sceptics, but also by economists at the various ministries.

The chapter of Donders and Graafland (1998, Chapter 2 in this volume) shows that important developments have occurred in the work of the CPB while, at the same time, there is a clear consensus of the limitations of models. Therefore I wholeheartedly agree with the new stress on international comparative and qualitative institutional studies. The role of the CPB as the economic conscience for government policy should not be overstated. Nevertheless, I just hope that the balance between international and scientific reputation on the one hand, and policy relevance on the other hand, will be kept, and that Tinbergen's idea about mission will continue to lead us. There is no use in reputation if it is not useful for improving policies.

2.4. Forecasting and policy-making

In the process of policy-making the forecasts of a macroeconometric model are still of relevance, although, as I explain later, its relevance in our country has decreased as the CPB always wanted. In the Netherlands, the yearly Budget Memorandum in September is accompanied by the yearly forecast of the CPB – the so-called Macro Economic Outlook – and the Memorandum is based on these insights. Technical information from other agencies such as the Ministry of Finance or the Ministry of Social Affairs are taken into account in order to come to a forecast. In addition, the Nyenrode Forum for Economic Research publishes their forecast, but until now the differences were rather small. The same holds for the secret shadow forecasts of the Central Bank.

In other countries a number of different organizations or independent research institutes publish annual forecasts. For example, there are seven different competing economic forecasts in the United Kingdom (e.g. Whitley, 1994). It should be noticed that the key features of these models differ substantially. In Germany, five institutes are engaged in forecasting, leading to a cry for a consensus forecast.

There has been a controversy about the usefulness of forecasting in the policy debate. Some economists argue that they do not have any faith in the forecasts of macroeconometric models (e.g. Gordon, 1984). In his Tinbergen lecture, however, Klein claims that in most cases during recent decades the forecast performance of macroeconometric models has been improved considerably and compared with their alternatives, such as naive models, time-series analysis, or judgemental forecasts, they do reasonably well (e.g. Klein, 1988). Nevertheless, forecasts should be treated with caution. Point estimates of important variables such as percentage change in GDP and unemployment are always surrounded by rather large confidence or prediction intervals.

Don (1993) argues that there are several sources of unpredictability due to uncertainty in policy and non-policy exogenous variables and mis-specification in the model. Especially for a small open economy as the Netherlands, the short-term forecasts are highly conditional on international developments and to a lesser degree on domestic policy measures (Van den Berg, 1986). One of the possibilities for dealing with uncertainty about the exogenous environment is to present forecasts in different scenarios, for example with respect to the guilder/dollar exchange rate or the growth of world trade.

To illustrate the changing role of forecasting, a few words on Dutch fiscal policy. In the 1960s, fiscal policy was seen as an instrument for stabilizing the economy. In practice, this so-called structural fiscal policy consisted of two parts. First, the acceptable budget deficit was calculated for a cyclically neutral base year. Second, given this net amount of borrowing, the yearly additional budgetary resources were defined as the trend growth of tax revenues. The calculation of these additional budgetary resources required forecasts about trend GDP and trend tax elasticities.

After the recession of the mid-1970s, there was a tendency to overestimate trend GDP and public finances deteriorated. A major change in fiscal policy was unavoidable. Fiscal policy was concentrated on following a yearly rule to lower the budget deficit. Accordingly, economic forecasts became even more important. Every change in economic forecasts influenced the ex ante deficit and led to a fiscal reaction in order to re-establish the deficit target. It is clear that such an approach is unsatisfactory and could sometimes work pro-cyclically.

Therefore, in 1994, the present coalition announced a new type of fiscal policy: the so-called trend-based fiscal policy, where the budget deficit may change in order to absorb non-structural deviations in revenue. To create room for cutting the deficit and tax cuts, the central government has set ceilings for real expenditures from 1995 to 1998. Economic forecasts derived from a cautious scenario were used for calculating the budgetary resources for the government period. Hereby, the need for repeated adjustments of the budget due to changing economic conditions is reduced. So, fiscal policy nowadays takes into account the downward risks of economic forecasts much more. The life of a Minister of Finance has become easier, as have the lives of his colleagues.

3. Macroeconometric modelling in the twenty-first century

If we look back at more than half a century since Tinbergen published his first macroeconometric model, the widespread applications and the usefulness of models for policy-making seem an achievement to me. A good example for the Netherlands is that political parties also rely heavily on the scenarios and the effects of changed policies as calculated by the CPB. This leads to an unusual discipline in political programmes as well as to the comparability of the different programmes. It is impossible to get away with grand promises that are impossible to realize.

For model builders, there are still many avenues to explore. First, the modelling of market behaviour is still rudimentary. More emphasis should be put on imperfections in financial and goods markets. Hereby, one could perhaps rely more on the appealing results of the industrial organization literature. In order to assess behavioural responses to government policies, the focus should be changed from a macroeconomic orientation towards a microeconomic orientation. Second, many current policies and policy proposals are aimed at improving the basic technological and ecological infrastructure of the economy. Therefore, it seems challenging to model the driving forces behind the process of economic development, such as infrastructure and technology, and I encourage the current efforts. For these issues the insights from the endogenous growth literature can be useful. Third, the effects of the ageing population in the years to come should be analysed in more detail in long-term models. Fourth, given the overwhelming problem of long-term unemployment, the efforts should be continued on modelling the effects of the welfare state and the institutions on the labour market. Finally, I could mention the problems of debts and deficits. But if I was a director of the CPB I would not concentrate on that as I am quite sure this will be taken care of effectively with or without models to support it. This may, of course, be arrogance on my part and perhaps he is wiser.

Acknowledgements

The author is grateful to R. H. J. M. Gradus and R. F. Zeeuw for their great help and the F. A. G. den Butter for his comments.

References

Van den Berg, P. J. C. M., 1986. 'De betrouwbaarheid van macro-economische voorspellingen', *Economische Statistische Berichten*, 1153–57.

Den Butter, F. A. G., 1991. 'Macroeconomic modelling and the policy of restraint in the Netherlands', *Econ. Model.* 8, 16–33.

Don, H. J. H., 1993. 'Forecast uncertainty in economics'. In: Grasman, J. and Van Straten, G. (eds.), *Predictability and non-linear Modelling in Natural Sciences and Economics.* Kluwer.

Donders, J. H. M. and Graafland, J. J., 1998. 'CPB Models and Employment Policy in the Netherlands', *Econ. Model.* 15, 341–56 (Chapter 2 in this volume).

Gelauff, G. M. M. and Graafland, J. J., 1994. *Modelling Welfare State Reform.* North Holland.

Gordon, R. J., 1984. *Macroeconomics.* Brown, Boston.

Klein, L. R., 1950. *Economic Fluctuations in the United States, 1921–1941.* Wiley, New York.

Klein, L. R., 1988. 'Past, present and possible future of macroeconometric models and their uses.' In: Klein, L. R. (ed.), *Comparative Performance of U.S. Econometric Models*, Chapter 1. Oxford University Press, 1991.

Lucas, R. E., Jr., 1976. 'Econometric policy evaluation: a critique'. In: *The Phillips Curve and Labor Markets, Carnegie-Rochester Conference Series on Public Policy, J Monet Econ.*, Suppl. 1, 19–46.

Stone, R. and Stone, W. M., 1939. 'The marginal propensity to consume and the multiplier: a statistical investigation', *Rev. Econ. Stud.* 6, 1–24.

Timbergen, J., 1936. 'Kan hier te lande, al dan niet na overheidsingrijpen, een verbetering van de binnenlandse conjunctuur intrede, ook zonder verbetering van onze exportpopsitie? *Prae-adviezen van de Vereeniging voor de Staathuishoudkunde en de Statistiek.* Martinus Nijhoff, Den Haag, pp. 62–108.

Whitley, J. D., 1994. *A Course in Macroeconomic Modelling and Forecasting.* Kluwer.

Chapter 2

CPB models and employment policy in the Netherlands*

Jan Donders and Johan Graafland

The CPB Netherlands Bureau for Economic Policy Analysis plays an important role in the preparation of economic policy in the Netherlands. This chapter addresses the interaction between CPB models and employment policy during the period 1950–97. We discuss several examples of the impact of CPB models on employment policies. At the same time, the specific needs of policy makers influenced model-building at the CPB. Several innovations of CPB models were needed to explain the actual developments on the Dutch labour market and to investigate the usefulness of various remedies addressing the disequilibria in this market.

JEL classifications: B49, E1, E24, E65

I. Introduction

This chapter discusses the interaction between CPB models and economic policy in the Netherlands. We focus on employment policy, because employment is an important target for economic policy. Since 1973, it even is the most important target. The chapter deals with two questions: how did CPB models affect employment policy and how did the needs and views of policy makers impact CPB models?

The organization of this chapter is as follows. To begin with, Section 2 sketches CPB's role in the preparation of economic policy. Section 3 discusses the interaction between labour market developments, CPB models and employment policy during the period 1950–97. During this period the focus of the CPB shifted from (Keynesian) demand side macroeconomic models in the 1950s and 1960s, via an early attempt in the 1970s to incorporate supply effects (VINTAF), to the development of a fully-fledged general equilibrium model based on microeconomic foundations (MIMIC) in the late 1980s. The fourth section deals with the MIMIC model in more detail. Our discussion of the history of MIMIC, its influence on policy-making and the impact of the needs and views of policy makers on MIMIC serves as a case study.

*Reprinted from *Economic Modelling*, 15, Jan Donders and Johan Graafland, 'CPB models and employment policy in the Netherlands', pp. 341–56, Copyright (1998), with permission from Elsevier Science.

2. CPB's role in the preparation of economic policy

Immediately after the Second World War, the CPB Netherlands Bureau for Economic Policy Analysis, as we like to call it today, was founded with Tinbergen, the founder of macroeconomic model-building,[1] as its first managing director. The CPB would be a strictly advisory body, operating both as a central source of economic information within the government and as an independent centre for applied economic analysis. The latter includes monitoring and forecasting economic developments as well as policy analysis. Policy-making is the task of the ministries, the parliament and the government. A distinctive feature of the CPB is that it analyses policy proposals for political parties and other public organizations like employers' and employees' organizations, as well as for government ministries.[2] These studies tend to be conducted mainly in a medium- or long-term framework.

Each year in April, the CPB publishes the Central Economic Plan. This publication gives a detailed overview of the economy and contains forecasts for the current and – since 1992 – the following year. Since the 1960s, the CPB prepares the Macro Economic Outlook every summer. Its forecasts help the cabinet to prepare the budget for the next calendar year. Updated with final decisions on fiscal policy, the Macro Economic Outlook is published in September simultaneously with the Budget Memorandum of the cabinet.

The Netherlands can be characterized as a consultation economy. One of the characteristics of the Dutch consultation economy is the need of all participants in the preparation of economic policy for factual knowledge and scientific analysis (CPB, 1992a, p. 95). This need explains the Netherlands' distinctive tradition of using econometric models to support economic policy-making. Policy co-ordination between the government and the organizations of employers and employees (the social partners) plays an important role in the Netherlands. Consultation bodies are the bipartite Foundation of Labour and the tripartite Social and Economic Council. The former is aimed at consultation between employers' and employees' organizations on labour conditions. The latter is an advisory body to government on social and economic policy. CPB's managing director is one of its independent members.

3. Labour market developments, CPB models and employment policy: a retrospect

This section discusses the policy questions raised by labour market developments during the period 1950–97. We show how these questions influenced model-building at the CPB. At the same time, we try to sketch the influence of CPB analyses on actual employment policies.

3.1. The 1950s and 1960s

After the Second World War, the Netherlands experienced remarkable economic growth. This favourable economic development can be attributed to a strong growth of both labour supply and labour productivity, the destruction of public and private capital during the war (that stimulated investments after the war), and the liberalization of international trade. Wage moderation also contributed to economic growth. Government and the social partners agreed on the need to limit the growth of real wages. Until 1963 the government set wage guidelines in close cooperation with and supported by employers' and employees' organizations.

In the early 1960s, the combination of fast economic expansion and labour time reduction led to a tight labour market, generating a stronger growth of wages. In 1964 the so-called wage explosion occurred: the average nominal labour costs per hour increased by more than 15 per cent. An increase in the burden of taxes and social security contributions also boosted the growth of labour costs in the second half of the 1960s. Consequently, profits fell and the competitive position of Dutch export industries deteriorated. These developments would contribute to the structural problems of the 1970s.

In the 1950s and 1960s, the CPB used annual models to assess short-term economic developments and the effects of alternative economic policies.[3] These models had Keynesian characteristics: effective demand was the most important determinant of production and employment. Keynesian policies to regulate the level of effective demand were based on simulations with CPB models. In this connection, we should mention 1952 and 1957. In both years, which were characterized by overspending, effective demand was reduced by a package of measures. These measures were implemented by the government after discussions in the Social and Economic Council. Both times, CPB's analyses played an important role in the Council's discussions. Looking back, however, it should be observed that in 1957 the measures to reduce domestic demand were implemented too late, after the start of the downswing. This experience illustrates that stabilizing the economy by discretionary demand policy is difficult.

The CPB did not focus exclusively on short-term economic developments. In the early 1950s the CPB had begun to analyse the long-term developments. This research project resulted in an outlook for the period 1950–70, published in 1955. Ten years later the CPB published its first medium-term outlook for the period 1965–70. The CPB developed models that could describe the interaction between the demand- and the supply-side of the economy. That's why model-building at the CPB was aimed not only at improving the short-term model. In 1967 CPB's then managing director, Van den Beld, presented his so-called CS model, a dynamic model suited to analyse the interaction between the business cycle and the structural development of the economy. The CPB used this model to make medium-term forecasts and analyses.

Policy makers also understood the importance of the structural development of the economy. We have already mentioned the centrally guided wage policy. This policy was an instrument not only to regulate the level of effective demand, but also to influence the structural growth of production and employment. Both government and social partners understood the need to contain the wage growth, because of its beneficial effects on investments and exports. CPB analyses supported this policy (Van den Beld, 1979).

3.2. The 1970s

The performance of the Dutch economy became very unfavourable in 1973, the year of the first oil crisis. As a consequence of the economic problems, CPB's contacts with the ministries and the cabinet became more intense in the 1970s, which enlarged CPB's influence on economic policy (Passenier, 1994, pp. 264–9). The Central Economic Commission, which normally prepares the macroeconomic policy of the government, also became more influential. The presidium of this commission consists of high-ranking officials of the five ministries involved in social and economic policy, CPB's managing director and, as a permanent adviser, a director of the Central Bank. Advice from the Central Economic Commission was often based on CPB forecasts and simulations with CPB models.

Although the Wage Act of 1970 limited the power of the government to interfere with wage negotiations, in the 1970s the government did interfere several times. Wage controls were aimed at reducing inflation and enlarging profits. The cabinet tried also to influence the distribution of income through these controls. Government interventions could not prevent, however, the rise in the labour share in enterprise income. As a matter of fact, government policy contributed to this rise since the gradual increase in the burden of taxes and social security contributions raised the growth of labour costs.

From 1973 employment in enterprises declined, although output still grew further. CPB models could not explain this development, since in these models the growth rate of employment in enterprises was usually linked to the growth rate of production by enterprises. Indeed, in the 1950s and 1960s, there was a strong correlation between employment and production. In the 1970s, however, this correlation did not hold any longer. As a consequence, CPB models overestimated employment.

In response, Den Hartog and Tjan tried to explain the fall in employment by means of a clay–clay vintage model.[4] In such a model the stock of capital equipment is supposed to consist of vintages of investment goods each of which has its own technical coefficients. Increases in the real product wage surpassing the growth of labour productivity embodied in the capital goods result in a reduction of the economic life span of capital goods and the related number of jobs. Such a reduction explained the fall in employment. The concomitant increase in average labour productivity, as a consequence of scrapping capital goods with a relatively low labour productivity, explained the further growth of output.

The study of Den Hartog and Tjan quickly had an impact on the discussions on economic policy. In February 1975, the cabinet published its Memorandum on employment. In an appendix the CPB presented the Den Hartog and Tjan view on the fall of employment. This analysis, however, did not yet lead to a change in macroeconomic policy. The cabinet was still convinced that the main cause of the economic problems was a lack of sufficient demand. That's why it decided to stimulate the demand for labour by employment programmes and by expanding the budget deficit.

In the summer of 1975, the CPB informed officials of the Ministry of Finance of its views with respect to the economic development in the medium-term. Assuming unchanged economic policy the CPB expected that unemployment would reach 300,000 persons (6 per cent of the labour force) in 1980. Next to that, the CPB expected a strong increase in the burden of taxes and social security contributions, that would raise labour costs and thus unemployment. Not only would strong wage increases shorten the economic life span of capital goods, but they would also reduce profits and, hence, the creation of new jobs by investments. At this time, the CPB message was taken more seriously. The Minister of Finance, Duisenberg, understood the need for a policy change. He proposed to limit the *increase* in the burden of taxes and social security contributions to 1 per cent of national income each year. After discussions, the cabinet agreed with this so-called 1 per cent-policy (see Toirkens, 1988, pp. 32–40).

In 1976, the Minister of Economic Affairs, Lubbers, published his Memorandum on economic structure. Lubbers endorsed the diagnosis of Den Hartog and Tjan. According to the minister, the structural problems of the Dutch economy originated from the rise in the labour share in enterprise income that had occurred since the mid-1960s, as a consequence of the tight labour market in the 1960s, the gradual increase in the burden of taxes and social security contributions and the deterioration of the terms of trade as a result of the oil crisis. To strengthen the supply-side of the economy, the government decided to reduce labour costs by wage subsidies and to stimulate investments by investment subsidies. Simulations with CSVIN (an adjusted version of Van den Beld's CS model with the vintage production function of Den Hartog and Tjan) showed the economic effects of these policy proposals. According to the then secretary-general of the Ministry of Economic Affairs (Rutten, 1984), these simulations had an important influence on the policy mix that was proposed in Lubbers' Memorandum.

The vintage production function was not only embedded in the CS model, but also in a new medium-term macroeconomic model, called VINTAF. The first version of this model was published in 1975 (Den Hartog et al., 1975). Two years later the CPB put into use a second version with endogenous social security contributions. Simulations with this model showed that an increase in the rate of unemployment results in an increase in social security contributions that raises labour costs and thus boosts unemployment further. In 1977, the Central Economic Commission based its projections and policy advice for the medium-term directly on the results of VINTAF. This model and its use for policy analysis incited a unique and vivid discussion among academics and government specialists.[5] Driehuis and Van der Zwan, who started this debate, criticized VINTAF for several reasons. They claimed, for example, that the vintage production function does not apply to all sectors of the economy and that not only labour costs, but also capital costs, determine the economic life span of capital goods. Moreover, they criticized the fact that VINTAF did not contain a financial sector. This debate led to further research on the specification and estimation of vintage models. Furthermore, the CPB decided to build a new version of the medium-term macroeconomic model with a financial sector.

In 1977 a new cabinet took office. This cabinet declared that it did not believe any more in Keynesian policies. Although the cabinet proposed to cut down government expenditure, it failed to do so. Consequently, it was not able to stop the simultaneous increase in the budget deficit and the burden of taxes and social security contributions, although the second oil crisis of 1979 led to a further increase in the natural gas revenues of government.

It is clear from the above that CPB analyses already showed the need for a change of economic policy in an early stage. In the 1970s, however, only a minor policy change occurred. Consequently, the labour share in enterprise income and unemployment kept rising. Yet, simulations with CPB models played an important role in the debate on economic policy and influenced actual government policies. Government defended wage controls by referring to simulations showing the beneficial effects of wage restraint; minister Duisenberg announced his 1 per cent-policy after the CPB presented its prospects for the second half of the 1970s; and minister Lubbers based wage and investment subsidies on model simulations. According to Den Butter (1991), even more important is the fact that the VINTAF models and the debate on the vintage production function have been instrumental in the general acceptance of the policy of wage restraint in the Netherlands. However, as we will discuss in the next subsection, it would take until 1982 before the labour share in enterprise income started to decline.

3.3. The 1980s

In 1981 a new cabinet took office, which would govern only until the next year. At the end of 1981, the Minister of Social Affairs and Employment, Den Uyl, proposed a 'jobs plan' to reduce unemployment, which led to heated discussions between the ministers involved in social and economic policy. The CPB estimated that the 'jobs plan' would raise employment by 5,000 jobs. This small effect disappointed Den Uyl and his officials. Ritzen, who was then with the ministry to co-ordinate the 'jobs plan', was not convinced. According to him, CPB's analysis showed the limitations of economic models (see Passenier, 1994, pp. 272–3).

In the early 1980s, the Netherlands experienced its most serious economic crisis since the Second World War. This crisis led to a boost in both the fiscal deficit and the unemployment rate. The huge fiscal deficit incited a debate on the necessity of a reduction of this deficit. Critics of CPB models argued that these models wrongly neglected the beneficial impact of a fall in the fiscal deficit on private investments, since these models did not contain a financial sector. This critique was expressed, among others, by academic researchers, such as the monetarists Bomhoff and Korteweg (see, for example, Bomhoff, 1982).

Already in the late 1970s, the CPB decided, as we have seen above, to incorporate a financial sector in its medium-term macroeconomic model.[6] This research project, that took approximately five years, resulted in the FREIA model (for a description, see Hasselman *et al.*, 1983). This model was based on modern portfolio theory. Indeed, according to simulations with FREIA, cuts in government spending aimed at a fall in the fiscal deficit indeed generate a decline in the interest rate. This fall would be so small, however, that these cuts would still have an unfavourable effect on production and employment in the short and medium-term.

The CPB used the FREIA model for the first time in 1982, when it gave technical assistance to the Central Economic Commission for the preparation of a memorandum which surveyed economic developments and the consequences of a number of policy measures for the next government period. The commission emphasized in its memorandum that a reduction in the fiscal deficit implies a short-term pain in order to realize a long-term gain. Although the latter effect was relatively small according to FREIA, the reduction in the fiscal deficit received high priority. Policy makers believed that the FREIA model did not capture all relevant effects of the extremely high fiscal deficit, like a loss in confidence of economic agents.

As we have observed in the preceding subsection, the CPB urged the necessity of a policy of wage restraint since the early 1970s. CPB's pleas for wage moderation, based on simulations with its models, bore fruit in the early 1980s. After its installation, the cabinet Lubbers I (1982–86) exerted considerable pressure on the social partners to reach an agreement to moderate wages. To that aim, it included a private-sector wage and price freeze in its proposed policy package. This threat of intervention contributed to the Wassenaar agreement that was reached in the autumn of 1982 by the central organizations of employees and employers. According to this agreement, the social partners aimed at an improvement of profitability by wage moderation and at a reduction in labour time. The cabinet subsequently dropped its threat to intervene. In the following years substantial wage moderation resulted, while the government kept its commitment not to interfere. The cabinet supported the policy of wage moderation by cuts in the minimum wage and related social security benefits and wages in the public sector. Consequently, the labour share in enterprise income (the ratio of wages plus imputed wage income of the self-employed to net value added at factor costs) declined from 95 per cent in 1981 to 82 per cent in 1989. The fall in the labour share in enterprise income raised the growth rate of employment and, to a lesser extent, also the growth rate of GDP, as simulations with CPB's medium-term macroeconomic model would show in the early 1990s (see CPB, 1991).

In the second half of the 1980s, policy makers stressed the significance of the supply-side effects of the high tax and social security premium rates and the generous social security benefits. At this time the issue of the tax wedge was also discussed at the OECD. CPB models, however, neglected these supply-side effects, with the exception of the influence of changes in tax and social security premium rates on the growth of labour costs. Officials of the Ministry of Economic Affairs, among them secretary-general Rutten, criticized the neglect of other supply-side effects (see Van Bergeijk and Van Sinderen, 1997, Chapter 3 in this volume). This was due to the methodology of the standard macroeconomic models, which were inappropriate to study the impact of such supply policies because of their weak microeconomic basis. Encouraged by the criticism, the CPB, on the one hand, decided to incorporate more of these effects into its macroeconomic models for policy analysis. On the other hand, more fundamental research was started by developing an applied general equilibrium model (MIMIC), which would be based on microeconomic theory. This model will be discussed in the next section.

One of the other topics in the second half of the 1980s concerned the investment subsidies that were introduced in the 1970s. These subsidies raised questions since they lead to substitution of labour by capital. It seemed irrational to stimulate this substitution since unemployment was still very high. The CPB analysed the consequences of a reduction in investment subsidies on the basis of simulations with FREIA-KOMPAS (CPB, 1986). It called attention to the fact that investment subsidies not only have a negative substitution effect on employment, but also a positive growth effect (since such subsidies raise investment and thus economic growth). Furthermore, the model simulations showed that the consequences of a reduction in investment subsidies depend on the use of the budgetary savings. According to these simulations, such a reduction would raise unemployment if these savings are used to lower the income tax. However, unemployment would be reduced somewhat if these savings are used to lower social security contributions paid by employers. In 1988 the cabinet decided to terminate the investment subsidies and to reduce both the social security contributions paid by employers and the tax rate on profits. As always, it is difficult to estimate the influence of CPB's analysis. It should be observed that an important reason for the cabinet's decision to terminate the investment subsidies was the fact that the subsidy outlays substantially surpassed the estimates.

Summarizing, the influence of CPB models on economic policy in the 1980s seems to have been more limited than in the 1970s. Policy makers became more and more convinced of the relevance of supply-side effects of both taxes and the social security system, which were weakly represented in the CPB models. Several policies were implemented of which not all favourable effects could be shown by the CPB models, such as the cuts in the social security benefits and the reduction of the fiscal deficit. CPB's analysis with respect to the necessity of wage moderation, however, was well acknowledged in the policy-making process.

3.4. The 1990s

The wage moderation of the 1980s resulted in a strong improvement of business profitability. In the 1990s, improved profitability had a beneficial impact on the growth of employment. After a temporary fall in employment growth in 1993–94 as a result of an international downswing, this growth has beenstrong again since 1995. Although the official unemployment figure is now far below the EU average, employment stays an important issue in the debate on economic policy because the total unemployment figure (inclusive of the hidden unemployed) is still very high. Furthermore, the ratio of employment to the potential labour force is relatively low in the Netherlands compared to other countries.

CPB's tool box contained several models, among them the applied general equilibrium model MIMIC and the medium-term macroeconomic model FKSEC (for a description of FKSEC, see CPB, 1992b). In particular, the former model was used to analyse various employment policies. That's why we will discuss the history of MIMIC and its use for policy analysis in detail in Section 4.

After the completion of FKSEC, the CPB decided to build a successor to this model. One reason is that the CPB felt the need to bridge the gap between the medium-term macroeconomic model and the (long-term) MIMIC model. While FKSEC is only suited for short- and medium-term analyses, the new model, JADE, is also suited for long-term analyses (for a description of JADE, see CPB, 1997). Furthermore, JADE provides a richer description of the labour market. This market is, as it is already in MIMIC, disaggregated by skill level. The high unemployment rate of low-skilled workers asked for such a disaggregation.

4. The MIMIC model: a case study

4.1. The history of MIMIC

In the sections above, we observed that, in the 1980s, policy makers got interested in the supply-side effects of the high tax and social security premium rates and the generous social security benefits. Partly in response to this interest and partly because of new developments in international research on economic modelling, the CPB decided to build a new model called MIMIC (Micro Macro model to analyse the Institutional Context). Work on MIMIC started in 1987. At that time, one of the most pressing policy issues in the Netherlands was the high rate of inactivity. In particular, every 100 people earning a wage had to carry the burden of financing the benefits of 86 people, of which 15 were unemployed, 17 disabled and 46 elderly. This created a high tax wedge distorting the labour market, for instance by reducing the labour market participation rate of women, which has been rather low in the Netherlands (41 per cent in 1985 against 50 per cent or more in other European countries). Not only the size of the tax wedge, but also the structure of both the tax and the social security system, is relevant for the labour market. Indeed, several policy questions arose, such as:

• How do marginal tax rates for different income groups affect labour supply and unemployment?

• What are the effects of an increase in the earned-income tax allowance that reduces the replacement rate, i.e. widens the gap between net wages and net benefits?

• How does abolishing the transferability of the basic tax-free allowance between spouses affect the participation rate of women?

• What is the impact of a reduction of the minimum wage, both with and without a concomitant reduction in social security benefits?

The instruments used by the CPB at that time were inappropriate to address these questions. To illustrate, the medium-term macroeconomic model contained only one tax variable. Hence, that model was unable to give a proper answer to questions about the impact of changes in the structure of the tax system. Indeed, the questions posed above require a model with a detailed description of the tax system and various labour-market institutions. For that purpose, the model should contain a highly disaggregated household sector that takes into account the fact that different groups of people respond to changes in the tax structure in different ways. Furthermore, CPB's macroeconomic models lacked a sound microeconomic theoretical base, which is required to get to grips with the supply-side effects of taxation.

In order to combine a large degree of disaggregation and a strong theoretical basis, the model was set up as an applied general equilibrium model. Although the model fitted in the international tradition of applied general equilibrium models as described by Shoven and Whalley (1984) and others, it also incorporated some new-Keynesian elements. Especially important is the notion of equilibrium unemployment, which is derived from a wage bargaining model.

In 1987 the MIMIC project started. Two and a half years later, at the end of 1989, the simulations with the first version of the model were represented at a conference in Noordwijk. It took another two years of further improvements before the model was actually used by the CPB for policy analysis. After that time, some other extensions were incorporated in the model which resulted in the version that was published in 1994 in the 'Contributions to Economic Analysis' series of North Holland (see Gelauff and Graafland, 1994).

From 1992 onwards, MIMIC has been used frequently for policy analysis. Most policy simulations are described in Gelauff and Graafland (1994) and some were published in economic journals. Besides, some results were reported in official CPB documents (CPB, 1992a, 1994). On several occasions the Ministries of Economic Affairs, Finance, and Social Affairs and Employment requested MIMIC simulations on policy measures. On one occasion, the MIMIC model was used for an analysis for the Ministry of Education of the effects of training programmes targeted at the low skilled. Furthermore, the model was more than once used for an analysis of policy proposals by unions and employers' organizations and for the Social and Economic Council. Political parties have also made specific requests for MIMIC simulations for their policy proposals. In some cases, the CPB also responded positively to requests from commissions and individual scientists. Finally, the CPB did some work for the European Commission (European Commission, 1994) and the International Labour Organization (Graafland, 1996).

After a period of intensive use of the model for policy analysis, several research projects started in 1995. On the one hand, empirical research was devoted to the production function with different skill levels of labour and the wage equation in order to improve the empirical basis of the model. Other research intended to extend the structure of, in particular, MIMIC's household model. This research is motivated by criticism of MIMIC simulation analysis concerning the impact of the marginal tax wedge on economic behaviour of agents (Bovenberg *et al.*, 1994). According to the critics, MIMIC did not take account of all the effects of changes in the marginal tax rate, since labour supply of breadwinners and single persons was exogenous, and the black economy and investment in human capital were not modelled. In order to meet this criticism, labour supply of breadwinners and single persons, investment in human capital, the black economy and household production are currently endogenized. The new MIMIC model became operational in the second half of 1997 and was used to analyse the consequences of several policy proposals, and support preparations for the elections in Spring 1998.

4.2. Impact of MIMIC on economic policy

While it is difficult to measure the impact of MIMIC analyses on economic policy, it can be noted that the model has become well known in the policy-making circuit, including academic circles, employers' and employees' organizations, bureaucrats and politicians. That does not necessarily mean that MIMIC convinces policy makers, but it at least suggests that they have found the results interesting.[7]

A further judgement of the impact of MIMIC might be derived by investigating how many actual policy measures are in line with MIMIC simulations on the effectiveness of these policies. For example, during the cabinet Lubbers III (1989–93), the basic tax allowance for wage earnings was raised significantly and the automatic increase in the tax bracket border values was suspended. Before this policy was implemented, MIMIC simulations in CPB (1993) had shown that, out of several alternative tax policies, this is the most effective way of stimulating employment and reducing unemployment because the tax allowance for workers reduces labour costs and, at the same time, increases the gap between net unemployment benefits and net wage income. (Former) minister De Vries, who knew MIMIC well, advocated this policy.

There are also examples of policy measures that are not effective according to prior simulation analysis of MIMIC and were indeed rejected by policy makers. For example, the tax reform proposed by the Stevens Committee was not implemented after the Social and Economic Council provided a negative report (Social and Economic Council, 1992). This report included some MIMIC simulations showing only a small impact of this drastic tax reform on the labour market. Another example concerns minimum wages. Abolition of or a reduction in minimum wages is repeatedly discussed in policy circles. However, no actual policy change has been implemented during recent years. MIMIC simulation analysis (Graafland, 1993) had shown that the employment effects of such a reduction are rather modest, unless unemployment benefits are also reduced. A third example concerns the individualization of social assistance benefits. After MIMIC analyses in CPB (1992c) showed the serious budgetary risks involved, this issue hardly receives serious attention anymore.

The increase in the general basic tax allowance in 1996 is a clear counterexample. According to the CPB (1993), this kind of tax reduction reduces employment instead of increasing it. This result stems from two mechanisms. First, the income effect implied by the increase of the (transferable) basic tax allowance generates a fall in labour supply by partners. Second, an increase in the basic tax allowance favours recipients of unemployment benefits, especially single persons, relatively more than wage earners. Hence, the replacement ratio rises. Both the fall in labour supply and the increase in the replacement rate generate wage pressure and reduce employment. Although these effects are not open to serious criticism by policy makers, still a rather large increase in the basic tax allowance was decided on in 1995. This decision was inspired by the political wish to raise the income of low income earners. Here we witness how in the political debate (short-term) social concerns can dominate (long-term) economic considerations. Indeed, MIMIC shows that there can be a trade-off between the full employment target and an equitable income distribution.

There are also examples of policies that can be recommended on the basis of MIMIC simulations but, nevertheless, have not seriously attracted the attention of policy makers. One example is the introduction of a negative income tax, which, according to MIMIC, might strongly reduce unemployment under certain conditions. However, no such policy measures have been implemented so far, although some political parties actually put forward some proposals in this direction. On the one hand, this can be explained by the drastic character of this policy measure. On the other hand, there may be some doubts about the reliability of MIMIC with respect to the effects of a negative income tax. In particular, as noted above, the MIMIC model might lack some important negative effects of the high marginal tax rate, implied by a high basic income. Still, the MIMIC simulations on basic income have surely contributed to the national debate on this topic.

Another example of a policy measure favoured by MIMIC but not actually implemented, relates to what has become known in the Dutch policy debate as Robin Hood policies. More specifically, according to MIMIC a budgetary neutral tax shift from low-income to high-income groups increases employment and reduces unemployment. This result follows from two mechanisms in the model. First, labour supply elasticities of married women working part-time and having relatively low incomes, are much larger than for other groups with higher incomes. Second, the wage bargaining model predicts that a rise in the marginal tax rate reduces wages, because wage increases generate a smaller growth in purchasing power if marginal tax rates are high. As a result, high wage claims are less attractive. Although these mechanisms are empirically well-based, policy makers doubted the reliability of these MIMIC outcomes. Their general perception was that MIMIC lacks some other relevant mechanisms that would show a more adverse impact of the marginal tax rate on employment and economic growth. Still, it can be argued that the MIMIC analysis has exerted some impact on the policy-making process. In general, in the 1990s the policy focus seems to have shifted from the possible detrimental impact of high marginal tax rates for top income groups to the problem of a high tax wedge for low-income groups. MIMIC may have contributed to this change in policy concern. Indeed, after MIMIC became operational in 1992, no reductions in tax rates for high income tax brackets have been implemented,[8] whereas the proposal of the Stevens Committee, containing such reductions, has been rejected. A further indication that MIMIC might have stimulated Robin Hood types of policies is the already mentioned strong rise of the basic tax allowance for workers during recent years which was partly financed by suspending the inflation correction to the income levels at which tax rates change.

Concluding, although it is difficult to give an exact estimate of the relevance of MIMIC for the policy-making process, we believe that MIMIC has been useful in informing policy makers about possible effects of their policy proposals. In some cases, this information seems to have had some impact on the decision to adopt or reject a particular policy, in other cases such an impact is less clear. Anyway, the MIMIC results have become well known to all kinds of parties participating in the policy arena. Although the CPB refrains from using the simulation results for specifying which concrete policy measures should be implemented, these results make policy makers aware of some important trade-offs between different social and economic goals and help to determine the borders of their playing field.

4.3. Impact of policy makers on MIMIC

As one can already detect from the foregoing discussion, the relation between MIMIC and the policy-making process has not been in one direction. On the contrary, the start of MIMIC was partly motivated by the desire to get a better grip on ideas of policy makers about the impact of taxation on the economy. That MIMIC has been rather successful in getting a firm position in the Dutch policy debate may well be due to its ability to reproduce many aspects of these intuitions of the policy makers in a systematic and scientific way. Current revisions of the MIMIC model, with respect to the impact of marginal tax rates on labour supply by breadwinners and single persons, the quality of labour supply and black labour are motivated by the desire to evaluate some ideas that are discussed in policy circles.

While one cannot deny that policy makers determine which economic ideas attract attention and, in this way, influence the research agenda for the MIMIC model, this does not imply that MIMIC cannot play an independent role in the policy-making process. Before including the ideas of policy makers in the model, their relevance is evaluated in light of the theoretical and empirical economic literature. The most significant illustration is, again, the Robin Hood discussion. Indeed, MIMIC results here run counter to the ideas of many policy makers (see, for example, Bovenberg et al., 1994) and policy makers have pointed to some missing links in the model. Yet, as we have argued above, even in this case the outcomes of the policy-making process were, in some respects, quite in line with the MIMIC results. It remains to be seen how the revised version of MIMIC, which repairs some missing links, will judge Robin Hood types of policies and how this will affect the policy-making process in the coming years.

5. Summary and conclusions

One of the characteristics of the Dutch consultation economy is the need of all participants in the preparation of economic policy for factual knowledge and scientific analysis. This need explains the unique role that CPB models play in the preparation of economic policy in the Netherlands. These models are used for the assessment of both the economic development in the short- and medium-term and the effects of alternative economic policies.

We focused on employment policy, because employment is an important target for economic policy. The CPB used various models to analyse labour market disequilibria. We paid special attention to several versions of the medium-term macro-economic model and the applied general equilibrium model MIMIC because most CPB analyses of employment policies were based on these models.

Employment policies are often evaluated with the help of simulations with CPB models. We discussed several examples of their impact. At the same time, the specific needs of policy makers for information influenced model-building at the CPB. Yet, the most important strength of CPB analyses is the independence of the institute. Thus, the CPB is not willing to adjust the *model outcomes* to the wishes of policy makers, but is ready to listen and improve its model in response to criticisms by policy makers of the way the economy has been modelled.

Several innovations of CPB models were needed to explain the actual developments on the Dutch labour market and to investigate the usefulness of various remedies addressing the disequilibria in this market. Among other things, we pointed to the incorporation of a vintage production function in CPB's medium-term macroeconomic model in the 1970s (to explain the fall in employment as a consequence of the gradual increase in the labour share in enterprise income and to show the benefits of wage restraint), the incorporation of supply-side effects of both taxes and social security benefits in the CPB models in the 1980s (because policy makers wanted to get more insight in the significance of these effects), and the disaggregation of the labour factor in the CPB models in the 1990s (because of the concentration of unemployment among lower skilled workers). Of course, progress in economic science also led to changes in the specification of CPB models.

Acknowledgements

This chapter presents our personal views. We benefited from the comments of Pierre Duguay, Mary Morgan and several colleagues.

Notes

1   In 1936 Tinbergen presented the first macroeconometric model ever made. He used this model to analyse which policy could reduce unemployment in the Netherlands. For an English version of his paper, see Tinbergen (1959).
2   Zalm (1998, Chapter 1 in this volume) discusses several examples of these analyses.
3   Barten (1988) discusses the models developed and used by the CPB during the period 1945–86.
4   The original chapter was published in 1974. For an English (somewhat revised) version of this chapter, see Den Hartog and Tjan (1976).
5   In 1977–78, several articles on this subject were published in the Dutch economic journal *Economisch Statistische Berichten* (ESB). See Driehuis and Van der Zwan (1978).
6   CPB's medium-term macroeconomic model would contain a monetary sector till the early 1990s. Since then the interest rate is exogenous again in the model, as a consequence of the gradual decline in the difference between the Dutch and the German interest rate that occurred during the 1980s in connection with the Dutch exchange rate policy.
7   The familiarity with MIMIC outcomes also appears from the large number of references in Dutch economic journals.
8   Except that the second tax bracket has been lengthened.

References

Barten, A. P., 1988. 'The history of Dutch macroeconomic modelling (1936–1986).' In: Driehuis, W., Fase, M. M. G. and Den Hartog, H. (eds.), *Challenges for Macroeconomic Modelling*. North Holland, Amsterdam, pp. 39–92.

Van den Beld, C. A., 1979. 'Het Centraal Planbureau: zijn invloed, zijn macht en zijn onmacht.' In: Van den Goorbergh, W. M., Van de Klundert, Th. C. M. J. and Kolnaar, A. H. J. (eds.), *Over Macht en Wet in Het Economisch Gebeuren: Opstellen Aangeboden aan prof.dr. D. B. J. Schouten*. Stenfert Kroese, Leiden, pp. 49–75.

Van Bergeijk, P. A. G. and Van Sinderen, J., 1997. 'Models and Macroeconomic Policy in The Netherlands', Tinbergen Institute Conference Paper, May 1997 (Chapter 3 in this volume).

Bomhoff, E. J., 1982. 'Models or markets: two approaches to employment policy.' In: Maddison, A. and Wilpstra, B. S. (eds.), *Unemployment: The European Perspective*. Croom Helm, London, pp. 125–47.

Bovenberg, A. L., De Mooij, R. A. and Van der Ploeg, F., 1994. 'Werkt een Robin Hood beleid?' *ESB 79*, 332–6.

Den Butter, F. A. G., 1991. 'Macroeconomic modelling and the policy of restraint in the Netherlands', *Econ. Model.* 8, 16–33.

CPB, 1986. Verlaging van WIR-premies, Lastenverlichting en de Prijsverhouding tussen Kapitaal en Arbeid: Een Macro-economische Analyse. Working Paper no. 6, The Hague.

CPB, 1991. De Werkgelegenheid in de Jaren Tachtig. Working Paper no. 41, The Hague.

CPB, 1992. *Nederland in Drievoud*. Sdu Uitgeverij Plantijnstraat, The Hague.

CPB, 1992. *FKSEC; A Macroeconometric Model for The Netherlands*. Stenfert Kroese, Leiden.

CPB, 1992. Belastingen en Sociale Zekerheid in Discussie: Individualisering en Ministelsel. Working Paper no. 42, The Hague.

CPB, 1993. Belastingverlaging, Heffingskorting en Overdraagbaarheid Belastingvrije Voet. Working Paper no. 50, The Hague.

CPB, 1994. Elections in The Netherlands: The Economic Consequences of Five Party Platforms. Working Paper no. 65, The Hague.

CPB, 1997. JADE: A Model for the Joint Analysis of Dynamics and Equilibrium. Working Paper no. 99, The Hague.

Driehuis, W. and Van der Zwan, A. (eds.), 1978. *De Voorbereiding van het Economisch Beleid Kritisch Bezien*. Stenfert Kroese, Leiden.

European Commission, 1994. 'Taxation, employment and environment: fiscal reform for reducing unemployment', *Eur. Econ.* 56, 143–70.

Gelauff, G. M. M. and Graafland, J. J., 1994. *Modelling Welfare State Reform*. North Holland, Amsterdam.

Graafland, J. J., 1993. Modelling the Effects of Minimum Wages and Unemployment Benefits. Research Memorandum no. 106, CPB, The Hague.

Graafland, J. J., 1996. 'Fiscal burden and employment: model simulations.' In: Van Ginneken, W. (ed.), *Finding the Balance: Financing and Coverage of Social Protection in Europe*. ILO, Geneva, pp. 77–90.

Den Hartog, H., Van de Klundert, Th. C. M. J. and Tjan, H. S., 1975. 'De structurele ontwikkeling van de werkgelegenheid in macro-economisch perspectief.' In: *Werkloosheid, Preadviezen van de Vereniging voor de Staathuishoudkunde*. Martinus Nijhof, The Hague, pp. 49–110.

Den Hartog, H. and Tjan, H. S., 1976. 'Investment, wages, prices and demand for labour: a clay–clay vintage model for the Netherlands', *De Economist* 124, 32–55.

Hasselman, B. H., Okker, V. R. and Den Haan, R. J. A., 1983. FREIA, een Macroeconomisch Model voor de Middellange Termijn. CPB, Monograph no. 25, The Hague.

Passenier, J., 1994. *Van Planning naar Scanning: Een Halve Eeuw Planbureau in Nederland*. Wolters-Noordhoff, Groningen.

Rutten, F. W., 1984. 'De betekenis van macro-econometrische modellen bij de beleidsvoorbereiding.' In: Den Hartog, H. and Weitenberg, J. (eds.), *Toegepaste Economie; Grenzen en Mogelijkheden*. CPB, The Hague, pp. 79–101.

Shoven, J. B. and Whalley, J., 1984. 'Applied general-equilibrium models of taxation and international trade: an introduction and survey.' *J. Econ. Lit.* 22, 1007–51.

Social and Economic Council, 1992. Herziening Belasting- en Premieheffing. The Hague.

Tinbergen, J., 1959. 'An economic policy for 1936'. In: Klaassen, L. H., Koyck, L. M. and Witteveen, H. J. (eds.), *Jan Tinbergen Selected Papers*. North Holland, Amsterdam, pp. 37–84.

Toirkens, J., 1988. *Schijn en Werkelijkheid van het Bezuinigingsbeleid 1975–1986*. Kluwer, Deventer.

Zalm, G., 1998. 'The relevance of economic modelling for policy decisions', *Econ. Model.* 15, 309–16 (Chapter 1 in this volume).

Chapter 3

Models and macroeconomic policy in the Netherlands

Peter A. G. van Bergeijk and Jarig van Sinderen

This chapter uses concepts of the industrial organization literature to investigate the Dutch macro modelling industry. For a long time, this industry was characterized by a virtual monopoly in the market for semi-official macroeconomic forecasts and policy analysis. We identify rents in terms of prestige, information and impact on economic policy. To a large extent, these rents explain why entry in this market occurred. Two case studies, on fiscal policy and competition policy, illustrate how policy makers and model builders interacted. These structural policies could not be analysed by the official model(s) and were only investigated in modelling exercises by relative outsiders. Finally, we discuss some policy implications of more competition in this modelling industry.
JEL classifications: A11, C5, E65

I. Introduction

Academic economists have *grosso modo* turned their backs on applied macro models, while policy makers in many countries often continue to rely on calculations and predictions based on detailed and large-scale models. In international organizations such as the IMF, the OECD and the EC, macro models are customarily applied. The academic position in the debate is well known (see, for example, Smith, 1997, Chapter 15 in this volume and Wren-Lewis, 1997, Chapter 11 in this volume). Policy makers, however, have been less explicit. We intend to fill part of these blanks in relation to our own experience with applied macro models in the policy process. A second motivation for this chapter is to get a better understanding of the Dutch macro-modelling industry. The products of this industry are used in the public policy debate, i.e. the market for economic diagnoses, ideas and policy prescriptions. This market is the topic of our investigation. One consequence of our choice of what is the relevant market for discussion is that we do not deal with forecasting activities, although – admittedly – forecasts often play an important role in policy processes. Our reasons to focus on this particular market are threefold. First, it concerns a *public* (i.e. readily observable) discussion on policy alternatives so that we have a relatively well-documented subject. Second, the exchange of ideas on policies should be an important element of the value that is produced by the macro-modelling industry. Third, the structure of this market is particularly interesting. Essentially one buyer (the government) is faced with one supplier (the Netherlands Bureau for Economic Analysis (CPB)). This mixture of monopolistic and monopsonistic elements leaves the market outcome in an *ex ante* sense undetermined, offering scope for (implicit) bargaining. A suboptimal market result cannot *a priori* be ruled out.

In the Netherlands, this market for 'what-if' questions could, for a long time, be characterized as a monopoly by the CPB. It remains the most important supplier of modelling exercises for policy purposes. In the Dutch academic debate, the role and dominant position of the CPB has been questioned, especially against the background of the discussion on the completion of a single European market (see, for example, Van Dalen and Klamer, 1997). Since the 1980s, however, contenders have emerged in the market and this raises the questions of why entry occurred and what the impact of this competition may be for the functioning of the industry.

Smith (1994) uses the structure conduct performance (SCP) paradigm and Porter's (1985) concept of the value chain, both well known from industrial economics, to analyse the macro-modelling industry in the UK, *inter alia*, illustrating that the combination of these analytical instruments may yield a very illuminating explanation of change and performance in this 'market'. Three key elements stand out in the SCP paradigm:

(i)   market structure (e.g. the number and size distribution of sellers and buyers, the degree of product differentiation, and the extent to which entry and exit barriers exist);

(ii) conduct (e.g. policies in the area of product differentiation including both research and development, and strategic or collusive behaviour); and

(iii) performance (e.g. productive and allocative efficiency, dynamic efficiency in terms of technological progress).

While it is useful to keep the SCP framework in mind as a check on whether all the potentially relevant elements have been covered by the analysis, it is the concept of the *value chain* that, in our opinion, adds the most value to our discussion. Figure 3.1 illustrates the production process (or value chain) for policy analyses. The products of the industry in which we are typically interested are quantifications of the effects of considered policies (including indications of the exactness, reliability and robustness of the investigated policy measures). Timing is also a very relevant dimension of the production process of the macro-modelling industry. On the one hand, the results of a new model may initiate the debate on a specific policy. On the other hand, model analyses will often be prompted by the policy agenda. Consequently, the ability to answer new questions (i.e. the industry's speed of innovation) will have to be an important element of any evaluation of the industry.

Typical inputs are computers, observations (data) and econometric tools, i.e. estimation of equations and core parameters, solution routines, etc. Combination of these inputs results in a model. Solving this model for a given set of exogenous

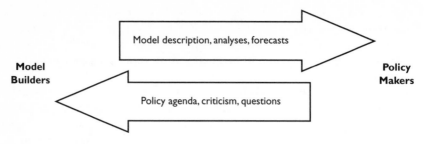

Figure 3.1 Value chain.

variables produces 'results'. The production process would seem to end when outputs (official forecasts and policy analyses) are supplied to the clients (decision makers). However, as Smith (1994) points out, the value chain in this industry is a process in which a second flow of information is equally important as policy makers express their demand, pointing out weaknesses in the assumptions, irregularities in the outcomes and new policy issues that need to be taken into account. It is in this sense that supply needs to meet demand in order for this market to be able to reach equilibrium. In this chapter we investigate how some 'new' ideas that could not (yet) be analysed in the available models are eventually dealt with by the different players in the market.

2. The Dutch modelling industry: stylized facts (1960s–1990s)

2.1. The 1960s to the 1970s

The relevant market of the Dutch macro-modelling industry in the 1960s could be characterized by the following stylized facts. The Netherlands has a long-standing tradition of empirically supported economic policy-making. This tradition started when Tinbergen (1936) built his first econometric model of the Dutch economy, and was institutionalized by the founding of the CPB in 1947 (see Barten, 1991 and Donders and Graafland, 1997, Chapter 2 in this volume). Given the available technology (in which the CPB at that time was a leading developer), a natural monopoly emerged that produced a benefit for the public and that was widely appreciated in the Netherlands. Generally speaking, policy makers agreed that models provided the foundation for a rational and well-documented discussion. One reason for this is that a monopoly on official forecasts helps to structure the policy debate, once policy makers accept the figures supplied by an independent body as the basis for negotiations and planning. This system helps to keep the political discussion as rational and consistent as possible. Essentially then, the demand side in the 1960s could be characterized as a 'monopsony by consent of the Dutch policy-making bodies'.

In regard to the interaction in the value chain, a number of observations are in order. The CPB was put at arm's length to the government so as to guarantee the Bureau's independence, creating a distance between, on the one hand, politicians and bureaucrats and, on the other, policy advisers that adhere to scientific standards. Policy makers were hardly consulted by the CPB during the model design phase and the value chain could thus be characterized as one-way communication. Generally speaking, communication consisted of the description and explanation of the final version of the model and the outcomes of a limited number of exogenous shocks. As a consequence, CPB models may have exhibited considerable inertia with respect to the analysis of specific policy demands. The impact, however, of econometric models on Dutch policy makers and politicians was still substantial. This is especially true in comparison with other countries. Just to illustrate this point: as far as we are aware, the Netherlands is the only country where political parties seek an econometric evaluation of the economic content of their electoral programmes (see, for example, Haffner and van Bergeijk, 1994). So the Dutch demand for model exercises is well developed and has a sound basis in Dutch society. Indeed, such analyses play a role in policy preparation by civil servants, in negotiations between the social partners, in parliamentary discussions and in decision-making by the Cabinet, and are accordingly well covered by the popular press.

2.2. Emerging competition

In the 1970s and 1980s, the structure of the industry changed when a competitive fringe of other model builders came into being. A number of universities, the Ministry of Economic Affairs and the Dutch Central Bank were involved in macro-econometric exercises and the results of their endeavours were published, but entry into the market of official analysis did not occur (see Verbruggen, 1992 and Van Els, 1997 (Chapter 6 in this volume) for an overview of modelling practices outside the CPB).[1] In our opinion, the exercises by universities lacked continuity, models were not maintained and no track-record was available that could allow policy makers to assess the performance of academic forecasters and analysts. One possible explanation for the academic behaviour is that institutional barriers that regulate the flow of (confidential) government information increase the costs for entrants outside government and the Central Bank. The limited size of the Dutch market may also have been a relevant factor. One further possible explanation is that the short-term rewards of model development (diversification and innovation) are too low, thus limiting the available funds for suppliers. Indeed, as Portes (1997) points out, one of the difficulties of getting good economic research funded is that economic research is by and large a public benefit, whereas users often desire privately appropriable results.

In respect to performance, the Dutch market for official forecasts showed some of the efficiency losses related to a lack of competition. The CPB was known for denouncing new academic trends (Barten, 1991).[2] Admittedly, high standards were adhered to and the quality of production was constantly being upgraded. The CPB, however, did not, generally speaking, publish confidence intervals for its forecasts. While most policy makers seemed quite satisfied with the output and efficiency of the CPB monopoly, the prestige of the CPB amongst academic economists substantially decreased over the years (Van Dalen and Klamer 1997). Based on a survey among Dutch economists, Van Dalen *et al.* (1998) found that 'young' PhDs (i.e. those economists that earned a doctorate since 1990) strongly rejected the methods and advice of the CPB. Moreover, not all policy makers were satisfied: the demand for analysis with respect to the impact of structural reform was initially not met by the CPB (as will become clear from the case study that we discuss in the next section), while policy makers wanted a real empirical evaluation of the whole policy spectrum, including structural change (Van Gent, 1997). These factors constitute so-called 'push factors' for entry in the Dutch macro-modelling industry that resulted in forward integration by policy makers.

During this process of forward integration in the value chain of the macro-modelling industry, it was increasingly being recognized at the policy institutions that building and maintaining a macro model may have significant advantages. These advantages were important pull factors that motivated structural change in the Dutch macro-modelling industry. The Netherlands Ministry of Economic Affairs and the Dutch Central Bank developed their own models which are now customarily being used in policy analysis and policy preparation, although not always in the Cabinet (see, for example, Van Sinderen, 1993 and Van Els, 1997, Chapter 6 in this volume). This suggests that it may be useful to take a closer look at the (potential) benefits of developing and maintaining such semi-official models in order to understand the Dutch macro-modelling market.[3] We suggest four sources from which benefits can be derived by a policy institution.

- Appropriable information related to a better understanding of the functioning of a model and the crucial parameters that essentially determine the outcome of modelling exercises. For example, potential benefits of forward integration may derive from the fact that the importance of modelling innovations and the uncertainties surrounding specific aspects of the analysis can only be fully understood if one knows the *métier*, i.e. if one is a model builder oneself.
- A model supplier puts his mark on the economic discourse by his choice to include some elements and to exclude others. Providing an alternative model is, then, an important way to get one's policy prescription on the agenda.
- One can apply one's own judgements about what is relevant or about what is to be considered an acceptable or sufficient standard of conduct. This allows the policy institution to make 'in-house' trade-offs between, on the one hand, logical and scientific standards and, on the other hand, the need to produce estimates of the potential impact of considered policies. One may sometimes not be able to make a full, detailed and completely satisfactory analysis in a decade's time although it is possible to produce a reasonable estimate, in a few weeks, on the basis of one or two *ad hoc* assumptions if you make the proper sensitivity analyses.

- Preliminary in-house assessment may, in addition, offer strategic gains as it may help to frame the proper policy questions and to prevent dead-end alleys.

The push-and-pull factors may offer an explanation to the question of why new players on the market were mostly of a non-academic nature. The number of individual modelling agents continued to increase as did forward integration in the value chain by institutions that demand or use the modelling exercises and are able to appropriate the results. In the private sector, banks and multinationals are involved in developing macro models (for example the Amsterdam-based brokerage firm IBS uses the CCSO model developed at the University of Groningen; see Jacobs and Sterken, 1995).[4]

3. How the supply side came to the Netherlands

Two short case studies relating to supply-side economics illustrate these push-and-pull factors. Motivated by the structural character of the problems of stagflation in the mid-1970s, the deteriorating situation of public finance and the high and persistent level of unemployment in the 1980s, the Dutch government recognized that well-functioning markets for goods and services provide the crucial underpinnings for a dynamic, high-income economy (Van Sinderen and Vollaard, 1999). As a consequence the Netherlands, like many other countries, embarked on a course of structural reform, aiming at improvements of the supply side of their economies through tax reform, trade liberalization, labour market reform and privatization, deregulation and competition policy. The available macro models, however, did not offer much guidance on these issues. A gap became apparent between, on the one hand, policy preparation based on macroeconometric models and, on the other hand, the policies that were perceived to be needed in order to implement structural change.

3.1. Public finances

In order to tidy public finances, a policy of reducing government expenditures was necessary. The available models (mostly based in Keynesian principles) showed the negative effects of reduced effective demand. Importantly, policy makers discussing the possible effects of a reduction in taxes only considered reductions of direct taxes *in combination* with a reduction of expenditures as a policy option (i.e. a balanced budget reduction in government expenditures and taxes). The CPB calculations at that time rejected such policies. In the early 1980s the VINTAF-II model predicted that a reduction in government expenditures would decrease economic growth and employment (see Netherlands' Government, 1978, p. 88), especially when income transfers were to be reduced.[5] The CPB models also influenced the policy discussion in another way. Generally speaking, microeconomic considerations of tax cuts (labour supply, human capital formation, increasing investment opportunities, etc.)

did not play an important role in the discussions, because these effects were not included in the models.

Rutten (1991, pp. 2–3), then secretary-general of the Netherlands Ministry of Economic Affairs, criticized the available models, arguing that

> the most important policy questions will relate to structural adjustment and structural reform. In such circumstances, general equilibrium models will be of great importance. In my view, they reflect the heart of economic science. They are highly relevant to important policy issues in many countries, such as high marginal tax rates, the functioning of the labour market, the social security system and the redistribution of income.

The CPB has taken up several of the research questions implicit in Rutten's exhortation. For example, the CPB developed a general equilibrium model MIMIC (Gelauff, 1994; Donders and Graafland, 1997, Chapter 2 in this volume) which produces a much more realistic picture of the policy issues related to public finance reforms.

3.2. Competition policy and deregulation

In the 1990s a new item was added to the research agenda ('structural adjustment and reform') implicit in Rutten's exhortation, namely the analysis of the macroeconomic impact of the functioning of markets. Generally speaking, macro models do not take changes in institutional arrangements into account. In the early 1990s the policy debate in the Netherlands focused on the economic consequences of cartels and other forms of (self) regulation. Consequently, the liberalization of the Shop Hours Act (proposed by the major political parties in the 1994 election campaign) and the plans to improve the functioning of markets in regulated and sheltered sectors, such as telecommunications, and the reduction of administrative compliance costs could not be covered by the CPB's econometric evaluation of the 1994 electoral programmes (Haffner and Van Bergeijk, 1994). The CPB explained that it did not take such changes in the legal framework into account because it could not quantify the effects of institutional change, pointing out that no modelling tools were available and criticizing political parties for not being sufficiently explicit and clear about their policy intentions (Zalm, 1994).[6]

Figure 3.2 illustrates this inertia for the case of empirical research into the functioning of Dutch product markets. Policy makers needed 'guidance' when they were considering the need to align Dutch regulations and competition law to European standards. Gradus (1995, p. 3), for example, stresses the importance of a clear-cut understanding of the economic effects of different regulation options. Kremers (1991) most clearly expressed the need to analyse the macroeconomic impact of product market inertia. In a sense, Kremers' (1991) article, discussing possible causes for the lack of economic dynamism in the Netherlands, triggered a large number of empirical studies (in the fields of both industrial organization and

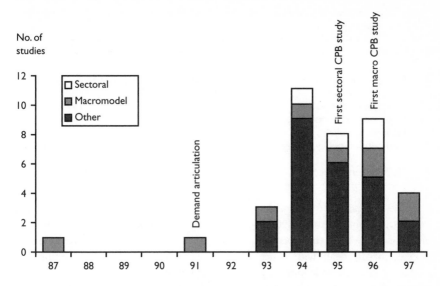

Figure 3.2 Dutch empirical studies on the functioning of markets (1987–97). Source: Van Gent (1997), Table 7.1.

macroeconomics). Kremers' analysis was widely debated and his 1991 article is one of the most quoted contributions in the Dutch economic discourse over the years 1992–97. This policy-oriented demand for research in the field of industrial economics (related to the issue of competition policy) was, however, initially not met by the CPB nor by academic economists. Only in 1996 did the CPB produce a first rough assessment of the potential impact of improved functioning markets in the sheltered sectors, adjusting the mark-up (price/marginal costs ratio) in two already-existing models (MIMIC and ATHENA, see Nieuwenhuis *et al.*, 1996).

3.3. Modelling in the competitive fringe

In order to get a first impression of the effects of supply-side policies, researchers at the Ministry of Economic Affairs included supply-side related elements in macro models (early examples are Knoester, 1983 and Knoester and van Sinderen, 1985). This modelling strategy was continued in the 1990s when the need to investigate the consequences of privatization, deregulation and more vigorous competition policy became apparent (Van Bergeijk *et al.*, 1993 and Van Sinderen *et al.*, 1994). The experience with modelling taxation provided new analyses and exerted an impact on the policy debate in part by stimulating the CPB to develop new models. This modest success stimulated the appetite of the modelling group at the Ministry of Economic Affairs and many new analyses were started (Table 3.1).

Table 3.1 Issues that have been analysed with the Ministry of Economic Affair's MESEM model

I	Taxation	Van Sinderen (1990, 1993); Bovenberg et al. (1990)
2	Growth accounting	Van Sinderen (1993); Van Sinderen and Waasdorp (1993)
3	Environmental taxation	Knoester and Van Sinderen (1993)
4	Investment in infrastructure; technology policies	Toen-Gout and Van Sinderen (1994); Van Bergeijk et al. (1997)
5	Competition policy, deregulation	Van Bergeijk et al. (1993); Van Sinderen et al. (1994)
6	Medium-term forecasts	Haffner and Van Bergeijk (1994)

So, in the cases of supply-side economics and public finances (early 1980s) and competition policy (early 1990s), policy makers took the lead in changing the modelling of policies and the process was policy driven. While the public finance discussion essentially dealt with issues related to 'mis-specification' (for example, the impact of taxation on labour supply), the question of competition policy and deregulation refers to changing certain aspects of the economic structure, i.e. to what Tinbergen (1952) labelled qualitative policies. Tinbergen (1952, p. 72) already pointed out that the 'scientific treatment of problems of qualitative policy meets with great difficulty'. This may provide an explanation for the slow response by the CPB. Interestingly, the analysis of issues related to competition policy appears to have spread to the academic world much quicker than in the case of supply-side economics. This may have been due to the success of the modelling strategy pursued by the ministries and the Central Bank in the case of public finance. In addition, the fact that the CPB had been challenged successfully on an earlier occasion may have reduced the perceived costs of entry.

4. A preliminary evaluation of the impact of competition in the modelling industry

In order to meet the demand for quantification of economic policy, a modelling agency – the Central Planning Bureau – was established within the government. This structure (monopolist versus monopsonist) was considered satisfactory by both demander and supplier for several reasons. First, the CPB was a pioneer and remained very much involved in the scientific discourse; there were major innovations in the 1950s and 1960s (as illustrated by the fact that the first director (Tinbergen) received the Nobel prize in economics (together with Frisch) in 1969). Second, the Dutch economy performed well, policy prescriptions were simple while supply-side problems were (perceived to be) less important. This system was challenged in the early 1980s when the results of the models strongly contradicted the necessary change in macro policy. At that time the co-operation between demanders and suppliers became less tight, resulting in forward integration in the value chain at the ministries and the Dutch Central Bank. Why did civil servants decide to do their own research instead of asking outsiders to build alternative models? We suggest three possible reasons. First, the monopoly of the CPB was so well established that a completely new analysis by outsiders (i.e. at the universities) would not have had any impact on policy-making. Second, the quality of models at the universities was disputable and/or the prevailing scientific paradigm was contested in policy circles. Third, the appropriable benefits of model-building means that doing research makes it possible to know all the ins and outs of the models of the monopolist and provides additional insights for policy-making and preparation.

Table 3.2 The cumulative impact of a tax shift from labour to energy (tax on bulk users of 1 per cent of GDP), in per cent deviations from base line, according to six models for the Dutch economy

	Model	Built at	Characteristics	Employment	Production
Dellink and Hofkens (1994)	ENTECH	U	D,X	1.4	−1.2
CPB (1992, 1994a and 1994b)	ATHENA	O	S,X	0.3 to	−1 to
	FKSEC	O	D,X	−6	−10
Knoester and Van Sinderen (1995)	MEOM	M	G	0	0
Kuper (1995)	CCSO	U	D,X	−0.1	−0.1
EC (1992)	QUEST	O	D,X	−0.3	−0.1
De Mooij (1993)	ENTAX	M	G	−1	−2.5

Key: D Disequilibrium macro model, G General equilibrium model, M Ministry of Economic Affairs, O Official forecaster, S Sector model, X Econometric, U University

The entry of modelling groups into the market has created a substantial diversity of analyses, covering the whole spectrum from (new) Keynesian via monetary to supply-side economics. Policy makers have started to use the products of the new suppliers, although the CPB is still a dominant supplier. This diversity (see Table 3.2) may, in addition, help the public to understand and appreciate the uncertainty and incompleteness of our economic knowledge. The diversity offers a unique opportunity to ascertain the robustness of policy advice independent of the prevalent economic regime. In this sense, economic policy-making is better informed as more and better knowledge is produced (although, paradoxically, this may have increased the feeling of uncertainty). Table 3.2 provides an example of the findings of six models with respect to the macroeconomic impact of a regulatory energy tax. At first sight, Table 3.2 appears to convey the message that economists disagree, as the range for the employment effects runs from +1.4 to −6 percentage points. However, a closer look reveals that, generally speaking, the modelling exercises agree that it is improbable that production will increase due to a greening of the tax burden (indeed it is rather probable that a regulatory energy tax reduces production). Second, although employment increases cannot be excluded on the basis of the modelling exercises, this would seem to be hardly probable while a clear downward risk exists according to most exercises.

This manner of information is valuable for policy preparation. We consider the increasing diversity of analyses an asset for the Dutch policy process as it makes it possible to provide for a cost-efficient assessment of both policy alternatives and their robustness. Diversity also diffuses the knowledge about macro modelling generating expertise outside the CPB. Also in this sense the increased competition in the macro modelling industry has added value to the policy process. It may very well have offered an indirect channel through which policy makers exerted influence on the CPB and the Dutch discourse of economic policy.

Acknowledgements

Preliminary versions of this chapter were presented at the Conference on the Use of Computable General Equilibrium Models for Policy Planning and Analysis, Copenhagen, October 1996, the second Lustrum conference of the Tinbergen Institute, Amsterdam, May 1997 and the Onderzoek op dinsdagmiddag seminar at De Nederlandsche Bank, Amsterdam, November 1997. Comments by Robert Haffner, Frank den Butter, Martin Fase, Mary Morgan, an anonymous referee and the participants of both conferences are gratefully acknowledged. This chapter does not necessarily reflect the opinion of our employers.

Notes

1   See Fase *et al.* (1992) and Van Sinderen (1993) for a description of these models.
2   It should be noted that CPB modelling substantially improved in the mid-1970s when Den Hartog and Tjan (1976) introduced neoclassical elements into VINTAF, the Dutch model.
3   The reader may wonder why forecasts by the Central Bank and the ministries do not count as 'official', but this is the perception of most Dutch policy makers and politicians.
4   Private sector modelling, however, by and large focuses on forecasting and is beyond the scope of this article.
5   Calculations, however, by Knoester and Van Sinderen (1985) showed that a minor change in the model specification (viz. including a feedback of the balance of payments on money growth) changed the sign of the impact of the multiplier, thus providing an analysis that underpinned the policy of cuts in government expenditures which was needed in policy preparation.
6   It is, however, important to note that demand for such macro model analyses was expressed well before the electional programmes were being drafted. Actually the importance and problems of the empirical analysis of structural (or regime) shifts was already recognized by Tinbergen in 1952.

References

Barten, A. P., 1991. 'The history of Dutch macroeconometric modelling 1936–86'. In: Bodking, R. G. *et al.* (eds), *A History of Macroeconometric Model-Building*. Edward Elgar: Cheltenham.
Van Bergeijk, P. A. G. and Haffner, R. C. G., 1996. *Privatization Deregulation and the Macroeconomy*. Edward Elgar, Cheltenham.

Van Bergeijk, P. A. G., Haffner, R. C. G. and Waasdorp, P. M., 1993. 'Measuring the speed of the invisible hand': the macroeconomic costs of price rigidity, *Kyklos* 46 (4), 529–44.

Van Bergeijk, P. A. G., Van Hagen, G. H. A., De Mooij, R. A. and Van Sinderen, J., 1997. 'Endogenizing technological Progress: The MESEMET model', *Economic Modelling*, 14, 341–367.

Bovenberg, A. L., Mulder, R. J. and Van Sinderen, J., 1990. 'Internationale integratie en belastingheffing.' *ESB*, 996–9.

CPB, 1992, *werkdocument* 43, Den Haag.

CPB, 1994a, *werkdocument* 63, Den Haag.

CPB, 1994b, *Vijf verkiezingsprogramma's*, Den Haag.

Van Dalen, H. P. and Klamer, A., 1997. 'Blood is thicker than water: The economist and the Tinbergen legacy.' In: Van Bergeijk, P. A. G. *et al.* (eds), *Economic Science and Practice*. Edward Elgar: Cheltenham.

Van Dalen, H. P., Letterie, W. A. and Swank, O. H., 1998. 'Economisch advies op het Binnenhof'. *TPE*.

Dellink, R. and Hofkes, M. W., 1994. 'Energieheffing, werkgelegenheid en technologische ontwikkeling' *ESB*, 159–61.

Donders, J. and Graafland, J., 1997. 'CPB models and employment policy in the Netherlands'. Paper presented at the Congress on Empirical Models and policy-making, Tinbergen Institute, Amsterdam, 14–16 May (Chapter 2 in this volume).

EC, 1992. European Economy nr 51 ('The Climate Challenge'), May.

Van Els, P. J. A., 1997. 'Policy-making and model development: The case of the Nederlandsche Bank's model MORKMON'. Paper presented at the Congress on Empirical Models and policy-making, Tinbergen Institute, Amsterdam, 14–16 May (Chapter 6 in this volume).

Fase, M. M. G., Kramer, P. and Boeschoten, W. C., 1992. 'The Nederlandsche Bank's quarterly model of the Netherlands economy', *Economic Modelling* (2), 146–204.

Gelauff, G. M. M., 1994. *Modelling Welfare State Reform*. Amsterdam: North Holland.

Van Gent, C., 1997. 'New Dutch competition policy: A revolution without revolutionaries.' In: P. A. G. van Bergeijk *et al.* (eds), *Economic Science: Art or Asset? The Case of the Netherlands*. Ocfeb, Erasmus Universiteit, pp. 59–72.

Gradus, R. H. J. M., 1995. The economic effects of extending shop opening hours in the Netherlands. Paper 11PF Congress, Lisbon, 21–4 August.

Haffner, R. C. G. and Van Bergeijk, P. A. G., 1994. 'The Economic Consequences of Dutch Politics', *De Economist*, 142 (4), 497–505.

Den Hartog, H. and Tjan, H. S., 1976. 'Investments, wages, prices and demand for labour', *De Economist*, 124, 32–82.

Jacobs, J. and Sterken, E., 1995, 'The IBS–CCSO quarterly model of the Netherlands: Specification, simulation and analysis', *Economic Modelling*, 12 (2), 111–63.

Knoester, A., 1983. 'Stagnation and the inverted Havlmoo effect: Some international evidence', *De Economist*, 131 (4), 548–84.

Knoester, A. and Kolodziejak, A., 1991, Effects of Taxation in Economic Models: a Survey, Research Memorandum 9102, Nijmegen University, Nijmegen.

Knoester, A. and Van Sinderen, J., 1985. 'Money, the balance of payments and economic policy', *Applied Economics*, 17 (2), 215–40.

Knoester, A. and Van Sinderen, J., 1995. 'Taxation and the abuse of environmental policies: A supply side view.' In: G. Boero and A. Siberson (eds), *Environmental Economics*. Macmillan: Houndsmill, 36–51.

Kremers, J. J. M., 1991. 'Naar een sterkere binnenlandse groeidynamiek', *ESB*, 76, 1228–32.

Kuper, G., 1995. Investment behaviour and vintage modelling. PhD thesis, Groningen University.

Kuper, G, H., 1994. The effects of energy taxes on production and employment. Paper presented at the annual conference of the European Economic Association, Maastricht, September.

Lucas, R. E., 1976. 'Econometric policy evaluations: a critique, *Journal of Monetary Economics*, Suppl. (April) (Brunner, K. and Meltze, E. (eds), 19–46).

De Mooij, R. A., 1993. 'Energieheffing en werkgelegenheid', *ESB*, 1100–4.

Netherlands' Government, 1978. *Bestek '81, hoofdlijnen van het financiël en sociaal–economische beleid voor de middellange termijn*, Tweede Kamer der Staten Generaal, 15081, no 1–2, The Hague.

Nieuwenhuis, A. *et al.*, 1996. *Marktwerking in beschutte bedrijfstakken*. Den Haag.

Porter, M., 1985. *Competitive Advantage*. Collier-Macmillan: London.

Portes, R., 1997. 'Users and abusers of economic analysis'. In: Van Bergeijk, P. A. G. *et al.* (eds), *Economic Science and Practice*. Edward Elgar: Cheltenham.

Rutten, F. W., 1991. 'Introduction'. *De Economist*, 1991, pp. 1–6.

Van Sinderen, J., 1990, Belastingheffing en groei. PhD thesis, Erasmus University, Wolters Noordhoff.

Van Sinderen, J., 1993. 'Taxation and Economic Growth', *Economic Modelling*, 10 (3), 285–300.

Van Sinderen, J., Van Bergeijk, P. A. G., Haffner, R. C. G. and Waasdorp, P. M., 1994. 'De kosten van economische verstarring op macro-niveau', *ESB*, 79 (3954), 274–9.

Van Sinderen, J. and Vollaard, B. A., 1999. 'The policy experience of structural reform in the Netherlands'. In: Van Bergeijk, P. A. G. *et al.* (eds), *Structural Reform in Small Open Economies*. Edward Elgar.

Van Sinderen, J. and Waasdorp, P. M., 1993. 'Het aanbodbeleid van drie kabinetten-Lubbers', *ESB*, 848–52.

Smith, R., 1994. 'The macromodelling industry: structure, conduct and performance'. In: Hall, S. G. (ed.), *Applied Economics Forecasting Techniques*. Harvester Wheatsheaf: New York, 68–88.

Smith, R., 1997. 'Emergent policy-making with macroeconometric models'. Paper presented at the Congress on Empirical Models and policy-making, Tinbergen Institute, Amsterdam, 14–16 May (Chapter 15 in this volume).

Tinbergen, J., 1936. 'An economic policy for 1936.' In: Klaassen, L. H., Koyck, L. M. and Witteveen, H. J. (eds), 1959. *Jan Tinbergen, Selected Papers*. Amsterdam: North Holland, 37–84 (original in Dutch).

Tinbergen, J., 1952. *On the Theory of Economic Policy*. Amsterdam: North Holland.

Toen-Gout, M. and Van Sinderen, J., 1994. *The Impact of Investment in Infrastructure on Economic Growth; Some Empirical Results for the Netherlands*. Confederation of European Economic Associations, Athens, 21–23 October.

Verbruggen, H. P., 1992. *Van Macro naar Meso*. Wolters-Noordhoff, Groningen.

Wren-Lewis, S., 1997. 'Conflicts between macroeconomic forecasting and policy analysis'. Paper presented at the Congress on Empirical Models and policy-making, Tinbergen Institute, Amsterdam, 14–16 May (Chapter 11 in this volume).

Zalm, G., 1994. Voorwoord, in CPB, 1994b.

Chapter 4

The IMF monetary model at 40*

Jacques J. Polak

A model reflecting the monetary approach to the balance of payments was published in the International Monetary Fund (IMF) in 1957. Its purpose was to integrate monetary, income and balance-of-payments analysis, and it became the basis of the conditionality applied to IMF credits. Extremely simple, with primary focus on the balance of payments effects of credit creation by the banking system, the model has retained its usefulness for policy purposes over time, as it was adapted to changes in member countries' priorities and in the international monetary system, in particular the disappearance of the par value system.
JEL classifications: B23, C30, E52, F41

I. Origin of the model

From the day in 1947 that the Fund opened its doors for business, member countries came to it to seek credit when they encountered deficits in their balances of payments that they found difficult to finance from their own reserves. To ensure that these countries would correct their payments positions within a reasonable period, the Fund had to have an understanding of the causes of the payments deficits and, both qualitatively and quantitatively, of the policy measures necessary to overcome them. Only then could it come to a judgement whether the actual or proposed policies of the member country would be sufficient to restore balance and, if not, to insist on a strengthened policy package as a condition for its credit. The model developed in the Fund to meet this need, first published in Polak, 1957 [1977][1] appeared to be still very much alive 30 or 40 years later. Approximately one-half of a 1987 IMF Occasional Paper (No. 55), attributed to no fewer than eight senior staff members of the Research Department and entitled *Theoretical Aspects of the Design of Fund-Supported Adjustment Programs* (International Monetary Fund, 1987, hereinafter referred to as OP55), was devoted to an exposition of the model and its implications for policy. In 1996, a workbook prepared as a

*Reprinted from *Economic Modelling*, 15, Jacques J. Polak, 'The IMF monetary model at 40', pp. 395–410, Copyright (1998), with permission from Elsevier Science.

training manual in the Fund's Institute (*Financial Programming and Policy: The Case of Sri Lanka*; International Monetary Fund, 1996, hereinafter referred to as Sri Lanka) focuses, as its title indicates, on the technique of financial programming, and its monetary chapter is built around the same model. Fund stand-by and other financial support arrangements continue to be designed around monetary targets serving as 'performance criteria' for the release of successive tranches or as 'benchmarks' that play a major role in the reviews of such arrangements.

2. The case for a simple model

One key characteristic of the model is its simplicity. For this, there were three good reasons.[2]

(i)　At the analytical level, a simple model was all that was possible at the time – the early post-war years – in view of the paucity of data (e.g. the absence of reliable national income or GNP figures) for many of the Fund's member countries and the total absence of econometric models to describe their economies. In these circumstances there were obvious advantages in the choice of a model that could produce some useful results with the input of only two sets of statistics, both generally available, banking and trade data. [Although GNP appears in Eqs. (1) and (2) of the model presented below, its structure is such that the reduced form of its import equation contains the coefficients m and k only in the combination m/k, that is the ratio of imports to money, if the marginal propensity to import can be assumed to equal the average propensity; but to estimate Y, a separate estimate of m is needed (Polak and Boissonneault, 1977, pp. 72–3).] Although the limitations on statistical data and on the practicability of interpreting these data by means of econometric tools have to a considerable extent subsided, it would still be a questionable undertaking to design an empirical, 'Lucas-proof' model for many of the Fund's customer countries, both in the developing world and among the 'transition economies'. Thus, while the Sri Lanka workbook contains a considerable number of behavioral equations fitted to annual data for that country, these do not add up to a country model and are used only, together with more ad hoc methods, in an iterative process to estimate future values of individual variables.

(ii)　Only a simple model, limited to a few crucial relationships, could be expected to have broad general applicability and therefore to be suitable to be loaded into the tool kits of the Fund economists sent out to a wide variety of countries as analysts and, as the occasion required, negotiators. Although over the years econometricians inside and outside the Fund have made valuable efforts to build more elaborate models both for individual countries and for groups of countries,[3] the Fund has generally had to rely, for its program design and control, on a simple model with a very limited number of standard variables subject to any elaboration on an ad hoc basis.

(iii) Most important from the policy point of view was the fact that this small model focused attention on the key variable that the authorities could control, domestic credit creation. That variable was seen in the Fund as crucial to the correction of the balance of payments problems for which its assistance was invoked, and therefore central to the conditionality of its stand-by arrangements. Reaching agreement with the governments concerned on acceptable numbers for credit creation often proved difficult, not primarily because of differences of view on the economics of the model, although the issue was often presented in those terms, but rather because adjustment is by its nature painful to a government in office. In some cases, failure to reach agreement led to a prolonged stand-off between the government and the Fund. Frequently, no doubt, governments swallowed their reservations and agreed to the Fund's conditions as a *sine qua non* for the conclusion of an arrangement. One particular case deserves mention. For years, officials in the UK had severely questioned the applicability to their country of the Fund staff's views on the effectiveness of monetary restraint. The resulting tensions between the UK and the Fund were, however, relieved as a result of a seminar on the subject in London organized by the UK Treasury in October 1968, that resolved most of the differences of view; and in his next budget speech the Chancellor of the Exchequer for the first time in many years stressed the importance of restraint on domestic credit creation (De Vries, 1976, pp. 442–3). But whatever the political or intellectual outcome of discussions of the model and its application between the Fund and member governments, there is no indication that the model itself was in any significant way modified as a result.[4]

Section 3 presents a simple version of the model, some of the general conclusions that can be drawn from it and a broad indication of its use in the Fund's relations with its member countries. Section 4 then explores the extent to which both the model, and the uses made of it, have been affected by developments in the world economy and by changes in member countries' policy priorities.

3. The model and its uses

The model was designed to study the effects on both income formation and the balance of payments of the two most important exogenous variables operating on the economies of the great majority of countries in the early post-war period: (1) autonomous changes in exports; and (2) the creation of bank credit. The linkage of domestic autonomous expenditure to credit creation, and of exports to additions to the money supply from abroad, required a model that explicitly recognized a demand-for-money function. The evidence from many countries suggested that the simplest form of such a function, namely demand proportional to GNP, would constitute a reasonable approximation.

Over the years, there have been a number of slightly different formulations of the model. The one presented below is probably the simplest; it derives from Polak and

Argy (1977, p. 206), slightly amended to make it more readily understandable in the light of OP55 (pp. 13 and 17). This model contains two behavioral and two definitional equations:

$$\Delta MO = k\Delta Y \tag{1}$$

$$M = mY \tag{2}$$

$$\Delta MO = \Delta R + \Delta D \tag{3}$$

$$\Delta R = X - M + K, \tag{4}$$

where

MO = money supply;
Y = GNP;
M = imports
R = reserves;
D = domestic credit of the banking system;
X = exports;
K = net capital inflow of the non-banking sector;
k = the inverse of the velocity of circulation of money; and
m = the marginal propensity to import.

The dynamic character of this model derives from the fact that it contains both Y (in Eq. (2)) and ΔY (in Eq. (1)). A solution of the four equations leads to expressions for the endogenous variables, such as ΔR and Y, as weighted averages of the values for the current and past years of the autonomous variables X, K and ΔD (Polak and Argy, 1977, p. 207). Statistical tests done in the Fund have shown that, 'on the whole, imports and income have been explained well by this model' (Polak and Argy, 1977, p. 210). The dynamic nature of the Fund model, in contrast to most of the academic monetary balance of payments models, yields not only the final equilibrium value of the endogenous variables but also the time path towards these values; the derivation of these short-term effects is essential if the model is to be used in the analysis of, and the prescription for, current policy problems (Rhomberg and Heller, 1977, p. 13).

In this general form, the model, assuming its validity, can be used to draw a number of inferences that are all to some extent counterintuitive and therefore constitute a useful bag of knowledge for international officials in their relations with national policy makers who may be more inclined to project first-round results (especially if they are favorable) into the indefinite future. These findings, it may be repeated, are based on the assumption of a constant income velocity of money, and while this assumption may not hold rigidly, there is enough evidence of its approximate validity to justify the expectation that it gives a good first stab at likely outcomes. I list here four such findings:

1   A permanent increase in output, for example as a result of a discovery of petro-leum, or the introduction of better agricultural techniques, while it raises income will provide only a temporary relief to the balance of payments.

2   A lasting increase in exports will produce a lasting increase in reserves but only a transitory improvement in the balance of payments. Probably the most strik-ing confirmation of this general proposition was provided by the complete, and to many unexpected, disappearance of the huge balance of payments surpluses of the oil exporters within a few years of the first oil shock.

3   Any once-for-all increase in credit will, over time, fully leak out through increased imports.

4   The stock of money is an endogenous variable; accordingly, while control over the expansion of credit can achieve a desired balance of payments result, control over the money supply can not. In the mid-1960s, the minister of finance of an industrial country that suffered from frequent balance of pay-ments difficulties advised a visiting Fund mission that the country was address-ing that problem by keeping the increase in its money supply to x per cent (I forget the figure) per year, and was truly surprised by the staff's comment that the policy stance adopted amounted to replacing any money that leaked out through the balance of payments so that the leakage could continue.[5]

For the further purpose of designing (or analyzing the adequacy of) the complex of a country's policies to deal with its balance of payments situation, it has been found useful to concentrate on the balance sheet of the central bank and its credit activ-ities, rather than on a consolidation of the balance sheets of the monetary system as a whole as in (3). This requires the introduction of the definition:

$$\Delta H = \Delta R + \Delta DCB, \tag{5}$$

and the behavioral equation

$$\Delta MO = q\Delta H, \tag{6}$$

where H is reserve money (currency plus reserves of commercial banks), DCB is domestic credit of the central bank and q is the 'money multiplier'.

The set of Eqs. (1), (2), (4)–(6) constitutes the logical core of the Fund's pro-gramming exercise, which has received the name of Financial Programming, and since the early 1950s has made up the center piece of the analysis leading to Fund conditionality: the stipulation of the policy actions on the part of the borrowing country that the Fund requested as conditions for the country's access to credit from the Fund. In the model's practical application, the validity of the behavioral equations is not taken for granted but tested, or, for the purpose of making projec-tions, amended as necessary in the light of any available information. Accordingly, projected numerical values for the relevant variables are not found by solving a set of equations but by making iterative calculations. There is a good reason for choosing the slow road of iteration in considering policy alternatives, namely that the choice of a target value, for example for ΔR, cannot be finally made until its consequences on the dependent variables are fully worked out. If the results of adopting one set of 'targets' turns out too harsh to be acceptable, targets may be adjusted, instruments may be reset and, perhaps, new instruments may need to be devised to bring about more favorable values for some of the 'exogenous' variables – such as pressure on donors to grant more aid, or the removal of some long-standing barriers to exports.[6] A particularly valuable by-product of this programming approach is that it forces the analyst to use (which frequently means: to construct) a set of consistent data on the balance of payments, government finance and the accounts of the banking system.

As one example of the model's attachment to simplicity, note that it stops at the explanation of ΔY and does not continue to an explanation of its real and price components (Δy and Δp). This may seem surprising, given the obvious interest of what Fund programs would do to real production and prices – or, as OP55 puts it, 'output and inflation targets are major factors in deciding upon the policy package' (OP55, p. 13). The origin of this apparent gap in the model lay in its focus on a monetary variable, the change in reserves, which could plausibly be argued (as it was in Polak, 1957 (1977)) to be independent of the quantity/price split of Y; so that from a prescriptive point of view it was possible to postulate a direct link between domestic credit creation and the change in reserves.

But why was this gap never filled? While one can think of a number of equations that would determine either Δp (the change in the price level) or Δy (the change in real GNP), it is questionable that any of these formulations would have the empirical validity that Eqs. (1), (2) have. For example, while it may be reasonable to assume that in some small open economies the domestic price level is fully dependent on the world price level and the exchange rate, we know that other small countries have succeeded in inflating themselves into an overvalued currency. Or again, one could postulate an assumption on the behavior of the price of domestic goods as a function of the ratio between actual and potential output (Khan and Montiel, 1990, p. 190), but unless the realism of such a postulate is established it would be rash to incorporate it in the model underlying the Fund's policy approach.

There are thus good reasons to leave Δy and Δp, as it were, dangling as quasi-exogenous variables in the Fund's operational model in its projecting mode. While there are elements in both Δy and Δp that may be susceptible to systemic projection, it is likely, especially in smaller countries, that special factors – crops, the opening of a new mine, the impact of recent exchange rate changes – have an influence that can better be estimated by a set of informed guesses than by the application of a formula which, at best, is known to hold for a broad group of countries on average over time (for an example, see Sri Lanka, pp. 105–22). To deal with a problem of this nature, a truncated model is to be preferred over one that pretends to be complete. In many practical applications, the price/quantity split could readily be brought in from outside the model. Thus the impact of a modest increase in the value of exports on an economy with some degree of slack could be anticipated to be essentially all reflected in Δy; a substantial increase in credit creation in an economy on the edge of inflation would probably all show up in Δp. One would know which scenario applied in an individual case and design policy recommendations accordingly.

4. The model over time

Although the Fund has continued to use essentially the same model as the foundation of its credit arrangements, these arrangements themselves continued over the years to broaden and deepen. But since none of these could conveniently be captured in econometric equations, no attempt was made to build them into the model. Thus while 'financial programming' and the underlying simple model continued to provide the packaging for the Fund's arrangements, the contents of the packages became increasingly complex over the years. A major effort was also made to set the Fund's programs against a medium-term background.[7]

In the remainder of this chapter I discuss the extent to which the model has (or has not) been modified to accommodate one additional policy variable, the exchange rate, and two new policy objectives, medium-term growth and the control over inflation.

4.1. The exchange rate

The design of the model in the early post-war years reflected two characteristics of the world economy in that period: the par value regime and a dominant upward trend in world demand. Balance of payments problems that brought countries to seek the assistance of the IMF were typically due to bursts of excessive domestic expansion, and could usually be cured by the introduction of financial restraint. If the expansion had festered long enough to raise the domestic price level above that in the rest of the world, there would be a need for a compensating change in the par value; and in the limited number of countries subject to chronic inflation, it might even be necessary to include a regular dose of compensating depreciation in Fund programs (Robichek, 1967, p. 9); otherwise, an adjustment program could be expected to succeed, usually quite quickly, without an exchange rate change (Polak, 1991, p. 36). In an age when the world was broadly on a full-employment path, there was, unlike the situation the 1930s, little incentive for countries to resort to currency depreciation as a means to raise their level of real income, quite apart from the fact that the Articles of Agreement banned 'competitive depreciation'. Thus, the same research in the Fund that stressed the importance of monetary policy for the balance of payments was bound to conclude that in a situation of full employment the effects of a devaluation on both the balance of payments and the real economy would likely be small, non-proportional and transitory (Alexander, 1952, p. 274). Indeed, the main outcome of that research was the discovery of certain ways in which devaluations could help to correct the excess demand that had caused the payments deficits in a full-employment economy. Among these ways were shifts in income toward groups that would save more or pay more in taxes (Polak, 1948

(1991)), real balance effects, and perhaps effects of money illusion (Alexander, 1952). In contrast to later concerns about the deflationary effect of currency depreciation (see, for example, Lizondo and Montiel, 1989), these causes of an expected downward shift in aggregate demand were seen at the time as welcome contributions to overcoming the excess demand that was assumed to be the cause of the country's payments difficulties, and which otherwise would have to be corrected by new policy measures.

As the par value system unraveled, the exchange rate became a frequent component of Fund standby arrangements.[8] But this did not require a radical change in the model. Exports already entered the model as an exogenous variable so that forecasting exports, whether with or without the exchange rate as one of the determining variables, was in any event performed outside the model (Sri Lanka, pp. 136–8). To the endogenous import equation an exchange rate term could readily be added (Sri Lanka, pp. 139–41). Indirect effects on prices and output and on government finance, as well as direct effects (if they can be ascertained) on capital movements, have to be taken into account in the reduced form equation of the system in which the demand for money, the change in net domestic assets and domestic credit creation converge (OP55, p. 41). Since, as noted, it is in any event not feasible to design a complete set of structural equations for the kind of economies with which the IMF works and solve this set for numerical policy numbers, the addition of the exchange rate as a variable had the effect of making the process of iteration more laborious rather than changing it in a fundamental way; it also, of course, made it possible to address explicitly a second objective in the Fund's arrangements, the pursuit of full use of the country's productive capacity.

Both the balance-of-payments and the short-term growth objective required not only that the exchange rate with which a country entered a stand-by arrangement was economically justified, but also that the rate would continue to meet that test in the face of uncertain external developments and – a more frequent concern – internal inflation. To achieve this objective, the conditionality of a stand-by arrangement typically includes a prescribed minimum *level* – or, if rebuilding of the stock of reserves is considered a necessity – a minimum *path* for net international assets that the country must observe to draw successive installments of its stand-by credit. The instrument by which countries ensure, if necessary, the observation of this limit is, normally, the exchange rate.

The standard conditionality of the Fund thus evolved toward the inclusion of a double monetary prescription: a ceiling on the expansion of domestic assets of the central bank to achieve an acceptable (flow) balance of payments result and a floor under its holdings of net foreign assets to bring about a satisfactory (stock) reserve outcome and, at the same time, make sure that the central bank would not use excessive intervention to counter market pressures toward a more depreciated exchange rate.

4.2. Medium-term growth

As the strongly expansionary trends that had characterized the world economy in the third quarter of the 20th century came to an end and an increasing number of developing countries had recourse to Fund finance and Fund programs, the members of the Fund and the institution itself became increasingly concerned about the impact of these programs on the growth prospects for the countries that needed to borrow under them. 'Growth' in this context meant two different things, not always sufficiently distinguished in the policy discussions, namely: (i) the increase in real GDP that could be achieved within the country's existing productive capacity, especially after it had experienced a negative shock; and (ii) the increase in output over the medium- or long-term to be achieved by the growth of capacity.

We have already noted, in the previous section, the potential impact of a change in the real exchange rate on capacity utilization. With respect to the second dimension, there has of course been no shortage of growth models going back to those developed by Roy Harrod and Evsey Domar in the 1940s. A variant of these models is still used in the World Bank (under the acronym RMSM, pronounced 'Rimsim') and in the Fund to make medium-term macroeconomic projections.[9] One may wonder at the survival of these models which omit what are nowadays considered the most important factors determining the growth of developing countries, such as outward orientation, realistic prices, privatization, reform of the financial sector and, in general, governmental attitudes toward the economy. But even if these models are accepted as simply spelling out one possible road to growth, their domination by long-term supply factors makes them too far removed from the short-term, demand-type monetary models to expect success in cross-breeding these two types of models.[10]

Instead, the Fund has pursued the double objective of stabilization with growth, not by an expansion of the model, but by an attempt to appraise the different items entering into the model on their potential contribution to growth. The movement in this direction started when the Fund created the Extended Fund Facility in 1974, under which it offered longer-term (10-year) credit to developing countries suffering from structural maladjustments or slow growth, and it intensified in the late 1980s when fostering economic growth became a primary purpose of Fund-supported arrangements under the Extended Structural Adjustment Facility (ESAF). In the application of the model to financial programming the analytically neutral variable 'credit creation' was split in its two sectoral components, credit to the private sector (usually to be encouraged) and credit to the government sector (usually to be discouraged). In a further specification, the Fund moved toward advice on specific types of taxes (with some taxes judged more acceptable than others) and on various types of expenditure, endorsing social safety nets and education (especially primary, not necessarily tertiary education) and frowning on military and other non-productive expenditures.[11] Beyond filling in with ever increasing precision the credit creation component of its conditionality, it also added further specifics of a non-monetary character, relying on 'a wide spectrum of policy instruments ... [that] also involved close collaboration with the World Bank in program design' (OP55, p. 29). Thus many programs in recent years have contained major policy understandings on structural adjustment, price and trade liberalization, deregulation of the labor market, privatization and many other policies.

4.3. Inflation concerns

The combination of monetary instruments used in Fund programs to guard against an unfavorable development in the balance of payments does not provide protection against deviations from the program in the opposite direction. A more favorable balance of payments than envisaged at the time of the program could lead to overperformance on the reserve target and hence, unless the level of domestic credit creation was kept correspondingly below ceiling, to a larger increase in the money supply than had been programmed. It is probably fair to say that up to the 1970s this possible outcome did not cause much concern. Countries enjoying temporary high export prices or manifestations of Dutch disease would not normally be users of IMF credit, but the Fund might caution them to restrain credit creation in order to build up reserves for a likely rainy day. For countries that had borrowed from the Fund, better than expected balance of payments or reserves performance were seen as welcome developments that might lead to early repayment of Fund credit. Moreover, the increase in the money supply might be welcome if it was provoked by a shift in the demand for money, perhaps as a result of a return of greater confidence in the currency as one of the results of the program. But the inflationary aftereffects of the debt crisis in the 1980s and even more strikingly the currency erosion that took place in many of the 'transition economies' in the 1990s have made it necessary to revise attitudes toward these issues. A study of the Fund's financial arrangements with 36 countries over the period 1988–1992 showed that 'targets for broad money growth were overshot by wide margins in approximately two thirds of the program years; in most countries this reflected mainly larger-than-expected increases in foreign assets ... *These developments illustrate the power of financial programs in general, and credit restraint in particular, for building reserves but* [equally] *their weakness for curbing money growth and, ultimately, inflation, particularly when the exchange rate is not used as a nominal anchor*' (Schadler et al., 1995, pp. 20–1; italics in original).

Rates of inflation not seen since the early post-war years made the control of inflation the first order of business in many countries, often ahead of dealing with potential balance of payments problems that had been made less threatening by the undervaluation of their currencies under the pressure of capital flight. In these circumstances controlling the money supply became an indispensable policy instrument, and the last decade has seen an active debate in the Fund on the circumstances in which, and the techniques by which, this could be achieved.[12]

These new developments present the countries affected by them, and the IMF in its task of providing advice and guidance, with a wide range of new challenges.

They also raise questions with respect to the continued relevance of a model that had been designed with substantially less taxing situations in view.

As the most striking example, the treatment of government deficits simply as elements in the magnitude of credit creation reflects a view on the structure of the capital market that is increasingly unrealistic for the great majority of countries. Governments in many countries may find it possible to finance deficits on local capital markets and thus, by raising interest rates, draw in capital from abroad and in the process to shore up the value of their currency. In order for the model to reflect these new realities of the financial conditions of some of the countries now seeking assistance from the Fund it would need to be expanded in at least three respects:[13]

1   The flexibility of international capital movements makes the treatment of that variable (K in Eq. (4)) as exogenous no longer tenable. K would have to be made at least in part endogenous, dependent on both the domestic interest rate and exchange rate expectations. Bearing in mind that an important component of K nowadays may be the outflow or the return flow of domestic flight capital, this change in the model alone would present a major challenge.

2   Allowance would have to be made for the fact that the domestic interest rate, which does not even appear in the simple model, may be strongly affected by the size of the government deficit, whether that deficit is financed from the banking system or in a nascent domestic capital market.

3   Yet another extension of the model would be needed to assist governments in the choice between two possible exchange rate policies, either of which may be appropriate in the circumstances described: a floating rate to block the inflationary impact caused by an oversupply of 'money of foreign origin', or a fixed exchange rate (or one moving at a predetermined crawl), to provide a psychological anchor to the price level, even though it may cause a competitive disadvantage if there remains some inertial inflation in the economy. To assist in this choice, the exchange rate would need to find a place in the model not only in terms of its effect on trade flows but also with respect to inflation expectations.

In a formal sense, it would not be particularly difficult to introduce these three extensions of the model. Indeed, versions of the model including the domestic interest rate and its effect on capital flows date back to its early days (Argy, 1977; Polak and Argy, 1977). But such extensions would not only destroy the simplicity of the model; they would also essentially be useless unless it were also possible to obtain some order of magnitude of the coefficients in the newly introduced equations. And that, unfortunately, is *not* possible.

In this setting, the Fund has had to forego the comfort of its old model and base its conditionality on a set of ad hoc instruments that seemed plausible in the circumstances.

With respect to government finance, the Fund has found it necessary in recent years to go behind ceilings on bank credit to direct restrictions on the government deficit, however financed, because government deficits, even if financed in a domestic capital market, crowd out investment by the private sector. Indeed, in the press reports on the Fund's relations with many countries (Russia, Argentina, Pakistan, to name a few) agreed limits on the deficit as a percentage of GNP have become the most prominent feature.

To stave off imported inflation caused by an expansion in the money supply, the Fund has favored a free (upward) float in many CIS countries, taking comfort from the fact that the currencies of many of these countries are so deeply undervalued that a measure of appreciation would not undermine their competitiveness, in particular since these countries were also experiencing a rapid increase in labor productivity. (In a number of transition countries in Central Europe, by contrast, the uncertainty created by widening of the exchange rate band has proved sufficient to calm the rate of inflow.) It should be noted, however, that governments that accepted a floating rate in principle (and whose fiscal policies were not always entirely solid) sometimes proved less than enthusiastic in its implementation and often tended to practice something close to a fixed rate.

While the prevention of excessive creation of domestic credit and the targeting of a desired increase in reserves are relatively straightforward, the avoidance of an excessive increase of the money supply raises more questions. In the first place, the normal effect of a successful stabilization after a period of high inflation is an increase in the demand for money. An inflow of money from abroad to meet this demand – and the corresponding overshooting of the reserve target – are entirely desirable, and to frustrate this demand by either a float or (with a fixed rate) putting a ceiling on the money supply would needlessly depress the economy.[14] A ceiling on base money would imply open-market sales of government paper at high domestic interest rates, which could be extremely costly. In addition, the resulting rise in domestic interest rates could attract more money from abroad, thus setting up a vicious circle.

Without much of a model to go by, the Fund has in recent years tended to adopt an 'all risk' policy, furnishing its arrangements with CIS and Baltic countries with a triple set of keys: a ceiling on domestic credit, a floor under net international assets and an indicative target for base money, reserving for periodic reviews a judgment as to the need for additional anti-inflationary action.

But for these countries, the exceptional situation described may be expected to subside as and when inflation comes down and the exchange rate stabilizes. In many of these countries the competitive advantage of an undervalued currency has been substantially eroded and while the concerns about inflation have to some extent abated, those about the payments position cannot safely be disregarded. At the same time, the continuing lack of confidence in banks has prevented the slowdown in velocity that has been typical of the end of inflation elsewhere. Thus, these countries may now increasingly find themselves in the position where the prescription offered by the simple version of the monetary model suffices: a ceiling on net domestic credit to protect the balance of payments plus a floor under reserves to ensure that the authorities do not overreach themselves in defending the stable value of their currencies. At some stage, confidence in the currency will rise and the resulting increase in the demand for money will pull in reserves. When that occurs, it will be possible to rejoice over the increase in reserves without feeling qualms about the rise in the money supply.

For an entirely different group of countries, however, the model would seem definitely to have lost most if not all of its applicability. Among the 14 Francophone countries that make up the Central and West African monetary and economic unions, there are no figures of (and indeed there is no meaningful concept of) country-by-country currency circulation nor, consequently, of a national money supply. The magnitude of credit extension is controlled by the common central banks for each region as a whole, and the development of regional money and interbank markets that could rapidly redistribute within the zone all credits expressed in the common currency (the CFA franc) has deprived the control of credit creation within any one country of economic meaning. Thus, for the Fund's operational purposes the government's domestic borrowing requirement has in practice become the only immediate instrument to influence the level of demand in individual countries (Clément, 1996, p. 76). Similar considerations would apply to the members of any other group of countries among which there was full effective movement of capital without any exchange rate risk, most particularly of course in the future the member countries of the European Monetary Union.[15]

Acknowledgements

The author, who was the Director of the Research Department of the IMF from 1958 to 1979, gratefully acknowledges comments and suggestions from David Burton, Michael Deppler, Joshua Felman, Christian François, Ernesto Hernandez-Catà, Anthony Lanyi, Leslie Lipschitz, José Lizondo, Henri Lorie, Jorge Marquez-Ruarte, Paul Masson, Susan Schadler, Van Can Thai and Christopher Yandle, as well as from the editors of this volume and a referee. An earlier version of this chapter is available as an IMF Working Paper (WP/97/49).

Notes

1 A version of the model was used as early as April 1950 in a paper prepared for the Executive Board of the IMF (Polak, 1994, p. xxv).
2 For a more detailed discussion of this aspect, see Rhomberg and Heller (1977).
3 Two of these were included in *The Monetary Approach to the Balance of Payments* (International Monetary Fund, 1977), the book that mainly served to bring together the original exposition of the model and the early attempts at its verification. Eleven further papers of this nature by Fund staff members were assembled in Khan *et al.* (1991).
4 The discussions with the British did lead to the introduction into the English, though not into the American, language of a new acronym, 'DCE' (domestic credit extension) for the variable called 'ΔD' in our model.
5 A more recent example of a similar fallacy is found in the claim that 'there is no evidence of a fundamental deterioration in Mexico's monetary and fiscal policies' as the cause of

Mexico's reserve losses, on the ground that the rate of growth of the money supply in Mexico in 1994 (at about 10 per cent) was significantly lower than in the previous year, when it had been about 30 per cent (Buira, 1996, p. 313).

6 OP55 (pp. 13–14) is, I believe, mistaken in attributing the need for an iterative procedure to the introduction into the model of the equation for imports, which that paper does not include in the simplest model it presents.

7 For a brief indication of the model used for medium-term projections, see footnote 10 below.

8 The proportion of Fund programs (for countries that did not belong to currency unions) that included exchange rate action increased from 32 per cent in 1963–72 to 59 per cent in 1973–80 to 82 per cent in 1981–83 and close to 100 per cent thereafter (Polak, 1991, p. 36).

9 The projections in these models are based on a combination of (i) a *target* growth rate for the economy with (ii) plausible *forecasts* for the outside world and (iii) the dubious *assumption* that any growth in output must equal the product of *new investment* multiplied by ICOR (the incremental/capital output ratio of that new investment, which is often assumed to equal that ratio in the recent past). If the exercise shows that the expected domestic saving and foreign capital do not produce the desired growth rate, the analyst is advised to think up various structural reforms that might in a general way, unrelated to the model used, ameliorate the outcome (Sri Lanka, Ch. VIII).

10 I have discussed attempts at integrating monetary and growth models in an earlier version of this chapter (Polak, 1997b).

11 For a discussion of the increasingly engaged nature of the Fund's conditionality, see Polak (1991).

12 The problem how to apply the model to situations in which inflation risks were an important concern of countries using Fund credit had arisen on some earlier occasion, of which the Philippines in the mid-1980s probably drew the greatest attention. The issue is discussed at length in OP55 (pp. 22–4).

13 What apparently would not need to be changed in the model is Eq. (1) which stipulates a constant marginal velocity of money. Available evidence suggests that that equation remained broadly valid. The Fund staff study referred to above noted that 'typically . . . velocity remained steady or rose . . .' (Schadler, 1995, p. 20). The experience of 25 countries in Eastern Europe and in the area of the former Soviet Union analyzed by Havrylyshyn (1995, pp. 22–5) found that in each of these countries, once the money supply was brought under strict control, inflation also fell to single digits per month in a matter of months. (Compared to the enormous magnitude of the percentage changes in ΔMO and Δp, any changes in Δy would be insignificant.) A sophisticated econometric calculation for Russia using monthly data for 1992–94 showed a close correlation, with a distributed lag of approx. 3–4 months, between broad money and the consumer price index (Koen and Marrese, 1995, pp. 60–1). But in the short-run there is evidence of a more complex relationship between changes in the rate of inflation and velocity (De Broeck *et al.*, 1997).

14 In its 1994 stabilization program, Brazil introduced slowly rising quarterly limits on the stock of base money as evidence of its commitment to bring down inflation. But the success of the stabilization effort, which brought inflation down from 47 per cent in June 1994 to a monthly average of 2 per cent per month in the last quarter caused a sharp increase in the demand for money which made the originally planned path for the growth in reserve money wholly unrealistic, and in November of 1994 the limit on base money was eliminated; but since the anti-inflation program had taken hold, the disappearance of a limit on base money did not undermine that program.

15 As long as countries participating in EMU remain individual members of the IMF they would be able to use Fund credit and the question of an appropriate model to set the conditionality for such credit remains relevant (Polak, 1997a).

References

Alexander, S. S., 1952. 'Effects of a devaluation on a trade balance', *IMF Staff Pap.* 2, 263–78.

Argy, V., 1977. 'Monetary variables and the balance of payments.' In: IMF (ed.), *The Monetary Approach to the Balance of Payments.* IMF, Washington, D.C., pp. 185–204 [reprint from *IMF Staff Pap.* 16, 267–88 (1969)].

De Broeck, M., Krányák, K. and Lorie, H., 1997. 'Explaining and forecasting the velocity of money in transition economies, with special reference to the Baltics, Russia and the other countries of the former Soviet Union.' International Monetary Fund, WP/97/108.

Buira, A., 1996. Reflections on the Mexican crisis of 1994. In: Calvo, G. A. *et al.* (eds.), *Private Capital Flows to Emerging Markets After the Mexican Crisis.* Institute for International Economics, Washington, D.C., pp. 307–20.

Clément, J. A. P., 1996. 'Aftermath of the CFA franc devaluation.' International Monetary Fund, Occasional Paper No. 136, Washington, D.C.

Havrylyshyn, O., 1995. 'Economic transformation: the tasks still ahead.' In: Per Jacobsson Foundation (ed.), *Economic Transformation: The Tasks Still Ahead.* Per Jacobsson Foundation, Washington, D.C.

International Monetary Fund, 1977. *The Monetary Approach to the Balance of Payments.* IMF, Washington, D.C.

International Monetary Fund, 1987. 'Theoretical aspects of the design of fund-supported adjustment programs.' IMF Occasional Paper No. 55, IMF, Washington, D.C.

International Monetary Fund, 1996. *Financial Programming and Policy: The Case of Sri Lanka.* IMF, Washington, D.C.

Khan, M. S. and Montiel, P. J., 1990. 'A marriage between bank and fund models? – Reply to Polak.' *IMF Staff Pap.* 37, 187–91.

Khan, M. S., Montiel P. J. and Haque, N. U., 1991. *Macroeconomic Models for Adjustment in Developing Countries.* International Monetary Fund, Washington, D.C.

Koen, V. and Marrese, M., 1995. 'Stabilization and structural change in Russia', 1992–94. In: Banerjee, Biswajit *et al.* (eds.), *Road Maps of the Transition – The Baltics, the Czech Republic, Hungary, and Russia.* IMF Occasional Paper No. 127, Washington, D.C., pp. 53–66.

Lizondo, J. S. and Montiel, P. J., 1989. 'Contractionary devaluation in developing countries: an analytical overview.' *IMF Staff Pap.* 36, 182–227.

Polak, J. J., 1948 [1991]. 'Depreciation to meet a situation of overinvestment.' In: Frenkel, J. A. and Goldstein, M. (eds.), *International Financial Policy – Essays in Honor of Jacques J. Polak.* International Monetary Fund and De Nederlandsche Bank, Washington, D.C., pp. 46–57.

Polak, J. J., 1957 [1977]. 'Monetary analysis of income formation and payments problems.' In: IMF (ed.), *The Monetary Approach to the Balance of Payments.* IMF, Washington, D.C., pp. 15–64 [reprint from *IMF Staff Pap.* 6, 1–50 (1957)].

Polak, J. J., 1991. *The Changing Nature of IMF Conditionality.* Essays in International Finance No. 184. Princeton University Press, Princeton, New Jersey.

Polak, J. J., 1994. *Economic Theory and Financial Policy, The Selected Essays of Jacques J. Polak*, vol. 1, Edward Elgar, Aldershot, UK.

Polak, J. J., 1997a, 'The IMF and its EMU members.' In: Masson, P., Krueger, T. and Turtleboom, B. G. (eds.), *EMU and the International Monetary System.* International Monetary Fund, Washington, D.C.

Polak, J. J., 1997b. 'The IMF Monetary Model at Forty.' IMF Working Paper WP/97/49.

Polak, J. J. and Boissonneault, L., 1977. 'Monetary analysis of income and imports and its statistical application.' In: IMF (ed.), *The Monetary Approach to the Balance of Payments.* IMF, Washington, D.C., pp. 65–131 [reprint from *IMF Staff Pap.* 7, 349–415 (1960)].

Polak, J. J. and Argy, V., 1977. 'Credit policy and the balance of payments.' In: IMF (ed.), *The Monetary Approach to the Balance of Payments.* IMF, Washington, D.C., pp. 205–26 [reprint from *IMF Staff Pap.* 16, 1–24 (1971)].

Rhomberg, R. R. and Heller, R., 1977. 'Introductory survey.' In: IMF (ed.), *The Monetary Approach to the Balance of Payments.* IMF, Washington, D.C., pp. 1–14.

Robichek, W. E., 1967. Financial programming exercises of the International Monetary Fund in Latin America. Rio de Janeiro (mimeo).

Schadler, S., 1995. 'IMF Conditionality: Experience Under Stand-By and Extended Arrangements, Part I: Key Issues and Findings.' IMF Occasional Paper No. 128, Washington, D.C.

Schadler, S. *et al.* (eds.), 1995. 'IMF Conditionality: Experience Under Stand-By and Extended Arrangements, Part II: Background Papers. IMF Occasional Paper No. 129, Washington, D.C.

De Vries, M. G., 1976. *The International Monetary Fund, 1966–1971.* International Monetary Fund, Washington, D.C.

Part II

The variety of experience

Chapter 5

Macroeconomic models and policy-making at the Bank of Canada*

Pierre Duguay and David Longworth

Operating in a flexible exchange rate regime, and managed by professional economists with a long experience within the institution, the Bank of Canada is one central bank where model-based projections play a central role in shaping and informing the internal deliberations about the formulation and conduct of monetary policy. As a result, the needs of policy makers are a foremost consideration for staff that develop and use models. This chapter describes the trends in policy formulation and model development at the Bank of Canada over the last 25 years, emphasizing the interactions between them, and explains the move away from large-scale disaggregated models towards a smaller, more focused model that can be used for both policy analysis and economic projections.
JEL classifications: C5, E52, E58, E37

1. Introduction

There is a long history at the Bank of Canada of building and using macroeconomic models for policy analysis and economic projections. This chapter examines the interaction between policy makers at the Bank and those who develop, change and use the models (especially RDXF and QPM).[1]

The Bank of Canada is in the forefront of central banks in the emphasis that is placed on the staff economic projection as part of a formal monetary policy framework that includes a schedule of meetings to discuss the projection and its implications for desired policy actions and to judge the significance of incoming economic data against the values consistent with the most recent projection (Duguay and Poloz, 1994; Poloz *et al.*, 1994; Longworth and Freedman, 1995). The management of the Bank is composed largely of professional economists who have worked as staff and, in many cases, have worked with models.[2] They value the use of theory to explain possible future economic developments and provide a clear story line. They also value empirical work to distinguish among various theories and to determine the size of important parameters.

*Reprinted from *Economic Modelling*, 15 Pierre Duguay and David Longworth, 'Macroeconomic models and policy-making at the Bank of Canada', pp. 357–75, Copyright (1998), with permission from Elsevier Science.

Empirical work that shapes model development can be initiated either by staff economists or by questions from management. The more interesting and/or robust the results, the more resources will be allocated by management for further research on that topic. In the end, both the policies that are adopted and the ideas about the monetary transmission mechanism that in part underlie those policies depend importantly on both cogent theoretical reasoning – tested in discussions within the central banking community and beyond – and a set of empirical work that would include single-equation estimation, models of a sector of the economy, and the results of policy analysis in full macromodels (whether estimated or calibrated).

This chapter covers only the complete macromodels that were used for policy analysis and/or economic projections; it thus typically does not cover the insights that were gleaned from other modelling exercises. The macromodels were generally developed by small groups of people from one section within the Bank. However, they were typically informed by a wide range of earlier empirical work that included testing theories against one another, testing parameter restrictions, and testing for stability over time.

Econometric model-building at the Bank began in the mid-1960s, with the hiring of part-time academic consultants and a new wave of economists trained in econometric techniques. The first model, RDX1 (standing for Research Department experimental), was intended as a research and learning tool. It was a relatively simple quarterly Keynesian model of price and income determination, with 48 stochastic equations (Helliwell *et al.*, 1969a, b). Progression to the more fully articulated RDX2 (with an extensive financial sector) started as soon as RDX1 was completed (Helliwell *et al.*, 1971). The new model contained 142 stochastic equations. The development of RDX2 took place during a period of momentous changes in the Canadian economy, with a major liberalization of the financial sector in 1967 and the return to a floating exchange rate regime in 1970.

Policy, model use, and model development are all interrelated. In Sections 2–5, we discuss these inter-relationships by focusing on four distinct episodes: forecasting during the M1 targeting period (1975–81); the search for a new monetary policy framework (1983–86); the adoption of a price stability framework (1987–88); and the development and use of QPM (the Bank's latest model) under inflation control targets. Section 6 summarizes the main trends and traces them to the interaction between policy makers and the staff.

2. Forecasting during the M1 targeting period (1975–81)

2.1. The policy background

Inflation in Canada rose to double-digit levels in 1974. In its effort to rein inflation in, the Bank of Canada started, in the autumn of 1975, to set target ranges for the rate of growth of M1, the sum of currency and demand deposits (Bouey, 1975). That decision was based on evidence from econometric research that: the demand for M1 had been a stable function of prices, real income, and short-term interest rates (White, 1975); swings in M1 growth 'explained' fluctuations in total spending (Duguay, 1979); and the rate of monetary expansion had accelerated well ahead of the rate of inflation.

The adoption of money-growth targets represented a clear shift away from the Keynesian paradigm embodied in the large-scale macroeconometric models of that time, including the Bank's own RDX2. The outbreak of inflation in the first half of the 1970s and the concomitant rise in unemployment[3] had exposed the shortcomings of that paradigm, particularly its neglect of the supply side and of the role of expectations. The monetarist paradigm was gaining widespread acceptance in central banking circles, both for its greater ability to explain inflation developments and for the persuasiveness of its logic. It also identified clearly the central bank's responsibility for inflation control.

Bank management continued to regard short-term interest rates as the main channel of transmission of monetary policy. What they hoped to get from M1 targeting was an objective guide to gauge the appropriate level of interest rates. The attraction of using M1 for that purpose was that it relied on only very short-term forecasts for prices and output, because the interest elasticity of the demand for M1 made it possible to achieve the target path over a reasonably short period, say 6–9 months; and yet, the approach appeared to provide the desired long-term nominal anchor for inflation.

Reality was not to be that simple (Thiessen, 1983). The high interest elasticity of the demand for money, which helped the Bank keep M1 on track, also allowed for wide deviations in total spending from the long-run trend consistent with money growth. That became clear when inflation began to accelerate again in the 1979–81 period, following the second oil-price shock.

2.2. Model development

Model development took new turns during the period of M1 targeting. A brand new version of RDX2 (dubbed the 'red book') had just been completed (Bank of Canada, 1976; Aubry *et al.*, 1977). It included major changes to the price, trade, and foreign exchange sectors in an attempt to improve the modelling of the international dimension of the inflation process (Aubry and Kierzkowsky, 1981). The focus was now on model validation (Maxwell, 1975, 1976), with particular emphasis on tracing the transmission of monetary policy (Freedman and Longworth, 1975) and the adjustment of supply to demand shocks (Maxwell, 1978). The dynamics of RDX2 held a number of surprises. For example, the working of the flexible exchange rate in the model was responsible for a much delayed aftershock that was nearly as large as the original shock (De Bever *et al.*, 1978). The model was used to generate medium-term scenarios to examine the effects of large domestic investment projects and new government budget initiatives.

While there was a desire to understand the dynamics of RDX2, there was also a recognition that the model had not kept up with the evolution of policy discussion at the Bank or with developments in monetary economics more generally. However, building a new macromodel or substantially altering an existing model is very expensive in terms of the allocation of financial and high-level human resources; the question always was whether to work on a full model or to allocate resources to examining economic theory and to estimating single-equation or sectoral models. Yet, there was a clear policy need to assess more explicitly the dynamic consequences for output and inflation of alternative target paths for money growth. Simpler simulation models, calibrated to capture the major features of the Canadian economy, thus began to be built for use in policy analysis (Freedman and Scotland, 1978). These models still tended to contain a lot of detail, but their structure was much simpler than RDX2, and their dynamics easier to figure out. They offered valuable insights about the implications of M1 targeting under adaptive expectations, particularly about the trade-off between goal (i.e. inflation) gradualism and instrument (i.e. money growth) gradualism.

Meanwhile, the Bank redeveloped its large-scale model for use in short-term forecasting. Large-scale models were increasingly being used elsewhere for that purpose.[4] Also an evaluation of the ex post forecasting ability of a number of publicly available econometric models, including RDX2, had shown some promise (Jenkins and Kenward, 1977). The fact that the medium-term properties of these models were being questioned seemed less relevant to their use in short-term forecasting than in policy analysis.

2.3. Nature of the projection exercise

The switch to a model-based projection occurred in 1979. Until then, the projection had been derived judgementally, from the input of a large number of sectoral specialists.

RDX2 was not suitable for forecasting. It would not be until the adoption of QPM in the 1990s that there was a model that Bank economists and Bank management felt relatively comfortable in using for both forecasting and policy analysis. Intended originally for policy analysis, RDX2 used data that provided the best approximation to the theoretical concepts being modelled; some of these data were available only after a very long lag; some required extensive manipulation. Thus, updating the database was a lengthy process; and whereas sector specialists worked with seasonally adjusted data, the model used unadjusted data. Nonetheless, the projection co-ordination group had begun using RDX2 (tuned to the judgemental forecast) to examine the consequences of alternative assumptions, or the implications of changes in fiscal policy.

The adoption of M1 targets increased the degree of simultaneity in the projection exercise. Until then, interest rates and the exchange rates were largely treated as exogenous variables. Targeting M1 endogenized interest rates, and that had direct consequences for the exchange rate. Factoring in the implications for prices and spending of projected movements in interest rates and the exchange rate required additional iterations. That simultaneity increased the demand for a model-based projection. What tipped the scale was the rapid depreciation of the Canadian dollar in the first quarter of 1977, which had made it necessary to turn to RDX2 simulations to obtain estimates of the full effects of exchange rate changes.[5]

After some discussion among staff and between staff and management, the decision was made to develop a model (RDXF, F for forecasting) that could be used to co-ordinate the input of sector specialists, rather than a model that would run in parallel with the judgemental forecast as had been done at the Federal Reserve Board. That meant distributing the ownership of the model among users and setting up a computer system that gave them easy access to the model, its database, and the estimation and simulation software (McDougall and Robertson, 1981).

In keeping with the bottom-up approach that had characterized model-building at the Bank, and to ensure that the model suited the needs of sector specialists, the latter were given primary responsibility for maintaining and developing individual sectors of the model. The projection-co-ordination group was responsible for documenting overall model properties and for ensuring that proposed changes did not have detrimental effects on other parts of the model. The result was a pragmatic, but rather a large model (some 200 stochastic equations and 200 identities) (McDougall and Robertson, 1982a, b).

Individual equations were judged primarily by their ability to track the data. Model properties suffered as a consequence.[6] This was evident almost as soon as the model became operational. The build-up of inflationary pressures in the early 1980s had pushed real interest rates to record highs, and Bank management became increasingly eager for medium-term (5-year) simulations showing how that situation would unwind. The model was inadequate for that task. Like all large-scale models at the time, it exhibited unreasonably weak monetary links[7] and paid insufficient attention to the formation of expectations[8] and to the resolution of imbalances between demand and supply.

A seminar convened to compare properties of various Canadian econometric models in use at the time showed that this was a fairly endemic problem (O'Reilly et al., 1983). There was broad agreement that the modelling of supply shocks and capacity constraints needed more work. Bank staff were inclined to believe that a small aggregated core model[9] with the details worked out in (block-recursive) satellite submodels, would be a key part of the solution; but there was not a clear view about what would constitute the core model.

The out-of-sample predictive ability of RDXF was not impressive. Large systematic constant-term adjustments had to be incorporated in the projections. Evidently, the focus on tracking historical data was responsible for considerable overfitting; and that raised questions about the wisdom of sacrificing long-run properties for some elusive forecasting ability.

2.4. New directions

In 1980, a small group of researchers embarked on the construction of a small (annual) macromodel with a strong theoretical base and a well-defined steady state, for the use in medium-term policy simulations. Their initiative was largely prompted by the need for a tool that could help address the medium-term questions that preoccupied management. The focus on rigour was also meant to answer deeper questions that preoccupied the economics profession more broadly (Masson *et al.*, 1980). Particular attention was paid to: maintaining an exact correspondence between model accounts and markets; imposing restrictions from theory, such as those linking labour supply, consumption, and asset demand; modelling the production technology, with energy as a factor of production, in the hope of explaining the slowdown in productivity growth; ensuring consistency of expectations; and achieving full stock and flow equilibrium. However, less attention was paid to short-term dynamics.

Although it contained only 25 stochastic equations, the resulting model (SAM, for Small Annual Model; Rose and Selody, 1985) was relatively complex and, like RDX2 before it, difficult to maintain.[10] The model possessed desirable long-run properties, but its short-run dynamics were very much at variance with the understanding of the transmission of monetary policy shared to this day by most staff and management. SAM was built around the notion of disequilibrium between supply and demand for base money. In the model, a reduction in money growth would lower interest rates immediately through its effect on inflation expectations (Fisher effect), thus raising the *demand* for real balances, even though simulated inflation fell only gradually, causing the *supply* of real balances to contract. The resulting disequilibrium in the money market would help speed up the adjustment of prices and spending. To many at the Bank, this seemed counterfactual since the bulk of base money is supplied passively, once decisions on short-term interest rates are made. SAM was used to address medium-term equilibrium issues, but it was not a substitute for RDXF. With a database that was difficult to update and unusual short-term dynamics, it was therefore bound to be eclipsed.

3. The search for a new nominal anchor (1982–86)

3.1. Policy background

On 29 November 1982 Governor Bouey made it known that the Bank no longer had a target for M1 because of the instability in its demand function.[11] In the 1982 Per Jacobsson Lecture, Governor Bouey (1982) had presaged the declining role of M1 and concerned himself with the 'search for a better analytic *framework* within which monetary *policy choices* are made'. The Governor noted that in the mid-1970s, 'We were aware of the important role of *expectations* in economic processes and were hopeful that the announcement of (M1) targets for policy would influence expectations and thereby speed the responses to policy. Moreover, the Bank would have a more solid *place to stand* in defending the actions that were undoubtedly going to be necessary to fight inflation' (emphasis added in each case).

The Governor came back to the topic of expectations a number of times in his lecture, as well as to the Bank's knowledge about how the economy functions:

Given the important role of *expectations* in perpetuating inflation, we in the Bank of Canada have found ourselves taking a view of policy that is more *forward-looking* than one based solely on monetary targets on the grounds that it is wise to respond immediately to any potentially inflationary shocks rather than to wait until such shocks are reflected in higher inflation and higher money growth. This is of course a bit different from the rather pessimistic view about the state of economic knowledge which influenced much thinking immediately after the outbreak of severe inflation in the mid-1970s and was one of the bases for the advocacy at the time of a monetary rule. We do know more about economic *processes* than is typically assumed by advocates of a strict adherence to such a rule. This is not to say we can forecast overall economic developments with any degree of certainty but we do know something about the implications of various kinds of *shocks. Exchange rate depreciation* has been the most important of these (emphasis added).

The rise in interest rates in the late 1970s and early 1980s did eventually bite as expected and, in spite of what large-scale models were saying, did produce a significant decline in inflation from double digits in 1981 to approximately 4 per cent by 1984. The orientation of policy was now fairly straightforward; with a large output gap, the goal was to encourage a recovery without re-igniting inflation.

For the time being, the staff economic projection using RDXF was loosely based on keeping 'predicted' (shift-adjusted) M1 on a steady growth path, with some attention to the behaviour of the exchange rate and some bounds on real interest rates.

3.2. The research program at the Bank of Canada

As the search for a new nominal anchor – monetary aggregate or otherwise – evolved over the 1982–86 period, it was guided in large part by the framework and concerns outlined in the Governor's Per Jacobsson Lecture. It was realized that M1 had played many roles in policy, but that there were three important roles that would be important to maintain with any future target: a *nominal anchor* as *medium-term guide to policy* (i.e. a target that would prevent cumulative policy error); a *place to stand* that would be used in communicating policy to the public and countering pressures to deal with short-term considerations; and an anchor with the potential to affect the formation of *expectations.*

The research program included an examination of the role of various monetary aggregates as targets, intermediate targets, and indicators, and an examination of the relative advantages of alternative nominal variables as possible targets for monetary policy.

3.3. Model development

The examination of the relative advantages of different nominal targets was carried out through literature surveys and discussions of the properties of individual targets.

However, the construction of a small model by Longworth and Poloz (1986) was the main vehicle for the comparison of alternative nominal targets and policy rules. All the policy rules considered were based on *nominal anchors* that would provide a *place to stand*. The focus was on monetary aggregates, nominal spending, the exchange rate, and (at an earlier stage) price-level targets.

The model had a number of key features, which allowed it to address the specific needs of policy makers and/or the strengths and weaknesses of previous models.

Its prominent feature was its simplicity: there were four behavioural equations (output demand, price Phillips curve, money demand, and exchange rate) plus a policy rule and identities. Simplicity was desirable for a number of reasons. First, so that the model could be understood both by the modellers and by the policy makers. Second, so that other key features could be put in place without too much difficulty: a coherent flow framework with a well-defined steady state, expectations that were model-consistent in the long run despite being adaptive in the short run, and exchange rate behaviour that was consistent with convergence to the steady state. Third, to reduce the time to do stochastic simulations.

The model was calibrated (rather than estimated), based on judgement using estimates by the modellers and others. This meant that modellers could concentrate on the effects of key variables and their parameters rather than expending considerable effort in the estimation phase of model-building to control for all the variables that might matter in explaining a given endogenous variable. Thus, for example, the output equation excluded foreign output, real commodity prices, and fiscal variables. The effects of shocks to these variables were implicitly subsumed in the shock term for output. Subsequently, two estimated versions of the model were produced and used to do shadow economic projections.

The stochastic nature of the exercise was seen by the modellers to be important in answering the policy makers' questions about which nominal target would be the 'best' in terms of responding to shocks.

3.4. Findings from the model

At an early stage in the project, the modellers found that the price level could not be stabilized in the short run without severe instrument instability. Thus, the exercise was pursued as a comparison among nominal income, money, and exchange rate targets. The overall conclusion was that 'policy directed towards the stabilization of nominal income dominates the other two rules in terms of minimizing the variance of real output and the price level. This result is in accord with those generated by static rational expectations models' (Longworth and Poloz, 1986). Interest rate reaction functions based on observed information and designed to stabilize nominal income were tested and found to be workable. Using information on the contemporaneous money stock proved not to be very useful in reducing the variance of prices or output.

4. Adoption of a more explicit price stability framework (1987–88)

4.1. Policy background

On 1 February 1987, John W. Crow became Governor. The output gap had largely closed, with inflation stabilizing at approximately 4 per cent. The economy was about to overheat, and it was more important than ever for the Bank of Canada to have a clear sense of direction: Where did it want to go? How would it get there?

The new Governor laid out his strategy in a lecture entitled 'The Work of Monetary Policy' (Crow, 1988). The goal of monetary policy was price stability.[12] This was not an arbitrary preference, but the way to generate confidence in the value of money and thus ensure the many benefits for the economy of a trustworthy monetary standard. Monetary policy worked through interest rates and the exchange rate, with uncertain lags and great imprecision. In particular, the results of monetary policy actions were greatly influenced by expectations. The Governor specifically referred to macroeconometric models as being useful in 'organizing our thoughts about the policy and the economy', but he stressed that they had their limitations. Monetary aggregates could be valuable in providing timely information about the trend of nominal spending in the economy, thus helping to 'keep us on the road'. However, uncertainty about the stability of their relationship to total spending or (in the case of the broader aggregates) about the Bank's ability to manage their rate of expansion over a relatively short period had militated against using them as formal intermediate targets. The Governor concluded with some remarks on the critical importance of maintaining confidence in the exchange markets. With the Canadian dollar on a downward trend from 1983 to 1986, there had been a number of episodes where extrapolative expectations in the exchange market had spilled over to the money market and had created difficulties in the conduct of monetary policy.

Thus, the Governor had taken an explicitly forward-looking approach that focused directly on the stated goal and skipped the intermediate target. That brought the staff projection to centre stage in the formulation of monetary policy. That also led the staff to take a more top-down approach in the projection, one that focused on the key macroeconomic relationships that were relevant to monetary policy. The role of the projection was well on its way to what was later documented in Duguay and Poloz (1994).

4.2. Changes to the projection exercise

A number of changes were made to support the role of the staff projection in helping achieve the goal of price stability.

Because the monetary linkages in RDXF were judged to be unrealistically weak, key RDXF equations were overridden to incorporate 'rule-of-thumb' effects of interest rate and exchange rate changes on aggregate demand, based on staff judgement and econometric evidence from reduced-form equations (later documented in

Duguay, 1994). The price and wage sector of the model was not quite accelerationist, but close enough for the immediate purpose.

Agreement was reached with management on a desired medium-term (7-year) path towards price stability, defined as a negligible rate of increase in the GDP deflator. The desired path for inflation was picked from a menu of simulations from RDXF, which included alternatives featuring smoother decelerating paths for M2 growth and nominal spending. However, these alternatives involved larger cycles in output, interest rates, and the exchange rate. While the desired path had been 'optimized' to a certain extent, it was understood that it would *not* be re-optimized (changed) from one projection to the next.

A convention was established to ensure timely reaction to shocks and to prevent cumulative errors. The staff projection would calculate the interest rates and exchange rate required to bring the level of nominal spending 6–8 quarters ahead to a pre-set path that would be revised infrequently and only with the concurrence of management. The reason for the convention was that the most important contribution of the staff projection to the conduct of monetary policy was the recalculation of the interest rate and exchange rate that the staff believed was necessary *in the first two quarters* of the projection to maintain progress towards price stability. Forcing a return of nominal spending to a prespecified path in a relatively short period of time purposely limited the ability of staff to adjust their recommendation about the policy setting to what they felt was acceptable to management.

Given the importance of the exchange rate in the transmission of monetary policy, as well as the notorious difficulty of making accurate exchange rate forecasts, the staff constructed an index of monetary conditions (MCI), which combined the interest rate and the exchange rate based on their estimated relative influence on aggregate demand, and Bank management started to use that index as a proximate target for its operations (Freedman, 1995).[13] The MCI provided the Bank with a kind of rule-of-thumb for dealing with unexpected movements in the exchange rate or unexpected changes in US interest rates. The desired MCI would typically be evaluated twice during a quarter – when the staff projection was presented to management, and halfway between projections, when staff would take stock of the information accumulated since the last projection and prepare a formal update of the outlook over the next two quarters for discussion with management. Management also received a weekly current-quarter GDP monitoring.

Although money demand equations in level terms were unstable over time, the growth rates of monetary aggregates (M1 and M2) had been found to be good leading indicators of growth in the volume and price components of total spending (Hostland *et al.*, 1988; Muller, 1990). Short-term predictions based on simple monetary indicator models were thus also regularly presented to management.

4.3. RDXF development survey

To guide future model development, a survey of RDXF users in the Bank was conducted in late 1988. The questions were grouped into three categories: How was the model being used? What level of detail was necessary? What was expected of a future model?

The results of the survey (Cozier *et al.*, 1988) indicated that there was a significant amount of dissatisfaction with the model and a good deal of agreement (among both users and developers of models) on the sources of the problem. Its large size and the absence of a theoretically tight core model made it difficult to interpret simulation results, and its properties were inconsistent with accepted theory. Users wanted a model that was consistent with their understanding of macroeconomic relationships, and comprehensible enough that they could have confidence in its simulations. The model would have Keynesian properties in the short-run, but would converge to a well-defined neoclassical steady state in the long-run. Expectations would at least be consistent with the model solution in the long-run, and any deviation from neutrality with respect to changes in inflation would have a logical justification. Such a model would provide a valuable common framework for policy analysis and for forecasting.

The Governor and Senior Deputy Governor were also asked for their views about the staff projection and use of RDXF simulations. They regarded the staff projection as *a basis for policy discussion*. They derived comfort from knowing that behind the macroeconomic story was a detailed scenario that could be monitored by sector specialists; but what mattered most for policy discussion was the macroeconomic picture and the analysis of the major issues facing the economy. They valued the projection as a consensus view from the staff. (The management did not influence the projection other than spelling out the monetary policy assumptions to avoid staff second-guessing monetary policy.) As well, they wanted the presentation to highlight the more contentious assumptions and the major risks. The explanation of why views had changed from one projection to the next was seen as particularly useful.

5. Development of QPM (1989–93) and its use (1993–present)

5.1. Policy background

Inflation pressures built up over the 1988–90 period, as aggregate demand moved beyond capacity, in part because of lax fiscal policy at both the provincial and federal levels. The staff economic projection was carried out with RDXF, but considerable top-down judgement was imposed so that the output from the projection process resembled what one would get from a reduced-form aggregate demand equation and a Phillips curve.

Informal discussions began in the summer of 1990 between officials of the Bank and of the Department of Finance on the possibility of establishing some type of inflation targets. This led to some work with small models of the Longworth–Poloz type, but with more forward-looking expectations in the exchange market. Based on the experience with using nominal anchor conventions in the staff economic projection in the 1987–90 period, it had become clear that returning to a nominal-anchor over a 1–2-year period was quite feasible in the models used in the Bank. Indeed, work with small models in the summer of 1990 showed that having nominal spending targets in level form and inflation targets (with price-level drift) had similar properties for most shocks if the horizon to return to target was approximately 1.5 year.[14] The staff working with such models became convinced that inflation targets were feasible.

In February 1991, the Governor and the Minister of Finance jointly announced the adoption of inflation-reduction targets (based on the consumer price index) with midpoints of 3 per cent for the end of 1992 (thus allowing almost 2 years to take into account the lags inherent in monetary policy), 2.5 per cent for mid-1994, and 2 per cent for the end of 1995. A band of ±1 per cent was to surround the midpoint. The Bank indicated that in response to shocks it would return towards the midpoint over 6–8 quarters (Bank of Canada, 1991). In December 1993, upon the appointment of Gordon G. Thiessen as the next Governor, the 1–3 per cent range was extended from the end of 1995 to the end of 1998.

The adoption of the inflation-reduction targets raised new questions about the establishment of credibility and the formation of expectations that would have to be addressed in model development.

With the announcement of targets, the staff economic projection shifted from a nominal spending convention to achieve price stability to a convention of aiming to hit the midpoint of the target range for inflation 6–8 quarters ahead.

5.2. Model development: QPM

The model development project for what was to become the Quarterly Projection Model (QPM) began in 1989 and lasted until 1993. Shadow staff economic projections were done in the first part of 1993 and QPM was adopted as the projection model in September of that year.

The results of the RDXF development survey noted above had a great influence on the development of the model, as did the conviction of the model builders that a tight theoretical structure with explicit stock-flow dynamics (thus drawing the best from the SAM model) was a necessity. The need to incorporate stock-flow dynamics meant that the exercise of constructing the model would be much more difficult than for a flow model like that of Longworth and Poloz. However, given the growing concern about the fiscal situation in Canada, it was becoming clear that the stock dimension was becoming all the more essential.

It was clear from the outset that if the project succeeded, QPM would be used for both economic projections and policy analysis. It was also clear that the model would be much smaller than RDXF and would have theoretical consistency imposed 'top-down'.

Midway through the project, in March 1991, the modellers described some of the key features of their prototype PAQM (for Policy Analysis Quarterly Model). The model was stable in that it converged to a well-defined steady state with damped cycles. It made a clear distinction between intrinsic and expectational dynamics, with expectations affected partly by the past, partly by the future (model-consistent expectations), and partly by the steady state; and it produced no free lunches.

The work on QPM benefited significantly from theoretical advances in the literature, as well as similar modelling of open economies that was being pursued at the IMF (Multimod), the Federal Reserve Board (versions of the multi-country model, MCM), and the McKibbin–Sachs Global model (McKibbin and Sachs, 1986).

At two key junctures in the development of the model, there were meetings of an Inter-Departmental Advisory Committee (IDAC) to get useful input from other experienced modellers and model users in the Bank's four analytic (i.e. economic) departments and to build a consensus that would lead to a general acceptance of the model for doing the staff economic projection. Although complete consensus was not reached on all issues (the subjects of calibration vs. estimation and the use of filters to determine 'short-run equilibrium values' were particularly contentious), the IDAC exercise eventually led to a much more successful launch of the model than otherwise would have been the case.

The modellers describe QPM as a system (see Poloz et al., 1994), with a long-run equilibrium model SSQPM (for steady-state QPM) that is well specified on the basis of rigorous economic theory (see Black et al., 1994) and the dynamic model QPM that provides paths to get from the starting point to the steady state (Coletti et al., 1996).

The steady-state model describes stock-flow equilibrium for household, firms, non-residents, governments, and the Bank of Canada. The key stocks in the model are household financial wealth, business fixed capital, net foreign assets, government debt, and the monetary base.

The major dynamics in QPM stem from three separate sources. First are those adjustments that are key elements of the economic structure, such as labour market contracts, the investments that move capital to its desired level, etc. Second are the adjustment of expectations (e.g. of wages, prices, and exchange rates) towards their steady-state rates and levels. Third is the reaction of monetary policy and fiscal policies to disturbances.

QPM is calibrated, not estimated. This allows other criteria in addition to the minimization of short-run prediction errors to play a role in assigning parameters. Such criteria include short-run and long-run economic properties (such as elasticities or shares), speeds of adjustment, and the ability of the parametrized model to replicate certain stylized facts. There is, of course, an inherent tension among the various criteria. However, the decision was made to give priority to the overall macroeconomic properties[15] and to the ability of the model to mimic the response to certain shocks, especially monetary shocks, that come out of vector autoregressions. As part of the trade-off, it was decided that judgement should heavily influence the first two quarters of the staff economic projection. Past errors are assumed to runoff at a rate based on the estimated first-order autocorrelation coefficient.

One complication in the modelling arises because the fundamentals in the

Canadian economy have not always been heading towards the same steady state. For example, government debt to GDP ratios, and net foreign asset to GDP ratios have changed significantly over time. This has necessitated the use of short-run equilibrium values (known as SREQs), which are filtered measures of the variables in question over the historical period and which converge to the long-run steady-state over the projection period.

The key monetary policy instrument in QPM is the yield curve spread: the difference between the 3-month and 10-year interest rate less its equilibrium value. This choice was made on the basis of a significant amount of work (including Cozier and Tkacz, 1994) which showed that the difference between short-term and long-term interest rates was a good measure of the real interest rate (for reasons set out by Clinton, 1994) and had significant impacts on output and consumption in reduced-form equations.

5.3. Projections with QPM and continuing issues with the model

After a few shadow economic projections run in parallel with RDXF, QPM was adopted as the model for the staff economic projection in September 1993. The role of the staff projection remained quite similar to that with RDXF. However, because of its strong theoretical underpinnings, QPM is much more easily used than RDXF for risk analysis and the analysis of alternative policies. Therefore each quarterly projection is accompanied by three or four risk analyses that focus either on alternative interpretations of the starting point, alternative assumptions about the behaviour of a sector or a variable over time, or alternative assumptions about monetary or fiscal policy. The management may ask for additional scenarios.

In models, like QPM, where the output gap plays a significant role, it is necessary to have a way of producing an estimate of the output gap that minimizes the chances of consistent biases in the prediction of inflation. Simple trend measures or Hodrick–Prescott filtered measures of potential output do not use all the relevant information. Thus the QPM modellers also came up with new multivariate filters to produce estimates of potential output and thus the output gap (Laxton and Tetlow, 1993; Butler, 1996). These methods implicitly put a greater weight on persistent supply shocks than had been the case earlier at the Bank. At the same time, they use structural information that is roughly consistent with QPM's structure.

QPM is a living, changing model. Improvements are constantly being made to it, although very rarely do these changes affect the theoretical structure of the steady-state model. Indeed, it is the tight theoretical structure of the steady-state that requires one to examine closely any proposed change. Items are added to the QPM work program based on problems, whether large or small, noted by those running the model or those required to sign off on the economic projections sent to management. As well, the questions asked by management also lead to investigations of alternatives.

Some areas where there was not full agreement when the model started to be used continue to receive attention. Examples include: the determination of the short-run equilibrium values, given the evidence of the problems with the use of filters (such as the Hodrick–Prescott filter), the question of whether highly constrained estimation should be used in some equations instead of calibration, a topic that is being considered in the context of model evaluation and testing; and the degree of asymmetries in the Phillips curve, especially with respect to the output gap (e.g. Laxton *et al.*, 1993).[16]

There are also areas of research outside the context of the QPM model where significant results could eventually be incorporated into QPM. These include: expectations and credibility; improvements in the measurement of potential output; monetary policy reaction functions in the context of stochastic simulations; and the effect of changes in trend inflation on total factor productivity.

6. Conclusion

The trend in macroeconometric model-building at the Bank of Canada has been away from the large-scale disaggregated models of the 1970s towards focused, well-articulated small- and medium-sized models, suitable for medium-term policy analysis and for short-term monetary policy setting under conditions of uncertainty about the future. This trend, evident in a number of other central banks (e.g. Bank of England, Federal Reserve Board, and the Reserve Bank of New Zealand), is consistent with what monetary policy is about. (It is, however, quite at variance with trends elsewhere, such as at the Netherlands Central Planning Bureau, towards disaggregated general-equilibrium, microeconomic modelling.)

Trends in model development and use at the Bank of Canada result from the interaction between policy makers and the staff:

- When policy makers wish to examine risks and alternative scenarios, they need a model that will provide a quantitative assessment.
- When policy makers look towards the medium-term, judgemental forecasting becomes more problematic (past the first quarter or two) and medium-term model properties become more important.
- When policy makers have a forward-looking target (such as the inflation-control targets first adopted in 1991), they need a mechanism to set instruments *today* in order to achieve that future target and they appreciate the need to have a model of expectations with forward-looking components.
- Staff economic projections that are integrated into the policy process (yet incorporate appropriate judgement about the short-term outlook) are most useful to policy makers.
- Those who develop and change models must be aware of which theoretical developments in the literature and modelling developments elsewhere can be helpful to the policymakers – either anticipating the needs of policy makers or reacting to concerns and criticisms offered by the policy makers. If the policy makers do not buy into a new paradigm they will not accept the policy advice

coming from a model built around that paradigm. Therefore cogent theoretical arguments and a wide variety of empirical evidence are likely to be necessary.

• Those who develop and change the model must be sensitive to the needs of policy makers: short-term vs. medium-term focus, atheoretical forecasting vs. policy analysis grounded in theory, details for many economic variables vs. broad forces in the economic projections, and the need for analysis of longer-term effects of fiscal policy. As well, they need to be aware of the ongoing tension between maximizing the fit of a model and imposing reasonable long-run restrictions that come out of economic theory.

Notes

1 That focus has led us to emphasize major policy decisions and to concentrate on their relationship to model use and development. Evidently, there were other influences on model development at the Bank, most notably from developments in macroeconomics and in econometric theory, and from interactions with other model-builders.

2 For example, 11 of the 16 individuals that have served as deputy governors over the last 25 years (including all three governors) have worked in the Research Department of the Bank. Only two were appointed from outside.

3 A major reform of unemployment insurance in Canada in 1971 increased the equilibrium rate of unemployment (see, e.g. Rose, 1988).

4 For example, staff at the US Federal Reserve Board were using the MPS model for forecasting. As well, a number of US commercial outfits (Chase, Wharton, DRI, to name a few) were offering model-based econometric forecasts. The Conference Board of Canada and the University of Toronto were also providing such services.

5 Ironically, McQueen (1997) reports that it was a question from Governor Rasminsky to staff about the consequences of the devaluation of the Canadian dollar for their economic projection in 1962 that had ushered in econometric modelling at the Bank of Canada.

6 For a UK perspective on how the bias towards forecasting has worked against policy advice, see Wren-Lewis, 1997, Chapter 11 in this volume.

7 For example, in the case of a permanent reduction in M1 growth, inflation had not adjusted after 10 years, with the result that real balances were still falling relative to control, nominal interest rates were still rising, and real spending was continuing to fall. Reduced-form models, on the other hand, showed that the adjustment was substantially completed after 4–5 years (see Duguay, 1979).

8 The importance of assumptions made about the formation of expectations is also featured in Boughton (1997, Chapter 8 in this volume), Edison and Marquez (1998, Chapter 12 in this volume), Mayes and Razzak (1998, Chapter 7 in this volume), Whitley (1997) and Wren-Lewis (1997, Chapter 11 in this volume).

9 The importance of having small models in which the macro properties can be more easily understood is also featured in Boughton (1997, Chapter 8 in this volume), Mayes and Razzak (1998, Chapter 7 in this volume), and Whitley (1997).

10 It took about 4 years to develop SAM. Subsequently, QPM also took 4 years to develop. The general impression gleaned from the Tinbergen Institute 10th Anniversary Conference indicated that there is a 'Law of 4 Years' for model development.

11 Instability in money demand equations was a feature in many industrialized countries that was much discussed in the literature at the time. The point was picked up in the discussion at the Tinbergen Institute Conference.

12 Although this goal is quite traditional for central banks, it had lost some of its currency as a result of the tumultuous inflation of the 1970s and a failure to make further progress towards price stability after 1984.

13 Other central banks subsequently adopted the MCI notion. See, in particular, Mayes and Razzak (1998, Chapter 7 in this volume) for the experience of the Reserve Bank of New Zealand. For a critical review of the econometrics underlying the weights in the MCI, see Eika *et al.* (1996); for a general overview of the concept see Ericsson *et al.* (1997).

14 Thus, there were two main differences with the work that had been done with the Longworth–Poloz model. First, the target was the rate of inflation, not the price level. Second, the horizon for hitting the target was 6–8 quarters, rather than 1–4 quarters.

15 In a model where many components of demand are modelled, and there is a complicated wage-price sector, it is often difficult to get reasonable macroeconomic properties without imposing certain restrictions. Moreover, there is evidence that some macro-relationships may be more stable than the functions determining individual components of GDP. For a related discussion, see Duguay (1994).

16 The modellers at the Reserve Bank of New Zealand have also been grappling with the topic (see Mayes and Razzak, 1998, Chapter 7 in this volume).

References

Aubry, J.-P., de Bever, L., Kenward, L., Kohli, U. and Longworth, D., 1977. Sectoral Analysis of RDX2 Estimated to 4Q72. Technical Report No. 6, Bank of Canada, Ottawa.

Aubry, J.-P. and Kierzkowsky, H., 1981. 'The transmission of foreign price inflation under alternative exchange rate regimes: a review of recent theoretical developments and experiments with RDX2 and MPS.' In: Courbis, R. (ed.), *Commerce International et Modèles Multinationaux*. Economica, Paris, pp. 259–77.

Bank of Canada, 1976. The Equations of RDX2 Revised and Estimated to 4Q72. Technical Report No. 5. Bank of Canada, Ottawa.

Bank of Canada, 1991. 'Targets for reducing inflation: announcements and background material.' *Bank of Canada Review*, March, pp. 3–21.

Black, R., Laxton, D., Rose, D. and Tetlow, R., 1994. QPM – Part 1: The Steady-State Model: SSQPM. Technical Report No. 72. Bank of Canada, Ottawa.

Bouey, G. K., 1975. 'Remarks to the Annual Meeting of the Canadian Chamber of Commerce. Saskatoon, 22 September 1975.' *Bank of Canada Review*, October, pp. 23–30.

Bouey, G. K., 1982. 'Monetary policy – finding a place to stand, the 1982 Per Jacobsson Lecture.' *Bank of Canada Review*, September, pp. 3–17.

Boughton, J. M., 1997. 'Modelling the World Economic Outlook at the IMF: A Historical Review'. Paper presented at the 10th Anniversary Congress of the Tinbergen Institute, Amsterdam (Chapter 8 in this volume).

Butler, L., 1996. The Bank of Canada's New Quarterly Projection Model: Part 4 – A Semi-Structural Method to Estimate Potential Output: Combining Economic Theory with a Time-series Filter. Technical Report No. 77. Bank of Canada, Ottawa.

Clinton, K., 1994. 'The term structure of interest rates as a leading indicator of economic activity: a technical note.' *Bank of Canada Review*, Winter, pp. 23–40.

Coletti, D., Hunt, B., Rose, D. and Tetlow, R., 1996. The Bank of Canada's New Quarterly Projection Model: Part 3, The Dynamic Model: QPM. Technical Report No. 75. Bank of Canada, Ottawa.

Cozier, B., Laxton, D. and Selody, J., 1988. RDXF Development Survey. Bank of Canada memo.

Cozier, B. and Tkacz, G., 1994. The Term Structure and Real Activity in Canada. Working Paper 94-3. Bank of Canada, Ottawa.

Crow, J. W., 1988. 'The Work of Canadian Monetary Policy, Eric J. Hanson Memorial Lecture. University of Alberta, Edmonton, 18 January.' *Bank of Canada Review*, February, pp. 3–17.

De Bever, L., Kholi, U. and Maxwell, T., 1978. An Analysis of the Major Dynamic Properties of RDX2. Technical Report No. 13. Bank of Canada, Ottawa.

Duguay, P., 1979. 'Bref aperçu d'un modèle à forme réduite de prévision de la dépense nationale brute au Canada', *L'actualité Économique*, 55, 411–25.

Duguay, P., 1994. 'Empirical evidence on the strength of the monetary transmission mechanism in Canada: an aggregate approach', *J. Monet. Econ.* 33, 39–61.

Duguay, P. and Poloz, S., 1994. 'The role of economic projections in Canadian monetary policy formulation. *Can. Publ. Pol.* XX, 189–99.

Edison, H. J. and Marquez, J., 1998. 'US monetary policy and econometric modeling: tales from the FOMC transcripts 1984–1991', **Economic Modelling** 15, 411–28 (Chapter 12 in this volume).

Eika, K., Ericsson, N. R. and Nymoen, R., 1996. 'Hazards in implementing a monetary conditions index', *Oxf. Bull. Econ. Stat.* 58, 765–90.

Ericsson, N. R., Jansen, E. S., Kerbeshian, N. A. and Nymoen, R., 1997. Understanding a Monetary Conditions Index. Paper presented to the Econometric Society European Meeting, Toulouse, August.

Freedman, C., 1995. 'The role of monetary conditions and the monetary conditions index in the conduct of policy', *Bank of Canada Review*, Autumn, pp. 53–9.

Freedman, C. and Longworth, D., 1975. Channels of Monetary Policy in RDX2. Paper presented to the Queen's University Conference on Canadian Monetary Issues, 17–20 August 1975.

Freedman, C. and Scotland, F., 1978. The Implications of a Change in Resource Prices: A Simulation Exercise. Bank of Canada memo, January.

Helliwell, J. F., Shapiro, H. T., Officer, L. H. and Stewart, I. A., 1969a. The Structure of RDX1. Staff Research Study No. 3. Bank of Canada, Ottawa.

Helliwell, J. F., Shapiro, H. T., Officer, L. H. and Stewart, I. A., 1969b. The Dynamics of RDX1. Staff Research Study No. 5. Bank of Canada, Ottawa.

Helliwell, J. F., Sparks, G. R., Gorbet, F. W., Shapiro, H. T., Stewart, I. A. and Stephenson, D. R., 1971. The Structure of RDX2. Staff Research Study No. 7. Bank of Canada, Ottawa.

Hostland, D., Poloz, S. and Storer, P., 1988. An Analysis of the Information Content of Alternative Monetary Aggregates. Technical Report No. 48. Bank of Canada, Ottawa.

Jenkins, P. and Kenward, L., 1977. The Comparative Ex-post Forecasting Properties of Several Canadian Quarterly Econometric Models. Technical Report No. 7. Bank of Canada, Ottawa.

Laxton, D. and Tetlow, R., 1993. A Simple Multivariate Filter for Measurement of Potential Output. Technical Report No. 59. Bank of Canada, Ottawa.

Laxton, D., Rose, D. and Tetlow, R., 1993. Is the Canada Phillips Curve Non-linear? Working Paper 93-7. Bank of Canada, Ottawa.

Longworth, D. and Poloz, S., 1986. A Comparison of Alternative Monetary Policy Regimes in a Small Dynamic Open-economy Simulation Model. Technical Report No. 42. Bank of Canada, Ottawa.

Longworth, D. and Freedman, C., 1995. 'The role of the staff economic projection in conducting Canadian monetary policy.' In: Haldane, A. G. (ed.), *Targeting Inflation*. Bank of England, London.

Masson, P. R., Rose, D. E. and Selody, J. G., 1980. Building a Small Macro-model for Simulation: Some Issues. Technical Report No. 22. Bank of Canada, Ottawa.

Maxwell, T., 1975. 'Validation of Macro Econometric Models: Some Reflections on the State of the Art.' *Bank of Canada Review*, November, pp. 9–16.

Maxwell, T., 1976. 'Assessing the Performance of Macro Econometric Models in Policy Analysis.' *Bank of Canada Review*, May, pp. 3–11.

Maxwell, T., 1978. 'The Dynamics of RDX2.' *Bank of Canada Review*, November, pp. 3–21.

Mayes, D. G. and Razzak, W. A., 1998. 'Transparency and accountability: Empirical models and policy-making at the Reserve Bank of New Zealand', *Econ. Model.* 15, 377–94. (Chapter 7 in this volume)

McDougall, M. and Robertson, H., 1981. Economic Projections and Econometric Modelling: Recent Developments at the Bank of Canada. Technical Report No. 23. Bank of Canada, Ottawa.

McDougall, M. and Robertson, H., 1982a. The Equations of RDXF, September 1980 version. Technical Report No. 25. Bank of Canada, Ottawa.

McDougall, M. and Robertson, H., 1982b. The Structure and Dynamics of RDXF, September 1980 version. Technical Report No. 26. Bank of Canada. Ottawa.

McKibbin, W. and Sachs, J., 1986. The MSG Model, Unpublished Memorandum submitted at the March 1986 Brookings conference on Empirical Macroeconomics for Interdependent Economies, Harvard University Department of Economics, February.

McQueen, D., 1997. 'Economic research at the Bank of Canada, 1935–1965', *Can. Bus. Econ.* 5, 89–95.

Muller, P., 1990. 'The information content of the financial aggregates during the 1980s.' In: *Monetary Seminar 90.* Bank of Canada, Ottawa.

O'Reilly, B., Paulin, G. and Smith, P., 1983. Responses of Various Econometric Models to Selected Policy Shocks. Technical Report No. 38. Bank of Canada, Ottawa.

Poloz, S., Rose, D. and Tetlow, R., 1994. 'The Bank of Canada's New Quarterly Projection Model (QPM): an Introduction.' *Bank of Canada Review*, Autumn, pp. 23–38.

Rose, D., 1988. The Nairu in Canada: Concepts, Determinants and Estimates. Technical Report No. 50. Bank of Canada, Ottawa.

Rose, D. and Selody, J., 1985. The Structure of the Small Annual Model (SAM). Technical Report No. 40. Bank of Canada, Ottawa.

Thiessen, G. G., 1983. 'The Canadian experience with monetary targeting.' In: Meek, P. (ed.), *Central Bank Views on Monetary Targeting.* Federal Reserve Bank of New York, New York, pp. 100–4.

White, W. R., 1975. The Demand for Money in Canada and the Control of the Monetary Aggregates: Evidence from the Monthly Data. Staff Study No. 12. Bank of Canada, Ottawa.

Whitley, J. D., 1997. Economic Models: a Flexible Friend for Policy Makers? Paper for the 10th Anniversary Congress of the Tinbergen Institute, Amsterdam. Published as 'Economic models and policy-making', *Bank of England Quarterly Review*, 1997, May, pp. 163–73.

Wren-Lewis, S., 1997. Conflicts Between Macroeconomic Forecasting and Policy Analysis. Paper presented at the 10th Anniversary Congress of the Tinbergen Institute, Amsterdam (Chapter 11 in this volume).

Chapter 6

Policy-making and model development: the case of the Nederlandsche Bank's model MORKMON

Peter J. A. van Els

This study offers an analysis of the interaction between model development and policy-making, with a special focus on the macroeconomic policy model of the Nederlandsche Bank, MORKMON. The interaction process is viewed against the background of modern developments in applied macroeconomics as well as the role of the model in the process of policy preparation. The study distinguishes between explicit and implicit linkages of policy-making and model development. Explicit linkages bear on the way policy itself and policy transmission channels are modelled, as well as to how views held by policy makers are embodied in the model. Implicit linkages are more subtle and indirect.
JEL classifications: C5, E5, E65

1. Introduction

Econometric research and model-building at the Nederlandsche Bank (the Dutch central bank) started in the early 1970s, initiated by the Board's explicit desire to have a separate econometric research unit to foster the conduct of up-to-date scientific research based on modern econometric techniques within the Bank. One of the tasks assigned to the research unit was to build a macroeconomic model for the Netherlands' economy to be used in support of the policy-making process. This model had to serve two purposes: providing forecasts for a short- to medium-term horizon, and providing a coherent framework for the analysis of policy and external shocks. The unit began its research activities on 1 January 1971 and gradually developed into the Econometric Research and Special Studies Department.

This chapter about policy-making and model development highlights the case of the Nederlandsche Bank's quarterly macroeconomic policy model of the national economy named MORKMON, which is the Dutch acronym for 'MOnetair-Reële KwartaalMOdel voor Nederland' (Monetary-Real Economic Quarterly Model for the Netherlands). The first version of this estimated model dates from 1981 (Fase, 1982) and several newer generations were to follow (Nederlandsche Bank, 1985; Den Butter, 1988; Fase *et al.*, 1990, 1992; Van Els and Vlaar, 1996).

In order to fully understand the interaction between the development of MORKMON and policy-making, other forces which influenced the process of model-building have to be taken into account. Among these forces are the changes in modelling trends in response to new developments in macroeconomic and econometric theory, and changes in the general attitude among academics towards the design and use of models, which do not necessarily reflect policy makers' tastes and preferences.

The chapter distinguishes between explicit and implicit linkages of model development and policy-making. Explicit linkages are taken to bear on the way policy itself and views held by policy makers have been modelled in MORKMON over the years. Implicit linkages are more subtle and indirect. They relate to interactions between policy-making and model development which often tend to remain unnoticed but are no less important.

The organization of this chapter is as follows. Section 2 describes the main stages in the development of MORKMON and addresses the role of external developments and general trends in applied macroeconomic modelling. This section merely serves to provide some background information on MORKMON and its position within the range of models which are currently in use at the Bank. Section 3 discusses the role of MORKMON in the policy-making process and hence will focus on the use of MORKMON rather than its development. The latter will be the subject of Section 4, which discusses the interactions between model development and policy-making. Section 5 concludes my argument.

2. MORKMON: some history and general background

MORKMON is a macroeconomic model for short- and medium-term forecasting and policy analysis. Like many models of its generation MORKMON is based on the new-Keynesian tradition. Its most distinguishing feature, however, is the strong focus on the monetary sector and the transmission channels of monetary policy. Figure 6.1 presents a schematic outline of these transmission channels, described in more depth by Boeschoten and Van Els (1995). The first channel, shown here for the pre-EMU situation, is the *exchange rate* which affects economic activity through the response of relative prices and real wages. The second channel, the *intertemporal substitution* effect, relates to the impact of interest rates on private consumption. The third channel, the *cost of capital*, operates through the impact of interest rates on investment, inventory formation and prices. The fourth channel relates to *wealth effects* on private consumption and investment, which include those triggered by changes in asset prices in response to interest rate changes. The fifth channel represents *income effects*, which influence expenditure through changes in the flows of interest and dividend payments between the various sectors in the model.

2.1. Stages in the development of MORKMON: an overview

Three stages in the development of MORKMON may be distinguished (see Table 6.1). During the *first stage* covering the 1970s and early 1980s, the emphasis was on

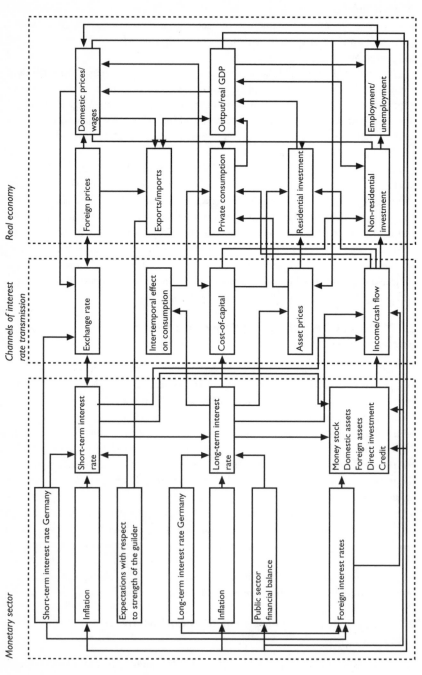

Figure 6.1 Interest rate transmission in MORKMON

modelling the financial sector of the Dutch economy. From the start, a research strategy was adopted in which individual studies concentrated on various aspects of the financial sector and monetary policy. These studies provided new empirical insights, in particular as financial and monetary behaviour in the Netherlands was a virtually unexplored territory in modern empirical research. In the early 1980s, they were combined to form a comprehensive model of the financial sector in the Netherlands. By and large the structure of this model, documented in Fase (1984), has been representative for later versions of the monetary submodel of MORKMON. Its central feature is a closed set of financial balance sheets for the major sectors of the Dutch economy, which numbered five at the time: non-bank private sector, commercial banks, central bank, public sector and the foreign sector. Private sector demand for financial assets is modelled according to Brainard and Tobin's (1968) dynamic multivariate portfolio approach, based on the theory of portfolio selection (see also Owen, 1986).

Table 6.1 History of MORKMON

Stage 1	
1971–80	Individual studies on financial and monetary behaviour in the Netherlands
1981	Complete model of monetary sector
Stage 2	
1981	MORKMON-I
1990	FYSIOEN
Stage 3	
1990	MORKMON-II
1991	Disequilibrium version MORKMON-II
1991	Rational (forward-looking) expectations version MORKMON-II
1993	PC-VARIANT: spreadsheet model based on impulse responses MORKMON-II
1996	MORKMON-III

Note that model-building activities started in a period in which macroeconometric models became exposed increasingly to severe criticism. Models of this type had failed to account for the joint rise of unemployment and inflation in the 1970s. Moreover, the Lucas (1976) critique made it clear that parameters of macroeconometric models are not invariant to policy changes, as these changes will alter the way households and firms form expectations about the future course of the economy. Partly as a result of these flaws, applied macroeconometric modelling gradually changed its character (see Whitley, 1994) and new trends developed. One such change was the stronger emphasis on sound microfoundations for macro models, which is also apparent in some of the more important parts of MORKMON, although the model as a whole is not derived from a single theoretically coherent framework but is based on a more eclectic modelling strategy. The portfolio approach to the private sector's demand for financial assets provides an example of this emphasis.

In the *second stage*, the focus of model-building activities shifted towards the real economic sector and the channels of monetary policy transmission. In 1981 the submodels of the monetary and real economic sectors were integrated (Fase, 1992). This resulted in a structural macroeconomic policy model of the Netherlands' economy, providing a single framework for both forecasting and policy analysis. An important landmark in this stage was the publication of MORKMON-I in 1984 (the English version can be found in Nederlandsche Bank, 1985). Thereafter the attention shifted towards the use of the model for policy analysis and short-term forecasting. Initially, model simulations were conducted on an *ad hoc* basis. In the second half of the 1980s, however, the use of MORKMON in the process of policy preparation intensified and model consultations began to take place regularly. We will come back to this issue in Section 3. During this time period, modelling activities also intensified. For instance, Bikker *et al.* (1986) subjected the model to a large number of econometric specification tests, and models of other institutions such as the Dutch Central Planning Bureau (CPB Netherlands Bureau for Economic Policy Analysis, CPB for short) were made operational, thereby broadening the scope of the Department's own modelling activities. The second stage in the development of MORKMON ended with the construction and publication of the graphic model FYSIOEN (Kramer *et al.,* 1990). FYSIOEN, which is based on MORKMON-I, seeks to visualize the interaction between various important macroeconomic variables by means of dynamic computer graphics. It has proved to be a powerful didactic and analytical instrument to convey information about the working of the Dutch economy and the Bank's policy model to the public.

Stage three, the final stage, started with the work on MORKMON-II in 1988/1989.[1] This stage can be characterized as one of intellectual deepening and refinement of modelling activities and consolidation and extension of what had been achieved with respect to model use. To the extent that these modelling activities were induced by the policy-making process, they will be looked at in more detail in Section 4. Four aspects of the changeover to MORKMON-II should perhaps be mentioned here. First, the wealth and income channels of monetary transmission were modelled more comprehensively and consistently than before. Second, the modelling of price and wage formation was based more firmly on economic theory. Third, the modelling of the public sector was extended in several ways so as to increase MORKMON's potential in handling fiscal policy issues. Fourth, in formulating and estimating the model there was more emphasis on equilibrium and error correction mechanisms. MORKMON-II became operational in 1990.

Intellectual deepening and model refinement were also manifest in two alternative model versions of MORKMON-II. The construction of these model versions was primarily driven by recent developments in macroeconomics but also with a view to their potential use in the process of policy preparation. The first alternative was based on the so-called disequilibrium approach in economic theory,[2] which takes nominal rigidities in prices and wages as a starting point. The disequilibrium approach accounts for the fact that multipliers of external shocks and policy actions are regime-dependent, i.e. they depend on the combinations of excess demand and excess supply that prevail in goods and labour markets (Fase *et al.*, 1992; Van Els and Keijzer, 1993). One lesson drawn from this exercise was that the simulation outcomes of the disequilibrium version broadly confirmed those obtained with the main model version. However, if the economy suffers from severe supply constraints, the main model is likely to underestimate the effects of shocks and policies that lead to an increase in potential output. The second alternative MORKMON model version considered the process of expectation formation, a topic which had and still has the interest of both policy makers and academics. In the main version of MORKMON-II expectations are either backward looking or captured by indicator variables. In the alternative model version the implications of using model consistent forward-looking expectations were explored (Bikker *et al.*, 1993a) and equations in which forward-looking expectation variables were deemed important were re-estimated. The model's simulation characteristics, however, changed only modestly and it was concluded that the simulation results of MORKMON's main version are quite robust to changes in the modelling of expectations.[3]

In 1993 the Bank issued two monographs to inform a wide audience, notably politicians, journalists, students and others with an interest in economic policy, about the model's simulation properties. Bikker *et al.* (1993b) compared the results of 25 different scenario analyses based on MORKMON to those obtained with CPB's FKSEC-model, whereas Boeschoten *et al.* (1993) provided background information on macroeconomic policy analysis in general. The latter publication included a diskette containing a small spreadsheet model, called PC-VARIANT, which consisted of some 30 standard impulse response analyses based on MORKMON for key macroeconomic indicators. These standard scenarios can be combined and hence provide information about the response of the Dutch economy to policy actions or external shocks.

The third stage in the development of the model also includes the changeover to the present version MORKMON-III as from July 1996, documented in Van Els and Vlaar (1996). The submodel of the banking sector was reformulated in order to yield a stronger link between credit demand and bank lending to households and firms, and between net foreign assets of banks and net foreign liabilities of the non-monetary sectors. The distinction between share capital and long-term debt became more explicit throughout the model. In modelling share prices, the implications of the issuing of new shares were taken into account. Confidence effects on consumer spending were introduced related to changes in the unemployment rate and the government's budget deficit. The latter implied the existence of some degree of Ricardian equivalence in the Netherlands, a result for which evidence had been documented earlier by Den Broeder and Winder (1992). Further model refinements were mainly related to the introduction of additional explanatory variables.

2.2. Proliferation of models

Before turning to the role of MORKMON in the policy-making process and discussing the linkages between model development and policy, it must be emphasized
that MORKMON is not the only model available for policy analysis in the Bank.
In particular since the mid-1980s a proliferation of models occurred, which was at
least partly induced by the severe criticisms to which macroeconometric models had
been exposed. Moreover, models are not the only research input in the policy-
making process. A substantial part of the resources for research in the Bank is allocated to individual empirical or theoretical studies. At the Nederlandsche Bank, at
least five different model types currently exist, each serving different purposes. For
short- and medium-term projections and policy analysis, *structural macroeconometric models* form the most important category. Next to MORKMON, a new quarterly multi-country model for the EU, named EUROMON, has been constructed
recently (De Bondt *et al.*, 1997), and will be further developed in the near future.
In addition, the CPB's policy model FKSEC and NIESR's world model NiGEM
have been operational for some years now. Since the early 1980s *leading indicator
models* have been developed and used to produce monthly forecasts of industrial
output, cyclical turning points, and real GDP growth in the Netherlands and other
industrial countries (Fase and Bikker, 1985; Bikker and De Haan, 1988; Berk and
Bikker, 1995; Van Rooij and Stokman, 1996). As from 1993, similar models have
been constructed for the purpose of inflation forecasting (Bikker, 1993a; Bijsterbosch and Hebbink, 1996). The third type of model available for policy analysis is
a *stochastic dynamic general equilibrium model* calibrated for the EU-area (Bolt and
Folkertsma, 1997; Folkertsma, 1999). This model is in the tradition of monetary
equilibrium models which are based on optimal intertemporal behaviour of agents
and incorporate inflation tax and liquidity effects in the spirit of Cooley and
Hansen (1989) and Christiano (1991). Because of optimizing behaviour and rational expectations, dynamic equilibrium models are less prone to the Lucas critique.
The model's main purpose is to provide a theoretically-sound framework for investigating the long-term (welfare) effects of policy changes or shocks to the economy.
VAR models form the fourth class of models, comprising Bayesian VARs as well as
structural VARs. In the early 1990s output growth forecasts obtained from a VAR,
which focused on the interaction between German and Dutch key economic variables, provided a point of reference for the outlook based on MORKMON (Bikker,
1993b). However, in general, VARs were not used for forecasting purposes but
merely served to study the empirical regularities of the process of monetary transmission (Boeschoten *et al.*, 1994; Garretsen and Swank, 1997; Vlaar and Schuberth, 1999; De Bondt, 2000), and to measure the monetary component of
inflation in both the Netherlands and Europe (Fase and Folkertsma, 1997). The list
of model types available for policy analysis also includes a *generational accounting
model* for the Netherlands (Hebbink, 1997). This model highlights the implications
of an ageing population and the effects of today's budgetary policy stance for future
generations.

3. Role and use in policy-making

Over the past two decades modelling activities and model use disappeared from universities to become more and more concentrated at policy institutions. Mankiw (1990) argues that this is mainly caused by recent developments in macroeconomic theory, which have not been of the sort that can be easily adopted in macroeconomic policy models. Another explanation is that practitioners and academics each exploit their own comparative advantages (Fase et al., 1992). Moreover, in policy analysis and forecasting it is common practice to incorporate relevant non-model or judgemental information.[4] Such information is likely to be available sooner in policy institutions than elsewhere. Whatever the cause of the shift is, it is clear that policy institutions still see macroeconomic models as major information sources and appropriate devices for structuring information in a coherent way.

This being said, what role does MORKMON play in the process of policy preparation at the Nederlandsche Bank? The pre-EMU intermediate target of Dutch monetary policy has been to stabilize the exchange rate of the guilder vis à vis the German mark. The Bank's main instrument to achieve this goal was the interest rate on special loans to the banking sector. Clearly, using a macroeconometric model such as MORKMON was not required for the daily implementation of the Bank's exchange rate policy. Model use merely aims at providing background information to members of the Board and others involved in the process of policy preparation on the cyclical stance of the economy, the economic outlook one to two and sometimes four years ahead, and on the effects of domestic policy and, as the Netherlands are a very open economy, changes in foreign variables. The precise role of MORKMON in the process of monetary policy preparation is rather difficult to pin down. Model information is not the only input but gets mixed with other sources of information, part of which will focus on institutional and political aspects. This will be the situation in most central banks, perhaps with the exception of the Bank of Canada where the model seems to play a central role in the discussions on policy design (see Poloz, Rose and Tetlow, 1994).

As from September 1988, forecasting exercises have been held twice yearly, in February and in August. The forecasts normally focus on the economic outlook for the Netherlands in the current and following year. Occasionally, when elections are due and a new cabinet's term starts, the forecast horizon is extended to a four-year period. The central economic outlook and alternative scenarios reflecting uncertainties and risks present in the base projection are based on assumptions about the world economy and domestic policies provided by the Bank's Monetary and Economic Policy Department and Financial Markets Department. These assumptions thus reflect views and expectations held by those involved in the process of policy preparation within the Bank. Based on these assumptions, the central economic outlook and the alternative projections are prepared by a small group of forecasters in the Econometric Research and Special Studies Department in charge of using MORKMON. A preliminary report is submitted for comments to the departments that provided the assumptions on which the outlook is based. The final report is discussed with members of the Board. As an outcome of the discussion sometimes additional scenarios are called for. While the Bank frequently informed the public about its model-building activities and simulation exercises with MORKMON, the forecasts themselves were not published externally until recently. However, as from October 1997 MORKMON-forecasts have been made available to the public regularly. Currently, they are published twice a year in the Bank's *Quarterly Bulletin*. It should be noted that MORKMON-forecasts were not the first macroeconomic forecasts to be published by the Bank. For some time already, the Bank has reported on the outcome of its leading indicator for industrial production in the Netherlands every month in *Economisch Statistische Berichten*, a widely-read Dutch weekly periodical for economists. Moreover, in September 1996 the Bank started the publication of forecasts and scenario analyses for the EU countries based on the multi-country model EUROMON in its *Quarterly Bulletin* twice a year.

The timing of the forecast exercises in February and August gives the Bank the opportunity to form its own views on the most likely future course of the economy and the risks which are involved, just before CPB launches the official forecasts (in March and September) on which the government bases fiscal policy. Moreover, as soon as the (still preliminary) CPB projections become available, a second MORKMON-outlook is prepared, based on the same assumptions the CPB used for the official forecasts, and the differences are evaluated. This evaluation exercise is meant to strengthen the Bank's role as an adviser to the government in social–economic matters, viewed from its position of responsibility for maintaining price stability.

The above-mentioned biannual internal forecast rounds are complemented by the so-called broad forecast exercises under the auspices of the European System of Central Banks (ESCB). The broad forecast exercises are held in autumn and spring. They contribute to the ESCB's assessment of the short-term economic outlook and the monetary policy stance in the Euro-area. Participating national central banks provide short-term forecasts based on a common set of external assumptions, taking unchanged interest and exchange rates as a point of departure. The exercise relates to a range of key macroeconomic variables. For the Netherlands, forecasts are based on MORKMON. The ESCB's broad forecast exercises are in fact the continuation of the so-called *ex ante* and *ex post* co-ordination exercises of the EU central banks under the auspices of the European Monetary Institute and, before 1994, the Committee of Governors of the EU Central Banks, which started already in 1992.

In between the regular forecasting rounds, updates of the economic outlook are provided when new information becomes available. MORKMON is used frequently for *ad hoc* policy and scenario analyses, both on request and on the Department's own initiative, depending on the occurrence of events that are likely to alter the latest economic outlook. One may think of issues such as sudden changes in commodity prices, changes in domestic fiscal policy, changes in foreign policies, and more recently, the Asian and Russian crises and concerns about asset price inflation. Two other examples may also be mentioned. In 1994, the macroeconomic implications of the election programmes of major Dutch political parties were simulated and compared, later followed by an evaluation of the intended economic policy of the newly-elected cabinet. The results of these internal exercises provided background information of potential relevance to the consultations with the Bank on economic policy issues during the process of the formation of the new government. Also in 1994, the Bank participated in a BIS model comparison project which focused on the transmission of monetary policies in the G10 countries according to the central banks' macroeconomic models (Boeschoten and Van Els, 1995). The objective of this project was to document cross-country differences in national transmission mechanisms and to investigate whether and how these differences can be related to elements of financial structure. The exercise showed that, in the Netherlands, changes in policy-controlled interest rates affect real output mainly through the cost-of-capital channel and the exchange rate channel of monetary transmission. The latter channel is particularly important for inflation.

To conclude this Section, I would like to make a final remark on the Lucas critique in relation to model-based policy analysis in the Bank. The Lucas critique clearly warns against a too mechanical use of models, in particular when exploring more radical policy changes. In such cases it has been common practice in the Bank to base policy advice not on one MORKMON-simulation exclusively but to consider a range of possible outcomes by conducting sensitivity analyses with respect to crucial parameter values. Another approach of showing ranges of possible responses, which has been followed at the Bank, is to consult different model-versions and models from other institutions. All in all, the Lucas critique has contributed to the awareness of the limitations of using structural macro models such as MORKMON. A prudential use of models, however, is likely to strengthen their role in the policy design process in the long run.

4. Model development and policy-making

In exploring the interaction of model development and policy-making, it is perhaps useful to draw a distinction between explicit and implicit linkages, although this distinction will always be arbitrary to some extent. Explicit linkages, addressed in Section 4.1, relate to the modelling of policy and policy transmission channels and to how views frequently expressed by policy makers are captured in the model. Implicit linkages between model development and policy-making, discussed in Section 4.2, are more subtle and hidden and, at best, seem to be only indirectly related to policy-making.

4.1. Explicit linkages

For a model to provide an analytical framework, which supports the process of monetary policy design, it has to meet several requirements. First of all, the model has to include a description of monetary policy itself. In MORKMON this has been reflected in the monetary authorities' reaction function which, for the pre-EMU era, explained how the Bank changes its policy instrument in order to stabilize the exchange rate of the guilder *vis à vis* the German mark, then the intermediate target of Dutch monetary policy. According to this reaction function, the policy-controlled short-term interest rate depended on the strength of the guilder, measured by the spot premium of the guilder against the Deutsche mark and the current account balance, the German short-term interest rate and the domestic inflation rate.

Secondly, the model has to explain how the economy responds to changes in the policy-controlled interest rate and, with price stability as the ultimate target of monetary policy, how monetary policy affects inflation. As a result, in model development there has been a strong focus on the channels of monetary policy transmission. In the changeover from MORKMON-I to MORKMON-II in 1989/90 an important novelty was the introduction of asset prices (shares, bonds and houses) and wealth revaluation effects in the model. This improved the model's ability to shed light on the implications of asset price inflation and stock market crashes such as the one in October 1987, which of course had attracted a lot of interest from policy makers both inside and outside the Bank. Another aspect of the changeover to MORKMON-II was the disaggregation of the private sector into households, firms and pension funds which made it possible to present a sectoral breakdown of private sector holdings of financial assets. The disaggregation also aimed to improve the modelling of the income channel of monetary transmission through a consistent framework of intersectoral flows of interest and dividend payments. In MORKMON, the modelling of prices strongly reflects the policy environment of a small open economy. As from the changeover to MORKMON-II in particular, prices are determined explicitly by the costs of production (mainly costs of commodity imports and unit labour costs) and a mark-up which depends on cyclical conditions (output gap) and pressures stemming from foreign competitors' prices measured in guilders. This implies that monetary policy affects inflation mainly through the response of the exchange rate, but also indirectly, through changes in the cost of capital, which affect unit labour costs and the output gap with some lag.

Thirdly, changes in monetary policy implementation have triggered model adjustments. A notable example of this has been the adjustment to MORKMON-I in order to cope with the introduction of the new monetary cash reserve arrangement, which was to be effected from July 1989 until April 1990 (Den Butter and Van Els, 1988). The new arrangement sought to reduce the excessive growth of the banks' net money-creating operations by acting on the price component of bank lending financed from short-term funds. This is achieved by levying a tax on the excess growth of money-creating operations above a certain threshold percentage. The arrangement replaced the use of direct credit ceilings, which suffered from a non-market-oriented nature and limited interbank competition. The adjusted model version in turn provided policy relevant information in showing that the new monetary cash reserve would support the Bank's exchange rate policy by reducing the net outflow of money.

Fourthly, model development is triggered by (changes in) the information requirements of policy makers and those involved in the policy-making process.

The size (400 equations) and elaborateness of MORKMON reflects this. We have already mentioned the policy makers' interest in the implications of asset price inflation, which, for instance, led to the inclusion of house prices in addition to prices of shares and bonds in MORKMON-II. Frequently, information requirements were also related to the implications of budgetary and fiscal policy for growth and inflation. Hence, over the years, the evolution of MORKMON has often been induced by attempts to meet these requirements. In MORKMON-I social security and pension premiums were still aggregated, and tax bases for income and corporate taxation were modelled only very rudimentarily, neglecting tax-deductible items. With the changeover to MORKMON-II, however, the model became better equipped for the analysis of fiscal and budgetary polices. Social security and pension premiums were treated differently, and a further distinction was made between employers' and employees' contributions. The latter distinction is important for a proper modelling of fiscal policy transmission on inflation, as employers' premiums exert a direct impact on wage costs different from the indirect, tax shifting effects of income taxes and social security premiums paid by employees. Reductions in employers' premiums have been used frequently by the government as a policy instrument to control wage costs to the benefit of employment. In addition, tax bases were modelled explicitly in MORKMON-II, taking into account the fiscal reforms which were effected in 1990. Other model adjustments reflected attempts to capture the impact of reforms in the social security system in the early 1990s. An example is the introduction of the replacement ratio (social security transfers in case of inactivity relative to wage income) as an additional determinant of wage formation in the Netherlands in later versions of MORKMON-II. A more recent novel element in budgetary policy, introduced when a new cabinet took office in August 1994, has been the so-called real expenditure scheme which aims to pin down public sector expenditure in real terms to previously agreed upon levels. This led to adjustments in the modelling of several government expenditure categories in MORKMON-III.

A final category of explicit linkages between policy-making and model development relates to views regularly expressed by policy makers and how these are captured in the model. For instance, monetary authorities frequently emphasize macroeconomic and monetary stability as a prerequisite for a successful economic performance. MORKMON-III has attempted to incorporate indicators of stability in various expenditure equations, provided the evidence was statistically significant. Confidence effects measured by changes in unemployment and government financial balances (elements of Ricardian equivalence) have indeed been found to be determinants of private consumption, whereas exchange rate volatility and the labour income share – the latter as a measure of the firms' competitive potential – significantly affect exports. In fact here the model has also been used as a research tool to investigate the empirical validity of certain policy presumptions.

4.2. Implicit linkages

Implicit linkages are only indirectly related to the process of policy design and the information requirements of those involved in policy preparation. Using the model in the policy design process requires maintaining its quality and up-to-dateness, and calls for regular checks on the model's out-of-sample forecast performance (Fase, 1992) and comparisons with other models. For instance, Mourik and Boeschoten (1994) have investigated forecast intervals at various horizons for key MORKMON variables by using stochastic simulation techniques. These intervals were found to be very wide for some variables. Forecasts may thus benefit from the prudential use of relevant non-model or judgemental information. On average, MORKMON's forecast performance has been similar to that of the CPB models FREIA-KOMPAS and FKSEC (Boeschoten and Van Els, 1994).

Safeguarding the model's quality also implies that new insights from economic theory be explored and, if relevant, incorporated into model development. Many of the smaller changes to MORKMON over the years should be seen against this background. One example is the modelling of hysteresis effects in the labour market which was introduced in MORKMON-II to replace the rather *ad hoc* modelling of wages in MORKMON-I (Blanchard and Summers, 1986). This example also highlights the more general argument that the interaction between model development and policy is difficult to disentangle from the impact of external trends and novelties in macroeconomic theory on model-building. Ultimately, however, these trends should perhaps be seen as policy driven to the extent that their intention is for models to become better equipped for policy use. The same holds for developments in econometrics. Error correction specifications were introduced when MORKMON-II replaced MORKMON-I. Through introducing equilibrium feedback, error correction formulations were helpful in improving the model's dynamics while, at the same time, strengthening its economic–theoretical and long-term properties. This enhanced the applicability of the model for policy simulations over a longer horizon.

Deeper issues such as the reasons for an institution developing its own model in the first place and the type of model to be constructed also belong to the category of implicit linkages. In-house model-building generates positive external effects on other research activities. Databases have to be constructed which can be used for other purposes as well. Knowledge of data and insight into the working of economies will be gained. The model itself may be used as a research tool. Building an own model brings with it full control over its operation. This enhances flexibility and decisiveness in model use, which are essential factors for a successful contribution of models to the policy design process. No doubt these issues played a role in the development of MORKMON.

5. Conclusions

This chapter addressed the issue of the interaction of model development and policy-making at the Nederlandsche Bank by focusing on the case of the macroeconometric policy model MORKMON, which has been in active use now for more than a decade. The experience at the Bank shows that structural models like MORKMON perform a useful role in the process of policy design. They offer a description of the full economy and hence provide a consistent framework for seeking answers to many policy questions. The interaction of policy-making and MORKMON's development has many faces and we distinguished between explicit linkages and implicit linkages. Explicit linkages are defined as the direct interactions between policy-making and the model development; at first sight, implicit linkages seem to be more loosely connected to the policy design process and include aspects of safeguarding the quality of the model.

It was stressed that MORKMON is not the only model available in the Bank for policy analysis. Over the years, partly in response to the Lucas critique and new developments in economic theory, there has been a proliferation of models, ranging from one-dimensional leading indicator models to a full-fledged stochastic dynamic equilibrium model. But the process of policy design has also called for the development of new models. A clear example of this is EUROMON, the Bank's macro-econometric multi-country model for the EU countries, its construction being triggered by the increased policy focus on European issues and EMU. In the near future, the further development of the latter model and extension of its use in the process of policy preparation will be important items on the agenda of model builders and model users in the Bank. In the longer term, a fringe benefit of the proliferation of models is that the future development of structural macromodels will gain from the work on general equilibrium models and VARs.

Acknowledgements

This chapter was presented for the congress on 'Empirical models and policy-making' organized and hosted by the Tinbergen Institute, Amsterdam, 14–16 May, 1997. Comments by Mary Morgan are gratefully acknowledged.

Notes

1   MORKMON-II was first documented by Fase *et al.* (1990). The English reference is Fase *et al.* (1992).
2   This version was inspired by the work of Sneessens and Drèze (1986) and Lambert (1988) for Belgium, and Kooiman and Kloek (1985) for the Netherlands.
3   It may be argued that this result hinges on the fact that for the exogenous German interest rates the implications of forward-looking expectations have not been taken into account. Hence, within a multi-country setting, rational expectations could make a bigger difference.
4   A justification for using non-model information in the form of add-factors or intercept corrections is the existence of large confidence intervals around forecasts (Mourik and Boeschoten, 1994). See also Clements (1995) for a formal treatment of the implications of judgemental intercept corrections for the rationality of macroeconomic forecasts.

References

Berk, J. M. and Bikker, J. A., 1995. 'International interdependence of business cycles in the manufacturing industry: the use of leading indicators for forecasting and analysis', *Journal of Forecasting* 14, 1–23.

Bikker, J. A., 1993a. 'A leading indicator of inflation for the Netherlands', *De Nederlandsche Bank Quarterly Bulletin* 1993/3, 43–57.

Bikker, J. A., 1993b. 'The interdependence between the Netherlands and Germany: forecasting with VAR models', *De Economist* 141, nr. 1, 43–69.

Bikker, J. A., Boeschoten, W. C. and Fase, M. M. G., 1986. 'Diagnostic checking of macroeconomic models: a specification analysis of MORKMON', *De Economist* 134, nr. 1, 301–50.

Bikker, J. A., Van Els, P. J. A. and Hemerijck, M. E., 1993a. 'Rational expectation variables in macroeconomic models: empirical evidence for the Netherlands and other countries', *Economic Modelling* 10, July, 301–14.

Bikker, J. A., Van Els, P. J. A. and Schuit, M. E. J., 1993b. 'Vijfentwintig spoorboekjes voor de Nederlandse economie' (Twenty-five standard scenarios for the Netherlands' economy), *Monetaire Monografieën* 13, Amsterdam: De Nederlandsche Bank/NIBE.

Bikker, J. A. and De Haan, L., 1988. 'Forecasting business cycles: a leading indicator for the Netherlands', *De Nederlandsche Bank Quarterly Bulletin* 1988/3, 71–82.

Blanchard, O. J. and Summers, L. H., 1986. 'Hysteresis and the European unemployment problem.' In: S. Fischer (ed.), *NBER Macroeconomics Annual*, Vol. 1. Cambridge, Massachusetts: MIT Press, 15–78.

Boeschoten, W. C. and Van Els, P. J. A., 1994. 'De voorspelkwaliteit van macro-economische modellen: een vergelijkende analyse voor het DNB-model MORKMON' (Forecast performance of macroeconomic models: a comparative analysis for the DNB-model MORKMON), *Maandschrift Economie* 58, 377–87.

Boeschoten, W. C. and Van Els, P. J. A., 1995. 'Interest rate transmission in the Netherlands: results for the Nederlandsche Bank's model MORKMON II'. In *Financial Structure and the Monetary Policy Transmission Process*. BIS, Basle, 452–72.

Boeschoten, W. C., Van Els, P. J. A. and Hemerijck, M. E., 1993. 'Macro-economische variantenanalyse met MORKMON-II' (Macroeconomic scenario analyses with MORKMON-II), *Monetaire Monografieën* 14. Amsterdam: De Nederlandsche Bank/NIBE.

Boeschoten, W. C., Van Els, P. J. A. and Bikker, J. A., 1994. 'Monetary transmission in a small open economy: the case of the Netherlands'. *Research Memorandum WO&E* 406, De Nederlandsche Bank, Amsterdam.

Bolt, W. and Folkertsma, C. K., 1997. 'The liquidity effects and the welfare costs of inflation in a monetary general equilibrium model of Europe'. *Research Memorandum WO&E* 513, De Nederlandsche Bank, Amsterdam.

De Bondt, G. J., 2000. *Financial Structure and Monetary Transmission in Europe: a Cross-country Study*. Cheltenham, UK: Edward Elgar (forthcoming).

De Bondt, G. J., Van Els, P. J. A. and Stokman, A. C. J., 1997. 'EUROMON, a macroeconometric multi-country model for the EU'. *DNB-Staff Reports* 17. Amsterdam: De Nederlandsche Bank.

Brainard, W. C. and Tobin, J., 1968. 'Pitfalls in financial models building', *American Economic Review* 58, 99–122.

Den Broeder, C. and Winder, C. C. A., 1992. 'Financing government spending in the Netherlands: an analysis from Ricardian perspective'. *De Economist* 140, 65–82.

Den Butter, F. A. G., 1988. 'The DNB econometric model of the Netherlands economy (MORKMON).' In: Driehuis, W., Fase, M. M. G. and Den Hartog, H. (eds.), *Challenges for Macroeconomic Modelling*. Amsterdam: North-Holland.

Den Butter, F. A. G. and Van Els, P. J. A., 1988. Analyse van kredietrestrictieregelingen met MORKMON (Analysis of credit restriction arrangements with MORKMON). *Internal note*, De Nederlandsche Bank, Amsterdam.

Bijsterbosch, M. and Hebbink, G. E., 1996. 'Inflatie-indicatoren voor Nederland (Leading indicators for Dutch inflation)'. *Research Memorandum WO&E 485/MEB-Series* 1996–23, De Nederlandsche Bank, Amsterdam.

Clements, M. P., 1995. 'Rationality and the role of judgement in macroeconomic forecasting', *The Economic Journal* 105, 410–20.

Christiano, L. J., 1991. 'Modelling the liquidity effect of a money shock', *Federal Reserve Bank of Minneapolis Quarterly Review*, Winter 1991, 3–34.

Cooley, T. F. and Hansen, G. D., 1989. 'The inflation tax in a real business cycle model', *American Economic Review* 79, 733–48.

Van Els, P. J. A. and Keijzer, L. M., 1993. 'Labour hoarding in a disequilibrium model of the Dutch labour market', *De Economist* 141, nr. 2, 256–78.

Van Els, P. J. A. and Vlaar, P. J. G., 1996. 'MORKMON III, een geactualiseerde versie van het macroeconomisch beleidsmodel van de Nederlandsche Bank (MORKMON III, an updated version of the Nederlandsche Bank's macroeconomic policy model)'. *Research Memorandum WO&E* 471, De Nederlandsche Bank, Amsterdam.

Fase, M. M. G., 1982. 'Geïntegreerd monetair reëel kwartaalmodel voor Nederland (Integrated Monetary–Real Economic Sector Quarterly Model for the Netherlands) (MORKMON-I-82)'. *Research Memorandum WO&E* nr. 8210, De Nederlandsche Bank.

Fase, M. M. G., 1984. 'The monetary sector of the Netherlands in 50 equations.' In: Ancot, J. P. (ed.), *Analysing the Structure of Econometric Models: Advanced Studies in Theoretical and Applied Econometrics*. Dordrecht: Martinus Nijhoff Publishers, 195–228.

Fase, M. M. G., 1992. 'Forecasting is an art, even for the central bank', *De Nederlandsche Bank Quarterly Bulletin* 1991/4, March 1992, 73–81.

Fase, M. M. G. and Bikker, J. A., 1985. 'De datering van economische fluctuaties: proeve van een conjunctuurspiegel voor Nederland 1965–1984' (Dating economic fluctuations: a test of a cyclical indicator for the Netherlands 1965–1984), *Maandschrift Economie* 49, 299–332.

Fase, M. M. G. and Folkertsma, C. K., 1997. 'Measuring inflation: an attempt to operationalize Carl Menger's concept of the inner value of money'. *DNB-Staff Reports* 8. Amsterdam: De Nederlandsche Bank.

Fase, M. M. G., Kramer, P. and Boeschoten, W. C., 1990. 'MORKMON II: het DNB kwartaalmodel voor Nederland' (MORKMON II, DNB's quarterly model for the Netherlands), *Monetaire Monografieën* 11. Amsterdam: De Nederlandsche Bank/NIBE.

Fase, M. M. G., Kramer, P. and Boeschoten, W. C., 1992. 'MORKMON II, the Nederlandsche Bank's quarterly model for the Netherlands' economy', *Economic Modelling* 9, April, 146–204.

Folkertsma, C. K., 1999. 'Nominal wage contracts, adjustment costs and real persistence of monetary shocks'. *DNB-Staff Reports* 30. Amsterdam: De Nederlandsche Bank.

Garretsen, H. and Swank, J., 1997. 'The transmission of interest rate changes and the role of bank balance sheets', *The Journal of Macroeconomics* 20, 325–40.

Hebbink, G. E., 1997. 'Generational accounting with feedback effects on productivity growth: an application to the public sector of the Netherlands'. *Research Memorandum WO&E* 506, De Nederlandsche Bank.

Kooiman, P. and Kloek, T., 1985. 'An empirical two-market disequilibrium model for Dutch manufacturing', *European Economic Review* 29, 323–54.

Kramer, P., Van den Bosch, P. P. J., Mourik, T. J., Fase M. M. G. and Van Nauta Lemke, H. R., 1990. 'FYSIOEN: macroeconomics in computer graphics', *Economic Modelling* 7, April, 148–60.

Lambert, J. P., 1988. *Disequilibrium Macroeconomic Models*. Cambridge: Cambridge University Press.

Lucas, R. E., 1976. 'Econometric policy evaluation: a critique', *Carnegie-Rochester Conference Series on Public Policy* 1, 19–46.

Mankiw, N. G., 1990. 'A quick refresher course in macroeconomics', *Journal of Economic Literature*, XXVIII, 1645–60.

Mourik, T. J. and Boeschoten, W. C., 1994. 'A check on the forecast performance of macroeconomic models: a case study for the Netherlands', *Economic and Financial Modelling* 1, 139–50.

Nederlandsche Bank, 1985. 'MORKMON, a quarterly model of the Netherlands economy for macroeconomic policy analysis.' *Monetary Monographs* nr. 2, Dordrecht: Martinus Nijhoff Publishers.

Owen, D., 1986. *Money, Wealth and Expenditure: Integrating Modelling of Consumption and Portfolio Behaviour*, Cambridge: Cambridge University Press.

Poloz, S., Rose, D. and Tetlow, R., 1994. 'The Bank of Canada's new Quarterly Projection Model (QPM): an introduction', *Bank of Canada Review*, Autumn 1994, 23–38.

Van Rooij, M. C. J. and Stokman, A. C. J., 1996. 'Korte-termijn indicatoren van de BBP-volumegroei voor zeven EU-landen (Short-term indicators of GDP growth for seven EU-countries)'. *Research Memorandum WO&E* 459, De Nederlandsche Bank.

Sneessens, H. R. and Dreze, J. H., 1986. 'A discussion of Belgian unemployment, combining traditional concepts and disequilibrium econometrics, *Economica* 53, S89–S119.

Vlaar, P. J. G. and Schuberth, H., 1999. 'Monetary transmission and controllability of money in Europe: a structural vector error correction approach'. *DNB-Staff Report* 36, Amsterdam: De Nederlandsche Bank.

Whitley, J. D., 1994. *A Course in Macroeconomic Modelling and Forecasting*. New York: Harvester Wheatsheaf.

Chapter 7

Transparency and accountability: empirical models and policy-making at the Reserve Bank of New Zealand*

David G. Mayes and W. A. Razzak

This chapter explains how the performance contract and clear accountability for monetary policy in New Zealand place strong requirements for transparent decision-making based on evidence and analysis. It explores the tension between the requirements of the policy maker and the constraints from evidence on the economic modeller in the context of the recent development of a Monetary Conditions Index. The chapter provides a detailed insight into monetary policy formulation in a central bank.
JEL classifications: E58, E52, E37

1. Introduction

Traditionally central banks have been fairly secretive and inexplicit in explaining their views about the future, the needs for policy and the evidence on which those decisions are based. The framework for monetary policy and its implementation in New Zealand place strong requirements for transparency by the Reserve Bank about its views on the future, how policy affects inflation and what policy should do. This means that research plays a particularly clear role in policy-making.[1]

However, the normal tensions exist in policy-making in New Zealand. The needs of policy can run ahead of the research. Policy decisions have to be taken under uncertainty, when the need arises, with the evidence to hand. They cannot wait until research can produce an incontrovertible answer. Furthermore, a central bank's decisions must be clear, well argued and generally accepted if the bank is to have the authority it needs to act effectively.

On other occasions it is research which produces the findings which then lead to a change in policy. Again here this process of development needs to be seen as a means of strength, increasing the central bank's authority, not revealing it to be fallible. The way the process of interaction between policy-making and research is

*Reprinted (with revisions) from *Economic Modelling*, 15, David G. Mayes and W. A. Razzak, 'Transparency and accountability: Empirical models and policy-making at the Reserve Bank of New Zealand', pp. 377–94, Copyright (1998), with permission from Elsevier Science.

managed is thus crucial in any central bank but it is particularly important when the process is carried out in an open and transparent fashion as in New Zealand.

It is the purpose of this chapter to explain that framework of transparency and accountability in formulating and implementing monetary policy in New Zealand. We illustrate the pressures this places in practice on policy makers and researchers alike by the case of indicators of monetary conditions.[2]

2. The framework for monetary policy and its implementation in New Zealand

Monetary policy in New Zealand has a specific objective, price stability, which is set out in Section 8 of the Reserve Bank Act, 1989. That objective is made specific in a Policy Targets Agreement (PTA) between the Minister of Finance and the Governor of the Bank, which is signed when the Governor is (re)appointed (for a 5-year term). It can be renegotiated. The current PTA was signed on 16 December 1999 following the election of a new government. In signing the PTA the Governor agrees to endeavour to achieve its terms and he can be dismissed if his performance is inadequate in this regard. This is a very real sanction and the Ministry of Finance demanded a report from the Reserve Bank's Board on the Governor's performance the first time that the Bank forecast that inflation would go outside the prescribed range (Mayes and Riches, 1996). Should the Governor's performance be judged inadequate those advisers and forecasters who had contributed to that inadequacy could also expect their jobs to be at risk.

The current (December 1999) PTA provides for inflation, as measured by the All Groups Consumers Price Index (CPI), to show 12-monthly increases of the range 0–3 per cent. There is, however, a set of 'caveats' to this requirement, in the event of:

- exceptional movements in commodity prices;
- changes in indirect taxes;
- significant government policy changes that affect prices;
- a natural disaster.

Then the Bank must detail the impact of these events on the price level and ensure that the effects on inflation are transitory. Section 15 of the Reserve Bank Act requires the Bank to produce statements at least every 6 months both accounting for its actions and explaining how it 'proposes to formulate and implement monetary policy to ensure that price stability is maintained over the succeeding 5 years'.[3] Furthermore, Clause 4 of the PTA requires that 'The Bank shall implement monetary policy in a sustainable, consistent and transparent manner'. (The 1999 PTA extends this clause with the words 'and shall seek to avoid unnecessary instability in output, interest rates and the exchange rate.')

It is thus necessary for the Bank not just to forecast inflation but to be able to explain how inflation is determined and how monetary policy can influence it over the future in such a way as to achieve outcomes consistent with the PTA all the time. All this has to be clear and not shrouded in the secrecy traditional among central banks so that the Governor can be held accountable. This arrangement is a very straightforward attempt to handle the principal-agent problem (Grossman, 1983) by making monitoring of the central bank's (agent's) performance as easy as possible. As Svensson (1997b) explains, it also gets rid of the problem of possible 'inflation bias' in the economy that Persson and Tabellini (1993), Rogoff (1985) and Walsh (1995a) try to solve, by tying the hands of government and giving the central bank the public task of maintaining price stability in a manner which cannot be secretly overridden. The Bank does this by openly applying the same preferences as laid down in the PTA and avoids the need for government to find 'conservative' central bankers, who have different preferences from society at large, and the problems this presents (Svensson, 1997a). While this contract may be optimal (Walsh, 1995b) it cannot be 'perfect' as parliament always has the right to override any agreement (McCallum, 1995), hence some doubt about price stability in the long run will always remain in any arrangement.

The Reserve Bank has chosen to achieve this transparency by producing and publishing quarterly projections of inflation, showing a quarter by quarter track 3 years ahead.[4,5] It also publishes sufficient detail of the projection for the rest of the economy so that the reasoning for the path of inflation can be readily understood. This in the main takes the form of figures for all of the main economic aggregates and components of inflation. These are labelled 'projections' rather than forecasts, as they are forecasts conditional on a set of straight-forward assumptions about fiscal policy, the rest of the world and rules for monetary policy.[6] The Bank then discusses in some detail what monetary policy needs to do in the light of these projections and how it should react when actual events turn out to be different from those in the artificial circumstances projected.[7]

Like all central banks the RBNZ needs to draw its conclusion for the appropriate level for current monetary conditions.[8] As New Zealand is an open economy, both interest rates and the exchange rate play important roles in the transmission mechanism from monetary conditions through to inflation. The Reserve Bank, therefore, explains the current monetary conditions it would like to see in the form of an index (MCI) that is a weighted average of those two components: the 90-day interest rate on bank bills (as a representative benchmark interest rate) and the trade weighted exchange rate (TWI), which is the normal reference measure used in New Zealand.[9] The weights are determined by computing the changes in the TWI and the 90-day rate that will have approximately the same impact on inflation 1–2 years ahead.[10] In more closed economies, such as the United States, the exchange rate element tends to be ignored and reference is made solely to interest rates as an indicator of what the central bank desires.[11]

The Reserve Bank thus takes a stance on the *level* of monetary conditions it wants to see but does not take a view on the desirable *mix* of interest and exchange rates as the two are jointly determined in an open economy and cannot in general be separately influenced. When looking over a period of time it is, of course, the level of real interest and real exchange rates that matters and the Reserve Bank uses the MCI in real terms when discussing the longer term requirements of monetary policy.[12] (It is the history of how the MCI was developed, driven by the needs of policy but guided by empirical investigation, which forms Section 4 of this chapter.)

In contrast to other central banks these statements regarding desired monetary conditions in the light of the published projections and views of how the economy works used to form the total of the normal 'signalling' mechanism to the market.[13] If views changed between projections, say, because of the occurrence of a major unexpected shock, then the Bank announced the new desired conditions and also explained why its views have changed. But it was very unusual to do this between projections, as usually there was insufficient new information to warrant a rethink. However, statements have been issued when actual market conditions have diverged from desired values in a manner that threatens the inflation target.[14] The Bank moved to the more normal practice of setting a short interest rate on March 17th 1999. It now sets an Overnight Cash Rate (OCR). It has also altered the reviewing process so that there is only one formal opportunity (mid-way) between forecasts for reviewing the setting of the OCR. In special circumstances the Bank can of course still alter the OCR at any time.

This method of setting monetary conditions by issuing statements has been described as 'Open Mouth Operations' (Guthrie and Wright, 1997). Although the Bank did not 'fix' an interest rate as such it had the ability to achieve any interest rate it wanted in the overnight (cash) market (Mayes and Riches, 1996). The mechanism is simple. The registered banks in New Zealand have to settle with each other each working 'day'.[15] This settlement is made through accounts held with the Reserve Bank. These accounts must not run into deficit and the cash available in the system was limited by the Reserve Bank to a target figure each day. This target was managed by daily Open Market Operations (see Huxford and Reddell, 1996). Because of the large size of daily government transactions the total liquidity available can be altered by large amounts very rapidly.[16] The Bank thus had a highly credible threat to be able to achieve the level of monetary conditions it wanted but did not normally have to exercise it. The last time the amount of settlement cash was changed was in August 1995 and prior to that, only in early 1993. The 90-day interest rate doubled from 4.5 to 9.5 per cent during 1994 without any need to change the cash target.

The key feature of this system is thus that the Bank has not merely to be completely transparent about how it sees the future for the economy and the needs of policy but that it has to be convincing in its exposition of that view.[17] This implies that the model used in forecasting needs to be public and that other key relationships which the Bank thinks apply to the operation of inflation determination need to be known and understood. Otherwise the Bank would have to intervene much more frequently to achieve the monetary conditions it wanted. The switch to the OCR, therefore, has very little implication for the general framework of policy. It merely enables the Bank to fix interest rates in the overnight market more precisely and simplify its operations.

2.1. The policy-making process and the interaction with research

As the Governor is personally responsible for the formulation and implementation of monetary policy, he makes his decisions with the advice of an *internal* body, the Monetary Policy Committee (MPC). The external Board of Directors,[18] appointed by the Minister of Finance, has a largely supervisory function, particularly in reviewing the Bank's performance in achieving the objectives of the PTA. MPC met weekly (and whenever required) to review economic and financial market news and to discuss the main issues of the formulation of policy. MPC, which is chaired by the Deputy Governor responsible for monetary policy, has a membership which includes the three governors and the senior managers of the departments involved in the policy process, a membership of about a dozen. When specific issues are discussed those who have done the work will join the committee for the meeting as full participants. The Bank has a very flat structure so that even quite junior researchers found themselves presenting their work directly to MPC and discussing it with the Governor face to face.

The policy process was deliberately structured so that the full debate was conducted at MPC rather than the main debate being undertaken within departments and only the one considered view then being presented to governors.[19] The Bank described the process it followed as providing 'contestable' advice.[20] It was thus the task of the Chief Manager of the Economics Department not just to present a personal or Departmental view of the needs of policy but to ensure that a broad range of choices was put forward and that minority views got through to MPC.[21] MPC does not vote although the Governor will normally go round the table getting people to be explicit about their personal views when there is considerable division of opinion. Indeed, at each of the regular weekly meetings the members of the committee were asked to state their personal views of whether desired monetary conditions should change and what action the Bank should take. Only after hearing those views would the Governor state his own views by way of conclusion or open up the debate. He did not attempt to achieve consensus although naturally he sought to persuade others to hold the same opinion.

The Bank treats Monetary Policy Formulation (i.e. what should be done) and Monetary Policy Implementation (doing it) as separate functions (see the Annual Report and Annual Plan). The Economics Department is responsible for the former and the Financial Markets Department for the latter function. It is for the departments to provide the necessary material and advice for the functions to be exercised efficiently and effectively. There is thus a very direct inter-relationship between the policy-making and the research that underlies it.[22]

In this chapter we are concerned solely with monetary policy formulation and hence with research work in the Economics Department and its relation with the policy-making by the Governor in the context of MPC.

3. The economic context

This requirement for clear and open forecasting and analysis could scarcely have come at a worse moment from an econometric point of view as New Zealand embarked on a comprehensive programme of macro- and microeconomic (structural) change in 1984, which has continued ever since (see Evans *et al.*, 1996). This has opened the economy up to external and internal competition, removed subsidies and distortionary taxes, involving sweeping deregulation, privatization and corporatization of the public sector, the establishment of fiscal surpluses and a small and declining public debt to GDP ratio and the replacement of double-digit inflation by price stability. It is difficult to exaggerate the scale of these changes, which moved New Zealand from being probably the most regulated OECD economy towards the other end of the spectrum in less than a decade. The sequencing may not have been ideal as financial markets were deregulated first and labour markets last (Bollard and Mayes, 1993), but all parts of the economy were affected.

This substantial structural change provides a major challenge for the econometric model builder. The Reserve Bank had traditionally developed a string of structural econometric models[23] that by 1990 had become quite large and advanced. The final model in this series (Model XII) used cointegration analysis in estimation. However, by the time testing of its properties had been completed and it was ready for use, the extent of the structural change meant that its forecasting performance was already too poor for it to be used in practice.

The Bank therefore responded to the consequences of structural change in three ways. It tried to incorporate the change into Model XII and to estimate new equations with time-varying parameters and structural shifts. It also placed more emphasis on its VAR models and key equations. Lastly it put much more emphasis on short-run forecasting methods, as these tend to be able to overcome structural shifts over short horizons. (This is well explained in David Hendry's Presidential lecture to the Royal Economic Society, Hendry, 1997.)

The attempts to restructure Model XII were largely unsuccessful and so the Bank implemented plans to create a new model of the economy in 1994. This had two steps. It began by estimating a core model with key relationships but this was superseded by a model (FPS)[24] with a strong element of calibration when a number of the key estimated relations still exhibited implausible characteristics. The model has many of the characteristics used in the Bank of Canada's QPM model, particularly stock-flow modelling and its attention to sensible steady-state properties and plausible dynamic responses to transitory and permanent shocks (Black *et al.*, 1994; Coletti *et al.*, 1996). It employs an overlapping generations approach, permits both forward-looking and rule of thumb expectation formation and incorporates forward-looking policy reaction functions for both the fiscal and monetary authorities.

From a policy point of view these developments have meant that the Reserve Bank has had to act in the 'wrong order' and make substantial changes to policy before the full empirical evidence to back it up could be in place. This has inevitably involved greater reliance on economic theory and the experience of other countries where this was comparable. However, this circumstance of having only partial evidence and having to make forward-looking assumptions is typical of policy-making. The structural change merely emphasizes the problem but not to the extent of that which the former COMECON countries have had to face, with small samples, poor quality and missing data and lack of experience with the new regime.

4. The monetary conditions indicator

The introduction of a monetary conditions indicator into the formulation of monetary policy provides an interesting story, driven by the needs of policy and constrained by the limits of empirical endeavour. Let us start from the policy side.

4.1. The demands of policy

The Reserve Bank of New Zealand viewed with interest the use of MCIs in Norway, Sweden and Canada. It had for some time been having difficulty in expressing to the market the bite that monetary policy is to have on the economy, given that both interest rates and the exchange rate form parts of the transmission mechanism and that they can move in reinforcing or opposing manners, depending upon the circumstances. It was concerned to get across the simple idea that for any given set of economic conditions different combinations of interest and exchange rates could have the same effect on inflation and hence that, since the Bank was concerned with the effect not the means, all such combinations would be equally acceptable/unacceptable.

It seemed virtually impossible to give the market messages related to both interest rates and exchange rates (e.g. that if the exchange rate rose substantially the Bank would be content to see some fall in interest rates). This problem was not primarily a function of New Zealand's unique signalling system. Had a short-term interest rate been used to signal, the Bank would have encountered exactly the same problem in trying to explain in words what the nature of the signal was. Mayes and Riches (1996) detail a number of occasions when it was found necessary to issue more than one statement to explain what was wanted. To give an unambiguous signal something relatively quantitative needed to be said.

Part of the problem has been that knowledge of the transmission mechanism has only grown slowly in quantitative terms. In mid-1994 the only transmission mechanism that the Bank quoted publicly was the direct effect from the exchange rate onto inflation [i.e. the feed-through from the exchange rate to import prices and hence into the imported component of the Consumer Price Index (CPI)]. This had a pass-through coefficient of about 0.3 over about 12 months.[25]

There was no indication of the degree of impact from interest rates or the 'indirect' effect of the exchange rate through decreasing the demand for exports and import-competing goods and services, whether in terms of size of impact or period over which the main impact was likely to be felt. In retrospect this short-run focus was an important contributor to underestimation of the inflationary potential that was being built up in the economy during 1993 and 1994, which ultimately led to exceeding the target range during 1995–1997.[26]

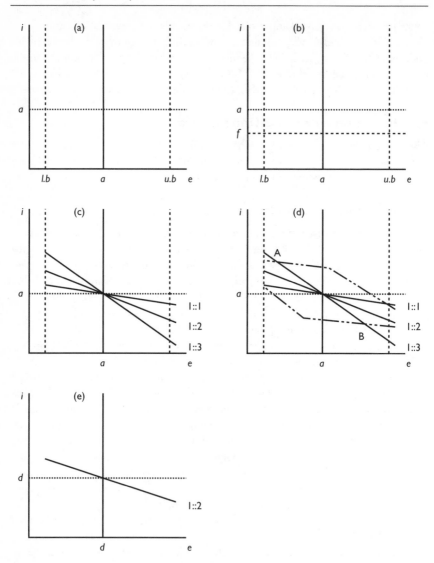

Figure 7.1 (a) 'Comfort zone'; (b) supposed 'floor'; (c) MCI lines; (d) MCI comfort zone; and (e) desired conditions. Abbreviations: *a*, assumed value for projection; *d*, published desired value; *e*, TWI (trade-weighted exchange rate index); *f*, supposed 'floor'; *i*, 90-day interest rate; *l.b*, lower bound of exchange rate below which inflation would be 'too high'; *u.b*, upper bound of exchange rate above which inflation would be 'too low'.

It is probably easiest to explain these developments in thinking visually. In each of the graphs in Figure 7.1 the interest rate, *i*, is shown on the vertical axis and *e*, the trade-weighted exchange rate (TWI), on the horizontal.[27]

Figure 7.1a illustrates the approach the Bank was using in 1994. Although it quoted a single value for the exchange rate, a, that had been assumed in the published projection, it made it clear that there was what came to be known as a 'comfort zone', delimited in Figure 7.1a by lower and upper bounds, $l.b$ and $u.b$, within which the exchange rate was free to vary without eliciting any intervention by the Bank. For a defined interest rate, the limits of the zone were determined by the values of the exchange rate which would generate outcomes uncomfortably close to the edge of the target band for inflation 12 months ahead.[28,29]

As the inflationary process developed during 1995 the market continued to take a more optimistic view of future inflation than the Bank did. As a result the Bank found it needed to counter sharp falls in forward interest rates by affirming an unwillingness to see interest rates fall. The Bank also observed that the major inflationary pressure was domestic and coming through the housing market. The continuing rise in the exchange rate over the period only had a very indirect effect on housing inflation whereas interest rates have a much more direct effect on the sector.[30] The Bank was therefore becoming increasingly concerned with nature of the inflationary process and the impact of the two main routes of influence on its components. This combination of events hence resulted in an important step forward (a) in talking about the mix of conditions and (b) in moving towards a longer-term view of inflation.[31] However, the market interpreted the worries about the minimum acceptable levels of interest rates because of the rate of rise of domestic inflation as introducing a 'floor' to the interest rate (Figure 7.1b).[32]

As 1995 developed evidence on the relative importance of interest rates and the exchange rate in controlling inflation increased. On the basis of the Bank's own research on New Zealand and results published for other countries, it concluded that the ratio lay probably within a range of 1:1 for the interest rate compared with the exchange rate and 1:3 as New Zealand is a fairly open economy. The 'best guess' was about 1:1.65.[33] Thus a line drawn in the i, e space shown in Figure 7.1 with this ratio, would represent combinations of interest and exchange rates where the impact on future inflation would be the same – i.e. monetary conditions would be the same. Three such (MCI) lines are shown in Figure 7.1c to cover the Bank's range of plausible values from 1:1 to 1:3 and the mid-point of 1:2.

In principle the Bank might have had to make choices between the short-run and long-run requirements for controlling inflation if inflation were not to bounce from one side of the target band to the other. With inflation at or above the upper edge of the band and inflationary pressures rising it needed a strong direct effect through the exchange rate to bring inflation down rapidly. However, once the indirect effects come into play as well, beyond the short-run horizon, there was the danger that demand could fall away so fast that the inflation rate could challenge the lower bound 18 months to 2 years ahead. While in practice the forecasts did not show a conflict the Bank became worried enough in October 1995 to issue a statement cautioning that, if the rapid slow-down in economic activity and consumer and business confidence continued, it would become necessary to ease monetary conditions.[34]

The next step was to draw up a zone of tolerance round the desired values for the MCI, in a similar manner to the exchange rate 'comfort zone'. This task was complicated by the limited confidence in the slope of the MCI.[35] The Bank deliberately took a very cautious view and traced in bounds, using whichever of the 1:1 and 1:3 slopes that would generate the smaller zone (as shown by the alternating dot and dash lines in Figure 7.1d).[36] The width of the band at the point of assumed monetary conditions reflected approximate bounds for the effect of changes in the *level* of conditions that would not challenge the edges of the inflation target range 1–2 years ahead.

However, this approach generates a problem if the *mix* of monetary conditions changes a lot, as the bounds of the 'comfort zone' and the plausible range of the MCI itself could, in theory, intersect (points A and B for example). It was only towards the end of 1996 that the Bank felt confident enough to publish its views. Initially it published a statement of the trade-off and conditions consistent with the middle of the target range for inflation (as shown in Figure 7.1e). This focus on the middle developed over the same period – partly because the previous indifference over where inflation was in the range, with the exception of avoiding being close to the edges of the target proved to be insufficiently severe to save inflation from going outside the range. The Bank now focuses on bringing inflation to the middle of the range 6 to 8 quarters ahead.[37] In June 1997, however, not only did the Bank begin to quote a numerical MCI, as explained in Section 2, but the Governor set approximate limits to acceptable fluctuation. These limits were to vary as the three-month interval between the publication of inflation projections proceeded, starting at plus/minus 50 MCI points immediately after publication and widening as the ensuing 3 months passed.[38]

We should emphasize that the Bank is using an MCI in a very limited manner. It shows the tolerance to portfolio shocks in the period between quarterly projections. The Bank decides on desired conditions quarterly. It would require quite substantial information that the projections were wrong for a change in desired conditions to be announced explicitly between forecasts.

4.2. The constraints encountered in research

The Bank produced six papers directly on the MCI including an article in the September 1996 *Bulletin* (Reserve Bank of New Zealand, 1996) – foreshadowing the changes introduced in December 1996. However, much of the relevant work relates to the ability to explain the transmission mechanism.

The initial work (Nadal-De Simone *et al.*, 1996) involved estimating a small model of an open economy, incorporating an IS curve with real interest parity a definition of the real exchange rate, a short-run aggregate supply curve, a definition of the CPI in terms of its foreign and domestic price components, a Reserve Bank reaction function for the nominal exchange rate as a function of the difference between the expected foreign inflation rate, expected inflation and the midpoint of the target band, a standard money demand curve and potential output as a random walk with drift.[39,40]

The model was developed as the simplest manageable representation that could be derived for an open economy, which included expectations formation, the main elements of the transmission mechanism including the separate but inter-related roles of interest rates and the exchange rate and a reaction function for the monetary authority. The authors felt it would be inappropriate to study the impact of policy in a model that did not allow for expectations, given the emphasis on having a transparent policy framework in New Zealand.

The results are rather different from the conventional MCI, which is typically derived from estimating a single equation IS curve, and show the importance of foreign interest rates and the expected exchange rate as well as the current exchange rate. These results confirm some of the difficulties suggested by Ericsson *et al.* (1997) in the conventional estimation of MCIs from a single equation IS curve [Hansson (1993) for example]. The model also emphasizes the importance of foreign demand in determining overall demand pressures in a small open economy. The estimates result in an MCI ratio less than unity. This is largely because the model incorporates all of the channels of influence of monetary policy on inflation, which we outlined in Section 4.1. These include the effects on expectations and the direct effect of the exchange rate on the CPI through import prices. Traditional MCIs only purport to measure the indirect impacts of interest and exchange rates.

The result indicates very clearly that when all the transmission channels are included the exchange rate seems to play a much greater role in the determination of inflation (compared with the interest rate) than is commonly thought from single equation work. This contrast with accepted results meant that the Bank felt it needed further work before it could proceed with publicly releasing an MCI.

Dennis (1996), therefore, attempted a different line of research that allows for a longer lag structure, by building a structural VAR. This six-variable model includes the output gap, domestic real interest rate, real effective exchange rate, domestic inflation, foreign real output growth and foreign inflation. The resulting MCI ratio was 1:1.7 (a 100 basis point increase in the real interest rate is equivalent in its effect on inflation a couple of years ahead as a 1.7 per cent increase in the real exchange rate). The model also suggested that the nominal interest rate has a more rapid impact on inflation than the exchange rate, emphasizing the point that the appropriate MCI may vary according to the time horizon being used. However, the model suffered from some implausible dynamics – and the short lag length required for stability meant that the impact of the exchange rate and interest rates could not be estimated accurately. The value of 1:1.7, however, seemed plausible in the light of estimates of 1:3 for Canada (Duguay, 1994), where the economy is somewhat less open and 1:2 for Norway and Sweden (Ericsson *et al.*, 1997) which are probably rather more similar to New Zealand, and hence the Bank began to operate tentatively assuming an MCI ratio in the range 1:1–1:3 but with the presumption that it lay somewhere towards the middle.

In view of the problems encountered with the multi-equation approach and the need to come up with some working results in the short-run, Dennis thought that the next sensible step would be to follow the more conventional approach and explore the results we could obtain from a single equation, reduced form model (Dennis, 1997).[41] However, this was based on the output gap rather than just output as is more common for an IS curve.[42] The resulting MCI ratios varied from 1.65 to 1.98. The evidence from other countries and these results led the Bank to the view that, while it was unlikely to be able to pin down an MCI ratio exactly, an approximation of the order of 1:2 would be appropriate provided it did not attempt to run policy too closely from it. Hence when it decided to publish an MCI in December 1996, 1:2 was the ratio specified.

However, while this gave a central line for desired conditions it does not have immediate implications for the width of the band for conditions that could be tolerated as not threatening the edges of the inflation target. In trying to establish this in a small calibrated model Dennis and Roger (1997) realized that there is a basic conundrum.[43] In order to be able to establish the appropriate bandwidth for the MCI we need to know the source of the shocks that disturb the model as their effect on demand and hence inflation varies. However, if we know the source of a shock and its magnitude the need for a bandwidth is rather irrelevant. An identifiable shock should lead the Bank to change 'desired' monetary conditions. The use of the band is appropriate when the 'shock' that has caused the actual conditions in the market to move away from their desired level cannot be identified. In these circumstances we can only choose some average value across the different sorts of identifiable shocks. The authors conclude that a bandwidth for the MCI of the equivalent of 75 basis points for the 90-day interest rate on each side of desired conditions might be appropriate.

The Bank did not give a clear indication of what the appropriate bandwidth might be but it did take two steps in this direction. First, in publishing the March 1997 *Economic Projections* it concluded that the tightening by the market of the equivalent of approximately 100 basis points on the 90-day rate was too much for comfort if it were maintained.[44] Second, as mentioned, in June 1997 the Governor limited tolerable, inexplicable, fluctuations to 50 MCI points in the period immediately after the release of projections.

More recently, Hunt and Razzak, 1997 have developed a small model to explore the robustness of policy to the choice of the MCI ratio. This research contrasts the performance that would be achieved if the Bank follows the dictates of a single equation model based on OLS with a model with a similar form to Nadal-De Simone *et al.* (1996) estimated by GMM.[45] It suggests, from stochastic simulations, that using the single equation model to drive policy would not merely result in a loss of output compared with the simultaneous equation model but that it would actually be impossible to remain within the inflation target. This research emphasizes why at present the Bank only uses the MCI to map out appropriate responses to unidentifiable or 'portfolio' shocks between quarters rather than to drive the setting of the level of desired monetary conditions.

5. Reflection

In the case of MCIs the needs of policy ran ahead of the empirical work and it became necessary to employ a rounded estimate of the MCI ratio before the consequences of doing so had been fully tested. The alternative of not specifying a ratio and letting the market guess what the Bank might actually believe would have been more harmful both to credibility and to the usefulness of market signals. Values of monetary conditions above the MCI line do at least tell us that the market feels it more appropriate to hold conditions tighter than the Bank feels necessary to return inflation to the middle of the target range. The market is aware of the Bank's caution and would not react adversely to new evidence suggesting that the MCI ratio should be changed.

With the benefit of hindsight it is possible to see that the MCI did not solve the Bank's communication problems. When the Bank took a very different view from the market over the impact of the Asian crisis in the second half of 1997, there was confusion of shifts in the MCI line and movements along it. This probably assisted the move to an OCR.

Acknowledgements

Revised version of a paper prepared for the 10th Anniversary Congress of the Tinbergen Institute Amsterdam, 14–16 May 1997. The views expressed in this chapter are those of the authors. We are grateful for the advice of colleagues, particularly Lars Svensson and Juha Tarkka, fellow participants in the Congress and the editors and a referee. The processes described here relate to the period 1994 to 1997 when the first author was responsible for monetary policy formulation at the Bank. There may have been changes since then.

Notes

1 It is not that other central banks do not go through similar processes, simply that in general they have neither felt nor had the need to be so explicit in public.
2 In an earlier version of this chapter (Mayes and Razzak, 1997, revised in this volume) we included a second example, drawn from the work on an asymmetric Phillips curve, which has not been incorporated into the Bank's policy and forecasting model, to illustrate a case where the research led the policy. Length precludes its inclusion here.
3 Clause 5 of the 1996 PTA.
4 In June 1997 there was a major change both to the forecasting methodology and to the form of the publication of the information. This was the first occasion that the forecast was based on the new FPS model (see Black et al., 1997a, b), outlined in Section 3 below. FPS (Forecasting and Policy System) enables the Bank to take a much longer and more clearly spelt-out view of inflation.
5 The data are now (May 2000) half-yearly not quarterly.
6 The current format of the rule for monetary policy is a reaction function to bring inflation back into the middle of the target range one to two years ahead. Prior to June 1997 projections were made on simple assumptions about the paths of interest rates and the exchange rate.

7 Prior to 1999 there were actually two forms for the publication. Twice a year they were the *Monetary Policy Statements* required by the Reserve Bank Act and in the intervening quarters, *Economic Projections*, which go into much more detail. Since 1999 they have followed the former format only.

8 This requirement is usually labelled 'desired conditions'.

9 Such indices are produced by central banks in a number of other open economies, including Norway, Sweden and Canada.

10 Prior to June 1997 the two components were stated separately along with an explanation of the weights. The use of the MCI greatly simplifies this explanation. The current MCI (for period t) is based on the average daily rates in the December 1996 quarter for the 90-day rate (r_0) (8.9 per cent) and TWI (TWI_0) (67.1):

$$MCI = \{(r_t - r_0) + 0.5[\log_n(TWI_t/TWI_0)] \times 100\} \times 100 + 1000.$$

This has the convenient property that a 1 basis point change in the 90-day rate changes the MCI by one point. The weights of 1 on r and 0.5 on TWI show that a 100 basis point change in the 90-day rate is treated as being equivalent to a 2 per cent change in the exchange rate.

11 Central banks that are seeking price stability by targeting the exchange rate rather than the CPI directly, such as those in the EU ERM2, will also express the needs of policy in terms of interest rates as the acceptable fluctuations in the exchange rate are limited.

12 See p. 11 of the June 1997 *Monetary Policy Statement* for the exact definition.

13 Unlike most other central banks the RBNZ did not signal its views by setting short-run interest rates or interest bands and it tries to avoid making other statements or taking actions which might be interpreted as expressing a new view of the needs of policy in between the quarterly projections.

14 There was in fact a hierarchy of statements made, starting with one issued over all the wire services by the Chief Manager of Financial Markets, through a Deputy Governor to the Governor himself if the message was intended to be particularly strong.

15 The 'day' actually ends the following morning.

16 The Bank paid 300 basis points below the market interest rate on positive balances in exchange settlement accounts to discourage banks from trying to corner the cash market and charged 90 basis points to rediscount Reserve Bank bills with less than 28 days to run to encourage banks not to be short of settlement cash.

17 This framework also encourages the Bank to be 'time consistent' and not to spring surprises, otherwise the credibility that it trades on would tend to be lost.

18 It meets monthly.

19 This is in contrast to some other central banks. In the Bank of Canada, for example, the 'staff' compile forecasts which are then presented to the equivalent committee to MPC and governors refer to these forecasts in a slightly arm's-length manner, as the 'staff forecasts' [Freedman (1994) for example]. In the case of the RBNZ, once the forecasts are adopted by MPC, they become the Bank's forecasts and the Governor takes full ownership of them, running the presentation to the media and explaining them in detail subsequently. The same is true for the methods the Bank uses in forecasting and analysis. Thus the Governor was very keen to make sure that he was fully aware of the new FPS model, the assumptions behind it and the properties that it exhibited. The FPS system was explicitly approved by Governors in outline before the main work started because of the extent of the investment involved and MPC went over its properties and performance in a number of sessions over a 6-month period before it was adopted as the main vehicle for policy analysis and forecasting.

20 One upshot of this contestability is the record, of what at times can be a very full and frank exchange, is not published. The research that underlies the policy advice is normally published in the Bank's *Bulletin* or as Discussion or Working Papers after external

review. These are now all available on the Bank's homepage on the Internet (http://www.rbnz.govt.nz). Where possible the finished versions are published in international refereed journals. The Bank wanted its thinking to be widely understood and to receive good feedback while developing its ideas. Approximately half the research budget was spent on external research, which was actively solicited, *inter alia*, through a publication called *Research News*. The Bank has even financed research by people with whom it disagreed in order to ensure a full debate.

21 The 'culture' of the Bank was such that people were not particularly reluctant to put minority views, as being in the minority was not in itself a barrier to advancement. However, human nature suggests that there must be a limit to people's willingness to disagree with the Governor. This culture of open debate does not, of course, extend to debating policy outside the Bank. The Governor determines the Bank's policy. However, where there is a very substantial debate, such as on banking supervision in the early 1990s or the change to a possible cash rate scheme in early 1997, the Bank may choose to issue a discussion paper first and the Governor will only make up his mind after listening to the public debate [see Reserve Bank of New Zealand (1997) for example]. (In this latter case the Bank actually withdrew its proposals after listening to the debate.)

22 MPC did not set the research agenda. The Bank has an annual planning round as well as a strategic look rather further ahead – this Annual Plan is published (the Annual Plan and Annual Report act almost as 'before' and 'after' documents in the process of accountability). Chief Managers were responsible for identifying the main issues on which work should focus. However, Governors set an agenda of around ten key issues and Chief Managers needed to set priorities in the light of them. Thus technical issues and basic research emerged from within the Department. However, issues of current interest were determined by a combination of Governors' requests and Departmental initiative. (The research programme was formally agreed by the Deputy Governor in charge of monetary policy every 6 months, prior to the release of *Research News*.)

23 See the Preface to Brooks and Gibbs (1991).

24 The model is a complete system with a core medium-term model, with calibrated parameters and a set of satellite models that link it into shorter-run and more detailed sectoral models. This complete system (known as FPS – Forecasting and Policy System) involves being able to combine forecasting techniques and running simulations readily. The model is described in detail in Black *et al.* (1997a, b).

25 Even this mechanism has been subject to change and progressive estimates have tended to fall. Disaggregated analysis shows considerable sectoral variation in how exchange rate changes are passed through into consumer price changes (Winkelmann, 1996).

26 It must be said that the Bank was not alone in underestimating the inflationary pressure that was building up. Not only did none of the other forecasters come at all close to forecasting the extent of economic growth in 1994–1995 but the Bank encountered considerable scepticism when in started projecting the problem in the second half of 1994.

27 Both can be treated in nominal terms as this discussion relates only to the next quarter.

28 Initially the market was merely told that this was how the Bank was operating (Nicholl, 1994) but ultimately they were actually told the values the process generated. These limits were not rigid in practice, as information coming to hand over the quarter would alter the view of appropriate monetary conditions.

29 For simplicity the bounds are shown as symmetric round *a* in Figure 7.1a. However, in practice the bounds would only be symmetric if the projected value for inflation 12 months ahead were in the middle of the target band. This was not normally the case so the 'published' comfort zone was not normally symmetric in practice.

30 The house price boom was due to a number of specific factors as well as reflecting the general improvement in the prospects for the economy (Bourassa and Hendershott, 1996; O'Donovan and Rae, 1996; Peters and Savage, 1996). It was amplified by house

price and mortgage debt levels being below trend compared with incomes, a surge in immigration into the Auckland region at the same time that several major construction projects reduced the supply of labour for residential construction and that interpretation of the Resource Management Act reduced the ease and increased the cost of releasing new development land (McShane, 1996). There may also have been some external factors at work as there was considerable co-movement among the housing markets of the Pacific region in this period.

31 Naturally the wish to take a longer-term view had been present throughout but, in the absence of clear quantitative results on the magnitudes of that longer-term feed through to inflation, the Bank had been reluctant to state its views. The practical difficulties in signalling made it increasingly easy to take that step.

32 This perceived 'boxing in' of the admissible range for market movements resulted in the Bank having to issue rather more statements than it wished (Mayes and Riches, 1996).

33 That is, a 1 percentage point change in the interest rate had the same effect as a 1.65 per cent change in the exchange rate.

34 In fact the decline was arrested partly perhaps in response to the statement and monetary conditions hence needed to remain tight. (This statement on 17 October 1995 is the only example of a statement indicating a change of view between forecasts since the beginning of 1994.)

35 The lines drawn are illustrative. The Bank did not operate off hard and fast rules and an actual or potential move outside the 'comfort zone' would generate debate rather than action initially.

36 Thus lower bound for falls in the exchange rates (rises in interest rates) used 1:3 while the lower bound for rises in the exchange rate (falls in interest rates) used 1:1 (and *vice-versa* for the upper bounds).

37 Thus the Bank has shifted its aim for policy from seeking to avoid challenging the edges of the target range to moving into the middle of the range.

38 See 'Speaking notes for briefing journalists on the release of the 27 June 1997 *Monetary Policy Statement*', which are available through the RBNZ web site. This idea appears to have been dropped subsequently.

39 A parameter is included to reflect how much weight is to be given, by monetary policy, to returning inflation to the middle of the band.

40 The model is estimated over the period 1987(Q1)–1995(Q2) using two-step, two-stage least squares (2S2SLS) (Cumby *et al.*, 1983) in both nominal and real terms using lagged values as instruments.

41 Dennis does attempt to deal with the endogeneity problems which have been identified in single equation work (Ericsson *et al.*, 1997) and suggests that weak exogeneity may actually apply in his model. Insofar as this judgement is incorrect the single equation estimates will be inconsistent. In any case such a model only focuses on the aggregate demand channel as an influence on inflation and ignores the expectations and direct price effects which have been described.

42 These output gaps are estimated by applying Hodrick–Prescott filters.

43 This point was already implicit in Nadal-De Simone *et al.* (1996).

44 In those projections the Bank was suggesting that inflation would fall to 0.8 per cent during the period 1–2 years ahead. A further tightening by 100 basis points would be likely to produce values of inflation too close to zero to accept.

45 The resulting MCIs are approximately 1:1.7 and 1:1, respectively. As the authors point out, the estimated MCI ratio is bound to put more emphasis on the role of the exchange rate when an open economy model is appropriately estimated.

References

Black, R., Laxton, D., Rose, D. and Tetlow, R., 1994. The Bank of Canada's new Quarterly Projection Model. Part 1: The steady-state model: SSQPM. Bank of Canada, Technical Report, no. 72.

Black, R., Cassino, V., Drew, A., Hansen, E., Hunt, B., Rose, D. and Scott, A., 1997a. 'The Forecasting and Policy System: an introduction.' Reserve Bank of New Zealand.

Black, R., Cassino, V., Drew, A., Hansen, E., Hunt, B., Rose, D. and Scott, A., 1997b. 'The Forecasting and Policy System: the core model.' Reserve Bank of New Zealand Research Paper 43.

Bollard, E. E. and Mayes, D. G., 1993. 'Lessons for Europe from New Zealand's liberalisation experience', *Natl. Inst. Econ. Rev.* 143, 81–96.

Bourassa, S. C. and Hendershott, P. H., 1996. Auckland, Christchurch and Wellington real house prices since 1980. Mimeo, University of Auckland.

Brooks, R. and Gibbs, D. T., 1991. 'The Reserve Bank econometric model of the New Zealand economy: Model XII.' Reserve Bank of New Zealand Research Paper 42.

Coletti, D., Hunt, B., Rose, D. and Tetlow, R., 1996. The Bank of Canada's new Quarterly Projection Model. Part 3: the dynamic model: QPM. Bank of Canada Technical Report 75.

Cumby, R. E., Huizinga, J. and Obstfeld, M., 1983. 'Two-step two-stage least squares estimation in models with rational expectations', *J. Econometr.* 21, 333–55.

Dennis, R., 1996. Monetary conditions and the monetary policy transmission mechanism. Mimeo. Reserve Bank of New Zealand.

Dennis, R., 1997. 'A measure of monetary conditions.' Reserve Bank of New Zealand Discussion Paper G97/1.

Dennis, R. and Roger, S., 1997. 'The role of monetary conditions indicator bands in monetary policy implementation.' Reserve Bank of New Zealand Discussion Paper.

Duguay, P., 1994. 'Empirical evidence on the strength of the monetary transmission mechanism in Canada: an aggregate approach.' *J. Monet. Econ.* 33, 39–61.

Ericsson, N. R., Jansen, E. S., Kerbishian, N. A. and Nymoen, R., 1997. Understanding a monetary conditions index. Mimeo, Federal Reserve Board.

Evans, L., Grimes, A., Wilkinson, B. and Teece, D., 1996. 'Economic reform in New Zealand 1984–95: the pursuit of efficiency.' *J. Econ. Lit.* 34, 1856–1902.

Freedman, C., 1994. 'The use of indicators and of the monetary conditions index in Canada.' In: Balino, T. J. T., Cottarelli, C. (eds.), *Frameworks for Monetary Stability.* IMF Institute and Monetary and Exchange Affairs Department, IMF, Washington D.C.

Grossman, S., 1983. 'An analysis of the principal-agent problem.' *Econometrica* 51, 7–45.

Guthrie, G. and Wright, J., 1997. Market-implemented monetary policy with open mouth operations. Mimeo. University of Canterbury.

Hansson, B., 1993. 'A structural model.' In: Franzen, T., Andersson, K., Alexius, A., Berg, C., Hansson, B., Nilsson, C. and Nilsson, J. (eds.), *Monetary Policy Indicators.* Sveriges Riksbank, Stockholm, ch. 5, pp. 55–64.

Hendry, D. F., 1997. 'The econometrics of macroeconomic forecasting', *Econ. J.* 107, 1330–57.

Hunt, B. and Razzak W. A., 1997. Model estimation and the formulation of monetary policy. Paper presented at the Money, Macro and Finance Group meeting, University of Durham.

Huxford, J. and Reddell, M., 1996. 'Implementing monetary policy in New Zealand', *Res. Bank New Zealand Bull.* 59, 309–22.

Mayes, D. G. and Razzak, W. A., 1997. Transparency and accountability: Empirical models and policy-making at the Reserve Bank of New Zealand. Paper presented at the 10th Anniversary Congress of the Tinbergen Institute, Amsterdam, 14–16 May (revised for this volume).

Mayes, D. G. and Riches, B., 1996. 'The effectiveness of monetary policy in New Zealand', *Res. Bank New Zealand Bull.* 59, 5–20.

McCallum, B. T., 1995. 'Two fallacies concerning central bank independence', *Am. Econ. Rev.* 85, 207–11.

McShane, O., 1996. The impact of the Resource Management Act on the housing and construction components of the Consumer Price Index. Report for the Reserve Bank of New Zealand.

Nadal-De Simone, F., Dennis, R. and Redward, P., 1996. A monetary conditions index for New Zealand. Reserve Bank of New Zealand Discussion Paper G96/2.

Nicholl, P., 1994. 'Intervention techniques under a deregulated financial environment', *Res. Bank New Zealand Bull.* 57, 130–43.

O'Donovan, B. and Rae, D., 1996. The determinants of house prices in New Zealand: an aggregate and regional analysis. National Bank of New Zealand.

Persson, T. and Tabellini, G., 1993. 'Designing Institutions for Monetary Stability'. *Carnegie-Rochester Conf, Ser. Pub. Pol.* 39, 53–84.

Peters, J. and Savage, J., 1996. Determinants of house prices in Auckland, Wellington and Christchurch: 1980–1995. NZ Institute of Economic Research.

Reserve Bank of New Zealand, 1996. 'Summary indicators of monetary conditions.' *Res. Bank New Zealand Bull.* 59, 223–8.

Reserve Bank of New Zealand, 1997. Monetary policy implementation and signalling: discussion document.

Rogoff, K., 1985. 'The optimal degree of commitment to a monetary target', *Quart. J. Econ.* 100, 1169–90.

Svensson, L., 1997a. 'Optimal inflation targets, "conservative" central banks, and linear inflation contracts', *Amer. Econ. Rev.* 87, 98–114.

Svensson, L., 1997b. 'Inflation forecast targeting: implementing and monitoring inflation targets', *Eur. Econ. Rev.* 41, 1111–46.

Walsh, C., 1995a. 'Optimal contracts for independent central bankers', *Amer. Econ. Rev.* 85, 150–67.

Walsh, C., 1995b. 'Is New Zealand's Reserve Bank Act of 1989 an optimal central bank contract?' *J. Mon. Cr. Bank.* 27, 1179–91.

Winkelmann, L., 1996. A study of pass-through elasticities for New Zealand import markets. Reserve Bank of New Zealand Discussion Paper G96/5.

Part III

Model products and model usage

Chapter 8

Modeling the World Economic Outlook at the IMF: a historical review

James M. Boughton

The World Economic Outlook (WEO) exercise at the IMF has grown in response to demands by policymakers in national finance ministries and central banks for objective and internationally comparable projections and policy scenarios. Policymakers came to view the discussion of WEO documents as an important element in their efforts to keep abreast of world economic developments, prospects, and policy options. Feedback from those discussions informed the IMF staff as to how the exercise should be improved. Driven by this policy relevance, the WEO evolved from a decentralized project that was only haphazardly model-based into a more rigorous and coordinated exercise.
JEL Classifications: B23, F47

The heads of state of the major industrial countries decided at the Versailles Summit in June 1982 to invite the Managing Director of the International Monetary Fund to participate in the regular multilateral meetings of their finance ministers and central bank governors. Accordingly, three months later, when the Fund's Governors gathered in Toronto for the Annual Meetings, the private (and then secret) G–5 meeting[1] began with a presentation by the Managing Director, Jacques de Larosière, on the Fund's view of the World Economic Outlook (WEO) and its implications for macroeconomic policies. From then on, de Larosière – and later his successor, Michel Camdessus – built their presentations in these semi-annual meetings around the global outlook.

The G–5 meetings were a nearly invisible but highly important vehicle for disseminating the projections and analysis made by the Fund staff. Eight years earlier, the WEO had been given a more public and more global platform when the committee of Fund Governors known as the Committee of Twenty initiated a review of the implications of the sharp rise in world petroleum prices of 1973–4. The staff was already producing global economic forecasts for informal discussion by the Fund's Executive Board; at the initiative of the Managing Director (then H. Johannes Witteveen), those forecasts were presented to the Governors for their meeting in Rome in January 1974. From that moment on, the Committee of Twenty and its successor, the Interim Committee,[2] always included the WEO as a major agenda item.

The interest in the WEO shown by policymakers at this high level induced the Fund's management and staff to devote substantial resources over the years to refining the forecasting process. The goal of this chapter is to describe how the WEO exercise evolved from a loosely structured set of ad hoc projections in the early 1970s to a more rigorous and far more detailed set of forecasts and 'scenarios', based primarily on econometric models, by the late 1980s. The focus is on the 1980s, because of the major changes that took place then; one should keep in mind that WEO models and procedures continued to evolve and mature throughout the 1990s. The evolution discussed here was driven by three interrelated developments: prodding from national policymakers (usually not directly but via the Interim Committee and Executive Directors) to deal with specific policy issues, shifting views in the economics profession, and the continuing development of econometric models at the Fund.

1. Evolution of the outlook exercise

The WEO originated with a staff chapter prepared as a background document for an informal discussion by the Fund's Executive Board in June 1969. The Organization for Economic Cooperation and Development (OECD) in Paris had been producing and publishing its *Economic Outlook* for industrial countries semiannually since 1967, but no official agency was doing an overall forecast of world economic conditions.[3] At the outset, the Fund staff merely reported the OECD secretariat's forecasts and offered its own interpretation of the policy implications for both industrial and developing countries. In January 1971, the Executive Board began holding regular 'informal' discussions of the WEO, based on increasingly detailed papers that included the staff's own projections for aggregated groups of developing countries. It then quickly became apparent that, notwithstanding the good working relationship between the IMF and the OECD, the Fund's research staff would have to do its own projections for the industrial countries if it wanted to produce timely and consistent forecasts for the world economy that reflected its own analysis and was consistent with its own policy advice to member countries. The forecasts were derived partly from single-country models maintained by Fund staff; partly from judgmental evaluations; and partly from official and other national projections. As the exercise evolved in the 1970s, the WEO staff began using a basic computer model (known as the 'WEO facility') to derive the global implications and to test the consistency of the forecasts generated by the country desks in area departments.

By the late 1970s, the exercise developed into a major Fund-wide forecasting project, complemented by analysis of key trends and policy developments. Both the forecasts and the analysis provided a global context for the Fund's surveillance over the macroeconomic policies and performance of individual countries. The exercise was conducted at least semiannually in the late winter and summer, and the conclusions of the informal Executive Board meetings were circulated as background papers for the Interim Committee meetings that followed soon afterwards. Beginning in 1980, the Board agreed that the papers should be published.

As early as the mid-1970s, it became clear to the staff that the WEO had the potential to become much more than a forecasting exercise. To play an important role in the Fund, it would have to focus as much on the policy options available to member governments as on the staff's views on how the world economy might evolve. That simple notion led to the idea of emphasizing 'scenarios': conditional medium-term projections, the character of which evolved substantially during the 1980s. These scenarios were a key to the success of the WEO for focusing the discussions on major policy issues. Rather than emphasizing short-term forecasts – in which cyclical and high-frequency fluctuations necessarily dominate – the WEO gave primary emphasis to medium-term considerations, notably the policy requirements for generating sustainable, noninflationary growth and for consistency between countries. As an unpublished 1984 paper summarized the point, the medium-term scenarios 'should be viewed not so much as a forecast of what will happen, but as an indication of the policy challenges that will need to be faced if a satisfactory outcome is to be achieved'. In Fund parlance, 'a satisfactory outcome' generally meant a rate of economic growth that could be sustained over several years without pushing inflation beyond a minimal level. With that in mind, the implicit goal of the scenarios was always to prod policymakers to adopt more stable and more sustainable policies.

Initially, the WEO scenarios were stylized presentations of how the pattern of current-account balances among industrial countries might evolve over a period of around three years under various assumptions. For two years starting in April 1978, the staff presented a 'recommended' or 'desirable' scenario based on the assumption that the major industrial countries would adopt the policies necessary to jointly achieve moderate, noninflationary growth. In that scenario, the large external imbalances observed in 1978 (notably a large current-account surplus in Japan and a large deficit in the United States) were projected to be substantially reduced over the medium-term.[4] This desirable outcome, however, was judged by the staff to be unlikely in the absence of significant policy improvements in several countries.[5] But the alternative scenarios, rather than projecting the consequences of specific deviations in policy from the assumed path, merely showed the effects of different assumptions about economic growth. Notably, if the U.S. economy were to grow more rapidly, and Japan more slowly, then the desirable outcome would be less likely to be achieved.

The first true medium-term scenarios were produced in 1980, in the form of projections for a specific period (1985–86) rather than for an undated comparative-static equilibrium. The impetus for this step was that the United States, Japan, Germany, and the United Kingdom were all embarked on an anti-inflation strategy to combat the effects of the second oil shock and (in the United States and the United Kingdom) the cumulative excesses of the late 1970s. Much of the public and internal discussion of economic policy was focused on the question of whether this reaction was excessive. Both the United States and the United Kingdom had slipped into recession with sharply rising unemployment, while Japan and Germany had developed large external surpluses. The major oil-exporting countries also were registering large external surpluses, and the non-oil developing countries were facing dangerously large deficits. Was it therefore time for the major industrial countries to ease up on the restraint?

To tackle that question, the Fund staff presented a summary of how the world economy might evolve over the next five to six years, (a) with a continuation of existing policies in industrial countries, (b) with more expansionary policies until inflation resumed, followed by a policy correction, and (c) with expansionary policies maintained even after inflation resumed. The staff's judgment was that countries should continue with contractionary policies in order to restore a reasonable balance to the global pattern of current-account balances while continuing to rein in inflation. Allowing inflation to heat up again would lead to a deeper and more prolonged downturn than the one that was then in progress, and failing to tighten policies after inflation heated up would only aggravate the eventual downturn. Thus the first global scenarios, although in retrospect they look rather primitive and unquantified, served – for better or worse – to bolster confidence in the use of contractionary demand-management policies to combat inflationary pressures.

The 1981 scenarios, which for the first time included projections of the debt-servicing burdens of developing countries through the mid-1980s, reflected the growing concerns among policymakers about the longer-run effects of the massive recycling of external surpluses from oil exporters to oil-importing developing countries. These scenarios are of particular interest because they foreshadow the problems that led, a year later, to a nearly global debt crisis. In the text as published in June 1981, the staff described the medium-term debt prospects of low- and middle-income oil importers as 'worrisome' and 'disturbing'; 'in the absence of adjustment measures, [many of these countries] would soon find themselves unable to finance their deficits' (pp. 16–17).

It may be noted in passing that to a reader of the published papers, the staff's analysis in the WEO might seem unduly timid. The preliminary chapters discussed by the Executive Board, however, often were more direct. In the case just described, the warning about the debt buildup was made more explicit in the version of the paper discussed by Executive Directors in April. That paper noted that the staff had prepared a scenario in which the non-oil developing countries did not carry out adjustment policies to reduce the buildup of external debt, but that such a scenario had not even been quantified because the implied financing requirements were completely infeasible. Because of the sensitivity of such conclusions, the published papers were always at least slightly bowdlerized.

The WEO scenarios were expanded slightly further in the fall of 1981: In addition to the baseline and more pessimistic scenarios, a 'favorable' Scenario C was now presented in the internal chapters. This seemingly innocuous extension was a response to the new-found optimism among many policymakers under the influence of the 'new' supply-side economists.[6] According to that school of thought, a combination of liberalization of markets and reduction of the size of governments would enable private-sector activity to expand rapidly to fill the vacuum left by contractionary demand-management policies. The 'favorable' scenario therefore assumed that inflationary expectations would fall rapidly, and real growth rise rapidly, in response to a cut in government expenditure. But the staff argued that such a favorable development was 'unlikely', and the chapter cautioned that if governments relied on the rosy scenario, they could be led into relaxing policies prematurely and falling inadvertently into the 'pessimistic' Scenario B.[7]

Not until 1985 did the Fund staff begin developing fully articulated medium-term scenarios for the world economy. That same year, both the Group of Ten (G–10) industrial countries and the Group of 24 (G–24) developing countries issued reports (reproduced in Crockett and Goldstein, 1987) calling on the Fund to strengthen its surveillance over the policies of the major industrial countries by more clearly explaining the consequences of pursuing unchanged policies and by specifying and evaluating options for policy adjustments. In response, the staff significantly expanded the scope of the scenarios in the spring 1986 exercise. For the first time, the staff made quantitative projections for each of the next four years, rather than just for a single medium-term period, for key macroeconomic variables for the United States, Japan, and Europe, as well as aggregate figures for industrial countries. These projections were produced under several different sets of assumptions, an exercise that earlier would have been impossibly complex to complete in the limited time available, because the staff lacked a fully articulated multicountry model.

For the 1986 experiment, the staff of the U.S. Federal Reserve Board, the OECD, and the Philadelphia-based Project Link agreed to provide econometric model simulations based on a common set of assumptions about economic policies and conditions. Those simulations were then combined, and extended to cover the implications for developing countries in more detail, using the newly developed MINIMOD system (see below). In essence, the exercise showed that an easing of fiscal or monetary policy could mitigate the short-term decline in output that was otherwise projected to occur, but at some risk of a rekindling of inflation.

As the staff's econometric modeling capabilities strengthened in the second half of the 1980s, the WEO scenarios became correspondingly more focused on specific policy options. For example, in August 1987, in an exercise that implicitly called into question the Louvre accord on key-currency exchange rates, the scenarios suggested that maintaining fixed rates might make reduction of the large external imbalances of the largest countries quite difficult. A few months later, after the October 1987 stock market crash, the staff for the first time since 1979 undertook to prepare a 'mini-WEO': a special review of the outlook in the light of a major shock. That review again suggested that the major industrial countries should allow exchange rates to adjust to absorb the differential effects of the decline in equity prices.

Another development of the late 1980s was the advent of the 'objective indicators' exercise. The idea, first proposed by the staff in 1985 as a means of strengthening Fund surveillance, was to introduce a set of normative benchmarks for the major industrial countries that would be comparable to the performance criteria used for monitoring progress under Fund-supported adjustment programs.

Although the G–7 flirted with but never did agree to any normative indicators, the framework survived in the WEO in the form of medium-term projections for a standardized set of macroeconomic variables. The published tables doubtless looked to readers like the grin of the Cheshire cat, but they did serve to focus the semi-annual discussions of the WEO by Executive Directors by linking projected fiscal deficits to shifts in current-account balances via the national saving-investment identity.[8]

2. The forecasting process

A key feature of the WEO exercise is the generation of forecasts that are conditional on standard assumptions. That is, the WEO forecasts are not necessarily the staff's best judgment of what will happen; they are the best judgment of what would happen, subject to certain assumptions. The standard 'technical' assumptions for the short-term forecasts (i.e. forecasts for the remainder of the current year plus the following one) are that exchange rates among industrial countries will remain fixed in nominal terms, that oil prices will remain fixed in terms of U.S. dollars, and that current economic policies will continue. The definition of current policies allows for announced changes, regardless of whether they have yet been implemented. (See, for example, WEO, October 1985, p. 1.) Overall, the short-term forecasts incorporate enough flexibility that they can be interpreted as if they were unconditional. Similar assumptions underpin the medium-term scenarios, except that exchange rates and key prices are fixed in real rather than nominal terms beyond the end of the short-term forecast horizon, and the possibility of cyclical disturbances is excluded after the end of the short-term horizon. In this context, the constraints are more fundamental.

The specification of policy assumptions for the medium-term scenarios becomes especially difficult when current policies are thought to be unsustainable. The projections will often become less and less believable as the forecast horizon lengthens, and the staff is forced either to hedge the forecasts or to derive complex explanations. This overdetermination problem first became acute in 1984, when the strength of the U.S. dollar was clearly unsustainable. Assuming both a continuation of the existing mix of fiscal and monetary policies and no change in real exchange rates led to unrealistic projections. The problem cropped up again around 1987, when the prevailing policy stance in the United States implied a growth in the stock of U.S. debt that was inconsistent with the maintenance of unchanged real exchange rates.

The staff solved the problem beginning with the fall 1986 WEO – and even made a virtue of it – by emphasizing the 'tensions' in the unrealistic scenarios. 'Circumstances may arise, of course, in which current policies appear to be either unsustainable or inconsistent with the underlying exchange rate assumption. In such cases, the analysis focuses on the alternative ways in which incompatibilities might manifest themselves, or be reconciled' (WEO, April 1987, p. 11). This approach acknowledged explicitly that the projections are overidentified: policies would have to be adjusted if the authorities hoped to keep exchange rates stable. By focusing on the 'tensions' in the overly constrained scenarios, the staff could discuss the requirements for a responsible policy stance without having to predict either policy changes or exchange rates.

The 'indicators' tables in the spring 1987 WEO paper for the Executive Board suggested that from 1986 to 1991, the U.S. general government deficit would be reduced by 1.8 per cent of GNP under the assumption of partial implementation of Gramm-Rudman. The counterparts of that deficit reduction were shown as a rise in gross private investment of 1.4 per cent of GNP and a fall in the current-account deficit by 0.4 per cent of GNP (with no change in the private saving rate).[9] The text pointed out that this scenario involved tensions, in that a strengthening of investment by that size seemed unlikely – whether on the basis of economic theory, econometric evidence, or historical perspective – while a larger reduction in the external deficit would seem to require a real depreciation in the dollar (which was inconsistent with the technical assumptions underlying the scenario).

The process by which these forecasts were produced was, for much of the 1980s, a cumbersome and unwieldy routine that imposed severe strains on the staff's limited resources. The Research Department, which had overall responsibility for the exercise, would initiate the forecasting round by circulating questionnaires to the area departments. Those questionnaires specified the main assumptions that were to underpin the forecasts (oil and other primary commodity prices, key-currency exchange rates, etc.) and asked the desk economists to provide initial projections for their countries on that basis. (Only the larger countries were included in this exercise; small countries were assumed to follow the patterns of their larger neighbors or trading partners.) These first-round forecasts were produced by whatever economic theories, methodology, models, and data that the desks believed to be relevant and appropriate for the country concerned. Some forecasts were derived primarily from official national projections, some were derived in part from models estimated and maintained by the area departments, and some were largely judgmental. The Research Department staff would then feed the results into the central WEO data base for processing by (mainframe) computer and would carefully analyze the global and regional outcome for consistency and credibility. The results would then be returned to the area departments for further review and revision. Normally, several iterations would be required to produce a consistent forecast for the world economy, and over time this iterative interaction between the country desks and the WEO staff became a year-round disciplinary influence on the Fund's forecasts and analysis.

The forecasting process gradually became more streamlined and efficient toward the end of the decade, partly because of the increased availability of computer technology and the successful development of multinational econometric models in the Research Department. The latter development is examined in the next section.

3. Modeling the world economy

The debate over the appropriate balance between individual judgment and the output of econometric models in macroeconomic forecasting has always been contentious. Even in the heyday of the large models of national economies in the 1960s, most successful forecasters used the models more for evaluating internal consistency than for making baseline projections.[10] During the 1970s, the preeminence of large-scale econometric models for macroeconomic forecasting was challenged by several developments, including a return to simpler, smaller, and more transparent models and the development of more sophisticated time-series techniques. In response to the Lucas critique (Lucas, 1976), the use of models for forecasting fell for a while into almost total disrepute. Not until the mid-1980s would econometric techniques advance to the point where forecasters could conclude comfortably that they had taken adequate account of the critique (at least in the absence of a major regime change), principally by allowing expectations to be determined by and consistent with the structure of the model.

3.1. Multilateral Exchange Rate Model

The first model to play a significant role in the WEO exercise was the Multilateral Exchange Rate Model (MERM).[11] The idea for the MERM, which was developed by Paul Armington in the late 1960s (Armington, 1969), was to derive equilibrium relationships between exchange rates and trade balances by reference to highly disaggregated production functions. The model provided a working framework for the preparations for the December 1971 ministerial meeting of the G–10 (the Smithsonian meeting) at which a new set of par values for the major industrial countries was to be negotiated. The staff's estimates of the pattern of rates that would equilibrate current-account balances were a major input into the negotiations, and the par values that emerged from the political negotiations were quite close to the MERM solutions (see de Vries, 1976, Chapter 26; and James, 1995, pp. 222–3). Although the agreed rates soon turned out to be unsustainable (the whole fixed-rate system collapsed just 15 months later), the problem was only partly with the initial pattern and was seriously aggravated by the lack of stabilization and coordination of macroeconomic policies afterwards.

The MERM was formalized first by Artus and Rhomberg (1973) and later by Artus and McGuirk (1981). It was a purely static but highly disaggregated system of relationships that explicitly recognized the multilateral dimension of the external adjustment process: a country's 'effective' exchange rate could be derived as a weighted average of bilateral weights, not by the traditional arithmetic based on the value of bilateral trade with each country, but by estimating the elasticity of trade in specific categories of goods to changes in exchange rates and by taking into account indirect competition between countries.[12] The MERM could be solved either for the pattern of exchange rates that would bring about a desired set of current-account balances (as for the 1971 Smithsonian discussions) or for the current-account balances that would result from an assumed set of exchange rates. It was in this latter mode that the MERM played a key role in quantifying the WEO forecasts in the 1970s and early 1980s (de Vries, 1976, pp. 125–6, 790, and 810). Shortly afterwards, however, the comparative-static nature of the model had rendered it obsolete for most WEO purposes, and it was gradually phased out.

3.2. World Trade Model

The second general empirical model developed at the Fund was the World Trade Model (WTM), which was introduced in the late 1970s as a complement to the MERM (see Deppler and Ripley, 1978). The WTM was a global, partial-equilibrium model designed to estimate the effects on international trade from changes in domestic economic activity. Like the MERM, it focused primarily on the larger industrial countries, but it did include more dynamic adjustment.[13] The model was used by the Research Department to check the area departments' forecasts for consistency and to start the iterative process by which a global economic forecast was to be produced. However, these initial trade forecasts were never accorded much credibility by the area departments and therefore had little real influence. The WTM was updated and expanded (see Spencer, 1984), but its basic limitations – the absence of expectations, limited dynamic adjustment, and minimal feedback from international trade to domestic activity – remained. It played less and less of a role in the WEO process over time and – like the MERM – was phased out completely by the end of the 1980s.

3.3. MINIMOD

The real breakthrough in the evolution of modeling at the Fund came in 1986, at a time when the effects of fiscal policy on economic growth were still much in dispute in policy discussions in the Executive Board, as elsewhere. Whether the subject was the WEO or the appropriateness of policies in individual countries, it was fashionable to argue that contractionary fiscal actions would 'crowd in' private sector activity by enough to stimulate aggregate economic activity quickly. Forecasts that showed otherwise were often dismissed as inconsistent with rational expectations or as tainted by the Lucas critique. That debate and the longstanding need for a more efficient means of producing policy analyses led the staff to devote substantial resources to the development of a dynamic, internally consistent, multicountry econometric model.

In 1985, in a first effort to tackle the Lucas critique head-on, the internal WEO papers had included a report on the results of a simulation study comparing policy effects with and without Muth-rational (i.e., model-consistent) formation of expectations about the economy.[14] That study showed that while fiscal multipliers were smaller when agents displayed perfect foresight about policy effects, most of the qualitative conclusions of the more conventional models still applied. To carry this type of analysis forward, the staff derived a scaled-down version of the Federal

Reserve's Multi-Country Model. The Fund version, dubbed MINIMOD, not only had far fewer equations to be solved and thus was more manageable; it also incorporated endogenous, forward-looking, model-consistent expectations and thus was relatively immune from the Lucas critique.[15] Relationships such as saving and investment functions depended in part on agents' expectations of future changes in interest rates, inflation, and exchange rates; and those expectations were formulated to be consistent with the long-run solution of the model (i.e. agents, on average, were assumed to forecast the eventual outcome of any policy or other exogenous action correctly).

3.4. MULTIMOD

The final step, a direct outgrowth of the MINIMOD project, was the development of MULTIMOD. Once the principle of generating alternative scenarios by running simulations with a global model was established and accepted, the Research Department staff set about estimating its own model. By the time of the spring 1988 WEO, MULTIMOD was ready for its debut. The new model (Masson *et al.*, 1988) differed from its predecessor in several respects. It was much larger (a total of 308 equations covering seven countries or groups of countries, compared with a total of 67 equations for the United States and the 'rest of the world' as a single bloc in MINIMOD);[16] the parameters were estimated by the staff using the Fund's own WEO data base, rather than being borrowed from other models; and the role of endogenous and model-consistent expectations was more extensive. Like MINIMOD, it was used by the staff to generate the *alternative* scenarios: the baseline projections were still based on the judgment of the country desks, and the model generated the deviations from the baseline in response to specified policy changes or other shocks.

When the Executive Board met to discuss the WEO in March 1988, the MULTIMOD projections immediately became the star of the show. The medium-term chapter now included, besides the baseline, 11 alternative scenarios predicated on specific shifts in policies or other conditions. Three scenarios detailed how the 'tensions' in the baseline might be manifested if the major countries did not change their policies in time. There might be another stock-market crash like that of October 1987, there might be severe deflation, or there might be a run on the U.S. dollar. The next five scenarios explained the types of policy changes that could avoid these dire consequences: improved structural policies in Europe, more fiscal consolidation in the United States, increased domestic investment and import penetration in Japan, or combinations of the above. The remaining exercises examined other possible actions such as increased financing for the heavily indebted developing countries and increased protectionist measures in industrial countries. These simulations – presented in detailed tables covering projections for each year from 1988 through 1992, with accompanying analysis – provided a much more concrete foundation for the Board discussion than had ever before been possible. This type of exercise became the standard for years to come.[17]

3.5. Developing-country models

The Fund staff constructed several partial- and general-equilibrium models of developing countries in the 1970s and 1980s. Two circumstances combined to spur this activity: Fund lending shifted heavily toward the developing world, which raised the demand by the Executive Board for detailed quantitative analysis of those economies, and the quantity and quality of data improved by enough to support the estimation of at least rudimentary empirical models. Several early studies, such as Khan (1974) on Venezuela and Otani and Park (1976) on Korea, focused on the linkages between monetary policy and economic activity and inflation. By the 1980s, more comprehensive macroeconomic models were appearing, such as Khan and Knight (1981). Simultaneously with the empirical studies, Fund staff were conducting basic theoretical research on the structure of developing economies and the differences between modeling industrial and developing countries. That work culminated in a series of papers in the early 1990s, collected in Khan, Montiel and Haque (1991).

For the WEO scenarios, the Research Department developed two independent models of the developing world in the late 1980s. One, the developing-country module of MULTIMOD, was used to project the implications of the industrial-country scenarios for developing countries taken together. The other, LDCMOD, was used to produce disaggregated projections that could be re-aggregated and studied for any geographic or analytical group of countries.[18] LDCMOD comprised some two dozen behavioral equations plus around 60 identities for close to 100 individual countries. Because of data limitations and the sheer size of the project, the structure and econometric sophistication of LDCMOD were far more rudimentary than those of MULTIMOD. The LDCMOD simulations took the industrial-country output from MULTIMOD as exogenous inputs; in principle, the LDCMOD simulations could have been fed back into MULTIMOD and so on through an iterative interaction to produce a globally consistent set of projections. The MULTIMOD team, however, preferred to iterate with their own highly aggregated developing-country blocs (which, like the rest of the model, incorporated forward-looking, model-consistent expectations) in order to produce an *internally* consistent outcome. This procedure was obviously inelegant, but it had a certain practicality that enabled it to endure well into the 1990s.

4. Evaluation

How useful were the WEO forecasts, and were they improved by the development of sophisticated models and the interaction with the policy interests of the Executive Board in the 1980s? Answering those questions is far more complicated than just comparing the forecasts with actual outcomes, because of the constraints in the forecast process. If countries' policies changed (as they inevitably did) in the interim, then the outcome would differ from the forecast even if the forecast was perfect on its own terms. Over a long enough period, however, such apparent errors should even out, and the forecasts should be unbiased. The two key questions, then, are whether a persistent bias has been evident – either in the observed forecast errors or in the qualitative approach taken by the staff – and whether the forecasts have been statistically efficient: that is, whether they have added significantly to the information that one could get simply by looking systematically at the historical time-series data without reference to an economic model.

In the policy discussions at the Fund, the question of bias arose primarily for the medium-term scenarios. The staff acknowledged that the medium-term reference scenarios contained an inherent optimism in that they ruled out both recessions and exchange-rate changes. That optimism was tempered by the construction of alternative scenarios that illustrated how the tensions in the baseline might be resolved, but the staff still ran into frequent criticism that it was viewing the world with rose-colored glasses. Even the alternative scenarios necessarily assumed that countries borrowing from the Fund would successfully carry out the economic pro-grams on which stand-by arrangements were conditional; since in practice many Fund-supported adjustment programs were not successfully completed, the poten-tial for serious imbalances and crises was inherently greater than recognized in the scenarios. Executive Directors often complained that the staff was failing to recog-nize the dire consequences that lay ahead like economic land mines.

Occasionally, the question of bias arose in the discussion of the short-term fore-casts as well. In February 1979, Executive Directors complained that the staff seemed to be overestimating likely growth in the industrial countries while underes-timating the inflation problem. At the time, the OECD's *Economic Outlook* was projecting 3 per cent growth in 1979–80 for the industrial countries as a whole, whereas the WEO was projecting 3.7 per cent. Executive Directors, on the whole, concluded that the OECD forecast was more realistic. (The outturn, incidentally, was 3.5 per cent.) That type of dispute, however, was uncommon.

Two intensive assessments of the basic track record have drawn mixed conclu-sions. Artis (1988) concluded that the forecasts of economic growth had been biased toward optimism in the 1970s but not in the 1980s, that in general the fore-casts were statistically efficient, and that overall the Fund had done no better or worse than national or other international forecasters during the 1970s and 1980s (pp. 1–3). Four years later, Barrionuevo (1992) concluded that although the WEO forecasts were not biased in the 1980s, they were less accurate than forecasts made with simple time-series methods.[19] In assessing that conclusion, however, one must keep in mind that time-series forecasting methods provide insufficient information for policy analysis and thus are not a viable option for a project such as the WEO.

No matter how one chooses to interpret the statistics, if one considers the size and complexity of the task it is clear that the World Economic Outlook has been a major success story for the IMF. Driven in part by constant feedback from the world's economic policymakers, by the beginning of the 1990s the WEO had become arguably the world's leading review of global economic trends and prospects. Without question, it was the polestar of the Fund's analytical work and of its communication with member countries and the public at large.

Acknowledgements

Prepared for the Tenth Anniversary Congress of the Tinbergen Institute, on *Empirical Models and Policy Making*, in Amsterdam (May 1997). I am grateful to Peter Hole, Flemming Larsen, Paul Masson, Jacques Polak, conference participants, and the Editors for many helpful comments.

Notes

1 From 1973 through 1986, meetings of the major-country finance ministers – held at least semiannually – were restricted to the Group of Five, or G–5 (France, Germany, Japan, the United Kingdom, and the United States). Separately, from 1976 on, the Heads of State and Government of those countries plus Canada and Italy (the G–7) met annually in public summits. The 1986 Tokyo summit led to a decision to expand the ministerial meetings to the G–7.

2 The membership of both committees comprised the Governors of the Fund (usually Ministers of Finance) from the countries represented on the Executive Board. Virtually all member countries are represented either directly or through constituencies. Views of policymakers are presented at the Fund on an ongoing basis by Executive Directors, who are either appointed by a national government (in the case of the largest countries) or elected by one or more countries. Terms of office for individual Directors range from two years to career service. The ministerial-level Interim Committee normally meets semi-annually and provides broad policy guidance for the work of the Executive Board, the Managing Director (who serves both as head of the staff and as Chair of the Executive Board), and the staff. Staff members are not government appointees.

3 Other international organizations had long produced periodic papers on world economic conditions, dating back to the League of Nations' 'World Economic Survey', published annually from 1932 to 1944. The United Nations began producing annual reports on global economic developments around 1948. In addition, the IMF Annual Report – which is a report of the Executive Board rather than the staff – has always included a review of world economic conditions, but its focus has been on the policy implications of current developments, rather than on the outlook. For a detailed description of the evolution of the WEO through 1978, see de Vries (1985), Chapter 40, pp. 785–97.

4 The length of the 'medium-term' was not defined precisely in that comparative-statics exercise, but it was understood to be around three years. The methodology involved allowing lagged effects that either were already 'in the pipeline' or were introduced by the assumed changes in growth rates to have their full effect on current-account balances. Thus the medium-term was the period over which equilibrium would be achieved in the absence of new shocks. For an exposition, see Artus and Knight (1984), Chapter 4.

5 That judgment was offered in February 1979. When the scenario was first presented a year earlier, the staff commented only that it 'would represent a very significant shift in strategy', notably through a 'more expansionary stance' of fiscal policy, without commenting on the likelihood of that shift taking place. The sharpening of the tone followed widespread criticism from Executive Directors and others that the staff was being too complacent.

6 The appellation 'new' is from a critical review by Feldstein (1986).

7 For an updated version of the rosy scenario, see WEO (April 1982), pp. 19–24.

8 Internal WEO documents presented data for each G–7 country and for the aggregate group. Published documents included only the aggregates.

9 The 1991 projections were not included in the published WEO.

10 Clive Granger (1980) summarized model-based forecasting experience as follows: '. . . the

forecasts produced by the model are not necessarily the forecasts issued by the model's constructors. If a forecast . . . seems strange or out of line with . . . the econometrician's own judgment, then it will probably be altered to look more reasonable. This application of "tender loving care" has been shown to result in improved forecasts . . .' (p. 119). For history and evaluation of policy analysis with econometric models, see Bodkin *et al.* (1990) and (specifically in a multi-country setting) Bryant *et al.* (1988).

11 Earlier partial-equilibrium empirical models were developed by Jacques Polak and others in the Research Department as early as the late 1940s; see notably Polak (1953), as well as the review in Frenkel, Goldstein, and Khan (1991). Also, as noted in Section 1, from the late 1970s the staff used a basic model (primarily a set of identities) to test the global consistency of the forecasts.

12 If two countries both sell the same good, or competing goods, to a third country, a change in either country's exchange rate *vis-à-vis* the third will affect the competitiveness of the other. That effect was captured by the MERM but not by models based on bilateral trade.

13 The model comprised blocks of equations for 14 individual industrial countries, plus four blocks for groups of countries: developed countries producing primarily primary commodities, major oil-exporting countries, other developing countries, and centrally planned economies (including non-member countries).

14 The study, Masson and Blundell-Wignall (1985), made use of a simplified version of the OECD's INTERLINK model, called 'Minilink'.

15 See Haas and Masson (1986) and Masson (1987). The model could be solved either with or without endogenous expectations, but once the staff became convinced that the fully consistent solution gave the more realistic and credible forecasts, the partial version was largely abandoned.

16 MULTIMOD was later extended to include a larger number of individual countries and greater disaggregation of the groups; the non-industrial world, however, remained highly aggregated. See Masson, Symansky and Meredith (1990).

17 For an independent (World Bank staff) evaluation of the analytical and forecasting properties of MULTIMOD, see Jamshidi (1989).

18 Analytical categories included countries grouped by level of per-capita income, type of principal exports, or degree of external indebtedness. For an exposition, see Adams and Adams (1989) and Kumar, Samiei and Bassett (1993); the name LDCMOD was introduced in the latter paper.

19 For an informal but independent analysis, see Worswick (1983). Artis (1996) updated and extended his earlier study and drew similar conclusions.

References

Adams, C. and Adams, C. H., 1989. 'A scenario and forecast adjustment model for developing countries.' In: *Staff Studies* (International Monetary Fund, Washington), 98–125.

Armington, P. S., 1969. 'A theory of demand for products distinguished by place of production.' *IMF Staff Papers*, Vol. 16, 159–76.

Artis, M. J., 1988. 'How accurate is the world economic outlook? A post mortem on short-term forecasting at the international monetary fund.' In: *Staff Studies* (International Monetary Fund, Washington), 1–49.

Artis, M. J., 1996. 'How accurate are the IMF's short-term forecasts? Another examination of the World Economic Outlook.' *Staff Studies*, December 1997, 1–39 (International Monetary Fund, Washington).

Artus, J. R. and Knight, M. D., 1984. 'Issues in the assessment of the exchange rates of industrial countries.' *Occasional Paper 29* (International Monetary Fund, Washington).

Artus, J. R. and McGuirk, A. K., 1981. 'A Revised Version of the Multilateral Exchange Rate Model.' *IMF Staff Papers*, Vol. 28, 275–309.

Artus, J. R. and Rhomberg, R. R., 1973. 'A Multilateral Exchange Rate Model.' *IMF Staff Papers*, Vol. 20, 591–611.

Barrionuevo, J. M., 1992. A simple forecasting accuracy criterion under rational expectations: evidence from the World Economic Outlook and Time Series Models, IMF Working Paper WP/92/48.

Bartolini, L. and Symansky, S., 1993. 'Unemployment and Wage Dynamics in MULTI-MOD.' *Staff Studies* (International Monetary Fund, Washington), 76–85.

Bodkin, R. G., Klein L. R. and Marwah, K. eds., 1991. *A History of Macroeconometric Model-building* (Aldershot, England: Edward Elgar Publishing Ltd.).

Bryant, R. C., Henderson, D. W., Holtham, G., Hooper P. and Symansky, S. A. eds., 1988. *Empirical Macroeconomics for Interdependent Economies* (The Brookings Institution, Washington).

Crockett, A. and Goldstein, M., 1987. 'Strengthening the international monetary system: exchange rates, surveillance, and objective indicators.' In: *Occasional Paper 50* (International Monetary Fund, Washington).

Deppler, M. C. and Ripley, D. M., 1978. 'The world trade model: merchandise trade.' In: *IMF Staff Papers*, Vol. 21, 147–206.

De Vries, M. G., 1976. *The International Monetary Fund 1966–1971: The System under Stress* (International Monetary Fund, Washington).

De Vries, M. G., 1985. *The International Monetary Fund 1972–1978: Cooperation on Trial* (International Monetary Fund, Washington).

Feldstein, M., 1986. 'Supply side economics: old truths and new claims', *American Economic Review: Papers and Proceedings*, Vol. 76, No. 2, 26–30.

Frenkel, J. A., Goldstein, M. and Khan, M., 1991. 'Major themes in the writings of Jacques J. Polak.' In: J. A. Frenkel and Goldstein, M., eds., *International Economic Policy: Essays in Honor of Jacques J. Polak* (International Monetary Fund, Washington), 3–39.

Granger, C. W. J., 1980. *Forecasting in Business and Economics* (Academic Press, New York).

Haas, R. D. and Masson, P. R., 1986. 'MINIMOD: specification and simulation results', *IMF Staff Papers*, Vol. 33, 722–67.

James, H., 1995. *International Monetary Cooperation since Bretton Woods* (Oxford University Press, Oxford).

Jamshidi, A., 1989. Evaluating Global Macroeconomic Models: A Case Study of MULTI-MOD, World Bank Policy, Planning, and Research Working Paper, WPS 298 (International Monetary Fund, Washington).

Khan, M. S., 1974. 'Experiments with a Monetary Model for the Venezuelan Economy', *IMF Staff Papers*, Vol. 21, 389–413.

Khan, M. S., Montiel, P. J. and Haque, N. U. eds., 1991. *Macroeconomic Models for Adjustment in Developing Countries* (International Monetary Fund, Washington).

Kumar, M. S., Samiei, H. and Bassett, S., 1993. 'An Extended Scenario and Forecast Adjustment Model for Developing Countries.' In: *Staff Studies* (International Monetary Fund, Washington), 47–75.

Lucas, R. E. Jr., 1976. 'Econometric policy evaluation: a critique.' In: K. Brunner and A. H. Meltzer (eds.), *The Phillips Curve and Labor Markets, Carnegie-Rochester Conference Series on Public Policy*, Vol. 1 (North-Holland, Amsterdam), 19–46.

Masson, P. R., 1987. 'The dynamics of a two-country minimodel under rational expectations,'

Annales d'Economie et de Statistique, Vol. 6/7 (Institut National de la Statistique et des Etudes Economiques) (France), 37–69.

Masson, P. R. and Blundell-Wignall, A., 1985. 'Fiscal policy and the exchange rate in the Big Seven: transmission of U.S. government spending shocks', *European Economic Review*, Vol. 28, 11–42.

Masson, P. R., Symansky, S., Haas R. D. and Dooley, M. P., 1988. 'MULTIMOD: A Multi-Regional Econometric Model.' *Staff Studies* (International Monetary Fund, Washington), 50–104.

Masson, P. R., Symansky, S. and Meredith, G., 1990. MULTIMOD Mark II: A Revised and Extended Model, Occasional Paper 71 (International Monetary Fund, Washington).

Otani, I. and Park, Y. C., 1976. 'A monetary model of the Korean economy', *IMF Staff Papers*, Vol. 23, 164–99.

Polak, J. J., 1953. *An International Economic System* (University of Chicago Press, Chicago).

Polak, J. J., 1995. 'Fifty years of exchange rate research and policy at the International Monetary Fund', *IMF Staff Papers*, Vol. 42, 734–61.

Spencer, G. H., 1984. 'The world trade model: revised estimates', *IMF Staff Papers*, Vol. 3, 469–98.

World Economic Outlook, various dates (International Monetary Fund, Washington). The full title of each WEO publication is World Economic Outlook: A Survey by the Staff of the International Monetary Fund, except for the autumn updates of 1984 through 1988. Those five were published as World Economic Outlook: Revised Projections by the Staff of the International Monetary Fund. The May 1980 and May 1985 papers were published as individual documents, not part of any other series. From 1981 through 1984, the WEO was published as part of the series of Occasional Papers. Beginning in 1986, a new series of World Economic and Financial Studies was established, comprising the WEO, related staff papers, and reports on capital market developments.

Worswick, G. D. N., 1983. The IMF's World Economic Outlook: A Critique; Report to the Group of Twenty-Four. UNDP/UNCTAD Project INT/81/046, UNCTAD/MFD/TA/24.

Chapter 9

Policy design and evaluation: EU structural funds and cohesion in the European periphery

John Bradley

Preparation for the Single European Market included a major reform and expansion of EU regional aid programmes designed to ensure that weaker EU member states would not lose out. Since these initiatives were likely to induce major structural changes in the developing economies of the periphery – mainly Greece, Ireland, Portugal and Spain – analysts were faced with the dilemma of using conventional economic models, calibrated with historical data, to address the nature and consequences of future structural changes. What emerged represented a learning process, based on guidance from EU and domestic policy makers as well as being informed by modelling studies.
JEL classifications: C53, E65, R58

1. Introduction

The reform of EU regional aid programmes into the so-called *Community Support Framework* (CSF) in the late 1980s presented EU as well as national policy makers and analysts with major challenges. The political rationale behind the CSF came from the fear that not all EU member states were likely to benefit equally from the Single Market, whose purpose was to dismantle all remaining non-tariff barriers within the Union. In particular, the less advanced economies of the Southern and Western periphery (mainly Greece, Portugal, Spain and Ireland) were felt to be particularly vulnerable unless they received development aid, although such distributional anxieties had found no expression in the Commission's own earlier *ex ante* model-based study of the impact of the Single Market (Emerson *et al.*, 1988).

Although the CSF expenditures were large (between 1–4 per cent of country GDP per annum) this in itself was not a problem for policy design or analysis. Indeed, evaluating the macroeconomic impact of public expenditure initiatives had been an active area of work since quantitative models were first developed in the 1930s. However, what was special about the CSF was its goal, i.e. to design and implement policies with the explicit aim of transforming the underlying *structure* of the beneficiary economies in order to prepare them for exposure to the competitive forces about to be unleashed by the Single Market. Thus, CSF policies moved far beyond a conventional demand-side stabilization role, being directed at the promotion of structural change, faster long-term growth, and real convergence through mainly supply-side processes.

To some extent the new breed of macroeconomic models of the late 1980s had addressed the theoretical deficiencies that had precipitated the decline of econometric modelling activity from the mid-1970s (Klein, 1983). However, policy makers and analysts were still faced with the dilemma of having to use conventional economic models, calibrated using historical time-series data, to address the consequences of future structural changes. In particular, the relationship between public investment and private sector supply-side responses – matters that were at the heart of the CSF – were not very well understood or articulated from a modelling point of view.

The revival of the study of growth theory in the mid-1980s had provided some guidelines to the complex issues involved in designing policies to boost a country's growth rate, but was more suggestive of mechanisms than of magnitudes (Barro and Sala-i-Martin, 1995). Furthermore, available empirical growth studies tended to be predominantly aggregate and cross-country rather than disaggregated and country-specific.[1] Another complication facing the designers and analysts of the CSF was that the four main beneficiary countries – Greece, Ireland, Portugal and Spain – were on the geographical periphery of the EU, thus introducing spatial issues into their development processes. With advances in the treatment of imperfect competition, the field of economic geography had also revived during the 1980s (Krugman, 1995). But the insights of the new research were confined to small theoretical models and seldom penetrated up to the type of large-scale empirical models that are typically used in realistic policy analysis.

Our chapter examines interactions that took place between policy makers and policy analysts during the design and evaluation of the CSF. In Section 2 we discuss issues related to the origins and design of the two CSF programmes: Delors-I covering the five years 1989–93 and Delors-II covering the period 1994–99. In Section 3 we describe how evaluations of the CSF were actually carried out, examining in particular the nature and consequences of the interaction between the policy makers and the policy analysts as both groups tried to work together. In Section 4 we explore the response of the economic modellers as they attempted to analyse the impacts of the CSF, describing how models were developed and changed as a result of exposure to new chains of policy influence. We conclude in Section 5 with a review of the lessons that have been learned.

2. Designing regional aid: the Community Support Frameworks

The conventional wisdom in growth theory is that regions should converge over time. Table 9.1 shows data for the four so-called 'cohesion' countries and indicates some convergence during the latter half of the 1980s – Greece being an exception – with a rapid acceleration afterwards in the case of Ireland and Portugal. Using Barro and Sala-i-Martin's average convergence speed (2 per cent p.a.), each country except Greece is found to have performed somewhat better than expected (in terms of GDP per head) since its accession to the EU. This may be partly attributable to the CSF programmes, though there is some empirical evidence that trade integration itself promotes convergence (Barry *et al*, 1997). If living standards are more accurately measured by private consumption per capita, however, relative living standards are found to have fallen in all four peripheral member states between 1973 and 1991 (Table 9.2). The pre-CSF convergence experience is therefore ambiguous.

Table 9.1 Relative GDP (GNP) per capita in purchasing power parity terms (EU12 = 100)

	1960	1973	1980	1985	1990	1993
Ireland	61 (62)	59 (59)	64 (62)	65 (58)	71 (62)	77 (69)
Spain	60	79	74	71	75	76
Greece	39	57	58	51	47	49
Portugal	39	56	55	51	56	61

Source: European Commission Annual Report (1994)

Table 9.2 Economic indicators in the periphery

	Greece	Ireland	Portugal	Spain	EU
Unemployment Rate (%)					
1960	n.a.	4.7	1.9	2.4	2.5
1973	2.0	6.2	2.6	2.6	2.6
1993	7.8	18.4	5.2	21.2	10.4
Private Consumption/Capita					
1973	57	67	65	80	100
1991	54	62	58	76	100

Source: European Economy No. 55 and Eurostat National Accounts (1970–91).

This was the background against which the reform of EU structural aid to the periphery took place. The fear was that the removal of non-tariff barriers to trade and factor mobility would create a situation where the weaker economies would become even weaker; fears that were reinforced rather than allayed by the lessons drawn from developments in trade theory during the 1980s (Helpman and Krugman, 1986). Introducing the possibility of increasing returns and imperfect competition into more traditional trade theory suggested that there were both potential gains from trade as well as risks that increased trade might actually be harmful in certain circumstances.

The CSF was intended to permit the peripheral countries to maximize the potential gains from trade liberalization while minimizing the potential losses. Since there was little or no political will to enlarge the total EU budget above 2 per cent of GDP, there was never any question that the aid to the weaker regions could take either the form or the magnitude of typical intra-state domestic budgets. Thus CSF aid was intended to facilitate a systemic range of targeted investment projects in specific member states that would promote structural reform and enhanced competitiveness, and was intended to be a transitory rather than a permanent feature of the EU budget.

The structural policies were grouped into five 'objectives', the first of which involved countries or regions whose general economic development was 'lagging' behind the EC average, defined as less than 75 per cent of average GDP per head. Greece, Ireland and Portugal were designated 'Objective 1', together with the southern regions of Spain and Italy, Northern Ireland within the UK, and the French overseas territories.[2] Our model-based work refers to the first four of the above countries (also referred to as the 'cohesion' countries).

Within the Objective 1 category, the CSF was to be organized in each country according to similar broad principles. Thus, a comprehensive investment plan had to be drawn up by national governments and submitted to the Commission for approval; the external aid element had to be accompanied by domestic public and private co-finance, with obvious implications for domestic fiscal policy; eligible CSF investments had to be additional to existing domestic programmes, putting further pressure on domestic fiscal policy; proposals had to be 'structural' in nature, with a high probability of promoting self-sustaining growth, thus excluding short-term income support schemes that would yield no longer term return.

In each of the Objective 1 regions the national governments drew up indicative proposals in early 1989 for aid under the reformed CSF. Negotiations between them and the European Commission took place over the following months and the formal CSF treaties were signed in late 1989. No model-based evaluation of the proposals were commissioned prior to the signing of the treaty, although some informal evaluations of the domestic proposals had been carried out.[3]

What emerged in each national CSF were programmes that could be classified into three broad economic categories: support for basic infrastructure (i.e. roads, telecommunications, etc.); support for human resources (training, re-training, etc.); support for productive structures (investment and marketing subsidies, etc.). These categories emerged from a pragmatic desire to create new investment programmes aimed at promoting faster growth rather than from any explicit influence of growth theory. Indeed, the formal connection of the CSF with growth theory only seems to have emerged during the subsequent model-based evaluation stages when the actual economic cause–effect mechanisms had to be identified and analysed.

Beneath this simple economic classification of the CSF lay a complex monitoring system. At the most aggregate level this involved many EU Directorates General as well as national finance and economics ministries; at an operational programme level it involved trade unions, employers, farmers, as well as the EC and domestic ministries; and at a regional level it involved local administrative structures in addition to the other layers. The overall macroeconomic impact analysis was co-ordinated from the most aggregate level, involving the Commission (DG XVI) and the national Ministry for Finance or Economic Planning, and we now describe how that process of evaluation was executed.

3. Evaluating the impact of the CSFs

Analysis of the impact and effectiveness of CSFs proceeded at many different levels, where the essential difference between levels is the extent to which the rest of the economy is assumed to remain unchanged while a specific policy initiative is investigated. These stages were denoted micro, meso, and macro in the CSF evaluations.

In the case of an individual project (e.g. a particular stretch of road), a conventional cost-benefit analysis could be carried out, with competing projects ranked in terms of increasing internal rate of return. Such analysis, however, gives rise to obvious difficulties in relation to the need to evaluate the impact of spillover effects and externalities in the context of the complete CSF. Moving up the scale of aggregation, the totality of projects targeted at a general or systemic problem (say, long-term unemployment or industrial competitiveness) could be evaluated in terms of how successful they are in attaining their overall priority objective. Finally, the effectiveness of the entire CSF can be evaluated as an integrated whole. Given the size of the funding in relation to the size of the economy, and the obvious implications for domestic fiscal policy, it was necessary to examine the impact of the CSF in a context that included economy-wide feedbacks and interactions, attempting to account for spillover effects and externalities. Here one needs to make use of formal national or regional economy models: input–output (I–O), macroeconometric, computable general equilibrium (CGE), growth, etc. Our chapter deals entirely with this higher level of analysis.

Since its inception, analysis of the aggregate impact of the CSF has been carried out to some extent at least using all four of the above model types: (I–O) models (Beutel, 1993), macroeconometric models (Bradley, Fitz Gerald and Kearney, 1992); CGE models (Bourguignon et al., 1992) and dynamic growth models (Gaspar and Pereira, 1991), all of which have particular strengths and weaknesses. Although there was potentially a wide range of model types suitable for aggregate CSF analysis, the actual state of availability of national empirical models in the four cohesion countries was far from ideal in the late 1980s.

The implementation provisions of the CSF treaties included an obligation for tight monitoring and control by the Commission and the responsible national authorities. Thus, the requirement for aggregate impact analysis arose out of these monitoring provisions, and was designed to be carried out by independent experts acceptable to Commission and national authorities alike. Thus, the interaction between policy makers and modellers took place at arm's-length, since the national ministries seldom had suitable models and expertise available for in-house use.

The first major problem that arose between policy makers and analysts was prompted by the two differing conceptual approaches to the aggregate CSF analysis: should it be built up from an accumulated series on individual micro- and meso-level evaluations, or should it be a top-down macroeconomic analysis? The earlier Commission analysis of the impact of the Single Market had appeared to do both simultaneously, using a micro-based approach and arriving at impacts that were very similar to a model-based macroeconomic evaluation (Emerson *et al.*, 1988, pp. 196–264). However, it was quickly clear that a micro-based approach was not feasible in the case of the CSF, since the basic research inputs for such analysis were not available. More seriously, even the 'reformed' macromodels of the late 1980s were still only able to quantify the demand-side impacts of public expenditure programmes, and not the 'structuring' effects, i.e. those having a lasting impact on economic and social structures that would endure even after the CSF policy aid ceased.[4]

The need to analyse structural policies pushed CSF evaluation into areas which were still at the frontiers of economic research, requiring fresh ways of translating the insights of new growth theory into modelling the long-term impacts of investment in infrastructure and human capital. For such model-based macro evaluation to be credible required that it be presented transparently, in terms of the logical chains of causes and effects illustrating how CSF policies achieve their stated cohesion goals.

Structuring effects can be described for a key CSF policy instrument – investment in basic infrastructure – as follows. In Figure 9.1 we illustrate the economic logic connecting the CSF policy and the desired intermediate target – competitive advantage. Thus, improvements to basic infrastructure lead to reduced production costs (cheaper transport), relaxed production constraints (smaller inventories), and a strengthened economic environment (growth in demand for output, easier access to labour). All three effects combine to improve competitive advantage.

Ways in which the improvement in competitive advantage promotes sustained benefits is illustrated in Figures 9.2 and 9.3. The more familiar sustainability mechanisms operate through fixed structures, with the gains through factor mobility being driven by relative cost advantages (Figure 9.2). These are not too difficult to incorporate into macromodels of small open economies through shocks to exogenous variables. Another set of mechanisms is more complex, and operates through specialization and diversification, thereby strengthening the local economic base (Figure 9.3). While these mechanisms can be explored in small theoretical endogenous growth models, they are difficult to introduce into larger empirical macro-

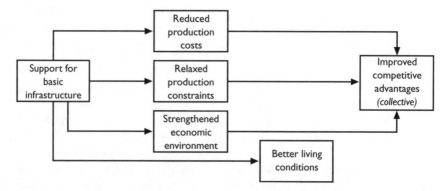

Figure 9.1 CSF impacts of investment in basic infrastructure.

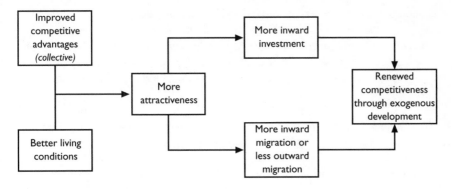

Figure 9.2 CSF long-term benefits: exogenous process.

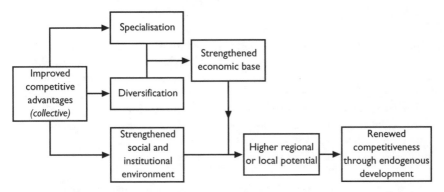

Figure 9.3 CSF long-term benefits: endogenous process.

models. These are typical of the types of logic chains that needed to be incorporated into the models, with analogous mechanisms for human resources and for productive structures.

3.1. The policy-model actors

However, before turning to details of how the models needed to be designed and used for CSF evaluation, we try to summarize the attitudes and expectations of the three main actors: domestic policy makers, Commission monitors and policy modellers.

Domestic policy makers: The design of the CSF was their prerogative, subject only to an overseeing role by the Commission. The actual package of measures put together in the CSF responded to national and regional political and economic priorities, extending many existing, but smaller domestic programmes. There was only limited interest in the finer details of mechanisms and impacts, possibly encouraged by the generous and relatively unconditional external aid element. Instead, crude measures of the likely immediate benefits of the CSF tended to be believed, derived by augmenting the public element of the CSF expenditure (the EU grant plus domestic co-finance) by a multiplier of between unity (pessimistic) and about one and a half (optimistic), with little thought initially given to exit strategies from the CSF aid programmes.

The Commission monitors: The overall size of the CSF budget and its allocation across countries was decided at the highest level of the EU, mainly in a political context. The bulk of the activity of DG XVI, the responsible Directorate-General, was focused on monitoring activity (i.e. ensuring that the EU aid was spent on what was approved within the CSF) rather than on macroeconomic evaluation (i.e. on finding out what impact was the CSF likely to have). Thus DG XVI itself financed little or no actual model development, although some was slipped into the evaluation contract budgets of the modellers as 'sectoral studies'.[5]

Policy modellers: The modellers, although reporting to national administrations and to the Commission, were outside the CSF design loop. The availability of models was uneven throughout the Objective 1 regions, with perhaps Ireland best, and Portugal least well served. Moreover, although the available models were suitable for evaluation of the expenditure (or demand-side) impacts of the CSF, they were not suitable for evaluating its structuring effects. Thus, modellers were aware that CSF analysis was not going to be an 'off-the-shelf' application of standard models, but would call for new research and model development.

The situation that prevailed during the early stages of analysis of the impacts of the CSF was that two of the three participants – the domestic policy makers and the Commission monitors – believed that it should be possible to give relatively straightforward answers to questions concerning the likely impact of the CSF on a recipient country's economy. The model-using analysts, on the other hand, were acutely conscious of both the scarcity of models in the Objective 1 countries and of the complexity of the channels of influence of CSF-type policies on the level and growth rate of output, a preoccupation that was treated with a certain degree of impatience by the two previous groups. The problem was compounded by the fact that both groups had different conceptual frames of reference. The policy makers/monitors thought in terms of a 'theory of action', i.e. a set of relatively simple cause-and-effect assumptions which linked CSF initiatives directly to the cohesion objective (MEANS, 1995). The analysts/modellers, on the other hand, worked with a 'global theory', which tried to describe all significant phenomena in the policy field, all the relevant effects of the CSF initiatives, and all the relevant causes of cohesion. In effect, a conceptual gulf opened up between policy makers/monitors, who saw issues in a straightforward cause–effect descriptive way, and the analyst/modellers, who needed to disentangle the CSF processes from a wide range of other complex factors.

4. Modellers' responses to CSF policy analysis needs

The first formal model-based evaluation of the impact of the CSF was carried out using the Irish version of the multi-sectoral HERMES model that had been developed during the mid-to-late 1980s as part of a trans-EU exercise financed by DG XII (Bradley, Fitz Gerald and Kearney, 1992). Since the time scale of the evaluation was compressed into just over one year, very little could be done to modify the model mechanisms in a way that would reflect how CSF policies would influence private sector behaviour, particularly since little was known about these mechanisms. A simple approach (in modellers' terms) had to be adopted, and the main components of the HERMES-based analysis are illustrated in Figure 9.4 below.

The key stages were as follows:

i. The aggregation of the wide variety of CSF programmes from the administrative and departmental categories used by the policy makers into categories related to the key economic mechanisms, i.e. physical infrastructure, human resources, productive structures;

ii. Definition of a suitable benchmark simulation for the economy in the absence of the CSF but with explicit assumptions about other policies like the Single Market, the Common Agriculture Policy, GATT, etc.;

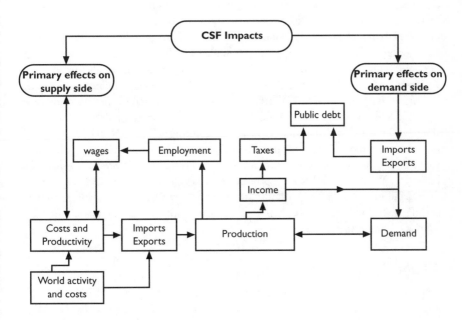

Figure 9.4 Model-based CSF evaluation: main causal links.

iii. Analysis of the standard Keynesian impacts of the CSF programmes, tracing out the impacts of domestic and EU financed investment expenditures on aggregate demand and the public sector finances;

iv. Implementation of a method of quantifying the long-term supply-side impacts of the CSF programmes, working through factor productivity and cost mechanisms;

v. Quantification of the CSF impacts in terms of deviations from the benchmark simulation.

Each of the above five stages involved quite complex explicit and implicit assumptions and choices. However, if there was a single innovation in the first Irish CSF evaluation it was the admittedly crude distinction made between transitory demand-side impacts and possibly enduring supply-side effects. Rather than modelling how long-term effects of CSF policies came about, the initial model-based CSF evaluation was forced to address a different question: i.e. what were the likely macro consequences if the long-term returns on CSF investments were of a specified size? There was a certain irony in the fact that the assumptions that were made – so crude as to be embarrassing to the modellers – were found to be very useful from conceptual and practical points of view to the policy makers/monitors.[6] After all, the supply-side consequences went to the heart of the CSF, while the demand-side effects, although providing welcome transient boosts to the economy, were not its ultimate goal. Nevertheless, there was a certain amount of unhappiness on the part of the policy makers/monitors with the crude rate-of-return assumptions, but no clear ideas as to how to improve on the evaluation methodology.

Turning to the other Objective 1 countries, the situation with respect to the non-availability of HERMES models for the Southern periphery would not have been serious if other, equally appropriate models had been available and were in the public domain. However, that was not the case. To remedy this modelling 'deficit', a project was funded by DG XII as part of the JOULE energy research programme having as its main objective the construction of comparable macroeconometric models for all the Objective 1 countries.[7] An account of these models is available in Bradley, Herce and Modesto, 1995. The resulting HERMIN models were of medium size (about 120 equations), had four sectors (manufacturing, market services, agriculture and government), and were motivated by the previous HERMES blueprint. Within the HERMIN project one was able to compare and contrast the four cohesion economies without arbitrary country-specific modelling choices getting in the way, as well as being able to carry out impact analysis of the CSF using a common methodology.

4.1. Modelling externalities

Since the crude rate-of-return assumptions used in the earlier HERMES-based analysis had been criticized by the Commission, an attempt was made in HERMIN to provide more justification by actually trying to model the association between

CSF investments and their long-run impacts. During the late 1980s, developments in 'new' growth theory had begun to provide a more adequate treatment of the processes of economic growth by moving beyond the earlier neo-classical growth theory to look at the externalities associated with human capital, public capital and technology. Externalities associated with public policy actions cannot be perceived by private agents in their optimizing behaviour. In the presence of externalities, many of the simple policy rules emanating from the orthodox neo-classical theory are invalid. Policy rules aimed at minimizing static efficiency losses may miss potential gains arising from policy links to externalities. Indeed, de Melo and Robinson, 1992 p. 60, go further and assert that: 'If there appear to be externalities to be exploited, policy makers should pursue them aggressively and not worry overmuch about getting the instruments just right.' Three types of externalities associated with the CSF expenditures were examined:

Factor productivity externalities: In HERMIN, a factor productivity externality was associated with improved supply conditions in the economy arising as a result of CSF investment in human capital and public infrastructure. They were incorporated by endogenizing the scale parameter, A, in the production function, which was modelled as a function of the stock of public and human capital.[8]

Consider the following production process:

$$Q = A * f(L,K),$$

where A is a scale parameter, which can be considered to represent the state of technology, L and K are the labour and capital inputs, respectively. The infrastructure factor productivity externality was incorporated into the production function of the non-traded sector as follows:

$$A_t = A_0 (KGINF_t/KGINF_o)^{\eta},$$

where A_t is the original estimated value of the scale parameter and η is an unknown externality elasticity that can be assigned different numerical values in the empirical model. KGINF is the stock of public infrastructure, computed as an accumulation of infrastructure investments. The baseline stock of infrastructure, $KGINF_0$, is taken as the stock that would have been there in the absence of the CSF increases decided for the period under consideration.

Industrial composition externalities: These refer to the increasing sophistication of manufacturing as a result of globalization. This externality can be viewed as operating directly through the multinational and indigenous firm location and growth process that is so important in the case of small open economies like Ireland and Portugal. The treatment of the tradable sector in HERMIN posits a supply-side approach in which the share of the world's output being allocated to, or generated within, the domestic economy is determined by a labour cost measure of international competitiveness (Bradley and Fitz Gerald, 1988). However, this neglects the fact that industries will require more than simply an appropriate level of labour costs before they locate in the periphery, or before they grow spontaneously. Without an available labour force that is qualified to work in these industries, or appropriate minimum levels of public infrastructure, many firms simply may not even be able to consider a country on the periphery as a location for production. Thus, a more realistic framework is one which posits a two stage process in which basic infrastructure and labour force quality conditions dictate the number of industries that could conceivably locate in the periphery, while competitiveness decides how many of the industries that could locate there actually do.

Labour market externalities: Another CSF-related externality which was introduced into the model alters the way in which the labour market functions. Many of the training programmes financed by the Social Fund component of the CSF are aimed at the long-term unemployed and school-leavers without qualifications. Empirical and theoretical work on hysteresis theories of the labour market suggests that these social groupings are likely to have little influence on wage bargaining (Lindbeck and Snower, 1989; Layard, Nickell and Jackman, 1991, pp. 173–213). Thus, one of the effects of the CSF human capital programmes is to increase the number of active and influential labour market participants.

One way to model this effect is to assume that the CSF expenditures increase the effect which better trained outsiders (such as the long-term unemployed) have on wage bargaining. This requires the wage bargaining mechanism to become more responsive to unemployment, both short and long-term, and can be modelled by increasing the size of the Phillips curve coefficient to represent a tightening of the labour market, thus altering the rate of adjustment of the unemployment rate to the natural rate.

Externalities: choosing parameter values: The magnitude of the externality effects described above are related to the relative improvement in a stock (e.g. infrastructure or trained workers) and to an elasticity parameter. In order to operationalize the process within a model one needs to assign numerical values to these elasticities. Aschauer's early work suggested that the impact of public capital on private sector output and productivity was very large, implying that an increase of 1 per cent in public capital could give rise to an increase of about 0.40 per cent in output (Aschauer, 1989). Of more relevance to CSF analysis, it was found that as the geographical focus narrows (from the whole nation, to States, to metropolitan areas in the U.S.), the elasticity falls because of leakages (i.e. it is impossible to capture all the benefits from an infrastructural investment within a small geographical area). In a survey of econometric results, Munnell (1993) showed that the elasticity with respect to public capital ranges from an upper bound of 0.39 for the entire U.S., through 0.20–0.15 for individual States, to lower bounds of 0.08–0.03 for individual metropolitan areas. The CSF analysis examined the case where the externality elasticities are zero, and involved a sensitivity analysis over the range of values indicated by the literature as relevant for small regional economies.

There is far less corresponding literature that examines the quantitative impact of human capital on growth, but much work examining the private and social returns to education and training (Psacharopoulos, 1994). Once again there is a wide range of estimates for the social rate of return, from high rates of 25 per cent to lower rates of 5 per cent. The international findings seem to imply that there is a law of diminishing returns: the social returns to education fall, by and large, as national income and aggregate spending on education rises. Psacharopoulos (1994) found that, even for the richer OECD countries, the social rate of return for higher education (the least beneficial case) is over 8 per cent. The empirical CSF analysis examined the case of zero human capital elasticities and involved a sensitivity analysis over a likely range of values.

Full details of the HERMIN-based model simulations of the CSF for the four 'cohesion' countries are reported elsewhere (Bradley *et al.*, 1995a; Barry *et al.*, 1997). Here we simply summarize some key qualitative findings of particular relevance to the policy makers. First, focusing on the purely Keynesian impacts of the CSF (i.e. under the assumption of zero externalities), the CSF impacts were broadly in line with the known multiplier properties of the models. Thus, the public investment multipliers are largest for Portugal (in the range 1.5) and smallest for Ireland (in the range 1.0). On the other hand, the multipliers associated with the transfer payments of the human resource programmes were less than unity for all models. Thus, to a certain extent these results validated crude *ex ante* views held about the impacts of investment policies (see above).

Second, as would be expected, increasing the size of the externality elasticities boosts the impact of the CSF programmes. This was most dramatically illustrated by the Irish simulations, which suggested that GDP impact is tripled relative to the zero elasticity case when elasticity values in the mid-range suggested by the literature were used. More modest improvements were found in the other three countries, basically because they are less open to the world economy.

Third, if the CSF is terminated and the externality effects are absent, then there are no long-term benefits. Thus, the withdrawal of the CSF simply reverses the previous Keynesian expansion, a rather trivial finding from the point of view of the modellers, but regarded with a degree of puzzled scepticism by the policy makers.

Fourth, even in the presence of positive externality elasticities, the beneficial impacts of the CSF programmes decay after its termination, since the incremental stocks of infrastructure and human capital also decay. However, there are modest positive effects even the long run, due to the increased stocks of infrastructure and human capital.

Fifth, the finding that the benefits from the CSF *in isolation* were modest drew attention to the fact that the real long-term benefits of the CSF were more likely to be associated with the way in which each of the peripheral economies responded to opportunities arising in the rest of the EU and world rather than with the CSF in isolation. This emphasized the need to work within the wider 'global theory' of macromodelling rather than the narrower 'theory of action' that tended to motivate policy makers who were focused on specific programmes.

Finally, when the HERMIN models were used more recently to examine the likely impacts of the Single Market on the four cohesion countries, the model-based analysis did not always bear out the original pessimism that gave rise to the CSF. Thus, neither Ireland nor Portugal appeared to loose out relative to the core economies, when the Single Market impact on the core economies was quantified as in Emerson *et al.*, 1988. Greece, on the other hand, did appear to be rather vulnerable to the Single Market, mainly due to the uncompetitive nature of its indigenous industries and the low actual and potential inflows of FDI (Barry *et al.*, 1997)

5. Lessons for policy makers and modellers

The experience of evaluating the impacts of the CSF provided some insights into the nature and benefits of interaction between policy makers and policy analysts in a situation where these occur at arms length rather than within an institution like a Central Bank or Finance Ministry. An key aspect of this process was that the work was monitored by the EU Commission, who insisted that the various national CSF programmes be evaluated impartially and publicly. Very little such analysis had ever been carried out for pre-CSF domestic investment programmes, tied up as they usually were with sensitive political budget and electoral cycles. As a consequence, almost no systematic international comparisons of public investment policy initiatives had ever been carried out.

The first lesson of the exercise concerned the tools of analysis. It pointed up a serious lack of well-documented economic models in the four cohesion countries. Thus, the capability of analysing even the Keynesian or demand-side impacts of programmes like the CSF was rather weak, particularly in the Southern periphery. Because of that, none of the four so-called cohesion countries had been included in the earlier EU model-based analysis of the impact of the Single Market (Emerson *et al.*, 1988). Many reasons could be advanced to explain the underdeveloped state of modelling in the periphery: the scarcity of the necessary skills in small countries; linguistic factors that tended to isolate non-English speaking countries from the main modelling centres; data problems, which were quite serious in the cases of Greece and Spain; the complex developmental nature of the peripheral economies, as they made a transition to greater openness and competitiveness. However, once the CSF evaluation studies were initiated, a series of fruitful developments occurred. First, it was possible to fund some model development through the European Commission, in situations where resources had not always been available domestically. The fact that the model developments were tied directly into the need to analyse the impacts of major public investment programme tended to direct research towards those aspects of the economy that were most exposed to the new programmes.

The second lesson concerned the relationship between the analytical requirements of the CSF evaluation and the body of research available to draw from. In order to achieve the cohesion objective in the context of transitional aid, there had to be a sustained increase in the growth rate of the peripheral economies for an extended period. However, the present state of growth theory, although it deals with cross-country comparisons, has only a limited amount to say about the empirics of growth within an economy (Fischer, 1991). The incorporation of externality mechanisms into the HERMIN econometric models represented an attempt to move towards this growth analysis, but a proper growth-theoretic analysis was impossible. In effect, the policy makers were posing empirical questions to the modellers that were almost impossible to answer adequately with the present state of knowledge.

The third lesson concerned difficulties that the policy makers and monitors experienced in absorbing whatever limited insights and advice that the modellers were able to offer them. Here the Commission moved decisively and set up the MEANS programme, designed to improve methods of evaluating structural policies and their practices within national administrations (Monnier and Toulemonde, 1993). There was an awareness of the diversity and compartmentalization of evaluation practices, and, based on an analysis of existing practices and experience within different administrations, the MEANS programme had three strategic aims: to establish zones of agreement concerning the proper use of tools to evaluate structural policies; to adjust evaluation methods to enable better co-ordination of partnership evaluations; and to promote acquired knowledge and thus increase the number and quality of qualified partners.

The MEANS programme acknowledged that models were potentially capable of extracting the pure CSF impacts from the background of all the other domestic and external shocks that were affecting the economy at the same time. It was also recognized that the distinction between the demand-side impacts and the enduring supply-side impacts was valuable, even if it was implemented in a crude fashion in the models. However, the model-based analysis was found to suffer from the 'black box' problem, where the answers given by the modellers to the policy makers were often more complex than the original questions. Thus, the strengths of the model-based approach were identified as the analytical framework to represent the economy; the ability to quantify feed-backs and policy linkages; and the ability to rank different policies in terms of their impacts on economic indicators like GDP per capita. Difficulties with the model-based approach were identified as the costs of building and maintaining models, where the Objective 1 countries were particularly vulnerable; the need to step outside the purely macroeconomic framework in order to identify and design the primary CSF impact channels; and the need to rely on inadequate results from micro-studies in order to quantify these mechanisms.

A final spin-off from the model-based analysis of the cohesion member states of the EU concerns the applicability to the transition economies of Central and Eastern Europe (Bradley, 1996). Indeed, the processes generating change in the CEE countries have begun to resemble forces familiar in the development of the EU periphery: progressive trade liberalization, foreign direct investment, technical change, fiscal and monetary policy reforms, and the market re-orientation of areas previously under state control. The encouragement by the EC Commission of cross-country co-operation and sharing of experiences within Europe has led to considerable insights and understanding. Nevertheless, the full potential of well-designed models to enhance the conceptualization, implementation and evaluation of the consequences of policy reforms in an increasingly inter-related world remains to be exploited.

Notes

1   Fischer, 1991 suggested that identifying the determinants of growth would require a switch away from simple cross-country regressions to time series studies of individual countries. Den Butter and Wollmer, 1996 is a rare example of a macroeconometric model with endogenous growth features.
2   The other objectives, which we ignore, involved areas experiencing de-industrialization (Objective 2), long-term unemployment (Objective 3), occupational integration of young people (Objective 4) and adjustment to agricultural structures (Objective 5).
3   For example, early model-based evaluations of the Irish government proposals indicated that the front-loading of construction activity would create inflationary pressures. The actual phasing in the subsequent CSF treaty was more evenly spread over the five years (Bradley and Fitz Gerald, 1989).
4   The term 'structuring effects' was coined to alert policy makers to the fundamental nature of the goals of the CSF (MEANS, 1995). Figures 9.1 to 9.4 are based on this work.
5   For example, the HERMIN modelling project for the four main Objective 1 regions, to be described below, was financed as part of the JOULE II energy-environment research programme of DG XII.
6   Some of the Commission's reactions to the distinction between demand and supply impacts are given in Spenlehauer and Toulemonde, 1993.
7   Although the funding for HERMIN came from DG XII, the modelling progress was followed closely, and perhaps a little impatiently, by DG XVI, who were responsible for CSF matters.
8   The trade effects of increased inter-country competition are ignored here, but have been examined by Barry et al., 1997 in the context of the Single Market and the CSF.

References

Aschauer, D. A., 1989. 'Is public expenditure productive?', Journal of Monetary Economics, Vol. 3, pp. 177–200.

Barro, R. and Sala-i-Martin, X., 1995. Economic Growth. New York, McGraw Hill.

Barry, F., Bradley, J., Hannan, A., McCartan J. and Sosvilla-Rivera S., 1997: Single Market Review 1996: Aggregate and Regional Aspects: the Cases of Greece, Ireland, Portugal and Spain. London: Kogan Page, in association with the Office for Official Publications of the European Communities, Luxembourg.

Beutel, J., 1993. The Economic Impacts of the Community Support Frameworks for the Objective 1 Regions 1989–93. Report prepared for DG XVI, Brussels: Commission of the European Communities, April.

Bourguignon, F., Lolos, S., Suwa-Eisermann, A. and Zonzilos, N. G., 1992. 'Evaluating the Community Support Framework with an Extended Computable General Equilibrium Model: The Case of Greece (1988–1995).' Paper presented at the Annual Conference of the European Economics Association, Trinity College Dublin.

Bradley, J. and Fitz Gerald, J., 1988. 'Industrial output and factor input determination in an econometric model of a small open economy', European Economic Review, 32, pp. 1227–41.

Bradley, J. and Fitz Gerald, J., 1989. *Medium-Term Review: 1989–1994*. Dublin: The Economic and Social Research Institute, June.

Bradley, J., Fitz Gerald, J. and Kearney, I., (eds.) 1992. *The Role of the Structural Funds: Analysis of the Consequences for Ireland in the Context of 1992*. Policy Research Series Paper No. 13, Dublin, The Economic and Social Research Institute.

Bradley, J., O'Donnell, N., Sheridan, N. and Whelan, K., 1995. *Regional Aid and Convergence, Evaluating the Impact of the Structural Funds on the European Periphery*. Avebury, Aldershot (UK).

Bradley, J., Herce, J. and Modesto, L., 1995. 'Modelling in the EU periphery, the HERMIN Project', *Economic Modelling*, Special Edition, 12(3).

Bradley, J., 1996. 'Macroeconomic problems of transition: lessons from the periphery of the EU.' Paper presented at the *International Conference to mark the 50th anniversary of the Faculty of Economics*, Ljubljana, Slovenia, 18–19 September.

Den Butter, F. and Wollmer, F., 1996. 'An empirical model for endogenous technology in the Netherlands', *Economic Modelling*, 13, pp. 15–40.

Emerson, M. *et al.*, 1988. *The Economics of 1992. The E.C. Commission's Assessment of the Economic Effects of Completing the Internal Market*. Oxford: Oxford University Press.

Fischer, S., 1991. 'Growth, Macroeconomics and Development.' In: Blanchard, O. J. and Fiscger, S. (eds.), *The NBER Macroeconomics Annual 1991*. Cambridge: The MIT Press.

Gaspar, V. and Pereira, A., 1991. 'The Impact of Financial Integration and Unilateral Public Transfers on Investment and Economic Growth.' Working Paper, Department of Economics, University of California, San Diego.

Helpman, E. and Krugman, P., 1986. *Market Structure and Foreign Trade: Increasing Returns, Imperfect Competition, and the International Economy*. Cambridge: The MIT Press.

Klein, L., 1983. *The Economics of Supply and Demand*. London: Basil Blackwell.

Krugman, P., 1995. *Development, Geography, and Economic Theory*. Cambridge: The MIT Press.

Layard, R., Nickell, S. and Jackman, R., 1991. *Unemployment: Macroeconomic Performance and the Labour Market*. Oxford: Oxford University Press.

Lindbeck, A. and Snower, D., 1989. *The Insider-Outsider Theory of Employment and Unemployment*. Cambridge, Mass.: MIT Press.

MEANS, 1995. *Identifying the Structuring Effects of Community Interventions*. MEANS Handbook No. 2, D.G. XVI/02 – Evaluation Unit, Brussels: Commission of the European Communities.

de Melo, J. and Robinson, S., 1992. 'Productivity and externalities: models of export-led growth', *The Journal of International Trade and Development*, Vol. 1, No. 1, pp. 41–69.

Monnier, E. and Toulemonde, J., 1993. *Methods to Give Meaning to the Evaluation Obligation: The Conclusions of the MEANS Programme*. Report No. MEANS/93/13/EN, CEOPS, France

Munnell, A. H., 1993. 'An assessment of trends in and economic impacts of infrastructure investment.' In: *Infrastructure Policies for the 1990s*. Paris: OECD.

Psacharopoulos, G., 1994. 'Returns to investment in education: a global update', *World Development*, Vol. 22, No. 9, pp. 1325–43.

Spenlehauer, V. and Toulemonde, J., 1993. *The Likely Impact of the CSF in Ireland: A Macroeconomic Evaluation, Case Study (I)*. Report No. MEANS/93/01/FN, CEOPS-Evaluations, Vaulx-en-Velin, France.

Chapter 10

Interaction between model builders and policy makers in the Norwegian tradition*

Olav Bjerkholt

Norway has a long tradition in the use of macroeconomic models for policy-making. This article traces this tradition to the direct and indirect influence of Ragnar Frisch and discusses the institutional features that distinguish the Norwegian tradition from that of other countries, in particular the role of the central statistical institution in model-building within government.
JEL classifications: C5, E6

1. Introduction

Since the early post-war period there has been in Norway a long and continuous tradition in the use of empirical models for economic policy-making within a remarkably stable institutional environment. The first comprehensive model, used in a real way for macro policy purposes, was constructed by the Central Bureau of Statistics in 1959, implemented on a first-generation computer, and used by the Ministry of Finance as the first in a series of models that were at the centre of macroeconomic policy preparation and co-ordination.

The Norwegian tradition in macroeconomic model-building and use differs from that of other countries in several respects, and the differences can be traced to the influence of Ragnar Frisch and to institutional features surrounding Norwegian post-war economic policy.[1] The latter can be briefly summarized as follows.

First, after 1945, the Norwegian government embarked (on a firm political basis) upon a programme of comprehensive macroeconomic planning, conceived as the *co-ordination of decisions taken within a large administrative system.* The institutional procedures put in place were, by and large, preserved under changing economic conditions and political regimes. In other countries macroeconomic planning more typically developed outside and parallel to the traditional decision-making bodies.

Secondly, policy-making and, at a later stage model-building, was from the first post-war years conducted within a 'national budgeting' format, closely tied to

Reprinted from Economic Modelling, 15, Olav Bjerkholt, 'Interaction between model builders and policy makers in the Norwegian tradition', pp. 317–39, Copyright (1998), with permission from Elsevier Science.

national accounts and input–output tables, when these were new and unknown within the administration and in the society at large, and still non-existent in many countries. Furthermore, models used for policy-making became *institutionalized* in Norway, i.e. embedded in the administrative structure of policy-making, and finally, the institutional solution found for the location of the *modelling unit*, namely, within the central statistical institution, was, and is, different from that of other countries.[2]

The type of model found suitable to serve in this environment was a large input–output model with much accounting detail, rather than the more aggregate type of econometric model that was adopted in other countries, inspired by the work of Jan Tinbergen in the Netherlands, Lawrence Klein in USA and others.[3] The differences in model-building tradition between Norway and other countries have diminished over time, but national characteristics both in model structure and model use may still be observed as distinguishing features of the Norwegian tradition.

There were also personal factors. Before the first model was taken into use, there existed a powerful paradigm of how models should be put to use for policy analysis, due to Ragnar Frisch who devoted his entire research programme at the Institute of Economics (University of Oslo) in the post-war period towards developing 'decision models', i.e. models for use in macroeconomic planning and decision-making. Frisch had conducted laboratory experiments in building decision models since the early post-war years and thus prepared the ground for taking models into use.

The first model may hence be considered as built to order to fit into an overall planning and policy-making format already established in Norway in the late 1940s (although the actual use would deviate from the prescription of the Frisch paradigm). In the following years, model developments and policy-making procedures interacted and influenced each other. Both would be affected by external events, theoretical innovations, and technical improvements. The stability and continuity of the relationship between model-building and policy-making and its firm institutional basis became preponderant features of the Norwegian tradition.

This article looks at this tradition retrospectively. The political and institutional background is set out in Section 2, including the emphasis on national accounting, the invention of the national budgeting approach, and the choice of modelling unit. Section 3 sketches the modelling views of Ragnar Frisch and the characteristics of the models that arose in Norway for short-term and long-term macroeconomic policy-making. Section 4 makes some observations on the interaction between model builders and policy makers in Norway, and Section 5 concludes.

2. The political and institutional background

Following the liberation of Norway in May 1945, a provisional cabinet was formed with representatives from all political parties. During the five-month lifetime of this cabinet, until elections could be held, a number of important decisions were made:

(i)   The system of direct control inherited from the war was to be upheld for the time being;

(ii)   in price policy, a stabilization of the cost-of-living index at its 1945 level was aimed at;

(iii) the parity rate of the Norwegian currency was fixed in conformity with the price stability goal;

(iv)   a system of forced arbitration in wage conflicts was introduced;

(v)   a monetary reform was carried out;

(vi)   steps were taken to achieve sizeable budget surpluses (Aukrust, 1965).

The first post-war elections resulted in a comfortable parliamentary majority for the Labour Party, which remained in power until 1965. The Labour government added a commitment to cheap money to the guidelines above and approached the post-war economic problems with a broad concept of national economic planning.[4] The immediate targets were economic reconstruction, full employment and fair and equal distribution.

The planning system which grew up to administer the post-war economy had few ideological overtones. The overall idea was to establish means for the co-ordination of the many decisions which, by necessity, had to be delegated to a wide range of government agencies. In this pragmatic approach a central planning agency was not found necessary. One reason was the almost desperate lack of trained economists. In 1945 there was not a single trained economist in the Ministry of Finance. A graduate study of economics at the University of Oslo had not been opened until 1935 and by the end of 1945 the cumulated number of graduates was only 74, but in the first years after liberation, Frisch's Institute became swamped with new students.

The Ministry of Finance would be in charge of economic policy and co-ordinator of the administrative planning apparatus of the new system of 'national budgeting'. A pattern established at this time – and still ruling – was that only one ministry would be responsible for economic policy, i.e. the Ministry of Finance, while most, if not all, Western European countries have had ministerial responsibility for fiscal policy separated from broader economic policy issues.[5] Within the Ministry of Finance a new *economy department* became the economists' bridgehead, as they rather abruptly took over the hegemony over economic policy and gradually replaced the lawyers (Lie, 1996).

2.1. National accounts

National accounts was, earlier than in most other countries, defined as the framework for the overall economic policy to be conducted within, and in a way which differed somewhat from the Anglo-American approach. This was overwhelmingly an influence by Frisch who already, in the late 1920s, had worked on a system of accounting concepts for describing the economic circulation (Bjerve, 1996), and Frisch (1933) had recommended the establishment of 'national accounts' (introducing this term for the first time in Norwegian). Frisch reworked his national accounting ideas several times in the ensuing years, adopting the *eco-circ system* as the name for his accounting framework (and elaborate *eco-circ graphs* as a way of presenting it). Frisch's national accounting ideas and his active role in the economic policy discussion in the 1930s led, through the intermediary of industrialists who wanted an end to the depression, in 1936 to a project in which Frisch, with colleagues at the University of Oslo, undertook to develop national accounts for Norway with funds provided by the Rockefeller Foundation and private Norwegian sources (Bjerve, 1996, 1998). In Frisch (1940) the eco-circ system had developed on a theoretical level into a quite sophisticated system of national accounts (Bjerve, 1996), while the empirical work had progressed less, when the University of Oslo was closed by the German occupational authorities in 1943.

The compilation of national accounts tables according to Frischian ideas continued covertly by some of his former students, the foremost being P. J. Bjerve, within the Central Bureau of Statistics (renamed Statistics Norway in 1991) and resulted in national accounts for 1935–43 being available soon after the liberation.[6]

In 1946–47, national accounting was at a preliminary stage internationally, only in a few pioneering countries had practical work got underway. The first international standard was still years away, hence, the early national accounting efforts had distinct national features. Frisch's efforts succeeded, perhaps through his pupils, in convincing the Labour Party government to give high priority to establish national accounts on a current basis to support the economic policy effort. The Frischian conception of national accounts (to some extent shared with that of Erik Lindahl) had distinguishing characteristics that separated it from Anglo-American thinking, above all that 'real phenomena' was what mattered. The accounts should distinguish clearly between the real sphere and the financial sphere and show the interplay between them. The entries in the accounts should represent flows (or stocks) of real and financial objects (Aukrust, 1994, pp. 35–6). This 'realist' conception of national accounting, supported by Frisch's detailed structure of concepts, was later modified by adopting elements from Richard Stone's work, and further enhanced by embracing the input–output approach of Wassily Leontief as an integral part. For years the Norwegian approach was one of very few accounting systems producing annual input–output tables. The accounting work took place in the Central Bureau of Statistics. The theoretical ideas that influenced it are reviewed in retrospect by the division head throughout the founding period in Aukrust (1994).

The result was a detailed set of accounts comprising thousands of entries, rather than just a few tables of aggregate figures, and giving the impression that an empirical representation of the entire economic circulation had been achieved and would provide a wholly new foundation for scientifically-based economic policy analysis.

2.2. National budgeting

The use of macroeconomic models for economic policy in Norway has been closely related to the reliance upon 'national budgeting' in the management of economic policy. Frisch had casually coined this catchword term and introduced the idea of a forward-looking policy pendant to national accounting at a meeting in 1940 (Bjerve, 1998). The national budget came to play a most prominent role in post-war economic policy. The idea was that of a budget, not for the government's fiscal accounts, but in real terms for the entire national economy, spelt out in the spirit and concepts of the Frischian national accounts. The national budget served as a conceptual framework as well as a quantitative instrument for economic planning. The national budgeting process was organized by the Ministry of Finance as a network of ministries, other government agencies, semi-official bodies, and co-ordinating committees, that either had decisions to make or information to convey of relevance for the national budget. Through this network the national accounting concepts became known throughout the administration years before GDP and other macroeconomic aggregates came into widespread use.

The various ministries and other agencies would contribute to the quantification of the national budget, adhering to the conceptual framework, in interaction with the Ministry of Finance. The national budgeting in the early post-war period took place in a highly-regulated and rationed economy, and called for the kind of detail that the new national accounts could provide. The value of the national budget was seen in its role as an integrating tool linking the sub-budgets of ministries, subordinate government agencies and semi-official bodies in the process of working out the economic prospects and economic policies for the coming year (Schreiner and Larsen, 1985; Bjerve, 1959, 1989).

When the government presented the national budget for 1947 as a White Paper (Ministry of Finance, 1947) to the Storting (Parliament), together with the fiscal budget, in January of the same year, there was no blueprint for what the national budget should be (and, needless to say, the parliamentarians were not prepared for it). The national budget document itself discussed the idea of national budgeting, distinguishing three alternative interpretations of the idea.[7] A *diagnostic budget* could be prepared simply as a summary of plans and expectations, which in general would not be consistent with the balance equations, but could serve to reveal gaps and inconsistencies. A *prognostic budget* could be conceived as a complete and consistent national budget based on assumptions about the behaviour of agents and assessment of exogenous influences. Both of these alternatives were discarded, however, in favour of the *programmatic budget* with targets of economic policy embedded in the national budget figures. The programmatic budget's range of targets must be supported by a set of instruments to make the targets achievable.

The adoption of the programmatic national budget as something different from a forecast of national accounting aggregates raised problems of interpretation and realism. The national budget would not constitute a plan in a meaningful sense unless it was based upon a realistic assessment of the functioning of the economy. The various sub-budgets had to be tied together in a way that took care of the inter-relations of the economy. This called for models, but the time was not yet ripe. With national accounts still in their infancy, large-scale models unavailable and computers in a modern sense non-existent, this was a daunting task and resolved by the 'administrative method', which at best was a highly-imperfect administrative iterative procedure. The introduction of the national budget and its success as a practical procedure in the post-war context thus created a demand for designated models to improve the process.

The National Budget for 1947 had argued against what it called the common misunderstanding that a programmatic budget is of interest only in an economy with extensive direct government controls, maintaining that a programmatic budget would be useful whenever a government intended to pursue a rational economic policy. This statement was borne out by later developments; the national budget was, indeed, found useful in circumstances rather different from those of the immediate post-war period with its tight constraints and special problems. As the economy recovered from the abnormal post-war situation and the external environment also changed, the rationing schemes and regulations were gradually dismantled, economic decision-making would rely primarily on monetary and fiscal policy, while the national budget retained its role as the single most important policy document, and has been prepared for every year since 1947.[8]

The introduction of the national budget in 1947 can be viewed as an exercise in macroeconomic education for politicians and civil servants alike, and as a vehicle for introducing national accounting, a wider role for the government in economic policy, and the new demand management theory of economic policy.[9] As such, it seems to have served well. The first national budgets met initially with some political opposition on the grounds of representing centralized planning, but the principles of national budgeting were never seriously challenged. When the Labour Party surrendered power in 1965 after an unprecedented 20 years in government, the transition to an anti-Socialist coalition went smoothly with practically no changes in the institutional system of economic policy-making and presentation.

The White Paper of 1947 also discussed the problem of time horizons in economic policy-making. The national budget had a horizon of only one year while several macroeconomic issues called for a longer time horizon. In the national economic policy context, the solution was found in the introduction of another policy document called the 'Long-Term Programme'. Norway has parliamentary elections strictly at four-year intervals. There is no option for calling elections at other times. The Long-Term Programme is presented in the last session of a parliamentary period and serves thus as the incumbent government's economic policy platform for the coming election period. The first Long-Term Programme was prepared at the request of the OEEC in connection with the Marshall Aid for the period 1949–52. Later a need arose for looking at macroeconomic policy options over a longer horizon. The Long-Term Programme for 1970–73 had annexed projections until 1990. The most recent Long-Term Programme, covering the period 1998–2001, included projections until 2050.

2.3. The choice of modelling unit

The Research Department of Statistics Norway (RDSN) has served as the model-building and operating unit for the government since models were taken into use.

Statistics Norway (known as the Central Bureau of Statistics until 1991) is the central institution of statistics and an old government institution (founded 1876) with a marked analytic tradition. It has traditionally kept close relations with the political community as well as with the university.[10] The Research Department was founded in 1950 and its tasks from the beginning consisted of national accounts, economic surveys (monthly and annual), and tax research. Econometric studies and model-building were still in embryo, but would expand and absorb the major part of the resources of the Department.[11] A range of other research tasks, foremost among them energy and environmental analysis, were added in the late 1970s.

Within the government administration, Statistics Norway was (and is) a directorate under the Ministry of Finance. By the law of public statistics, Statistics Norway is *not* under instruction from above in statistical matters. This 'protection' was interpreted to hold also for the research activities and thus provided an opportunity for a research environment to flourish within the otherwise strict confines of the central government. This role in macroeconomic model-building and analysis for a central statistical institution seems unique in the world.

An advantage of the Norwegian solution was the very close relationship that was established between the modelling effort and the national accounting at an early stage. The model builders were thus offered an opportunity of a more profound understanding of the macroeconomic data. The proximity to the statistical work in general was an advantage both with regard to access and to the understanding of the data generating processes. It also opened up the possibility for suggesting concrete improvements in the national accounts for modelling purposes, and naturally made the national accounting experts highly aware of the macroeconomic data needs.

RDSN is today one of the largest economic research institutions in Norway and regularly serves several ministries, government-appointed committees and the general public using its arsenal of models, while retaining its special role for the Ministry of Finance. It may well be considered as an institution within an institution, and the symbiotic relationship between statistics and policy-oriented economic research has been preserved (and also survived without much discussion the fads of governmental and research establishment reforms of the 1980s and 1990s).

The establishment of a separate research department within Statistics Norway was not a premeditated move by the government. The general view was rather to avoid establishing units that might attract economists as a scarce resource away from tasks of higher priority.[12] Frisch had most likely expected that his Institute should be the model-building unit, and may have taken that for granted. Statistics Norway's responsibility for providing updated national accounts and input–output tables for the government's national budgeting and an analytic tradition provided a good background for the development of a model to serve in national budgeting. At least it did so for Statistics Norway and the new Research Department. The idea of an input–output model figured prominently from the early 1950s, in close contact with Frisch who worked on prototypes using Statistics Norway's data. A bottleneck was the computational aspect. Only after Statistics Norway got the government's permission to procure the first commercially available first-generation computer in

Norway (DEUCE, produced by English Electric) in 1958 was there a practical possibility of replacing the opaque administrative method by an explicit solution of the input–output model that lay at the core of the national budgeting procedure.

3. The Norwegian modelling tradition

After 1945 Frisch embarked on a comprehensive programme of developing 'decision models'. After an early attempt at developing what may best be described as a disequilibrium model (Frisch, 1949), suited to the immediate post-war shortage and rationing situation, Frisch embraced the input–output model of W. Leontief in the early 1950s, put great emphasis on it in his lectures and incorporated it, together with enhanced accounting relationships and other elements, into his decision models.[13] The Institute of Economics was a laboratory of modelling experiments under Frisch's direction from the late 1940s until Frisch retired in 1965 (Bjerve, 1998).

3.1. Frisch's model-building philosophy

Ragnar Frisch was a visionary in several respects; he must be counted among those who foresaw the future reliance of economic policy-making upon macroeconomic ideas and model tools provided by economists. Frisch had played an active role internationally in establishing econometrics as a discipline and in founding the Econometric Society in 1930. He was appointed a Professor at the University of Oslo in 1931 (in an effort to forestall Frisch accepting an offer from Yale University). He founded the Institute of Economics as a privately financed research institute at the University of Oslo. Frisch was Editor of *Econometrica* since the journal appeared in 1933, and his return to the editorial chair after wartime imprisonment was marked with an article on the 'responsibility of the econometrician' (Frisch, 1946).

In this article Frisch noted that the '*econometric attitude* will gradually come into its own, not only in theory, but in practice as well'. The demand for economists in government service would increase significantly: '. . . one feels the need of men who understand how the big economic issues, employment, investment, labor, living costs, fiscal policies, etc. *gear into each other* . . . essentially a quantitative problem . . . belonging to *general macroeconomics*', noting the somewhat different need in market economies and centrally-planned countries.[14] But 'men who can handle general macroeconomic problems cannot be produced at short notice'. What is needed is 'free research work . . . opportunity to follow out *in tranquillity* the avenues of approach suggested by intuition and imagination'. Research must be undertaken on a realistic basis, but 'it is inevitable that the realism that the free research worker stands for . . . will differ from what is considered the right kind of realism in certain very practical quarters'. The remedy is 'large organizations where young economists can be trained in free research work in general economics and . . . econometrics', adding somewhat ominously that econometrics is a powerful tool and dangerous when abused: '. . . it should only be put into the hands of really first-rate men. Others should be absolutely discouraged from taking up econometrics' (Frisch, 1946, pp. 1–4).

Frisch's modelling philosophy was expressed *inter alia* in his classification of four stages in modelling, denoted by him the *on-looker approach*, the *ad hoc instrument approach*, the *feasible instrument approach*, and the *optimization approach* (Frisch, 1962).

- The **on-looker approach** may cover a wide range of methods, but it is an outside approach with regard to the policy-making. The on-looker analyst 'simply tries to guess at what will happen without making any systematic attempt at finding out what somebody – the Government or a private organization or a coalition of private organizations – *ought to* do if they want to influence the course of affairs' (Frisch, 1962, p. 250).

- In the **ad hoc instrument approach** the analyst is concerned with the existence of instruments which may be changed at will to induce change in the course of affairs. His understanding of the inter-relations of the economy has not reached the stage, however, where it can be formulated as a complete model with a definite number of degrees of freedom. The ad hoc instrument approach is thus an intermediate stage, '. . . a very first and tentative preparation for a *further analysis* that does lead to a precise dynamic model with a well-defined number of degrees of freedom' (Frisch, 1962, p. 252).

- In the **feasible instrument approach** the analyst thinks in terms of a complete model with degrees of freedom corresponding to instruments and truly exogenous (uncontrollable) influences. For each set of values given to exogenous influences there is a set of alternative fixations of the instruments which span the feasibility space. The analyst has to co-operate with the decision makers 'to map out to the authorities the feasible alternatives and to help them understand which ones, or which one, amongst the feasible alternatives are the most desirable from their own viewpoint. To develop a technique of discussing feasible policy alternatives in such a scientific way is one of the most burning needs in economic policy-making today' (Frisch, 1962, p. 253). This is highly reminiscent of Tinbergen's (1954) *Theory of Economic Policy*, but Tinbergen credits Frisch as the originator of this approach (see end note 15).

- The final stage is the **optimalization approach** which includes a preference function and a mathematical programming technique for locating the most preferred solutions among the feasible alternatives. 'When the effort to map out a spectrum of feasible alternatives has gone on for a while, the conclusion will inevitably force itself upon the public and the authorities that the number of feasible alternatives is so great that it is impossible to keep track simply by listing them and looking at them' (Frisch, 1962, p. 254).

Frisch here clearly takes a stand on whether models should be forecasting devices or policy-making tools: 'How can it be possible to make a projection without knowing the decisions that will basically influence the course of affairs? It is as if the policy maker would say to the economic expert: "Now you expert try to guess what I am going to do, and make your estimate accordingly. On the basis of the factual information thus received I will then decide what to do". The shift from the on-looker viewpoint to the decision viewpoint must be founded on a much more coherent form of logic. It must be based on a *decision model*, i.e. a model where the possible decisions are built-in *explicitly* as essential variables' (Frisch, 1962, p. 253).[15]

Frisch never lost this perspective on the future of model-building and continued to devote most of his energy and ingenuity to attacking the problems of the final stage in model-building: the establishment of a preference function (by interviewing decision makers) and the solution of the mathematical programming problems. Frisch found relatively little support among his colleagues and Norwegian policy makers in this endeavour; his disappointment was expressed in occasional outbursts of scorn over model builders and users who did not have a proper understanding of what they were doing. Again and again Frisch reiterated his never faltering belief in the possibilities for improving the material conditions of mankind as well as promoting a true democracy by appropriate use of scientific economic programming at the national and international level.

The use of macroeconomic models in Norway has never aimed higher than at a moderately reasonable satisfaction of the feasible instrument approach.[16] On the other hand, in the absence of an explicit preference function, one is left with precisely the problem stated by Frisch, that a model may be used to generate far too many feasible alternatives to be sorted out and evaluated in a wholly intuitive manner in the minds of the policy makers. Frisch's views of the interaction between modellers and policy makers were later replaced by the more pragmatic approach of Leif Johansen as set out in his textbooks (Johansen 1977, 1978).

3.2. The short-to-medium-term model

The first model to be established and used in policy-making was an input–output model (120 industries), named MODIS, with an adjoined consumption demand structure (Sevaldson, 1964). The model had strong affinities to Frisch's Oslo Median Model (Frisch, 1956). The model was constructed and operated by Statistics Norway (then CBS), and used by the Ministry of Finance in the preparation of the national budgets from 1960 until 1965 and also for the Long-Term Programmes 1962–65 and 1966–69. The operation of the model required that the Ministry sent filled-in forms of exogenous assumptions to Statistics Norway and received tabulated results in return; hence, the Ministry made direct use of the model.

It is somewhat unclear how the changeover from the 'administrative method' to the computer-based solution actually took place. The advantage of the model was that it could actually solve the system of simultaneous equations that was at the core of the national budget co-ordination. The administrative method could at best give only an approximation. But equally, or perhaps more important for the policy analysis was the fact that the model could be used to generate 'impact tables' giving the effects of changes in exogenous assumptions. It seems that the model at a very early stage was declared a success, with no question of going back to the previous method.

The first MODIS model was replaced in 1965 by a successor version which comprised more industries (150), and with the input–output relations extended to comprise the Leontief price model. The model, furthermore, had a complete system of demand functions, and a very detailed representation of the taxes and transfers, income components, and financial flows (Sevaldson, 1968). The price relations of the model reflected an early version of the Scandinavian model of inflation, imposed upon the Leontief price system (Aukrust, 1970, 1977). The vast improvement in size and scope of the second version of the model was made possible by the use of the first second-generation computer in Norway (UNIVAC 1107).

The first two model versions were costly and cumbersome to operate and constructed on the (rather unrealistic) assumption that it would suffice to run them only very few times per year. A third version in 1967 was a breakthrough in efficient calculation and allowed intensive use of the model, especially for studying policy alternatives. The separation between the role of Statistics Norway in building and maintaining the model and the role of the Ministry of Finance in using it in the preparation of official policy documents was strictly maintained. In principle, Statistics Norway would only be involved in a technical capacity of operating the model, not in making exogenous assumptions and in policy analysis. Statistics Norway was, however, free to use the model for its own purposes and in rendering services to others. In practice it turned out that the modellers had to become more involved in the Ministry use of the model on an informal basis, especially in view of the limited competence the Ministry had for utilizing a tool of such complexity. The informal interaction would often lead to improvements in the model.

The fourth version, completed in 1974, was a completely redesigned model, incorporating the new UN Standard of National Accounts of 1968 with commodity-by-industry input–output tables. The level of detail had increased further as the model now comprised approximately 200 commodities, for each of which the model distinguished between an import price, a domestic price and an export price. The overall size of the model was inflated by the attention to fiscal and sectoral detail and a straight count showed that it comprised roughly 5000 variables (of which 2000 variables were exogenous). The 1974 version was a vast improvement in the representation of the empirical structure of the economy, but to some extent at the price of losing the simplicity and transparency of the original Leontief model (Bjerkholt and Longva, 1980).

MODIS survived, surprisingly, as the main macroeconomic tool of the Ministry of Finance until 1993, but had then been retained for several years against the advice of RDSN which in the meantime had developed both a quarterly and an annual macroeconomic model with much more elaborate behavioural relationships. The new models were large by international comparison, but much smaller than the mammoth-sized MODIS model. The Ministry was hesitant in surrendering a modelling framework that had served it well.

It appears from this rather sketchy description of the MODIS series of models that the use of macroeconomic models for short-term policy-making in Norway emphasized accounting relationships, information handling, sectoral and fiscal detail within an administrative system and left important behavioural relationships to be taken care of outside the macroeconomic model itself, often by auxiliary models. The lack of simultaneity that this might cause could to some extent be compensated by iterative calculations. For this purpose great effort was put into achieving a user-oriented model, especially with regard to the two-way communication between policy makers and the model. The general idea was that the shortcomings of the model with regard to the theoretical content, as well as the lack of formal procedures for evaluation of alternative results and other weaknesses, had to be compensated for in some way or other within the administrative environment of the model. It seems clear that the Ministry view was that such an incomplete model and a procedure of groping for acceptable outcomes was much preferred to Frisch's optimalization approach.[17]

The Scandinavian model of inflation, originated by Aukrust in the early 1960s[18] was incorporated in the structure of the MODIS model and played a considerable role in forming the general perception of Norway's economic situation, and also in the design of model-based policies for combating inflation in the 1970s (Bjerkholt, 1986). That it was difficult to corroborate Aukrust's model econometrically (Aukrust, 1977, pp. 135–42) did not detract much from its value for economic policy.

Aukrust's inflation model provided the basis for a new institutional element in the interaction between modellers and decision makers, namely the Technical Calculation Committee for Income Settlements, established in 1968 with Aukrust as chairman and high-level representatives from the trade unions, the employers' federation, farmers, fishermen and the ministry responsible for income affairs as members. The RDSN served as secretariat for the committee which prepared reports on issues of particular relevance for upcoming income negotiations. The purpose was to forge a common view on the economic situation before income negotiations took place and to foster an agreement on the effects of alternative outcomes of income settlements. Thus through the use of models, incomes policy became closely integrated with the macroeconomic policy analysis.

The inflation forecasting can be illustrated by the national budget inflation forecasts for 1975–77 which were the first years the government dared to publish such forecasts. The forecasts as published in October the previous year (with actual inflation in parentheses), were 11.6 (11.7), 8.7 (8.6) and 8.3 (8.6) (Bjerkholt, 1986, p. 46). This may seem like remarkable forecasting for these rather turbulent years, but the results may be more due to the detailed model's ability to allow the policy maker to fine-tune instruments to achieve the published targets, which in practice meant increased subsidies to prevent wage escalations. Norway is the only OECD country for which the 1970s, in terms of macroeconomic aggregates, looked much like the 1960s, only better. Whether that to any extent can be related to proficiency in model use, is hard to say.

The experience of the 1970s convinced the RDSN modellers that future macro-economic modelling had to abandon the strategy of extending the already large model with more relationships and behavioural modules. More economic content embedded in the model would require a downsizing of the unwieldy MODIS model. The current short-to-medium model, MODAG, was developed around 1980 and finally adopted by the Ministry of Finance as the workhorse for the national budget in 1993.[19] The transfer also implied that the Ministry operated the model without assistance from RDSN, which remained in charge of maintenance, updating and further development. Moving to MODAG implied a scaling down of sectoral detail (to around 30 commodities), but remaining considerably more detailed than models of the other Nordic countries that generally had been scaled *up* in sectoral and other detail.

3.3. The long-term model

The model adopted to fill the need for long-term policy analysis was the MSG model of Johansen (1960). In 1957, Johansen had embarked on a project to develop 'the model basis for a study of the relationships between production sectors under economic growth', with the intention of constructing a model that could perform calculations 'with numbers which in order of magnitude correspond to Norwegian conditions' (Schreiner and Larsen, 1985). The outcome was Johansen (1960), later enlarged and reissued as Johansen (1974). Johansen was a brilliant economist, who had worked as Frisch's assistant since he was an undergraduate, and took over his chair at the university in 1965. Frisch seems to have held a sceptical view of the MSG model on the ground that it was not a proper decision model, and thus not really suited for policy-making purposes. Frisch had an ingrained scepticism towards the performance of free markets in capitalistic economies and may not have liked the emphasis of Johansen's model compared to his own decision models.

Johansen's model can with considerable justification be considered the original prototype of the family of 'applied general equilibrium' models.[20] Johansen made it clear, unlike many of contributors in this field, that he aimed at more empirical validity than just a reasonable calibration of parameters.[21] The model had not, unlike MODIS, been designed for government use, but even before publication there was contact between Johansen and the Ministry of Finance about the possibility of using the model for the Long-Term Programme 1962–65. Johansen seemed to hold the view that the model would be too difficult for the Ministry to cope with at the time (Schreiner and Larsen, 1985, pp. 248–49). Instead the Institute and the Ministry embarked on a joint project to develop a second version of the model, completed in 1968. The model's first official use was in long-term projections until 1990, annexed to the Long-Term Programme 1970–73. Soon after the responsibility for operating the model was transferred to the RDSN as the only practical solution for maintaining the model for the Ministry's use along similar lines to the short-to-medium model.

The MSG model was used extensively in the ensuing years and became, like MODIS, an institutionalized model, that would be a common reference for policy-making in several areas. Every Long-Term Programme after 1969 had annexed long-term projections prepared by means of successive versions of the model.[22] But the model also got used for many other purposes, including sector-related analyses, both within central government and by non-government interests.[23] The interaction with users resulted in successive rounds of model enhancements.

While the early long-term projections were little related to policy matters (and also had little predictive value), more recent long-term exercises have addressed important policy matters in a Norwegian context related to inter-temporal issues of substantial magnitude, such as oil policy and use of oil revenues, demographic waves and pension funds, *et al.* Another application area for the MSG model emerged in the 1980s in assessments of structural reforms, such as tax reforms and trade regimes.

A later development of the MSG model was its adaptation for energy and environmental policy studies. RDSN extended its research field to comprise energy and environmental studies from the end of the 1970s. Energy sets Norway apart from all other OECD countries, both in regard to petroleum production (Norway is the second largest exporter of crude oil in the world) and electricity production (100 per cent hydro power). The line pursued was to utilize the long-term model MSG as the basis for integrated economy–environment modelling.[24] By and large this was a line of development initiated by the modelling environment and ran ahead of the demand from the government administration, which in the wake of the Brundtland Commission instructed all ministries to study the environmental consequences of major policy proposals. Hence, environmental analysis became from the outset firmly integrated in the existing modelling framework.

4. Observations on the interaction between model builder and policy maker

The interaction between policy makers and model builders can be viewed in a larger context as between government ministries broadly conceived on the one hand and academia and relevant research institutes offering model tools or model-based insights on the other. At a more operational level it is the interaction between the key policy-making body, say the Ministry of Finance, and its designated model-building unit, in the Norwegian case the Research Department of Statistics Norway. An important aspect of the latter relationship was that the RDSN was not under instruction by its superior Ministry, and thus provided an enclave of 'free research work' in the sense of Frisch (1946). RDSN considered its mandate to be to build models that would be found useful for the Ministry of Finance in the conduct of economic policy (and later extended to other ministries). Sometimes it missed, building models for which there was little demand. This dedication was also a limitation in the sense that RDSN would hesitate to embark upon major model-building projects that were considered as without appeal to policy makers.

4.1. Model builders versus policy makers

To make the institutional relationship between model builders and policy makers viable, there have to be degrees of freedom. Policy makers may not like to be confined to discussing policy within a model framework defined by others, while model builders may like even less having to adapt to the whims of policy makers. Priorities in model-building and model improvements might thus differ. Policy makers would often be concerned with more trivial improvements like updating procedures, reconciliation of results from different (sub-)models, details of specification of no theoretical interest, etc. In the Norwegian context such needs were accommodated by the Ministry offering additional resources on a contractual basis. On the other hand, the model might in certain situations be perceived by the policy makers as being too much of a straitjacket. The MODIS model was much structure and little behaviour, and allowed the Ministry much discretionary judgement, while the MODAG model in recent years may have appeared less amenable in the confrontation between econometric evidence and the Ministry view of how the economy functioned. Generally, the Ministry seems to have stuck to a very disciplined use of the models with no fiddling with the results, but on some occasions it is known to have 'disconnected' certain relations while operating the model.

4.2. Links to universities and the research frontier

Norway is a small country and has perhaps a more tightly-knit community of economists than most countries, due to the dominating role of the Institute of Economics at the University of Oslo as a supplier of economists for government service. This may have facilitated links, both formal and informal, between policy makers and the econometric and model-building research frontier.

An important formal channel for interaction in Norway was the *Modelling Committee*, established by the Ministry of Finance soon after 1960 to discuss and coordinate modelling issues between the Ministry, the Institute of Economics and the Research Department of Statistics Norway. The Ministry has been represented by the Heads of Department of the two major policy-making departments. Until his untimely death in 1982, Leif Johansen was the leading member of the committee. The committee, which still exists, would regularly review experiences in modelling, discuss new proposals for extending or major improvements of the modelling system, discuss the relevance and possible incorporation in the model of new theoretical advances, etc. The Central Bank was given one representative on the committee after it started model-building of its own and later the Norwegian School of Business Administration was also invited to join.

To play the servant role in a relationship with a basically conservative client like the policy makers of the Ministry of Finance may, however, involve a danger of losing touch with new developments and fossilizing established models. The RDSN realized this danger, perhaps belatedly, and tried to counteract it by extending the range of clients and emphasizing the academic criteria and links in its work. From having served primarily the Ministry of Finance as its subordinate agency over the first 25 years of its existence, the RDSN offered model tools and services to other ministries and the general public. The academic links were emphasized through dual appointments, external university-style evaluations of seniority qualifications, departmental doctoral scholarships, incentives to publish internationally and take part in international research co-operation.

4.3. Comparing RDSN and the Dutch CPB

The roles played by RDSN in Norway and CPB have similarities, but also differences. In both cases, a model-building environment was established within the central government administration at an early stage. The mode of operation in the interaction with policy makers was, however, different. CPB built *and* used the models on requests for policy advice from the Ministry of Economic Affairs, while in Norway the Ministry of Finance was the direct user of the model. The integration of model use and model-based thinking in the actual policy analysis within the relevant Ministry thus may appear to have progressed further in Norway. CPB had, on the basis of the law which established the institution, a mandate to provide forecasts and policy advice and became a highly-visible institution, while RDSN has kept a rather low profile. CPB published forecasts based on privileged access to the government's policy intentions (Donders and Graafland, 1997, revised as Chapter 2 in this volume), while RDSN played a merely technical role in the preparation of the national budget forecasts. The opinions of RDSN on policy-relevant issues might nevertheless have seeped through in the annual economic survey published in February every year. RDSN did not publish its own forecasts for the Norwegian economy until as late as 1987.[25]

Other differences comprise the proximity of RDSN to the statistical work, which allowed the modelling needs to influence priorities in the national accounts and other statistical data, and thereby enhanced their user value for modelling purposes, not least with regard to the use of preliminary data for updating purposes.

Both RDSN and CPB seem to have been successful in achieving a high reputation for their modelling work in the political world (cf. Zalm, 1998, Chapter 1 in this volume), although in the Norwegian case the actual reliance upon model analysis in the political decision-making may perhaps have been higher.

4.4. Side effects

The model reliance of the policy-making units within the Ministry of Finance has most likely strengthened its position both versus other ministries and relative to the political level. The model, and the fact that the Ministry of Finance was in charge of both the fiscal budget and the economic policy in general, became a basis for disciplining other ministries into relating all major issues to the national accounting and modelling framework. The modelling may also have served to prevent opportunities for outsiders with unorthodox modelling ideas or policy advice to penetrate directly to the political level over the heads of civil servants.[26]

An indirect effect of the Norwegian solution that may have had considerable impact has been the channelling of personnel. The modelling unit has over time served as a recruiting pool for the Ministry of Finance and other policy-making ministries. Senior researchers, often attracted to RDSN in the first place from academic interests in econometrics and model-building, would leave the RDSN to become Heads of Ministry Departments and influence policy-making and promote the further use of models within the government administration.

Governments of all countries are inclined to a high degree of secrecy with regard to budgetary information at the pre-publishing stage, and for good reasons. Even after budgets or policy documents have been published, the government may find its interest best served by keeping all material used in the preparation closed to public access. What about the models? In the Norwegian case the line pursued by Statistics Norway as the model operating unit was to apply the general policy of non-exclusivity: the models should be available to any interested party. This was made easier by not being directly involved in the policy analysis.

In practice it was not as easy as it might seem. The macroeconomic models were large, requiring hundreds of exogenous variables and assumptions, while the user interest was often only in studying the effects of a small handful of variables. In practice, arrangements were worked out under which the user would be allowed to have the differential changes made to a reference path prepared by the Ministry of Finance, calculated without revealing the policy implicit in the reference path. Hence, the institutionalized use of the model was extended to benefit also outside users, such as the political parties or interest groups.

A special case of outside user was the opposition parties in the Storting. Since the 1950s, RDSN had calculated revenue and income distribution effects of tax proposals for the government and, from the 1960s, allowed opposition parties access to the same tax models as the government, using exactly the same assumptions as in the budget preparation. This was a sophisticated business because the government would insist (and still does) that prior to the publication of the budget its assumption about income and price changes, necessary for tax calculations, are privileged information. RDSN accommodated opposition party requests, using the privileged information without revealing it. Hence, all tax proposals are calculated on exactly the same basis and their revenue or income distribution effects are never contested, and no tax proposal would be put forward without having been calculated this way. This system was carried over to cover also the macroeconomic models.

5. Conclusions

The origin of the Norwegian tradition in the use of models for macroeconomic policy-making owes much to the legacy of Ragnar Frisch, the dominant figure in Norwegian economics in the twentieth century, and perhaps more than he has been credited with. Frisch's direct influence on economic policies was limited by comparison with, for example, that of Tinbergen in the Netherlands (and certainly much less than he would have preferred). Frisch may have been viewed by the Norwegian policy makers and politicians at the time as a 'man not constrained by the maxim of politics as "the art of the possible" ' (Frisch (1995, p. xviii)), but his indirect influence may have been under-rated. In retrospect it seems that his overall impact on Norwegian economic thinking, modelling, and policy-making was far-reaching as a result of his role in the development of econometrics in a broad sense, his pioneering efforts in national accounting and modelling, and his role as a teacher to generations of economists. Perhaps his appeal to moral obligations in stating the role in society of the macroeconomist and the econometrician left a strong mark on his pupils, including those who did not share his political convictions (Frisch 1995, pp. xiv–xxiii).

The distinguishing features of the Norwegian approach have been the institutional solution found for the arena of interaction between modellers and policy makers and the concept of macroeconomic policy as a system of co-ordination, rather than in the choice of economic policy targets and instruments. The actual conduct of economic policy may, however, be viewed as much influenced by the use of models. Perhaps it would be justified to say that macroeconomic models in Norway have served more to maintain an infrastructure around the economic policy-making than as a direct contributor to policy changes and source for policy innovations. Consistency, coherence and co-ordination in economic policy have been emphasized more than any pretence of optimality. This is in line with Smith's account of why models have survived as practical tools (Smith, 1998, Chapter 15 in this volume).

Acknowledgements

I am most grateful for very helpful and constructive referee comments from the joint organizers of the *Empirical Models and Policy-Making* meeting, Mary Morgan and Frank den Butter, and from an anonymous referee. I have drawn substantially on the collective memory of colleagues in the Research Department of Statistics Norway and benefited from the access to the Ragnar Frisch archive at the University of Oslo. I would furthermore like to thank the former Head of Statistics Norway, Petter Jakob Bjerve, and the former Head of CPB, Pieter de Wolff for very enlightening conversations.

Notes

1 Donders and Graafland (1997, revised as Chapter 2 in this volume) call the role played by the Dutch Central Planning Bureau 'rather unique in the Western world', an assessment that may be doubted in view of the fact that the institutional solutions found in the Netherlands and Norway were rather similar. There were also differences, as commented upon in Section 4.

2 Except in Statistics Denmark, which copied the Norwegian solution on a diminutive scale many years later, and in France with the role played by INSEE.

3 The differences were thus observed by Waelbroeck (1975): 'A completely different tradition in model-building exists in Norway, stemming from the model-building work of Frisch and Johansen, the Central Statistical Bureau has, under the direction of Aukrust, built a series of "Modis" and "Prim" models, to predict industrial output,

prices, and income distribution by means of input–output analyses. These models, in which the major final demand aggregates are predicted exogenously, and in which coefficients are not estimated econometrically, are completely different from the other models surveyed; no comparable work exists elsewhere: in other countries input–output has found applications in long-term rather than in short-term planning' (p. 425).

4 Frisch had played a role in influencing the view of the Labour Party towards planning. He had contact with leading Labour Party representatives in the 1930s, had been an intermediary in bringing Keynes' views to the Norwegian parliamentarians' attention, and been the anonymous drafter of a Crisis Plan which became the Labour Party's electoral platform in 1935 (see Andvig (1986)). Frisch had been convinced in the early 1930s of the need for a planned economy to overcome depression, and in Frisch (1934) described the 'encapsulating phenomenon' of an unregulated capitalistic system, an article he would often refer to.

5 For a brief period in the late 1940s the national budgeting was allocated to the Ministry of Trade, and in 1979–81 there was a separate Ministry of Planning. In both cases the changes were person-related, and of no future consequence.

6 An early publication by two Frisch pupils applying a national accounting approach in assessing the costs of the German occupation was Aukrust and Bjerve (1945).

7 Ministry of Finance (1947). P. J. Bjerve was Head of the Monetary Policy Division (later renamed the National Budget Division) in the Ministry of Finance, which prepared the National Budget for 1947 and presumably the author of these passages in the white paper. Trygve Haavelmo, having returned from the USA, took over after Bjerve and was responsible for preparing the national budget for 1948. Haavelmo left quickly after that for the University of Oslo. He was for many years informally an adviser on economic policy to the Labour Party, especially to its former prime Minister Trygve Bratteli, but took less interest in modelling.

8 Since the Fiscal Budget was aligned with the calendar year in 1961, the National Budget and the Fiscal Budget for the coming year are presented to the Storting at the opening of the parliamentary session in October each year, with a Revised National Budget presented in May.

9 In optimistic disregard of Keynes' dictum that those over 30 years would be uninfluenced by new theories (Keynes, 1936, pp. 383–4).

10 Of the five Director Generals of Statistics Norway over its first 100 years, three had spells as members of the Cabinet (two as Ministers of Finance), one became Governor of the Central Bank.

11 The national accounting work was later moved to the regular statistical units of Statistics Norway, but not until 1991.

12 The establishment came about after the Minister of Finance, Mr Erik Brofoss, put pressure on P. J. Bjerve to accept the directorship of the Central Bureau of Statistics, having secured the support of Frisch as an intermediary. Bjerve was firmly set for an academic career, but yielded to pressure on the condition that he was allowed to establish a research department within Statistics Norway.

13 Frisch claimed to have originated the input–output analysis in his article, Frisch (1934), ahead of W. Leontief. The claim is found unwarranted in Bjerkholt (1995).

14 This was, incidentally, the first time the term 'macroeconomics' was used in *Econometrica*.

15 Frisch's decision model approach may be viewed as an attempt at establishing a stringent 'theory of economic policy', a view clearly held by Tinbergen who in his seminal and influential book on the subject, modestly stated in the preface that 'the core of the theory in this book is nothing but an application of the notion of "decision models" as introduced by Ragnar Frisch' (Tinbergen, 1954).

16 Except as isolated exercises, such as the attempt of Aslaksen and Bjerkholt (1985) at deriving implicit preferences of policy makers.

17 Similar views of preferring incomplete models rather than a formal pretence of optimalization seem to have been held on good pragmatic grounds also in other model user environments, see, e.g., Siviero *et al.* (1997).

18 The short-run version originated in a three-person government appointed committee chaired by Aukrust in 1966 (Aukrust, 1970), and was later followed by the long-run version explaining the wage and price trends in terms of world market prices, foreign exchange rates and productivity in the exposed and sheltered industries. Similar studies were soon after undertaken for other small countries (e.g. Sweden, the Netherlands). Aukrust (1977) expressed the core of the model as 'the basic idea of the Norwegian model is the purchasing power doctrine in reverse' (Aukrust, 1977, p. 114).

19 Cappelen and Longva (1987), Cappelen (1992). In Bergman and Olsen (1992) the MODAG model is reviewed together with models from other Nordic countries by Whitley (1992).

20 Standard references are usually given to more recent work, such as Shoven and Whalley (1984), except in Australia where applied general equilibrium models are still denoted 'Johansen type' models.

21 'Again it has become a habit among economists who are quantifying their models to say something like the following: "The principal aim of the present study is methodological. The statistical data are very scanty and unreliable. The quantitative analysis should therefore be considered merely as an illustration of method". Having given this statement, the author could hardly be blamed for using the statistical data uncritically. I should therefore like to characterize the quantitative analysis contained in this study in a way which differs somewhat from the usual one: the data and the quantitative analysis serve the purpose of illustrating the method and the model. But, at the same time, if I were required to make decisions and take actions in connections with relationships covered by this study, I would (in the absence of more reliable results, and without doing more work) rely to a great extent on the data and the results presented in the following chapters' (Johansen, 1960, p. 3).

22 How useful these projections were is another matter. Bjerkholt and Tveitereid (1985) compared long-term projections for the period 1980–90 undertaken at different times and concluded that the differences reflected short-term changes in the economic climate and mood rather than real differences in the evaluation of growth factors. The current 'mood' was primarily expressed by the value set for the Hicks-neutral technical progress parameters.

23 Later versions of the model are Bjerkholt *et al.* (1983), Longva *et al.* (1985) and Holmøy (1992). A list of uses of MSG until 1985 is given in Schreiner and Larsen (1985).

24 The history and current status of MSG as a general equilibrium model adapted for energy and environmental analyses is set out in Alfsen *et al.* (1996).

25 The first attempts to venture into this area did not pass quietly, as they resulted in public rebukes by the Prime Minister (Ms Brundtland) and her Minister of Finance for forecasting a surge in unemployment. Statistics Norway's right to publish forecasts was not put in question, and as it soon turned out that the unemployment forecasts were 95 per cent correct, there were few other similar incidents.

26 When a conservative government came into power in 1981 (for the first time in 55 years) there may, in the wake of the Thatcher and Reagan victories, have been a brief opening for Laffer-type advice, but of no consequences.

References

Alfsen, K. H., Bye, T. and Holmøy, E. (eds.), 1996. 'MSG-EE: An Applied General Equilibrium Model for Energy and Environmental Analysis', *Social and Economic Studies*, 96. Statistics Norway, Oslo.

Andvig, J. C., 1986. Ragnar Frisch and the Great Depression: A Study in the Interwar History of Macroeconomic Theory and Policy. Ph.D. Thesis, Norwegian Institute for International Relations.

Aslaksen, I. and Bjerkholt, O., 1985. 'Certainty equivalence procedures in decision-making under uncertainty: an empirical application.' In: Førsund, F. R., Hoel, M. and Longva, S. (eds.), *Production, Multi-Sectoral Growth and Planning*. Contributions to Economic Analysis 154. North-Holland, Amsterdam, pp. 289–329.

Aukrust, O., 1965. Tjue års økonomisk politikk i Norge: suksesser og mistak. Articles from the Central Bureau of Statistics 15, Statistics Norway, Oslo.

Aukrust, O., 1970. 'PRIM I – A Model of the Price and Income Distribution Mechanism of an Open Economy', *Rev. Income Wealth* 16, 51–78.

Aukrust, O., 1977. 'Inflation in the open economy: a Norwegian model.' In: Krause, L. B. and Salant, W. S. (eds.), *Worldwide Inflation: Theory and Recent Experience*. Brookings Institution, Washington D.C., pp. 109–66.

Aukrust, O., 1994. 'The Scandinavian contribution to national accounting.' In: Kennessey, Z. (ed.), *The Accounts of Nations*. IOS Press, Amsterdam, pp. 16–65.

Aukrust, O. and Bjerve, P. J., 1945. *Hva krigen kostet Norge*. Dreyers Forlag, Oslo.

Bergman, L. and Olsen, Ø. (eds.), 1992. *Economic Modeling in the Nordic Countries*. Contributions to Economic Analysis 210. North-Holland, Amsterdam.

Bjerkholt, O., 1986. 'Experiences in using input–output techniques for price calculations.' In: Sohn, I. (ed.), *Readings in Input–Output Analysis*. Oxford University Press, New York, pp. 35–48.

Bjerkholt, O., 1995. 'When input–output analysis came to Norway', *Struct. Change Econ. Dyn.* 6, 319–30.

Bjerkholt, O. and Longva, S., 1980. 'MODIS IV – A Model for Economic Analysis and National Planning', *Social and Economic Studies*, 43. Statistics Norway, Oslo.

Bjerkholt, O., Longva, S., Olsen, Ø. and Strøm, S. (eds.), 1983. 'Analysis of Supply and demand of Electricity in the Norwegian Economy', *Social and Economic Studies 53*. Statistics Norway, Oslo.

Bjerkholt, O. and Tveitereid, S., 1985. 'The use of the MSG-model in preparing a "Perspective Analysis 1980–2000" for the Norwegian economy.' In: Førsund, F. R., Hoel, M. and Longva, S. (eds.), *Production, Multi-Sectoral Growth and Planning*. Contributions to Economic Analysis 154. North-Holland, Amsterdam, pp. 271–87.

Bjerve, P. J., 1959. *Planning in Norway*. Contributions to Economic Analysis 16. North-Holland, Amsterdam.

Bjerve, P. J., 1989. 'Økonomisk planlegging og politikk.' Det norske samlaget, Oslo.

Bjerve, P. J., 1996. Contributions of Ragnar Frisch to National Accounting. Paper presented at the IARIW Conference, Lillehammer, 1996. Documents 96/21. Statistics Norway, Oslo.

Bjerve, P. J., 1998. 'The influence of Ragnar Frisch on macroeconomic planning and policy in Norway.' In: Strøm, S. (ed.), *Econometrics and Economic Theory in the 20th Century: The Ragnar Frisch Centennial Symposium*. Econometric Society Monographs no. 30, Cambridge University Press, New York.

Cappelen, Å., 1992. 'MODAG – a macroeconometric model of the Norwegian economy'. In: Bergman, L. and Olsen, Ø. (eds.), *Economic Modeling in the Nordic Countries*. Contributions to Economic Analysis 210. North-Holland, Amsterdam, pp. 55–93.

Cappelen, Å. and Longva, S., 1987. 'MODAG A – a medium-term macroeconomic model of the Norwegian economy.' In: Bjerkholt, O. and Rosted, J. (eds.), *Macroeconomic Medium-Term Models in the Nordic Countries*. Contributions to Economic Analysis 164. North-Holland, Amsterdam, pp. 153–211.

Donders, J. and Graafland, J., 1997. CPB models and employment policy in the Netherlands. Tinbergen Institute Conference Paper, May 1997 (revised, Chapter 2 in this volume).

Frisch, R., 1933. *Sparing and cirkulasjonsregulering*. Fabritius, Oslo.

Frisch, R., 1934. 'Circulation planning: proposal for a national organization of a commodity and service exchange', *Econometrica* 2, 258–336 and 422–35.

Frisch, R., 1940. Nasjonalregnskapet (National Accounts). Report from the Third Nordic Meeting of Statisticians, Oslo, 1939.

Frisch, R., 1946. 'The responsibility of the econometrician', *Econometrica* 14, 1–4.

Frisch, R., 1949. Price-wage-tax Policies as Instruments in maintaining Optimal Employment. Memorandum from the Institute of Economics.

Frisch, R., 1956. Main Features of the Oslo Median Model. Memorandum from the Institute of Economics.

Frisch, R., 1962. 'Preface to the Oslo Channel Model – A survey of types of economic forecasting and programming.' In: Geary, R. C. (ed.), *Europe's Future in Figures*. North Holland, Amsterdam, pp. 248–86.

Frisch, R., 1995. *Foundations of Modern Econometrics. The Selected Essays of Ragnar Frisch*. 2 vols. (Edward Elgar, Aldershot, UK) (edited, selected and with an introduction by O. Bjerkholt).

Holmøy, E., 1992. 'The structure and working of MSG-5, an applied general equilibrium model of the Norwegian economy'. In: Bergman, L. and Olsen, Ø. (eds.), *Economic Modeling in the Nordic Countries*. Contributions to Economic Analysis 210. North-Holland, Amsterdam, pp. 199–236.

Johansen, L., 1960. *A Multi-Sectoral Study of Economic Growth*. Contributions to Economic Analysis 21. North-Holland, Amsterdam.

Johansen, L., 1974. *A Multi-Sectoral Study of Economic Growth*. 2nd enlarged ed. Contributions to Economic Analysis 21. North-Holland, Amsterdam.

Johansen, L., 1977. *Lectures on Macroeconomic Planning. Part 1: General Aspects*. North-Holland, Amsterdam.

Johansen, L., 1978, *Lectures on Macroeconomic Planning. Part 2: Planning under Uncertainty*. North-Holland, Amsterdam.

Keynes, J. M., 1936. *The General Theory of Employment, Interest and Money*. Macmillan, London.

Lie, E., 1996. *Ambisjon og tradisjon. Finansdepartementet 1945–65*. Norwegian University Press, Oslo.

Longva, S., Lorentsen, L. and Olsen, Ø., 1985. The multi-sectoral growth model MSG-4. Formal structure and empirical characteristics. In: Førsund, F. R., Hoel, M. and Longva, S. (eds.), *Production, Multi-Sectoral Growth and Planning*. Contributions to Economic Analysis 154. North-Holland, Amsterdam, pp. 187–240.

Ministry of Finance, 1947. Om nasjonalbudsjettet 1947 [On the National Budget 1947]. White Paper, No. 10, Ministry of Finance, Oslo.

Schreiner, P. and Larsen, K. A., 1985. 'On the introduction and application of the MSG-model in the Norwegian planning system.' In: Førsund, F. R., Hoel, M. and Longva, S. (eds.), *Production, Multi-Sectoral Growth and Planning.* Contributions to Economic Analysis 154. North-Holland, Amsterdam, pp. 241–69.

Sevaldson, P., 1964. 'An interindustry model of production and consumption in Norway.' In: *Income and Wealth,* Series X. IARIW, London, pp. 23–50.

Sevaldson, P., 1968. 'MODIS II – A macro-economic Model for short-term analysis and planning.' In: *Macro-Economic Models for Planning and Policy-Making.* United Nations, Geneva, pp. 161–71.

Shoven, J. B. and Whalley, J., 1984. 'Applied general equilibrium models of taxation and international trade: An introduction and survey', *J. Econ. Lit.* 22, 1007–51.

Siviero, S., Terlizzese, D. and Visco, I., 1997. Are model-based inflation targets used in policy-making? Paper presented at Empirical Models and policy-making. 10th Anniversary Congress of the Tinbergen Institute, Amsterdam.

Smith, R., 1998. 'Emergent policy-making with macroeconometric models', *Econ. Model.* 15, 429–42 (Chapter 15 in this volume).

Tinbergen, J., 1954. *On the Theory of Economic Policy.* Contributions to Economic Analysis 1. North-Holland, Amsterdam.

Waelbroeck, J., 1975. 'A survey of short-run research outside the United States'. In: *The Brookings Model: Perspective and Recent Developments.* North-Holland, Amsterdam.

Whitley, J. D., 1992. 'Comparative properties of the Nordic Models'. In: Bergman, L. and Olsen, Ø. (eds.), *Economic Modeling in the Nordic Countries.* Contributions to Economic Analysis 210. North-Holland, Amsterdam, pp. 3–53.

Zalm, G., 1998. 'The relevance of economic modelling for policy decisions', *Econ. Model.* 15, 309–16 (Chapter 1 in this volume).

Chapter 11

Conflicts between macroeconomic forecasting and policy analysis

Simon Wren-Lewis

Econometric macroeconomic models are used by policy makers for two purposes: forecasting and policy simulation. In the early days of macroeconomic modelling, there was no perceived conflict between these two activities: a model that was good at forecasting would give good policy advice and vice versa. However, this chapter argues that as models develop, important conflicts can emerge between forecasting and policy analysis. It is argued that the low status of macroeconometric models within academic macroeconomics in the UK and US indicates that the development of macroeconometric models in these countries may have been biased towards the needs of forecasting. The chapter suggests that in the UK these trends contributed to important policy errors in the 1980s and 1990s. The solution to these problems is to develop different models for forecasting and policy simulation, and the chapter discusses some of the issues that might arise from this division of labour.

JEL Classifications: C50, E17

1. Introduction

Most institutions that conduct both policy analysis and forecasting have traditionally used the same model for these two activities. This chapter suggests that serious conflicts may arise between forecasting and policy analysis in the development of these macroeconometric models. The suggested solution to this problem is to use separate models for forecasting and policy analysis, and the chapter discusses some of the issues that might arise from such a 'division of labour'. Recent developments in multi-country modelling and in the Bank of England suggest that this process may be currently underway.

The chapter has three main sections. Section 2 examines the sources of potential conflict between forecasting and policy analysis. Section 3 argues that this conflict, and an emphasis on forecasting, contributed to major macroeconomic policy errors in the UK in the 1980s and early 1990s. It also suggests that a focus on forecasting has diminished the role that macroeconomic analysis has had over debates on European Monetary Union. Section 4 examines some of the issues that might arise for policy-making if separate models were used for forecasting and policy analysis. A final section concludes.

2. Forecasting and policy analysis

Before discussing conflicts between forecasting and policy analysis, it is important to define the two activities clearly. The definition focuses on outputs, rather than the means of producing those outputs. A forecast is an unconditional prediction of what will happen to the economy. Policy analysis is more diverse, but it includes a *ceteris paribus* analysis of the effects of changing policy instruments, and the design and consequences of alternative policy regimes. Now of course the two activities can be linked: the government is part of the economy, and so a forecast can involve an analysis of the effects of government actions. However, the two activities need not be linked at all: a VAR model producing forecasts need not even include policy variables, and even if it does, it is very unclear how to identify policy shocks using it.

The idea that there might be *a critical* conflict between using the same model for policy analysis and forecasting is at first sight surprising. Indeed the idea seems counter intuitive: surely if a model cannot predict, then it cannot be trusted to suggest policy changes. This is still the widespread view among modellers themselves, commentators on modelling (e.g. Kenway, 1994, p. 5), and the general public. When macroeconomic models were first built, the presumption was that the process of forecasting would encourage model improvement which would enhance policy analysis.

However, to academics the idea of a single, all embracing model that can do everything is not at all natural. Theoretical macroeconomics contains a large number of rather small models, and the differences between these models often (although not always) reflect the question the model is attempting to answer. An individual macroeconomist, who held a consistent view of the way the economy worked, would not think it odd to use one macromodel to answer one question, and a different model to answer another.

The idea that a model has to be able to predict before its policy advice can be trusted is severely compromised once we recognize the stochastic nature of macro-models. The problem in a highly stochastic environment is that prediction is relatively uninformative: there is too much else going on, too much noise. The fact that a particular macroeconomic model does well in forecasting in any one year is largely down to luck. To assess whether it was due to the model, we would need a run of forecasts over at least a decade, and control for judgemental input. However, models do not stand still for decades, and so even this information would be of limited value.[1] (See Wallis, 1989, for a general discussion.)

There is therefore no necessary reason why forecasting and policy analysis have to be done with the same model. To see why there might be advantages in using separate models it is worth noting exactly what is involved in the process of forecasting, and how different it is from policy analysis (or an econometric forecasting test). Much of the time of a forecaster involves monitoring the data, and particularly the recent data. They also need to monitor what other forecasters are forecasting. When it comes to running the model, a great deal of time will be spent 'massaging' the output to generate 'smooth' quarterly paths for some variables, or to generate 'plausible' numbers for others. The spur to model development that arises from forecasting comes from reacting to prediction errors, or equation errors over the recent past. The forecaster qua forecaster may not be very interested in simulation properties of the model as a whole, and even less in competing theoretical approaches.[2]

Those involved in policy analysis, on the other hand, have no direct interest in the latest monthly data release for consumer prices. They will tend to place more emphasis on the overall fit of an equation rather than focusing on its tracking ability over the last few years. They will be even more interested in the theoretical properties of a specification, and they will tend to view this within the context of the properties of the complete model.[3]

A practical example of the type of conflict I have in mind involves the choice of specification for a new equation for a model. Suppose there are two candidates: one does better at tracking the recent data, but one has more desirable theoretical properties. Ideally, given this choice we would want to ask many more questions; were the more desirable theoretical properties tested in the other equation? are there encompassing tests etc. etc. But suppose limited resources mean that this information is not available and the choice needs to be made now? (In my experience such resources are always limited, if only by time, and so a trade-off of this kind often exists.) Will the needs of short-term prediction prevail over theoretical properties?[4]

The development in macroeconomics that made conflicts of this kind critical was the rational expectations revolution in macroeconomics.[5] The attraction of rational expectations to most academic macroeconomists was not that it explained the data better, but rather that it made sense within the dominant 'rationality' paradigm. There are indirect indications that the introduction of rational expectations does not bring forecasting benefits. For example, rational expectations tends to be absent in models used by institutions that specialize in forecasting. When the forecasting performance of UK models has been compared by the ESRC macromodelling bureau at Warwick (see Wallis and Whitley, 1991, for example), there has been no tendency for models which make greater use of rational expectations to perform better. I doubt whether many would now claim that adopting the Rational Expectations Hypothesis would significantly improve forecasting performance, except perhaps after regime shifts.

The rational expectations hypothesis is critical for policy analysis rather than forecasting. The key role that rational expectations can play in policy design is now so familiar that it does not need repeating here. However, implementing the Rational Expectations Hypothesis in macromodels is costly: not only does it take time to do, but rational expectations solution techniques make the whole business of forecasting and policy analysis far more complex and time consuming.

The introduction of rational expectations became extremely difficult, if not impossible, for some models that had grown very large in size. It is a well known in modelling that model size is not normally correlated with a model's theoretical complexity. Instead large models are typically disaggregated models. By making the model larger and more detailed, the forecaster could incorporate more information which would, it was hoped, help improve short-term forecasting. Partly as a result, most econometric macromodels became large – sometimes very large.

Incorporating more information to improve short-term forecasting was not the only factor leading to greater model size, and it may not have been the critical motive. Pressure from clients for disaggregated information was also very important, leading to a large number of equations describing public sector activities in government models, and extensive industrial disaggregation in models used by institutions selling forecasts to the private sector.[6]

Whatever the precise motives for the trend to greater size, it did have a critical effect on the ability of large models to provide comprehensible policy advice. All too often the behaviour of these models, even in the long run, could not be satisfactorily explained or related to basic theory (Turner, 1991). They became 'black boxes'. The implications for their users are discussed below, but it is worth noting that a large size also made theoretical development much more difficult. It is complicated enough implementing rational expectations consistently in a 25 equation macromodel – it becomes virtually impossible in a 1000 equation model.

This conflict between policy analysis and forecasting is mainly a conflict between theory and predictive ability, but it is not the only source of conflict. Recent work by David Hendry and colleagues has shown how the concept of a single 'best' model capable of fulfilling different types of prediction is problematic. For example, Clements and Hendry (1995) examine circumstances in which adding additional structure potentially crucial for conditional policy analysis, could lead to a deterioration in unconditional forecast performance because the extra structure is itself unpredictable. Forecasting models may also differ depending on the required forecasting horizon. Hendry has explicitly noted that his results are uncomfortable for those who want to use the same model for policy analysis and forecasting.

Given that such conflicts exist, will forecasting or policy analysis win out? Important here is the structure of the national macromodelling 'industry' and the associated funding regime. Three generic types of institutional structure can be identified:

1   Research is done within government or a government agency (i.e. in the Treasury, finance ministry or Central Planning Bureau) on its own model.
2   Research is done outside government (in academia or research institutions), perhaps in the context of other models, with a view to the government absorbing 'best practice' in its own model. This comes close to the UK framework.
3   Research is done outside government, and the government uses outside models rather than maintaining a model of their own. This comes close to the US experience.

The importance of private sector forecasting depends on the nature of the research funding regime noted above. In the case where model development is largely funded by the private sector, then this sector will call the tune. The interest of the private sector is in forecasting, not policy advice. Now of course getting the forecast right will depend in part on predicting what the government will do, and what effect its actions will have, but that is only one part of the complete picture – and perhaps on some occasions a relatively unimportant part. I believe it is no accident that in the US, where the influence of the private sector on model development can be dominant, we see large, highly disaggregated national models (e.g. DRI, Wharton), with little or no trace of rational expectations.[7]

Even within the other two funding regimes noted above, there remains an important bias towards forecasting coming from the private sector. In the UK, for example, the two most long-standing non-government modelling institutions (the London Business School and National Institute for Economic and Social Research) receive a large part of their funding from the private sector, directly or indirectly as a result of their forecasting activity. The key difference from the US, however, is that UK funding also comes from the Economic and Social Research Council, which provides research money to the academic community. There is countervailing pressure, which is partly why both of these institutions' models include rational expectations to some degree.

Even within government, the existence of private-sector forecasts puts reactive pressure on these institutions. Ministers and their advisers need to have a forecast, and the analysis behind it, in order to react to claims of doom and gloom coming from private sector forecasts. The countervailing pressure from academia on policy analysis is slight by comparison.

What is the evidence that macroeconometric models have developed with a bias towards forecasting rather than policy analysis? I will limit myself to the situation in the UK and US, and experience in other countries may be quite different, owing to the importance of the institutional structure noted above.

In the UK and US, most of the main modelling groups compete directly in the forecasting market, and so they have to produce a product that commands respect to survive. The main group of economists other than macromodellers who are involved in policy analysis are academics, and here the story is very different. Mankiw (1990) suggests, for example, that large econometric macromodels have become something of a joke in US academic circles. While the position is less polarized in the UK, it remains the case that few academic macroeconomists would look to existing econometric macromodels if asked to give policy advice (as noted in Smith, 1994, for example). When asked why, they would typically reply that these existing macromodels are out of date and difficult to understand. There may also be a view that these models are too large. However, the dominant criticism tends to be that the models have failed to incorporate theoretical developments that academic macroeconomists now regard as standard. (Section 3 provides some specific examples.)

Model builders sometimes respond to this academic criticism by suggesting that current theory is too diverse and controversial, and that the model builder should use the test of time to see what current academic fashions have lasting value. Unfortunately, as I have argued elsewhere (Wren-Lewis, 1993), this excuse does not stand up to examination. For example, one element of macroeconomic analysis that has been regarded as standard by nearly all macroeconomists for the last ten or more years is a consumption function based on intertemporal optimization, which allows current consumption to depend on future labour income. However, econometric macromodels that incorporate such an approach remain in the minority even today.

The growing distrust and antagonism of academic macroeconomists to econometric macromodels is a very strong indication that forecasting rather than policy analysis has been the dominant force in the development of these models. The next section uses events in the UK over the last twenty years to provide further evidence, and also to suggest that a bias towards forecasting has had significant costs.

3. Forecasting models and policy errors: a UK case study

If the development of macroeconometric models has been guided more by the needs of forecasting than policy analysis, does this matter? After all, I have suggested above that this development may have reflected the demands of policy makers or the private sector. In this section I want to use the experience of the UK over the last 20 years as a 'case study' to examine this question. The section ends, however, with a very topical issue that is central to much of Europe, where I believe there is a critical deficiency in the advice coming from macroeconometric models.

In the macroeconomic history of the UK over the last two decades, three episodes stand out. The first was the monetarist experiment of the early 1980s, and the associated collapse of UK manufacturing industry and massive rise in unemployment. The second was the failure to foresee and counteract the consumer boom of the late 1980s. The third was the deep recession of the early 1990s, which occurred while the UK was briefly a member of the Exchange Rate Mechanism of the EMS. One reason for looking at these major events is that they are associated with changes in policy regime, and changes in regime are precisely the moments when models geared to forecasting that do not embody rational expectations are likely to be weak, for reasons familiar from the Lucas critique of these models.

To understand the role of macromodels in the UK 'monetarist experiment' of the early 1980s, we need to start a decade earlier. As Kenway notes: 'By 1973, the short-term income-expenditure model dominated UK macro-modelling' (Kenway, 1994, p. 34). The limitations of that approach were made evident by the traumatic events of the 1970s. From our point of view, the key issue became the modelling of the exchange rate, following the breakdown of Bretton Woods in 1971. Modellers were faced with a new problem: a variable that had previously been exogenous was now endogenous. It was the inability of UK macromodellers to solve this problem for many years that was important in the events of 1980/81.

The way this problem is, almost without exception, solved today in a structural macromodel is by using Uncovered Interest Parity (UIP), with or without a risk premium. Together with rational expectations and a terminal condition tying down the long run real exchange rate (Power Parity Purchasing or something more sophisticated: see below), this endogenizes the exchange rate under free floating. The key, and possibly only, free parameter to estimate is the risk premium (see Fisher *et al.*, 1990).

By the end of the 1970s, however, nothing like this existed in any of the main UK macromodels. The 'industry leader' in terms of modelling the exchange rate was the London Business School (LBS) model. The 1978 version of the model endogenized the exchange rate by taking an 'International Monetarist' view, which in practice meant that movements in the exchange rate were determined by the ratio of UK to world money (Kenway, p. 128). This model, and its operators, were influential in devising the macroeconomic policy that would be adopted by the newly elected conservative government in 1979. '. . . by giving form to Monetarism, this model can be seen as lending credibility to the three major tenets of economic orthodoxy in the 1980s' (Kenway, op. cit., p. 131). The director of the Centre for Economic Forecasting at the LBS, Terry Burns, became Chief Economic Adviser at the Treasury in the early 1980s.[8]

This model suggested that a gradual reduction in money growth would produce a relatively painless reduction in inflation. The Medium-Term Financial Strategy (MTFS) adopted by the new Conservative government had at its centre piece a gradual decline in money growth. What actually occurred in 1980/81 was a substantial 'overshooting' of the exchange rate, and this massive real appreciation helped reduce the size of the UK manufacturing sector by about 20 per cent. Unemployment rose to levels unprecedented since the war.

The story that is now widely accepted about why this happened is based on the Dornbusch overshooting model (Dornbusch, 1976). It is generated by a combination of UIP, rational expectations, and nominal inertia. The UK macromodels at the time had the last ingredient, but not the first two. As the date of the Dornbusch paper suggests, this theoretical model was available to UK macromodellers, yet none adopted it. While the fact that the LBS chose to use an alternative framework was important in the evolution of policy, it is also noteworthy that other models continued to treat the exchange rate in an even cruder manner, and so provided no counterweight to the LBS analysis.

Currie (1985) argues forcibly that the ideas behind exchange rate overshooting were being widely discussed in academic and policy circles at the time of the monetarist experiment. So what can account for the delay in adopting or even experimenting with UIP in UK econometric macromodels? All the UK models were involved in conducting short-term forecasting exercises as well as in giving policy advice. We have already noted that, from a forecasting point of view, there was little if anything to be gained in devoting resources to embodying rational expectations in macromodels. (This was not done in the UK until Patrick Minford developed the Liverpool model in the early 1980s.) Exactly the same can be said of UIP: its predictive ability is weak, as Meese and Rogoff (1983) have argued. So a delay in implementing UIP and rational expectations that seems incredible from an academic point of view, seems much more understandable if the model was mainly a forecasting tool.

The failure of macroeconometric models to provide helpful advice during this period also had consequences for policy makers' views about these models. To quote Whitley (1997, p. 164): 'By the early 1980s it became clear that policy makers had little confidence in macroeconometric models in general. This can be attributed partly to the failure of forecasts, but also to the perceived theoretical shortcomings of the models (and particularly the absence of a key role for money).' This lack of trust was to have important consequences a decade later.

In the real UK economy the 1980/81 recession was followed by a slow but steady recovery. By the end of the 1980s, however, this recovery had become an unsustainable consumer boom fuelled by borrowing (rather than higher incomes), leading to a monetary contraction and recession in 1990–92. The consumer boom reflected a universal forecasting failure: no modelling group predicted its onset or strength. It might appear odd to attribute a forecasting failure by models to an emphasis on forecasting rather than policy advice within those models, but again the absence of current macroeconomic theory from these models was critical.

There are still a number of competing theories about what led to the late 1980s consumer boom, but two of the leading contenders rely critically on modern intertemporal theories of consumption. The first focuses on the substantial degree of financial liberalization that took place in the UK in the 1980s (Muellbauer and Murphy, 1991). In an open economy this would allow previously credit constrained consumers to borrow more, and immediately increase their consumption, with no offsetting reduction in consumption elsewhere. Darby and Ireland, 1994, present econometric evidence that credit liberalization in the context of an intertemporal consumption model could account for the magnitude of the UK consumer boom. A second account argues that consumers were over optimistic about future rates of income growth, perhaps believing in the widely reported 'Thatcher supply side miracle'. In the intertemporal model, an increase in expected income growth leads to a jump in current consumption.

In the late 1980s, however, none of the UK macromodels embodied a consumption function based on intertemporal optimization. This was despite the fact, noted above, that by the mid-80s the intertemporal consumption model had become standard within academic macroeconomics. Rational expectations was no longer a key problem: by this time – following exchange rate overshooting and the example of Minford's Liverpool model – most of the major UK models had incorporated rational expectations to some extent. Yet none had yet incorporated the then standard theoretical model of consumption.[9]

If the main focus of these models had been policy analysis, then the fact that *no* UK model had adopted intertemporal consumption would be incredible. This model is crucial for fiscal policy analysis because of Ricardian Equivalence. It might have been unfortunate if *all* the models had adopted intertemporal consumption, given the serious empirical debates about its validity, but the fact that none did shows how dislocated UK macroeconometric models had become from mainstream academic analysis. (The situation was much the same in the US.) However, this omission is much more understandable if UK macroeconometric models had been primarily geared to forecasting. In *normal times*, expectations about future income would be a stable function of past income, and so a traditional Keynesian type consumption function would be adequate from a forecasting point of view and a lot simpler to use.

If the models had been geared to policy advice rather than forecasting, and had as a result adopted a consumption function based on intertemporal optimization, would this have avoided their failure to forecast the UK consumer boom? As the accounts based on hindsight noted above indicate, an intertemporal model alone is not enough: an analysis of financial liberalization or optimistic income growth expectations would also have been required. However, anyone working with intertemporal consumption models will quickly realize that this framework can generate large movements (in fact 'jumps') in the savings ratio, and so once the first signs of the consumer boom had emerged, using intertemporal models might have made forecasters more aware of the upside risks.

In both these episodes, the models were unprepared to meet events and new ideas, and so failed to provide useful advice to policy makers. While it would be fanciful to lay to blame for either episode entirely at the door of these models, their failure did play a part in shaping events. As the quote from Whitley above suggests, these failures meant that by the end of the 1980s the models were not seen by most economists and government advisers as useful tools for providing policy advice. This became important in 1990, when the UK signalled its intention to join the ERM.

A key question in 1990 was what exchange rate sterling should enter at. In general, macroeconometric models did not play a central role in this debate *at the time*.[10] On this occasion the problem was not so much that the models had nothing to contribute, but instead that their credibility at giving useful policy advice was so low that few regarded it worth using them to analyse this issue. Instead most analysts fell back on a very simple theory, Purchasing Power Parity. PPP calculations suggested that an equilibrium rate for sterling was around 3 DM/£, and the UK entered at 2.95 DM/£.

The fact that the UK was forced to leave the ERM in 1992 as sterling fell below its lower 6 per cent band around 2.95 DM/£ does not *prove* that PPP was wrong, although the general presumption today is that sterling is overvalued at 3 DM/£ (see Fisher and Whitley, 1998). What is clear is that leaving the ERM gave a substantial boost to (and may even have generated) the UK recovery from recession, without any cost in terms of a rise in inflation. My own research among others has shown that the attempt to maintain 2.95 DM/£ both intensified and prolonged the recession of the early 1990s (Hughes Hallett and Wren-Lewis, 1995).

When the major models were *subsequently* used to examine the sustainability of the UK entry rate, most said quite clearly that sterling was seriously overvalued in the ERM (see Church, 1993). The ERM episode is therefore rather different from the monetarist experiment ten years earlier. In 1980/81 the models were unable to provide a credible critique of policy, whereas in 1990 they were. Unfortunately this is not because the models had necessarily improved during this period, but simply that the theory that went beyond PPP in UK models was some 20+ years old. (The models essentially used the Fundamental Equilibrium Exchange Rate approach formalized by Williamson, 1983, that was itself based on trade equations of the type popularized by Houthaker and Magee, 1969). However, the failure to provide policy advice in the past, together with their inability to keep pace with theory, made the models vulnerable to attack and easily ignored.[11] In addition, in the public view the models were associated with the failure to forecast the earlier consumer boom, and were therefore not to be trusted. Common to both 1980 and 1990, however, was that policy makers resorted to crude, reduced form type relationships (money to price regressions and PPP) as an alternative to model-based output, and that these reduced forms proved unreliable.

To conclude, on all three occasions events exposed the theoretical inadequacies of most UK econometric macromodels. The key point is not that the models necessarily embodied the wrong theory – with ERM entry they did not – but that their failure to address theoretical issues that had been current in academic thinking for some time made them very vulnerable to attack and easily ignored. The failure to keep pace with theory is understandable if the focus of model development had been on the needs of forecasting rather than policy advice, although it is of course impossible to *prove* this connection. Model failure in one case led directly to policy errors (the delay in reacting to the consumer boom), while in the other two policy makers relied on other advice which proved costly in terms of unemployment.

3.1. European Monetary Union

Are these examples from the past unusual episodes with no necessary implications for the future? Is the UK experience atypical? The debate around the costs and benefits of European Monetary Union suggests otherwise. Macroeconomists and macroeconomics have played an important role in the debates over EMU, although most economists believe that political rather than economic factors have played the critical role in actual decisions. However, the economic argument has been lacking one critical piece of evidence.

The main economic costs and benefits of EMU are fairly clear. The most obvious benefit is a reduction in transaction costs and uncertainty. Estimates have been made of both, although clearly they cannot be precise. The main cost is a sacrifice of macroeconomic flexibility in the face of asymmetric shocks. Very little work has been done to *quantify* these costs. Significantly, most of the work that has been done has used the IMF's Multimod, which is a multi-country model that is used for policy advice and not for forecasting. (See Masson and Symansky, 1992, in particular.) We therefore have no number to compare the numerical estimates of the benefits of EMU with, and so economists have resorted to judgement.

To quantify the costs of EMU we need an econometric model. We need to use the evidence of the past to assess the scale of demand shocks, supply shocks and exchange rate 'bubbles', and to assess the degree of both real and nominal inertia in goods and labour markets. In addition, we need to do this allowing for any changes in fiscal policy regime brought about through currency union. Such an analysis is not easy, but it can be done using available techniques, *if* the models are up to the task (see Bryant *et al.*, 1993). Given the importance of the issue, we have to ask why work of this kind is not more widely available. Once again macroeconometric models are not being used to provide important policy analysis, even though there is no obviously superior source of information available. One possible reason suggested by the UK experience is that many multi-country models are geared towards forecasting, and so cannot easily be used to provide this key piece of policy analysis.

4. A division of labour: recent developments in UK macromodelling

The previous section argued that an emphasis on forecasting had led to models that were weak – and perceived to be weak – at policy analysis, and that this could have contributed to policy mistakes. The message, however, is not to steer existing econometric models away from forecasting, but instead to allow a division of labour. We need to build separate models for forecasting and policy analysis.

Recent trends in the UK (and to some extent elsewhere) have been moving in this direction. I should at this stage declare a personal interest. After working on the Treasury model, and being responsible for the development of the National Institute's domestic and world models, I then constructed a domestic macromodel – COMPACT – from scratch from within the UK academic sector.[12] The focus of this model was in incorporating recent developments in macroeconomic theory in a way that was consistent with UK history. Given the analysis above, I decided that forecasting with COMPACT would hinder this goal, and so COMPACT is only used for policy analysis.

Within policy-making institutions, recent developments at the Bank of England reflect the same trend. The Monetary Policy Committee of the Bank now has responsibility for monetary policy, so the Bank's short-term forecasts are critically important. However, in recent years it has moved away from maintaining a single macroeconomic model, and instead operates a suite of models, of which the forecasting model is just one (Whitely, 1997; Fisher and Whitely, 1998).

A similar trend is evident among multi-country models. We have already noted that Multimod, maintained at the IMF and widely used, is primarily a simulation rather than forecasting tool. Masson, 1998, defines what he calls the 'new breed' of multi-country models as those 'tightly specified from theory and hence more homogenous across countries, and relied on rational expectations'. (The group includes MSG, John Taylor's model, MX3 as well as Multimod.) He notes that none of this new breed is used for forecasting.[13]

One of the objections that is often raised to maintaining different models for forecasting and policy analysis is that policy-making would lose consistency. However, this objection does not stand up to analysis, especially when the need for robust policy is recognized. Consider actions within a given 'regime'. The 'pre-budget' forecast would take place using the forecasting model. Ministers would then explain what they would like to change, and the policy model would suggest the direction and scale of instrument changes that could achieve this.

The forecast that governments have traditionally presented to the public, however, have been 'post- Budget', i.e. after taking into account their instrument changes. Here there appears to be a problem: as the policy and forecast models differ, implementing the budget forecast on the forecasting model will imply different outcomes for this intervention than in the policy model. Unless the two models are the same, they will give different answers about the post-Budget outcome. However, this is not a problem in practice, because any forecast is a mix of model prediction and forecaster intervention. It would therefore be very easy to produce a post-budget forecast using the forecasting model that was consistent with the advice of the policy model, using residual adjustments on the forecasting model.

This practical problem becomes even less important when it is recognized that good policy-making does not rely on a single model to forecast or a single model to give policy analysis. No one method of forecasting clearly dominates all others, and so it makes sense to 'pool' forecasts to some extent. Those advising policy makers incorporate this diversity of view routinely in forecasting through judgemental intervention. Equally, policy advice should be based on looking at the output of more than one macromodel. As there are bound to be different views of the world, embodied in different models, with non-zero probabilities of being correct, then policy needs to be robust across these models. It is inevitable, therefore, that any post-budget forecast should also involve judgemental intervention and not be based on a single model. The need for a diversity of view is given by Whitley, 1997, as the key reason for the Bank of England's move to using a range of models. Nevertheless, he describes one of these models as the 'forecasting model', which is also the model that remains 'in the mainstream of macroeconomic models'. Recent developments at the Bank are therefore consistent with the need to differentiate forecasting and policy models, as well as corroborating the argument of this chapter that the emphasis of traditional UK macroeconometric models has been on forecasting.

The need for separate models for policy analysis and forecasting therefore sits very easily with the need to make policy robust by using a range of models. There are, however, limits to the number of alternative models that should be used. It is important not to lose sight completely of one of the rationales for using a single model, which was to achieve consistency across policy decisions. The problem of how to weight the results of different models when they conflict needs to be addressed. There are also dangers in having too many 'problem specific models'; that is a separate model (or models) for each policy issue. One is that important interactions between different issues will be missed. Another is that such plurality is costly in terms of resources, and a result may be that model calibration rather than model estimation becomes standard. While investigating the properties of models using calibration is undoubtedly informative, it does not and should not become a substitute for econometric estimation and testing.

If different models are used for forecasting and for policy analysis, then conflicts over resources between forecasting and policy analysis will not go away, but such conflicts would become more open. However, policy analysis would still improve, because it would be based on models that had been built with policy in mind, and had not had their properties compromised by the need to produce short-term forecasts. It is also possible that forecasts would also improve, to the extent that the forecasting abilities of models had been compromised by the needs of policy simulation.

In addition, the development or use of models designed for policy analysis rather than forecasting should greatly improve interaction between government and academic economists. Econometric macromodels built for policy analysis might still be complex by academic standards, because for reasons noted above it makes sense to build models that can answer a broad range of policy questions. However, because the components of these models will have firm theoretical foundations, it will be possible to understand the complex model's properties using techniques like 'theoretical deconstruction' (e.g. Wren-Lewis *et al.*, 1996; Masson, 1988; or Deleau *et al.*, 1984).

In conclusion, therefore, the use of separate models for use in forecasting and policy analysis appears to present no serious practical difficulties. Indeed something similar to the changes proposed above have recently occurred at the Bank of England, where a forecasting model is operated alongside a separate suite of policy orientated models. The argument of this chapter is that the advantages of this type of division of labour are overwhelming.

5. Conclusions

This chapter has argued that over the last two or three decades important conflicts have arisen in the development of macroeconometric models between the needs of forecasting and the needs of policy analysis. In the UK and the US the theoretical development of models appears to have been compromised by the needs of forecasting, and partly as a result, macroeconometric models have become increasingly divorced from academic macroeconomists.

To what extent is a bias towards forecasting a problem? The chapter looks at the role of econometric macromodels in UK policy over the last twenty years. The analysis suggests that at key points in the UK's macroeconomic development, UK models generally failed to give advice that policy makers found useful or convincing. That failure reflected an inability to keep pace with developments in macroeconomic theory, which may in turn have reflected a bias towards forecasting in the development of these models. This model failure contributed in part to policy failure.

The solution to this problem that the chapter suggests is to use different models for forecasting and policy advice. This represents a radical departure from the mainstream tradition, which envisaged a single model being used for both activities, but it does follow recent trends in UK and multi-country modelling. It also fits in with the need to make policy robust by examining alternative models. This chapter suggests that there are no serious practical problems involved in using separate models for forecasting and policy analysis, while the substantial advantage is that models will no longer represent an uneasy compromise between the needs of the two activities.

The limitations of this chapter should also be noted. Although the tensions between forecasting and policy advice described in the first section are general, the evidence presented is limited geographically (focusing on the UK and to some extent the US rather than Europe or elsewhere), and relies more than I would wish on my own experience of modelling within both government and quasi-academic institutions in the UK. In mitigation I would argue that the UK experience is particularly interesting, as the interaction between macromodelling and policy-making has at times been a close one. In addition, the reasons I give for the UK experience are not country specific and could apply elsewhere, and it would be a very interesting exercise to see if they do.

Acknowledgements

My thanks to conference participants, two anonymous referees, and Frank den Butter and Mary Morgan, for extensive comments on earlier drafts. The usual disclaimer applies.

Notes

1   A graphic if imprecise analogy is with doctors and heart attacks. If you had a heart attack, you would want a doctor to be as near as possible. We also generally accept that medical research can tell us some of the factors that make heart attacks more likely. In a recession, a macromodeller can give useful advice about how to get out of recession. In addition, they can give advice on policies that might make recessions less likely. However, to insist on the macromodeller being able to predict when a recession will occur is a bit like insisting that your doctor tells you exactly when you will have a heart attack, and discounting all his other advice when he refuses to do so.

2   I do not want to suggest that forecasters are only interested in numbers. It is often important to be able to justify forecasts using some plausible economic story to convince policy makers, and for that reason forecasts using theory-based econometric models (as opposed to purely data-based exercises) are likely to remain central in most institutions. In my own experience, however, forecasters are generally unwilling to sacrifice much predictive ability for the sake of theoretical consistency.

3   Of course particular individuals may have interests in both forecasting and policy analysis, but my argument need not necessarily involve conflicts between individuals, but between activities and how that influences model development.

4   Such a trade-off will not always be present in model selection, of course, as in some cases the best equation dominates in all departments. Where a trade-off does occur, it normally involves issues of degree: the equation that has a better short-term forecasting record will not be completely atheoretical, while the equation with the more desirable properties will not be completely hopeless at prediction. Nevertheless, an important trade-off remains.

5   Earlier debates within macromodelling also involved similar issues, but in some cases (such as the development of 'LSE econometrics' and the Neo-classical Synthesis itself) there appeared to be a progressive resolution of the conflict.

6   I doubt, however, if client pressure of this kind can completely account for the tendency for these models to grow. To take just one example, many macroeconomic models in the 1970s and 1980s contained a variety of different price variables. These different measures were not all required as outputs, and they were generally explained using similar equa-

tions. They did, however, allow the forecaster to incorporate detailed information (e.g. high seasonal food prices) which would improve a short-term forecast.

7 Of course not all models developed in the U.S. eschew rational expectations, particularly if we include multi-country models. However, as we note in Section 4, some of the more influential multicountry models developed in the U.S. are used for policy analysis and not used for forecasting.

8 The LBS model was not the only justification for the MTFS of course. Proponents relied on simple reduced forms linking money to prices: see Wren-Lewis 1984. However, these reduced forms carried weight partly because most existing UK models were incapable of providing credible simulations of the effect of changes in the money supply.

9 Martin Weale did develop a version of the National Institute's model which incorporated intertemporal consumption as part of the Meade project (Weale *et al.*, 1989). Significantly, however, this model was never used for forecasting.

10 An exception was Wren-Lewis *et al.*, 1993, which used the National Institute's model. However, the public discussion of this analysis did not involve comparing the Institute's model with other macroeconometric models, but with PPP.

11 At least one model proprietor used the critique of traditional trade equations provided by Krugman (1989) to suggest to me that, once again, the output of his own model could not be trusted.

12 See Darby *et al.*, (1999) and Wren-Lewis *et al.*, 1996. I also constructed the first version of the National Institute's world model, GEM (now NIGEM), but in this case the UK Treasury's world model was used as a template.

13 Not included in this group, for example, is OECD's Interlink, which is a larger model which does not incorporate rational expectations. Interlink is used as part of the OECD's forecasting process.

References

Bryant, R. C., Hooper, P. and Mann, C., 1993. *Evaluating Policy Regimes*. Brookings, Washington, D.C.

Clements, M. P. and Hendry, D. F., 1995. 'Macroeconomic forecasts and modelling', *Economic Journal* 105, 1001–13.

Church, K. B., 1993. 'Properties of the fundamental equilibrium exchange rate in models of the UK economy', *National Institute Economic Review* 141, 62–70.

Currie, D., 1985. 'Macroeconomic policy design and control theory – a failed partnership?', *Economic Journal* 95, 285–306.

Darby, J. and Ireland, J., 1994. Consumption, Forward Looking Behaviour and Financial Deregulation. International Centre for Macroeconomic Modelling Discussion Paper No. 20.

Darby, J., Ireland, J., Leith, C. and Wren-Lewis, S., 1999. 'Compact: A Rational Expectations, Intertemporal Model of the United Kingdom Economy', *Economic Modelling* 16, 1–52.

Deleau, M., Malgrange, P. and Muet, P. A., 1984, 'A study of short-run and long-run properties of macroeconometric models by means of an aggregative core model.' In: P. Malgrange and P. A. Muet (eds), *Contemporary Macroeconometric Modelling*. Basil Blackwell, Oxford.

Dornbusch, R., 1976. 'Expectations and exchange rate dynamics', *Journal of Political Economy* 84, 1161–76.

Fisher, P. G. and Whitley, J. D., 1998. Macroeconomic models at the Bank of England. Paper given at a NIESR/ESRC Conference, London.

Fisher, P. G., Tanna, S. K., Turner, D. S., Wallis, K. F. and Whitley, J. D., 1990. 'Econometric evaluation of the exchange rate in models of the UK economy, *Economic Journal*, 100, 1230–44.

Houthakker, H. and Magee, S. P., 1969. 'Income and price elasticities in world trade', *Review of Economics and Statistics* 51, 111–25.

Hughes Hallet, A. and Wren-Lewis, S. 1995. 'Is there life after the ERM: the UK experience', *Economie Internationale* 63, 31–54.

Kenway, P., 1994. *From Keynesianism to Monetarism: The evolution of UK Macroeconometric Models* (Routledge).

Krugman, P. R., 1989. 'Differences in income elasticities and trends in real exchange rates', *European Economic Review*, Vol. 33.

Mankiw, N., 1990. 'A Quick Refresher Course in Macroeconomics', *Journal of Economic Literature*, 28, 1645–1660.

Masson, P. R., 1988. 'Deriving small models from large models.' In: R. C. Bryant *et al.*, *Empirical Macroeconomics for Interdependent Economies*. Brookings Institution, Washington, D.C.

Masson, P. R., 1998. Macro-Modelling: Where do we stand? A Personal View. Paper given at a NIESR/ESRC Conference, London.

Masson, P. and Symansky, S., 1992. 'Evaluating the EMS and EMU Using Stochastic Simulations: Some Issues.' In: R. Barrell and J. Whitley (eds), *Macroeconomic Policy Cooperation in Europe*. SAGE.

Meese, R. A. and Rogoff, K., 1983. 'Empirical exchange rate models of the seventies: do they fit out of sample?', *Journal of International Economics* 14, 3–24.

Muellbauer, J. and Murphy, A., 1991. Measuring Financial Liberalisation and Modelling Mortgage Stocks and Equity Withdrawal. Mimeo, Nuffield College, Oxford.

Smith, R., 1994. 'The macromodelling industry: structure, conduct and performance.' In: S. Hall (ed.), *Applied Economic Forecasting Techniques*. Harvester/Wheatsheaf.

Turner, D., 1991. 'The determinants of the NAIRU response in simulations of the Treasury model', *Oxford Bulletin of Economics and Statistics* 53, 225–42.

Wallis, K. F., 1989. 'Macroeconomic forecasting: a study', *Economic Journal* 99, 28–61.

Wallis, K. F. and Whitley, J. D., 1991. 'Sources of error in forecasts and expectations: UK economic models, 1984–88', *Journal of Forecasting*, 10, 231–53.

Weale, M., Blake, A., Christodoulakis, N., Meade, J. and Vines, D., 1989. *Macroeconomic Policy: Inflation, Wealth and the Exchange Rate*. London: Unwin Hyman.

Whitley, J. D., 1997. Economic Models: a Flexible Friend for Policy Makers? Paper for the 10th Anniversary Congress of the Tinbergen Institute, Amsterdam. Published as 'Economic models and policy-making', *Bank of England Quarterly Bulletin*, 1997, May, 163–73.

Williamson, J., 1983. *The Exchange Rate System*. Institute for International Economics.

Wren-Lewis, S., 1984. 'Omitted variables in equations relating prices to money', *Journal of Applied Economics* 16, 483–96.

Wren-Lewis, S., 1993. Macroeconomic Theory and UK Macromodels: Another Failed Partnership?. International Centre for Macroeconomic Modelling Discussion Paper No. 20.

Wren-Lewis, S., Westaway, P. Soteri S. and Barrell, R., 1993. 'Evaluating the UK's Choice of Entry Rate into the ERM'. *Manchester School Money Study Group Conference*, 59, 1–22.

Wren-Lewis, S., Darby, J., Ireland, J. and Ricchi, O., 1996. 'The macroeconomic effects of fiscal policy: linking an econometric model with theory', *Economic Journal* 106, 543–59.

Part IV

The interaction process and institutional arrangements

Chapter 12

US monetary policy and econometric modeling: tales from the FOMC transcripts 1984–91*

Hali J. Edison and Jaime Marquez

This chapter uses the transcripts from the FOMC meetings to characterize the interactions between policy makers and macro models in the formulation of US monetary policy. We develop a taxonomy of these interactions and present two case studies. The first case focuses on the debate on the choice of monetary target and the second case focuses on the 1990/1991 recession. The analysis reveals that US monetary policy relies on models for information. Models give estimates of both the outlook and the response of the economy to policy changes. Models also evolve to recognize the changing context in which policy makers operate: exchange rate flexibility, financial deregulation, and international trade agreements.

JEL classifications: C5, E52

Our short-term models are poor but our intermediate-term models are really extraordinarily difficult to deal with. In these different and separate models, to which I think you are referring, are a lot of very interesting results. But they give you really quite different scenarios as to what would happen under various conditions. I think what we're dealing with is a very difficult conceptual problem of how our economy functions, especially in the growing world environment, under these different scenarios. I think what you succeeded in doing was getting some idea of dimension on some of the areas, but the range of error has to be awfully high. And I think all we can do is pick up one or two major notions.

Chairman Greenspan,
December 1989 FOMC meeting, p. 3.

1. Introduction

How is US monetary policy formulated? The Federal Reserve Act states the goals of monetary policy by specifying that, in conducting monetary policy, the Federal

*Reprinted from *Economic Modelling*, 15, Hali J. Edison and Jaime Marquez, 'US monetary policy and econometric modeling: tales from the FOMC transcripts 1984–1991', pp. 411–28, Copyright (1998), with permission from Elsevier Science.

Open Market Committee (FOMC) should 'promote effectively the goals of maximum employment, stable prices, and moderate long-term interest rates'. There is, however, considerable debate among economists about translating these goals into a coherent description of US monetary policy. One reason for the debate is the secrecy surrounding the details of how such policy is formulated. Detailed information about the FOMC meetings is necessary to understand the conduct of US monetary policy; the FOMC transcripts offer such information. These transcripts, however, have only recently been made available to the public and we use them here to examine interdependencies between econometric models and policy makers.[1]

To our knowledge, no one has used transcripts of past FOMC meetings to examine the formulation of monetary policy at the Fed. Several papers, including Reifschneider et al. (1997), Brayton et al. (1997), Duguay and Longworth (1998, Chapter 5 in this volume), and Whitley (1997), examine the development of models and their use in monetary policy at the Federal Reserve and at other central banks. Our chapter differs from previous work by drawing on FOMC transcripts and thus offering an unprecedented look at the role of econometric models in the policy-making process.

The chapter is organized as follows: Section 2 summarizes the structure of the FOMC and how models are used in the policy discussion. Section 3 provides a taxonomy of the interactions between policy makers and models. Section 4 deals with the role of models in the debate on disinflation. Section 5 examines the role of models in policy discussions regarding the 1990–91 recession. Section 6 gives our conclusions.

2. The Federal Reserve Board and the Federal Open Market Committee

2.1. Background

The Federal Reserve System, created in 1913, consists of the Board of Governors (Board) and 12 regional Federal Reserve Banks.[2] The Board of Governors consists of seven members appointed by the President and approved by the US Senate. These governors have 14-year appointments (with one appointment ending every two years), and one governor is the Board's Chairman and another is the Vice Chairman. The Federal Open Market Committee (FOMC) is made up of the Board of Governors, the president of the Federal Reserve Bank of New York, and presidents of four other Federal Reserve Banks who serve on a rotating basis. All of the presidents participate in the FOMC discussions but only the five presidents who are members of the Committee vote on policy decisions.

FOMC decision-making involves two stages: setting annual objectives for monetary and credit growth, and adopting an FOMC directive to give operating instructions to the trading desk of the Federal Reserve Bank of New York. These decisions are taken in formal meetings held eight times each year in Washington, D.C.

(When necessary, telephone consultations are used to amend the operating instructions.) In the February and July meetings, the FOMC adopts the annual objectives for money and credit growth which are reported to Congress.[3] At these meetings the staff reports on recent developments and presents both the macroeconomic outlook and its sensitivity to different monetary policies. The July meeting updates the forecast and extends it one year.

The Federal Reserve System conducts monetary policy using three tools: (1) open market operations – the buying and selling of US government securities in the open market to influence the level of reserves in the depository system; (2) reserve requirements – regarding the amount of funds that commercial banks and other depository institutions must hold in reserve against deposits; and (3) the discount rate – the interest rates charged to commercial banks and other depository institutions when they borrow reserves from a regional Federal Reserve Bank. The FOMC oversees open market operations, whereas the Board of Governors oversees reserve requirements and the discount rate.

2.2. The structure of FOMC meetings[4]

2.2.1. Preparations for the meeting

The FOMC policy process begins with the preparation of two key documents which are circulated before the meeting (see Lindsey, 1997): The *Greenbook* and the *Bluebook*. The *Greenbook* contains a detailed forecast of the US and foreign economies which serves as a baseline for the FOMC discussion; this forecast is the view of the Board's staff and not of the members of the FOMC. This forecast is referred to as a 'judgmental' projection because it does not rest solely on projections from any large-scale econometric model. The Federal Reserve staff's models play a role, however, by (1) providing a baseline from which staff develop their judgmental *Greenbook* forecasts; and in (2) constructing alternative scenarios. The *Bluebook* presents the staff's view on the behaviour of reserves, interest rates, and gives alternative paths for key monetary aggregates.

2.2.2. Presentations and discussions at the FOMC meeting

During the 1984–91 period, FOMC meetings began with a report by the manager for foreign exchange operations on developments and associated actions regarding foreign exchange operations. Then the manager for domestic open market operations reports on trading desk activity under the committee's instructions since the last meeting. The committee then discusses these reports and votes on approving them.[5]

Following these presentations, senior staff report on the economic outlook. The director of the Monetary Affairs division then comments on recent behavior of monetary and credit aggregates and reports on the alternative paths laid out for money growth in the *Bluebook*. Each alternative specifies a different growth rate for the key monetary aggregates and an associated range for the federal funds rate. Each presentation is followed by a discussion in which policy makers focus on those elements that suggest a stronger, or weaker, outcome than that projected by the Board staff. The committee's discussion gives rise to an FOMC directive over which FOMC members vote. The directive contains the instructions to the trading desk in New York for pursuing the policy objectives.

The entirety of the meeting is taped to produce a transcript which includes, as appendices, the material presented by the staff to the FOMC. Thus the transcripts are a complete official record regarding the conduct of monetary policy.

3. Taxonomy of the interactions between policy makers and model developments

The transcripts are simply a record of the discussion at the FOMC. Therefore we develop a taxonomy to interpret the record and assess the interactions between policy makers and model developers. There are no numbers, no test statistics, or other quantitative measures to judge the extent of interactions between policy makers and model builders. In our chapter, the written word rules, but we hope to minimize the effect of our choice of words by quoting extensively so as to give the reader an opportunity to disagree with our interpretation. Moreover, the transcripts are publicly available and thus our interpretation can be challenged. Our interpretation of the official record also benefits from our direct responsibilities in developing and maintaining the international models and using them for implementing simulation scenarios during the period under examination.

3.1. Policy makers influencing modeling

Policy makers can influence model-building through their requests for model respecification and we group them into three categories.

3.1.1. Direct requests

Policy makers are said to make direct requests for model respecification when they request that the model incorporate a certain feature: explaining a particular variable, modeling a particular transmission channel, or adding a particular country to the model. We did not find this sort of request in the FOMC transcripts.

One explanation for this absence is that the Board staff uses relatively standard models, embodying well-accepted economic relationships. Another, less obvious, explanation would involve FOMC members placing their direct requests for model changes outside FOMC sessions, which would not be reflected in the transcripts. Those requests, however, would have to be implemented at some point by the model managers and, as 'model managers' of the Multicountry model (MCM) over the period covered, we did not implement such requests, so we rule out this channel during the 1984–91 period. However, the absence of direct requests in these transcripts does not rule out their presence in future transcripts and, unless such a possibility can be satisfactorily ruled out, we allow for them in our taxonomy.

3.1.2. Persuasive requests

Policy makers are said to make persuasive requests for model respecification when their concerns involve modifying the model. As questions of this sort arise with some regularity, senior staff request research from economists to investigate these questions. Upon completion, the research is presented in a briefing to the Board and often is incorporated into the model(s).[6] Our analysis of the cost of disinflation (Section 4 below) offers an instance of persuasive requests.

3.1.3. Idiosyncratic requests

Policy makers are said to make idiosyncratic requests when their questions are best answered with tailor-made models. For example, the appreciation of the dollar during the 1980s generated requests for examining the predictive accuracy of alternative exchange-rate models (see Edison, 1991).

3.2. Models influencing policy-making

Models can influence the conduct of policy-making by providing information. We postulate three roles depending on the effect of that information on the decision process.

3.2.1. Institutional role

A model is said to have an institutional role when it provides routine information about the future state of the economy or about its response to hypothetical changes in assumptions. One example is senior staff's presentation on the state of the economy at the February/July FOMC meeting. Another example is the discussion of the *Bluebook* examining recent behavior of monetary aggregates and model-based paths for money growth. The role of models at the Fed may differ from the role of models at the other central banks.

3.2.2. Influential role

A model is said to have an influential role when its results are discussed extensively. Extensive discussions of model results normally take three or four pages of a 40-page document. Our analysis of the role of models during the 1990–91 recession (Section 5 below) reveals instances where the models exercised this role.

3.2.3. Decisive role

A model is said to have a decisive role on policy when information based on model properties alters the course that monetary policy would have taken in the absence of that information. As evidence of a decisive role one would like to see unambiguous statements from FOMC members indicating that the decision is solely based on the model or that, out of all considerations, model simulations were decisive. We did not find such statements. This category is, nevertheless, useful because one cannot rule out *a priori* such a role as new transcripts become available.

4. Case study 1: policy makers, models, and the price-stability debate

This section considers how the models developed by Board staff were used in a special briefing (December 1989) to address the question of whether price stability should be the main objective of monetary policy.[7]

4.1. Historical perspective

Congressman Neal, Chairman of the House Banking Subcommittee on Domestic Monetary Policy introduced legislation (H.J. RES 409, September 25, 1989) requiring

> ... that the Federal Open Market Committee of the Federal Reserve System shall adopt and pursue monetary policies to reduce inflation gradually in order to eliminate inflation by not later than 5 years from the date of this enactment of this legislation and shall then adopt and pursue monetary policies to maintain price stability.

To consider the ramifications of such a change for monetary policy, Vice Chairman (of the FOMC and New York Fed President) Corrigan proposed at the October 1989 FOMC meeting that the Board staff prepare for the Committee a special briefing on the question of achieving price stability in five years. In framing his proposal, Corrigan (p. 45) indicated that

> ... I'm not suggesting a forecast but alternative scenarios, problems, obstacles, and costs, so that we could really get a systematic feel of what kinds of problems would be involved in that kind of underlying policy goal.

This quote suggests that the models should be used to give 'a systematic feel', highlighting one role models play – influential.

The implementation of the special briefing faced two concerns. First, how to quantify the adjustment cost and its sensitivity to the time horizon. Second, how to ensure that the transmission channels embodied in the model did not assume, implicitly, the answer. As an example of the role of the model in addressing this question, Angell [F][8] (p. 47) notes that

> ... the model that we're going to use is going to be rather important. It seems to me that if you're going to use the Phillips curve trade-off model you're going to defeat the Neal Amendment.

Statements such as the one above suggest that these special briefings provide a venue to initiate model changes, an example of a persuasive request.

4.2. Highlights of the special presentation

The special FOMC presentation focused on identifying the macroeconomic consequences of stabilizing the price level by 1995 using monetary policy. To address the concerns of the FOMC on the choice of model, the Board staff used three different models in their presentation.

A first set of simulation results was based on the P-star model in which the equilibrium price level depends on M2, given velocity and output. The model suggests that prices adjust when the equilibrium price differs from the actual price level. The model, thus, can be used to solve for the path of M2 growth that yields an inflation rate close to zero. The results suggested that a five year horizon is too short a time period to eliminate inflation gradually.

A second set of simulation results was provided using an experimental multi-country system with forward-looking expectations – MX3. Two cases, differing in the degree to which monetary policy announcements are viewed as credible by workers and firms, were examined. In the case of high credibility, people alter their beliefs about the behavior of the central bank whereas in the weak credibility case they do not alter their beliefs. For both cases, the analysis assumed that the FOMC announces in advance its intention to slow money growth to rates consistent with attaining price stability by 1995.

A third set of simulation results was presented using the global model, FRB/GLOBAL, which combines the US model (MPS model) with models for foreign economies (MCM). The structure of the combined model is similar to MX3 except that expectations are adaptive, implying the absence of credibility (see Brayton et al., 1997 for a description of the evolution of modeling at the Federal Reserve).

To compare the costs of lowering the inflation rate across models, the presentation used the 'sacrifice' ratio – a measure of the amount of excess unemployment over a period associated with each one percentage point decline in inflation. The larger the sacrifice ratio, the greater the cost for each percentage point of disinflation. The sacrifice ratio generated by the FRB/GLOBAL model was 2.2 whereas the ratio generated by MX3 ranged from 0.2 for the strong credibility to 0.6 for the weak credibility. These results suggested that the more forward-looking and flexible expectations are, the lower the costs of disinflation will be.

Costs of Achieving Zero Inflation Under Alternative Scenarios

		Cumulative Losses 1989–95		
		Shortfall of GNP from potential[1] (percent) (1)	Excess of unemployment over natural rate[2] (percent) (2)	Sacrifice[3] ratio (3)
1.	Zero inflation base case	20	8-1/2	2.2
2.	With weaker dollar	24-1/2	9-1/2	2.5
3.	With higher oil prices	25-1/2	10-1/2	2.7
4.	With unchanged full–employment budget deficit	20	8	2.1

1. Calculated as the cumulative percentage gap between potential GNP and actual GNP from 1989 to 1995 .
2. Calculated as the cumulative gap between the actual unemployment rate and the natural rate (assume to be 5-1/2 percent) from 1989 to 1995.
3. Calculated as the cumulative excess of unemployment over the natural rate divided by 3.9 (the reduction in inflation between 1989 and 1995).

Exhibit 12.1 Source: Material for Special Presentation to the Federal Open Market Committee, 18–19 December, 1989; Exhibit 14.

To give the FOMC some indication of how the sacrifice ratio would differ if economic conditions became less favorable, three alternative scenarios were considered: a weaker dollar, higher oil prices, and higher budget deficit. Relative to the base case, achieving zero inflation with the weaker dollar increases the loss of output and the sacrifice ratio (Exhibit 12.1). Losses in the scenario yielded results similar to those of the base case.

4.3. Highlights of the policy discussion

The issue that received the most attention is the sensitivity of the cost of disinflation to both the policy horizon and the degree/impact of credibility. Specifically, Parry [F] (see endnote 8) asks (p. 3):

> I'd like to ask an opinion about the credibility issue. If one had a Neal resolution, and in addition to that had publicly announced some kind of multiyear path on something such as either nominal GNP or money, do you think that that would have a significant impact on credibility? And, therefore, would that lead you more in the direction of faster adjustment than was incorporated in the model?

No single test can provide an unambiguous answer to this question. Thus Stockton [S] (see endnote 8) (pp. 3–4) replies:

> My own view is that it would be difficult to expect an immediate adjustment and a response to that. If you look back at inflation expectations survey data, for example, in 1979 there wasn't an immediate reaction to the announcement of a change in Federal Reserve operating procedures . . .

With respect to the sensitivity of the sacrifice ratio to the horizon, Angell [F] (p. 4) asks:

> . . . Since we're already getting something we don't know about, maybe we might as well go ahead and do another 5 years because we're only doing more of that which we don't know about; and thereby, we would have a base case movement to zero inflation in 1995 and then [we could] look at the adjustment to the natural rate of unemployment. And that would also give us an opportunity to look at the current account deficit . . .

Though not transparent from Angell's remark, the question of horizon is important because the costs and benefits of disinflation do not materialize at the same pace. Hoskins [F] makes this observation (p. 8):

> . . . Having said all that, one observation I'd make, which I think Governor Angell was getting at, is that we are measuring the cost of reducing inflation. If one is trying to make a decision about whether or not it's worthwhile doing, one needs to measure the benefits of having a zero rate of inflation – that is, in the next 5 years out or 10 years – and then compare that with the cost of the transition, because many of us believe there are some gains to maintaining price stability in terms of economic performance.

But Melzer [F] places the issue in its influential context (p. 13):

> . . . what would happen to the sacrifice ratio if the time frame were longer? I think I know what would happen to the expectational effects and the credibility and so forth. But do you have any sense of that? If you made it 10 years instead of 5, does the sacrifice ratio come down materially?

Thus this record reveals that the model had an influential role in the policy process by providing estimates of the sensitivity of the cost of achieving price stability. Moreover, the record contains neither evidence contradicting the models' predictions nor remarks about using methods not based on models. The overall position is best summarized by Black [F] (pp. 21–2):

> . . . I know no one would have a lot of confidence in the econometric measures that one would use to determine what the costs of eliminating inflation are,

but what to me comes out as most important is the qualitative differences between these various approaches. The backward-looking model, which is the traditional way we've looked at it here, makes the cost very, very high. But if we can assume that we have something like rational expectations and forward-looking expectations and if we can assume that we have some kind of credibility and strength in that credibility, then the cost becomes considerably less . . .

In the end, the Neal Resolution was not passed in Congress and the Federal Reserve Act of 1978 remains relevant. Nevertheless, the sensitivity of the results to both credibility and policy makers' emphasis on long-term goals called for models with forward-looking expectations. This capability, available on experimental basis in 1989, is now operational in 1997 (see Brayton *et al.*, 1997; Levin *et al.*, 1997). This modification of the models provides an example in which policy makers exerted a persuasive influence in the respecification of the models.

5. Case study 2: policy makers, models, and the 1990–91 recession

From 18 December, 1990 to 20 December, 1991, the discount rate declined by 350 basis points – one of the largest one-year declines in the discount rate in the post-war period. During 1991, policy makers faced: a military conflict in the Persian Gulf; the strains stemming from the disintegration of the Soviet economy; the international ramifications of German re-unification; and a recession in the United States. This section examines the role models played in this decline in interest rates.

5.1. Phase I: December 1990–January 1991

The December 1990 FOMC meeting was concerned about the sluggish growth rates for the various monetary aggregates as well as the relatively small growth rates predicted for the next two years. In that context, M2 was viewed as the key policy indicator and, as the following exchange reveals, the institutional role of the model was key to the discussion:

> Mr Mullins [F] (p. 28): What interest rate elasticities do we assume for money demand, roughly speaking?
> Mr Kohn [S] (p. 28): I can give you some numbers on what if the funds rate changes by x basis points, that kind of thing.
> Mr Mullins [F] (p. 28): Yes.
> Mr Kohn [S] (p. 28): A 50 basis point decrease in the funds rate – now this is a quarterly average, so it won't show up the way it would in the monthly numbers – gets you about $\frac{3}{4}$ of a point for the year, but it's loaded into the first and particularly the second quarters.

Just prior to the discussion for the vote on whether to cut the discount rate, Chairman Greenspan [F] states his views (p. 34):

> ... I would suspect the two percentage point difference that Don [Kohn, S] is getting between the growth of M2 and that in his model may in fact reflect something we don't measure – namely, the inclination of individuals to hold liquid deposits which in the previous calculations are all presumed to be risk free ...

This remark suggests that the model, in its institutional role, estimates the systematic behavior of the economy which allows policy makers to formulate hypotheses about the unsystematic behavior and thus to craft the associated response. Specifically, when Greenspan identifies the gap between the data and the model's predictions as arising from individuals' propensity to hold risky assets, he is formulating a hypothesis which can then be used as the basis for a discussion on lowering the discount rate. The discount rate was lowered by 50 basis points immediately after the December 1990 FOMC meeting.

Immediately before the February 1991 meeting, the Board decided to lower the discount rate by 50 basis points due to the worsening of the credit situation as envisaged in the FOMC directive of December 1990.

5.2. Phase II: February–April

After lowering the interest rate by what was thought then to be an aggressive magnitude, FOMC members devoted the February 1991 meeting, which sets monetary targets for the year, to a thorough examination of the effects of past policies. Exhibit 12.2 displays the outlook presented at that meeting and how it would change under alternative policy options. To put these results in perspective, Prell [S] (Appendix, p. 26) argues:

> ... Admittedly, these scenarios are quite arbitrary constructs, but they do seem relevant in light of the differences between the staff and FOMC forecasts that I presented earlier. I hope that, in combination with the model simulations presented in the Bluebook, they will at least give you some rough indication of the sensitivity of the economy to your policy decisions.

This remark illustrates the sense in which models exert an influential role. The design of the different scenarios are left to the staff, but the ultimate decisions remain with the FOMC. Interest rates were kept unchanged as committee members saw the economic situation as marked by 'heightened uncertainties' and that not enough time had elapsed for the effects of the lower interest rates to be felt in the economy.

At the March meeting there continued to be uncertainty about the outlook for the economy and the FOMC examined another round of model results. The major question related to the extent to which the effects of monetary policy could be offset by the

WHAT IF THE FED WERE TO EASE SUBSTANTIALLY IN THE NEAR TERM?

SCENARIO 1:   FOMC judges, _correctly_, that the economy is "one percent weaker" than Greenbook suggests; it lowers fed funds rate to achieve the same output level in late 1992 as in the Greenbook.

SCENARIO 2:   FOMC judges, _incorrectly_, that economy is weaker than Greenbook suggests; it eases now, but realizes by midyear that the Greenbook was right and reverses course to avoid seriously overshooting the Greenbook output path in 1992.

	1991	1992
Real GNP, Q4/Q4		
Greenbook	1.9	2.6
Scenario 1	1.6	2.9
Scenario 2	2.3	2.2
Unemployment rate, Q4		
Greenbook	6.1	6.0
Scenario 1	6.2	6.0
Scenario 2	6.0	6.0
CPI, Q4/Q4		
Greenbook	3.9	3.9
Scenario 1	3.9	3.8
Scenario 2	3.9	4.0

	1991				1992			
	Q1	Q2	Q3	Q4	Q1	Q2	Q3	Q4
Federal funds rate								
Greenbook	6.75	6.75	6.75	6.75	6.75	6.75	6.75	6.75
Scenario 1	6.25	5.0	5.0	5.0	5.25	5.5	6.0	6.75
Scenario 2	6.25	5.0	6.25	7.5	8.0	7.75	7.25	6.75

Exhibit 12.2 Source: Material for Staff Presentation to the Federal Open Market Committee, 5 February, 1991; Chart 17.

effects of the dollar appreciation that had been taking place in the first quarter of 1991. Specifically, Siegman [S] (Appendix, p. 4) reports that

> In order to offset the impact of a 10 per cent appreciation on real GNP and bring the economy back on track by the end of the year, the staff's model suggests that US short-term interest rates would need to decline by about 100–125 basis points by the end of 1992, depending on the pace of offsetting the impact on GNP.

By estimating the trade-off between interest rates and exchange rates consistent with a given path of GDP, the statement reveals an instance in which the model has an influential role. Once again, interest rates were left unchanged.

However, before the next FOMC meeting on 30 April the discount rate was lowered by 50 basis points. Explaining the decision to the non-Board members of the FOMC, Chairman Greenspan [F] argued (in a telephone conference call dated 30 April, p. 1):

> ... In summary, I would say that, in line with the FOMC discussion on how events might or might not materialize, clearly what is happening at this stage is a slowing in the rate of decline but virtually no useful evidence in the order books or in the advance indicators of activity that suggests we are coming out of this [recession] any time in the immediate future ...

Greenspan's statement suggests a disappointment with the speed of recovery or a reaction to the realization that earlier forecasts were optimisitic. Though the statement does not provide unambiguous evidence of a decisive role for models, the February FOMC meeting examined model simulations (see Exhibit 12.2) contemplating further interest-rate reductions should the economy appear weaker than what was forecasted. Though no formal statistical test exists to discriminate among the various pieces of information, the transcripts provide the closest evidence of a model exerting a decisive influence.

5.3. Phase III: May–August

The discount rate remained unchanged from May to end August. Nevertheless, there are plenty of examples of the interaction of the FOMC and models.

At the July 1991 meeting, when members can update the targets for the monetary aggregates, attention was focused on the extent to which movements in the dollar were offsetting movements in interest rates. Specifically, Exhibit 12.3 reports the sensitivity of the forecast to factors perceived to be contributing to the relatively slow recovery of US economic activity: the appreciation of the dollar and the weakening of foreign economic activity. One scenario that was not included among the charts, but that was discussed in the staff presentation, involved the trade-off between interest rates and exchange rates. Specifically, Truman [S] (Appendix, p. 9) reports:

> ... We tried a modification of the February dollar scenario in our econometric models. In it, the dollar remained at its February level, but the federal funds rate was adjusted to leave the path of US real GNP essentially the same as in the baseline forecast. Our models suggest that to achieve this result, the federal funds rate today would have to be about 130 basis points higher now and increase another 20 basis points or so over the course of 1992. Given all the factors that can affect our forecasts, this correspondence of judgmental and model-based results is remarkably close. In essence, it can be said that the decline in the funds rate has offset the unexpected strength of the dollar.

Alternative Scenarios

Baseline: Greenbook forecast extended through 1993; M2 growth at 5-1/2
                             percent in 1992 and 1993.

February Dollar: Dollar at the level projected in February, almost 15 percent
                             below level now projected; federal funds rate unchanged from
                             baseline.

Weak Foreign Growth: Foreign growth remains at about 1-1/2 percent; federal funds rate
                             unchanged from baseline.

	1991	1992	1993
Percent change, Q4 to Q4			
Real GNP, U.S.			
Baseline	1-1/2	2-3/4	2-1/2
February Dollar	2-1/2	4-1/4	5
Weak Foreign Growth	1-1/2	2	1
GNP Prices			
Baseline	4	3-1/2	3-1/4
February Dollar	4-1/2	4-1/2	5
Weak Foreign Growth	4	3-1/4	2-1/2
Real GNP, Foreign *			
Baseline	2-1/4	3-1/2	3-1/2
February Dollar	2-1/4	3-1/4	4
Weak Foreign Growth	1-1/2	1-1/2	1-1/2
Q4 Level, $ billions			
Current Account			
Baseline	-45	-52	-56
February Dollar	-37	-20	-32
Weak Foreign Growth	-48	-73	-95

* Average of 22 industrial and 8 developing countries weighted by bilateral shares in U.S. non-agricultural exports.

Exhibit 12.3 Source: Material for Staff Presentation to the Federal Open Market
Committee, 2 July, 1991; Chart 14.

This statement suggests that, based on the model, the lack of recovery expected
by the FOMC was due to an unexpected appreciation of the dollar and the influential role of the model in its implications for interest rates is clear: they would have
to decline again to offset this unexpected appreciation.

Interest in quantifying the role of the dollar in the slowing of economic recovery
using model-based results reappears in the 20 August meeting. Specifically, Parry
[F] (p. 18) asks:

The assumption made in the forecast with regard to the dollar is that it remains
constant. Is that an exogenous determination? And if it is, what, for example,
would the MPS model give for the dollar and what would be its implications?

To this question, Truman [S] (p. 18) responds:

> Well, viewing the forecast as a whole, it is not an assumption that is part of the projection process. It is endogenous to our outlook for interest rates here, which is where we start from, our outlook for interest rates abroad, and what else is going on in the forecast . . .

Though Truman does not report the estimates from the MPS model, he indicates:

> . . . The MPS model has a slightly different exchange rate equation than most others, none of which does very well . . .

The remarks from Truman illustrate the manner in which persuasive requests from policy makers lead to changes in the model. Specifically, addressing the adequacy of exchange-rate models led to permanent modifications in the exchange-rate equations of the operational models (see Edison and Pauls, 1993).

5.4. Phase IV: September–December

The Board lowered the discount rate by 50 basis points on 13 September. The discussion motivating that reduction relied only on data developments and not on model predictions. Nevertheless, the magnitude of the reduction in interest rates matches closely the one that, at the February meetings, was reported as being needed (Exhibit 12.2, scenario 1) to raise output in 1992 to the level forecasted in February of 1991.

The discount rate declined again on 6 November by 50 basis points. Prior to this date, the FOMC had two scheduled meetings and a conference call. The first of the scheduled meetings (1 October 1991) revealed continuing concern about the extent to which the unexpected behavior of the dollar was offsetting the easing of monetary policy. Prell [S] (p. 8) notes:

> Ted Truman presented an interesting econometric result – I think it was in the chart show – which indicated in essence that to a first approximation the decline in interest rates that had occurred since the beginning of this year had effectively offset the surprise we have seen in the dollar, which we had not anticipated to appreciate as it did. Thus, if you looked at where output would be sometime out in 1992, these were compensating forces . . .

Thus models are playing an influential role by identifying the factors that account for the gap between the functioning of the economy and the expectations of the FOMC. Indeed, the initial decision to lower interest rates implicitly relied on an exchange-rate response that would, if anything, accentuate the expansion of income. The dollar, contrary to expectations, appreciated and the models were then used to quantify the resulting offsetting effect on income.

Model estimates are clearly not the only input to the policy formation process but no other analytical tool could provide a quantitative estimate of the extent to which different forces in the economy offset changes in monetary policy. In this regard, Chairman Greenspan expressed his views in the 30 October Conference Call (p. 1):

> ... I've concluded from this myself that we probably have to do something further, but I'm uncomfortable about a variety of different alternatives. What I'd like to do is to get a sense of this Committee with respect to: (1) an update on how all of you view your various Districts and the nation as a whole; and (2) any suggestions you might wish to offer regarding various alternative ways we might move. For example, we could, were we to choose to do so, do a 25 basis point reduction in the federal funds rate today. We could wait perhaps until Friday and do a [cut in the] discount rate and 50 basis points [on the federal funds rate]; we could wait until after the FOMC meeting and do either or both of those; ...

Changes in interest rates were delayed until the next meeting. That meeting revealed continued disappointment between expectations and performance. A question posed by Syron [F] (p. 2) succinctly summarized this disappointment:

> Mike, I have two questions. Is it fair to say, looking at the probability distribution in your forecast now, that you still would consider the negative tail fatter, even after your revision?

Some of that disappointment might have been 'home grown' as Lindsey [S] (Appendix, p. 3) indicates:

> ... Indeed, when we prepared the previous bluebook, we concluded that the near-term sensitivity of M2 to changes in short-term interest rates was lower than we had previously thought. We did so in recognition of the heightened importance of partially offsetting movements in the yield curve ...

The discount rate was lowered 50 basis points on 6 November. This timing, however, was influenced by considerations generally neglected in theoretical papers but crucial for actual decisions: the timing of quarterly auctions and the meetings of Federal Reserve Banks Presidents with their respective boards.

The last decrease in the discount rate in 1991 took place on 20 December. At the FOMC meeting, Truman [S] (Appendix, p. 4) offered a 'worst case' scenario:

> ... We have estimated the effects on our outlook for the US external sector of a 'worst case' scenario in which there is little or no growth abroad in the near term and only a weak recovery in 1992, producing growth over the four quarters of next year about 1 per cent lower than we are now projecting. Our

model simulation suggests that such a scenario would chop almost $\frac{3}{4}$ of a percentage point from the level of US real GDP by the fourth quarter of 1992 ...

Once again, for meetings that involve absorbing substantial amounts of data, conjectures, and estimates, one cannot tell unambiguously the weight of model simulations in the crafting of the FOMC directive. Did the results of the model change monetary policy or did it merely provide empirical support for decisions that would have been taken anyway? Though our reading of the record does not suggest a clear-cut answer to that question, we do not see how a reading of the record would deny an influential role of the models in the interest-rate reductions of 1991.

6. Conclusions

This chapter shows that the conduct of US monetary policy relies on models for information. Models give estimates of both the outlook and the response of the economy to policy changes. Just as clear, models evolve to recognize changes in the context in which policy makers operate – exchange rate flexibility, financial deregulation, and international trade agreements. What has not been clear until now, however, is how this model-based information gets channeled to policy makers and how models evolve to recognize the character of the questions faced by policy makers? This chapter examines these questions with the transcripts from the FOMC meetings and provides an insiders' look at the formulation of monetary policy.

The transcripts indicate that models are shaped by the judgment of policy makers. Indeed policy makers can influence model-building through their requests for the models to address issues central to the conduct of monetary policy. The debate on how to conduct monetary policy to attain price stability led to modifications of the treatment of expectations in the models (Section 4).

The transcripts also indicate that, as informational devices, models play an institutional role, as reflected in the regular reporting of forecasts and their sensitivity to hypothetical changes in policies (Section 2.2). Models also exert an influential role by estimating the systematic component of economy and allowing policy makers to craft policy responses to address the unsystematic component. This role, previously undocumented in the literature, is reported in our analysis of the 350 basis points decline in interest rates in 1991 (Section 5).

On the whole, we conclude that far from being mechanistic providers of policy constraints, models shape and are shaped by the judgment of policy makers, at least in the conduct of monetary policy in the United States from 1984 to 1991.

Acknowledgements

Edison and Marquez are senior economists in the Division of International Finance at the Federal Reserve Board. Comments from Joseph Coyne, Frank den Butter, William Helkie, Dale Henderson, Karen Johnson, David Lindsey, Mary Morgan,

Adrian Pagan, Peter Tinsley, and Ted Truman are gratefully acknowledged; Molly Wetzel cross-checked our quotations and Katherine Vanderhook provided editorial comments. This chapter was written for the Conference on Empirical Models and policy-making at the Tinbergen Institute, Amsterdam, 14–16 May 1997. We also thank the participants of the conference for many useful comments, especially Ralph Bryant and Ken Wallis. The views in this chapter are the responsibility of the authors and should not be interpreted as reflecting the views of the Board of Governors of the Federal Reserve System or other members of its staff.

Notes

1 On 18 May, 1976 the FOMC voted to discontinue its policy of releasing to the public a detailed memorandum of discussion of its meetings. This was a controversial decision at the time, but was motivated by the threat of 'Sunshine Legislation' – which called for prompt public disclosure of government meetings – and a lawsuit challenging the 45-day delay in releasing the domestic policy directive. Since 1976, the Federal Reserve has issued 'policy record' or 'minutes', which is released 6 or 7 weeks after each meeting, a couple of days after it is approved at the next FOMC meeting. This document is a summary of the substance of the discussion at the meeting and does not indicate the individual FOMC members' policy position. In the autumn of 1993 in the course of conducting hearings, the House Banking committee learned that the FOMC continued to tape FOMC meetings in their entirety and retain transcriptions of the tapes. The Federal Reserve has issued, with a 5-year lag, transcripts of the FOMC meetings. At present the years 1984–91 have been issued [see Board of Governors of the Federal Reserve System (1984–91)]. (See the Committee on Banking, Finance and Urban Affairs, 1994.)

2 For more details see Board of Governors of the Federal Reserve System (1994).

3 This reporting follows The Full Employment and Balanced Growth Act (Humphrey–Hawkins Act) of 1978. This Act specifies that each February the Federal Reserve must announce publicly its objectives for growth in money and credit and that at mid-year (July) it must review its objectives and revise them if appropriate.

4 For more details see Meek (1982).

5 Currently, FOMC meetings begin with one review of both foreign and domestic financial developments and the actions of the trading desk. This report is usually given by the Manager of the System Open Market Account at the Federal Reserve Bank of New York.

6 Examples of such briefings over 1984–91 include Long-Term Perspective on External Position of the US Economy (May, 1984); Economic and Monetary Policy Issues raised by the Weakening of the Dollar (November, 1985); Treatment of Special Situation and Seasonal Borrowing in Desk Operations (October, 1987); Description of the P-Star Model (November, 1988); The Effects of Large Oil Price Increase (August, 1990).

7 See Mayes and Razzak (1998, Chapter 7 in this volume) for a discussion on price stability and the interaction of models and policy makers at the Reserve Bank of New Zealand.

8 An F in brackets denotes an FOMC member; an S in brackets denotes a staff member.

References

Board of Governors of the Federal Reserve System, 1994. *The Federal Reserve System: Purposes and Functions*, 8th ed. Board of Governors of the Federal Reserve System, Washington, D.C.

Board of Governors of the Federal Reserve System, 1984–91. (various volumes) Transcripts of the Federal Open Market Committee Board of Governors of the Federal Reserve System, Washington, D.C.

Brayton, F., Levin, A., Tryon, R. and Williams, J., 1997. 'The Evolution of Macro Models at the Federal Reserve Board.' *Carnegie Rochester Conference on Public Policy*, December, 47, 43–82.

Committee on Banking, Finance and Urban Affairs, 1994. The Federal Reserve's 17-year Secret: with Examples of Federal Open Market Committee transcripts. 103rd Congress 2nd Session, Washington, D.C.

Duguay, P., Longworth, D., 1998. 'Macroeconomic models and policymaking at the Bank of Canada', *Econ. Model.* 15, 357–75 (Chapter 5 in this volume).

Edison, H., 1991. 'Forecast performance of exchange rate models revisited', *Appl. Econ.* 23, 187–96.

Edison, H. and Pauls, D., 1993. 'A re-assessment of the relationship between real exchange rates and real interest rates: 1974–1990.' *J. Monet. Econ.* 31, 165–87.

Levin, A., Rogers, J. and Tryon, R., 1997. 'Evaluating international policy with the Federal Reserve's global model', *Fed. Reserve Bull.* 83, 797–810.

Lindsey, D., 1997. How Monetary Policy is Made in Practice in the United States. Board of Governors of the Federal Reserve System, Mimeo.

Mayes, D. G. and Razzak, W. A., 1998. 'Transparency and accountability: Empirical models and policy-making at The Reserve Bank of New Zealand,' *Econ. Model.* 15, 377–94 (Chapter 7 in this volume).

Meek, P., 1982. *U.S. Monetary Policy and Financial Markets.* Federal Reserve Bank of New York, New York.

Reifschneider, D., Stockton, D. and Wilcox, D., 1997. Econometric Models and the Monetary Policy Process. *Carnegie Rochester Conference on Public Policy*, December, 47, 1–38.

Whitley, J., 1997. Economic Models – a Flexible Friend for Policy Makers? Paper for the 10th Anniversary Congress of the Tinbergen Institute, Amsterdam. Published as 'Economic models and policy-making', *Bank of England Quarterly Bulletin*, 1997, May, 163–73.

Chapter 13

Economic models and economic policy: what economic forecasters can do for government

Robert Evans

This chapter examines the interaction between economic models and policy-making through a case study based on the UK government's Panel of Independent Forecasters. The Panel of Forecasters met for the first time in February 1993 and was the government's response to the policy vacuum created by the decision to leave the European Exchange Rate Mechanism (ERM) in September 1992. The focus of the chapter is on the policy recommendations made by the Panel of Independent Forecasters, their foundations in economic modelling methodologies and their links to wider socio-economic issues. It is argued that, because of their ambiguity, economic models have the potential to legitimate a range of possible social futures, thereby re-politicizing economic policy by re-connecting it to wider social and moral debates within society. As a result, the uncritical use of any single macroeconomic model is likely to stifle rather than encourage thought and limit debates about economic policy to questions about preferences. The chapter concludes by considering the implications of this for the making of economic policy and argues that citizens and policy makers need to re-think their own roles in order to actively (re)shape social institutions, structures and policy choices.

JEL classifications: A11, A14, E61, E65

I. Introduction

This chapter presents a sociological perspective on the use of knowledge generated by macroeconomic models in policy-making.[1] It is not therefore about the institutions which support and produce macroeconomic modelling research but about the social processes through which economic knowledge is produced, validated and used. My empirical window on this interaction between economic models, knowledges and policies, is the UK government's Panel of Independent Forecasters. Appointed to advise the Chancellor of the Exchequer after the UK's exit from the European Exchange Rate Mechanism (ERM) in 1992, the Panel of Independent Forecasters brought together a diverse group of economic forecasters and asked them to produce policy recommendations for the Chancellor.

Although the sociology of scientific knowledge has typically focused on the debates which take place *between* scientists, it is important to remember that scientific knowledge claims often form the basis of interventions in the world. From this perspective, it is the interaction between scientists such as economists and policy makers that is important and interesting.[2] However, the success of this process – the 'translation' of policy makers needs into economic modelling procedures and vice versa – depends critically on economic agents accepting the 'roles' specified for them within the macroeconomic models. In other words, for economic analysis to be effective as policy advice it will need to be credible not only as economics but also as a social and political strategy for the future. In this way, a successful forecast has the character of a self-fulfilling prophecy – the various economic agents behaved as expected and so the actual out-turn matched the expected outcome.[3] If this is not the case, then presumably forecasts are right only by chance. Examples of the way in which the models suggest behaviours include: policy makers adopting certain 'reaction functions'; workers agreeing certain wage agreements or productivity targets; non-workers accepting certain benefit levels and so on. If these groups refuse (or are otherwise unable) to become the 'intended agents' postulated by the modellers, then the analysis and recommendations will be difficult (if not imposs-ible) to apply in practice.[4]

The aim of the chapter is to illustrate this argument by examining the range of theories and models which lay behind policy advice given by the Panel of Independent Forecasters in 1993 and the range of socio-economic futures which their models claimed to legitimate. Although, as elsewhere in this volume,[5] it is accepted that a diversity of models is a 'good thing,' this is not because policies pro-duced in this way are more 'robust' in the way that economists typically understand the term. Rather, it is argued that using a plurality of models enables a decision-making process which is able to be reflexive about the kinds of human subjects and social institutions which it seeks to enrol. By this I mean that using a range of eco-nomic models and experts problematizes the ways in which different economic models (re)draw the boundaries around policy issues (e.g. by (re)defining responsibilities, channels of influence or transmission mechanisms in different ways). However, this sort of expert deconstruction is not a negative consequence of the Panel's intellectual diversity. Instead, because it allows the articulation of new knowledges about the interests, values and assumptions which underpin the scient-ific representations of the economic models, this expert debate actively promotes an understanding of the 'interpretative flexibility' of economic data which is as import-ant for policy-making as 'getting the facts right'.[6]

However, it may well be that economists, trying to establish their own preferred interpretation of the available data, are not the best people to produce such reflexive insights.[7] Indeed, in practice, the Panel of Forecasters did not serve this function at all and tended, instead, to emphasize where it agreed. Whilst this had the advantage of providing a single piece of policy advice, the cost was that the Panel failed to communicate the diversity and excitement of its economic (and econometric) models. This is important because the Panel had the expertise to legitimate shifting debates about economic policy towards more inclusive agendas of social, political and moral responsibilities.[8] Indeed, their models suggested that a range of policies had the potential to make sense as economics. By choosing to resolve and minimize their differences in private, the Panel did little to encourage political and public debate about the wider social dimensions of economic policies – for example, the relative costs and benefits of European Monetary Union. Instead, perhaps bounded by the concept of 'long-run equilibrium', the policy recommendations remained narrowly focused on the (national) economic orthodoxies of fiscal sustainability and so the openness of the economic future was lost.[9]

The chapter is structured as follows. In the next section, I provide some background information on the economic events which led to the inauguration of the Panel and set the policy agenda for 1993. Next I outline the theoretical and interpretative models which the Panel members used to analyse and understand the economy, focusing on the 'big picture' and identifying two main sets of theories. Section 4 looks at a particular application of these models and theories – forecasting and producing policy advice in October 1993, and examines how the general (conceptual, but also empirical) models were applied in a particular instance. The analysis highlights the wide range of views which can underpin economic policy choices and shows how consensus and convergence are achieved, despite the uncertainty of econometric criteria. Section 5 compares the recommendations made by the Panel with the policies announced by the Chancellor and shows how, perhaps as a result of the Panel's decisions about presentation, issues which they had identified as important failed to make the policy agenda. In conclusion I argue that the value of economic models (and modellers) lies not in their ability to quantify, but in their potential to provide a level epistemological basis for the range of social, political and moral theories which can be used to frame economic policy and that citizens and policy makers need to re-think their own roles if they are to actively shape the economic future.

2. The Panel of Independent Forecasters and UK economic policy

To understand fully the Chancellor of the Exchequer's decision to appoint the Panel of Forecasters at the end of 1992, it is necessary to go back to the economic cycle which preceded it. In the mid-to-late 1980s, the UK economy experienced strong economic growth, particularly in consumers' expenditure, and a rising rate of inflation. In an attempt to slow this boom and contain inflation, the government, with the support of a significant proportion of the UK economics profession, took the decision in October 1990 to formally join the ERM and fix the exchange rate between sterling and other European currencies. Later, as the boom turned to bust, the government found itself presiding over what turned out to be a sustained contraction in economic output. Unfortunately for the government, the seriousness of the situation was not clear at the time because, as with the boom phase of the economic cycle, the recession was not forecast particularly well.[10] Thus, although some economists believed that the recession was being prolonged by the need to maintain the exchange rate, others were forecasting its imminent 'end'. Eventually, in September 1992 (approximately two and a half years after the recession began), the UK government left the ERM and allowed the exchange rate to fall, thus permitting further cuts in the interest rate and hopefully stimulating some sort of recovery.

Although popular with its supporters, the government's decision also had a significant cost – the UK no longer had an economic policy. Moreover, a large proportion of economics community in the UK had backed the ERM policy and were similarly at a loss. The Panel of Independent Forecasters were introduced into this political vacuum as a way of bolstering the credibility of economic policy-making and rebuilding the reputation of the government. As Alan Budd, the Chief Secretary to the Treasury explained:

> Associated with [leaving the ERM] was the feeling that the Treasury in particular had produced appallingly bad forecasts and that this was one of the reasons why we had made this ERM mistake ... So what the Chancellor does to, if you like, appease the wrath of those people who say he ought to be sacked ... and also that the Treasury forecasters should be sacked ... [is to say] 'Well, actually we never paid that much attention to our forecasts, and it isn't the only thing we do. But, just to demonstrate the extent to which we do take account of outside views, I shall have this Panel of Independent Forecasters and I shall let them supplement what my own guides tell us.'[11]

This Panel of Independent Forecasters, which met for the first time in February 1993, was required to produce three reports a year. The idea was that they would act as a public check on the Treasury by providing a yardstick against which any policies announced by the Chancellor could be measured. The Panel itself was composed of seven economists and its members, who were all regular economic forecasters, were deliberately chosen to reflect a broad spectrum of views, backgrounds and analyses. Theoretically they ranged from traditional Keynesianism, through (mainstream) neo-Keynesianism to New Classical economics and Friedman-style monetarism. Institutionally, the Panel members worked in organizations ranging from universities to merchant banks, although most had previously been involved in giving policy advice.[12] In practice, especially after the initial novelty had worn off, the Panel had a fairly low public profile and the time its members were expected to devote to each meeting was quite small – each report was the product of two meetings (each of which lasted for one day) – and the members were free to publish their own forecasts and analysis at other times. The Panel and its role are summarized in Figure 13.1.

The Panel's meetings and reports covered the usual elements of economic forecasting – assumptions, domestic demand, net trade, prices, unemployment, monetary conditions, and so on. The published reports included a discussion of the main factors affecting the economy and short-term forecasts covering the main economic indicators for up to two years ahead. Medium-term projections covering a five-year horizon were discussed in a separate section, and the reports generally concluded with recommendations for fiscal and monetary policy. The format adopted was that each report consisted of a common front section which summarized the discussion

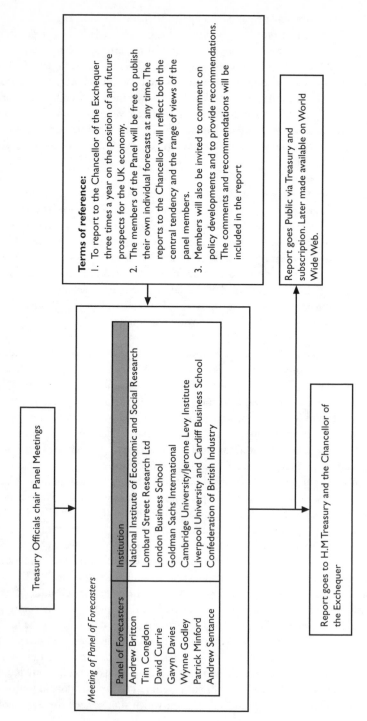

Treasury Officials chair Panel Meetings

Meeting of Panel of Forecasters

Panel of Forecasters	Institution
Andrew Britton	National Institute of Economic and Social Research
Tim Congdon	Lombard Street Research Ltd
David Currie	London Business School
Gavyn Davies	Goldman Sachs International
Wynne Godley	Cambridge University/Jerome Levy Institute
Patrick Minford	Liverpool University and Cardiff Business School
Andrew Sentance	Confederation of British Industry

Terms of reference:

1. To report to the Chancellor of the Exchequer three times a year on the position of and future prospects for the UK economy.

2. The members of the Panel will be free to publish their own individual forecasts at any time. The reports to the Chancellor will reflect both the central tendency and the range of views of the panel members.

3. Members will also be invited to comment on policy developments and to provide recommendations. The comments and recommendations will be included in the report

Report goes Public via Treasury and subscription. Later made available on World Wide Web.

Report goes to H.M Treasury and the Chancellor of the Exchequer

Figure 13.1 Members of Panel of Forecasters and their Relationship to Government.

and indicated where various Panel members agreed and what they recommended (whilst also identifying key disagreements). This front section also included tables showing the arithmetic mean of the individual forecasts for the main economic variables (for those economists who forecast that variable) as well as the maximum and minimum values forecast. The second section of the reports consisted of appendices which tabulated the Panel's forecasts for wider range of economic variables over both short- and medium-term horizons as well as the seven individual submissions in which the Panel members outlined their own views and concerns in more detail. However, there was no attempt to standardize the forecasts by using common assumptions in order to improve comparability. As a result, differences between the forecasts and policy recommendations reflected a mixture of different models, different assumptions and different judgements.

3. Different ways of understanding the economy

At their first meeting in February 1993 the Panel of Independent Forecasters showed that the available economic data were consistent with a wide range of interpretations and their forecasts ranged from fairly bleak to reasonably optimistic (e.g. forecasts for GDP growth in 1993 ranged from 0.2 per cent to 2.0 per cent). The need for policy intervention was similarly variable. Thus, although there was a consensus that the economy was more likely to resume some sort of economic growth as a result of leaving the ERM, there remained a range of views regarding the scale of this recovery and what, if anything, ought to be done to ensure it. In fact, a closer examination of the individual forecasts reveals that the apparent consensus (i.e. that GDP growth in 1993 will at least be positive and that the recession is over) concealed very different views about the character of this economic growth. For example, the relative contributions of domestic demand and net trade to overall economic growth varied considerably, and, in the case of domestic demand, the differences were not just of magnitude but of direction.

There were therefore very different ways of making sense of the available data. For simplicity, I am going to begin by distinguishing between two main sets of stories and models – the 'Devaluationists' and the 'Classicals' – and make this distinction on the basis of where the economists *started* their analysis. Devaluationist stories and models are those which emphasized the importance of the devaluation which occurred after the UK left the ERM and a typical account began: 'Following the devaluation of sterling and the subsequent falls in interest rates . . .' The 'Classical' stories, on the other hand, emphasized the ideas of equilibrium and deviations from natural rates, and generally began: 'Because of the recession the economy is now a long way below trend, output is some way below potential and unemployment is well above the natural rate . . .' From these two starting points, the Panel members then developed two distinct styles of analysis and policy futures which are summarized in Table 13.1 below. The rest of this section outlines main features of the two groupings, including the differences within each group and the similarities between them, in more detail.

Table 13.1 Summary of theories and policies

Theoretical framework	Proponents	Policy issues	Policy solutions	Economic prospects
Devaluationists	Andrew Britton David Currie Gavyn Davies Wynne Godley Andrew Sentance	• Net exports and trade deficit • Unemployment and budget deficit • Inflation • Investment	• Fiscal tightening • Training and education • Boost investment • Reduce consumption	Bleak
Classicals	Tim Congdon Patrick Minford	• Weakness of economy • Output gap • Budget deficit	• Fiscal prudence • Monetary boost	Good

3.1. The 'Devaluationist' stories

The 'Devaluationists' represent what can be thought of as mainstream economics in the UK. The principal proponents were the National Institute and the London Business School. In addition, I have included Gavyn Davies, Wynne Godley and Andrew Sentance amongst its members. The models used by this group tend to be broadly Keynesian (at least in the short-term) and typically include hysteresis effects in the labour market. The group was generally pessimistic about the future, being particularly concerned about the growth-inflation trade-off, net exports and unemployment.

According to the 'Devaluationist' economists, the UK economy would recover during 1993 as growth resumed following the devaluation of the sterling exchange rate. In addition, the low level of interest rates was expected to bring about a modest expansion in consumer spending. However, over the longer term problems were expected to appear as the forecast economic growth led either to falling unemployment which would then cause wages to rise (hence forcing deflationary policies) and/or rising consumption which would increase imports and reduce net exports (again forcing deflationary policies). The Devaluationists were thus forecasting a difficult future in which economic growth would be constrained by either the Budget deficit or the Trade deficit.

However, despite this common structure there were also differences between the various Devaluationist accounts. One example is their selective appeal to precedent (in particular the 1967 devaluation) as a justification for their pessimism. Thus, some of the forecasters (e.g. Britton and, to a lesser extent, Currie) made explicit appeals to historical precedent and talked about the 'characteristic response' of the British economy. In other words, the persuasiveness of these forecasts, and their relevance for policy-making, rested upon the plausibility of the idea that the economy is subject to regular and predictable sequences of events and, perhaps more importantly, that these patterns had persisted. They were thus, implicitly, suggesting that events during the 1970s and 80s had not significantly changed the way in which economic agents (especially workers and wage bargainers) would behave.[13]

However, this assumption is not one which all the Devaluationists shared. For example, others, such as Wynne Godley, argued that the important thing about 1993 was that the 'present conjuncture contains a number of well known features which, taken together, make it very different from the later stages of all previous recessions'.[14] In other words, it was the *unique* context of the 1992 devaluation – in particular the high levels of indebtedness – which had to be appreciated if it was to be properly understood. In this context, in which the novelty of the situation is emphasized, one might expect a much more important role for judgement in forecasting and policy.

3.2. The 'Classical' stories

The other way of analysing the recovery was to refer directly to the economic cycle itself. In contrast to the 'Devaluation' stories, these forecasts and policy recommendations were based on more monetarist economic models. The most important idea was that of movements away from an equilibrium generating powerful forces which tended to restore it. As a result, both 'Classicals' tended to be optimistic about the growth-inflation trade-off and future export performance. However, because the economy was so far from its trend position, they both expected problems to arise in the near future if the government did not act to reinforce the recovery.

The simplest version of this 'Classical' story was put forward by Tim Congdon. Congdon argued that the recession had pushed the economy a long way from its long-run trend position, and that, because the 'output gap' was 'exceptionally large', the economy would be able grow at an above-trend rate for several years.[15] Like Britton and Currie, Congdon therefore offered an account of events in which the economic cycle was explained using concepts and exemplars well known to economists. The difference, of course, was that, in Congdon's case, the intellectual and empirical pedigree of his analysis comes from 'Friedman's 1967 presidential address to the American Economic Association and the associated literature.'[16]

The other monetarist on the Panel was Patrick Minford. Like Congdon, Minford believed that the economy was a long way beneath trend, that inflationary pressures were weak, that above trend growth would not be inflationary and that prompt action was needed to ensure recovery.[17] However, like Godley, Minford made his forecasts conditional on there being something very different about this economic cycle which meant that analyses based on precedent could not tell the whole story. It was Minford's contention that, because of a sea-change in popular culture within the UK, inflationary expectations in the 1990s (and hence wage and price behaviour) were very different from previous economic cycles. As a result, inflation was 'down and out' in the UK.[18] and the analysis of Currie and Britton was very wrong.

3.3. Summary

The aim of this section has been to introduce some of the variety of economic analyses which the Panel of Forecasters offered the Chancellor at their first meeting in February 1993. Not only were there (predictable) differences in theoretical approach but there were also differences amongst those economists who appeared to share much of the same theoretical framework over the differing weights which should be given to precedent and present. Conversely, despite their theoretical differences, Congdon, Britton and Currie all argued that the future would be like the past, with the implication that the successful policy solutions would be those that had worked in the past. In a similar way, Godley and Minford, despite their possibly even more profound differences, also found themselves agreeing that analysts and policy makers needed to be attentive to the particular characteristics of the current situation if they were to really understand what was going on. The sociological insight is that, in the forecasts based on precedent, the 'economic agents' postulated in the models of Britton, Congdon and Currie are the 'same' in the 1990s as they were in the 1970s. For Godley and Minford, on the other hand, the 'economic agents' in the 1990s are very different from those of the past and need to be treated as such.

4. Creating a policy consensus

This section moves forward in time from February 1993 to October of that year when the Panel met for the third time. This meeting was significant because it preceded the UK's first unified Budget in which taxation and expenditure plans would be announced simultaneously. Economic policy was therefore at the forefront of the political agenda. This context was clearly influential because, although the Panel, as individuals, continued to express the range of views outlined in the previous section, their report nevertheless produced a consensual policy recommendation. Indeed, in many ways it is the epitome of what economists might consider a 'robust' policy. However, I want to argue the point from the other direction and emphasize what is lost when economic advisers agree not to differ. In particular, by agreeing a consensus recommendation around the sustainability of government borrowing, the Panel also agreed *not* to make unemployment and net exports a major policy concern. As a result, several reforms identified as important by the majority of Panel when speaking as individuals were not pursued as economic policies by the government.

The first part of this section therefore draws out in more detail some of the social and political implications of the economic models and theories used by the Panel and, hence, some of the debates which were glossed over in the search for consensus. The second part describes some of the reasons for this outcome and argues that although the consensus was, in part, due to the relatively non-doctrinaire nature of the problem they chose to solve, another, sociologically more interesting, factor was the effort made by some of the Panel members to achieve it.

4.1. The difference differences make

The starting point for the Panel's policy recommendations in October 1993 was their agreement that 'the overriding imperative of policy is to ensure a sustainable fiscal position'.[19] However, 'there [was] no consensus whether further fiscal tightening will be necessary in practice'.[20] Rather, the Panel's position was that they:

> would all support further fiscal tightening over the next three to four years *if it became necessary* to ensure sustainability . . . However, the risks are clearly not symmetric . . . We would therefore all support the announcement of tax or spending reforms, *desirable in their own right*, which should secure a net reduction in the PSBR [Public Sector Borrowing Requirement].[21]

When put like this, their recommendations seem little more than a statement of the obvious and it might be argued that the consensus is unimportant. After all, a policy which is unsustainable or undesirable makes little sense in any kind of economics. However, such a conclusion is rather unfair and obscures what the Panel had to do in order to achieve it.

The first point to note is that the Panel's agreement that 'the overriding imperative of policy is to ensure a sustainable fiscal position'[22] constructed the problem in a certain way. This was, in part, contingent on the absence of Wynne Godley from the October meeting[23] but one can also imagine that if the Panel had set the imperative of policy as being 'full employment' or 're-entering the ERM in 1998' then its recommendations might have looked very different. In any case, even when this policy goal is accepted, the individual submissions to the Report made it clear that a wide range of policy actions were justifiable. In addition, even amongst the Panel members who agreed that some sort of fiscal tightening was needed, the size, timing and aims of these measures varied considerably, as outlined below.

The most straightforward fiscal policy recommendations came from Tim Congdon who stated that 'there is no doubt that public sector borrowing is unsustainably high and that steps must be taken to reduce it'.[24] In other words, despite the tax increases announced in the March Budget, Congdon still believed that the 'structural Budget deficit probably remains at over 3 per cent of GDP (i.e. roughly £20 billion)'.[25] In terms of the necessary policy response, he stated that '3 years is surely quite long enough'[26] to reduce this to zero.

Although several of the other Panel members took a similar view to Congdon and doubted that the policies announced in the March Budget would reduce the PSBR sufficiently (i.e. like Congdon they believed that the Budget deficit was, to some extent, structural), others disagreed and thought that it was (or might have been, or could have been made to be) cyclical.[27] For example, Gavyn Davies believed that 'given the immense uncertainty in all projections of this type [i.e. of government borrowing in the medium-term], there is obviously no compelling case from a PSBR/financing point of view for further fiscal tightening.'[28] This aspect of Davies's argument was also supported by Andrew Britton who, in his submission, argued that:

Our projections of the public sector financial position do not suggest the *need* for any further tax increases in the November Budget. The level of debt and borrowing implied for the medium-term – in so far as this can be calculated with any degree of accuracy – does not appear imprudent.[29]

Finally, Patrick Minford's contribution also rejected the idea that the budget deficit was structural. However, unlike Britton and Davies who were agnostic about a structural deficit, Minford's central expectation was that the PSBR was cyclical (i.e. had no structural component). In fact, Minford believed that (with appropriate monetary policies) unemployment could fall to such an extent that:

the public borrowing we see would melt away [so that] there would be no need for the public spending programmes allegedly needed to boost competitiveness.[30]

On the other hand, even amongst those who agreed with Congdon that fiscal policy should be tightened there were important differences over the aims, timing and scale of any additional policy measures. For example, David Currie argued that any measures should be 'phased in to avoid undue impact on [the] recovery during 1994'[31] whereas Congdon wanted to implement them straight away. Currie's more cautious position reflected his own understanding of the recovery as basically weak with competitiveness likely to be eroded through inflation.

However, there were also other reasons, apart from the reducing the Budget deficit, which were used to justify tighter fiscal policies. For example, Currie, as noted in the previous section, believed there was a need to shift the 'mix' of policy, by placing more of the restriction on fiscal policy, in order to 'rebalance' the economy by restricting consumption and boosting investment and net exports through lower interest rates and better exchange rates. There was therefore an implied idea of a 'healthy' distribution of resources within the economy – a distribution which successful competitor countries were seen to have – and which Currie used to construct economic success for the UK as being dependent on it becoming a high(er) investment economy. In terms of policy actions, Currie recommended 'Budget measures to curb borrowing amounting to some £3–4bn over and above [those] announced by the previous Chancellor'.[32]

Currie was not alone in this view. Andrew Sentance provided a very similar analysis and, like Currie, argued that 'a further fiscal tightening is [needed] to change the balance of fiscal and monetary policy in a way which is favourable to sustaining a higher level of investment and net exports'.[33] This argument was also important (and ultimately more compelling) for Gavyn Davies who also agreed that 'a further shift in the fiscal/monetary [mix] looks desirable in order to control consumption, boost investment and maintain a competitive real exchange rate'.[34] In terms of policy, Davies suggested (as he did in July 1993) that the Chancellor should introduce 'consumption-reducing measures [which] should probably build up to at least 2–3 per cent of GDP over the next 4 years'.[35]

There were therefore real policy choices to be made and, what is more, there was more to these issues than just the economic analysis. Each of the different 'policy worlds' outlined by the Panel members required the emergence of a certain kind of social future if it was to hold true (this is the normative project of economics). In Congdon's story, net trade was forecast to grow strongly under existing market conditions, with the economy strong enough in turn to eliminate the Budget deficit in three years. This replicates the social and political priorities of the early Thatcher governments in which the responsibility of the state was to manage its own finances prudently – private sector capital flows on the other hand are not a concern of government, and neither is employment.[36]

Of those forecasters advocating a different sort of social future, the most radical alternative (in a European context) was proposed by Patrick Minford who argued the way forward for the UK was through a deregulated economy characterized by minimal public spending and the policy regimes of the 'Asian Tigers'. Thus, in Minford's future world, it was only the European economies who undid their post-war social legislation which would be able to compete effectively in the world markets. This, in turn, is radically different to the policies proposed by the mainstream economists who, nevertheless, recognized the need for change if the UK was to be able to compete successfully in globalizing world markets. In the Devaluationist's world, because the gain to competitiveness was expected to be quickly threatened by higher inflation, competitiveness could only be maintained through interventionist policies which boosted training, productivity and investment. The sort of conclusion that Minford draws was rejected and the solution instead was to move to a higher wage, higher productivity economic future. The implied social model was thus more in line with European social-democratic policies and implied a very different set of social institutions, economic actors and policy priorities.

4.2. Pulling it all together

The policy recommendations of the Panel's October Report began by presenting the relatively uncontroversial premise that 'the overriding imperative of policy is to ensure a sustainable fiscal position'.[37] However, the previous section has demonstrated that this consensus cannot be attributed to the Panel starting off with similar forecasts or beliefs. As we have just seen, they did not. Indeed, as Gavyn Davies pointed out, even if there were some 'motherhood-and-apple-pie' statements in the report about the importance of fiscal sustainability, 'you would not have got most Keynesians to write that down 10 years ago'.[38] In any case, even when the principle of fiscal sustainability *was* accepted, this was not enough to ensure consensus because the policy recommendations related to how sustainability should be achieved in practice and here there was a wide range of views available. However, the Panel did reach a consensus and this section looks at some of the reasons why. In essence, my argument is that the Panel reached a consensus because they were prepared to work at it. Thus, for example, Andrew Britton noted:

Patrick [Minford] ... who had the very optimistic projection of the borrowing requirement, was quite prepared to concede that there was a serious risk and that the whole question of sustainability ought to be discussed. Even though, in his projection, it was a problem that disappeared almost immediately he was quite prepared to use other people's forecasts as a basis for discussion.[39]

Thus, there was more to the consensus than the question itself and although not everyone on the Panel felt pressures to reach agreement and compromise, some certainly did. For example, in an earlier interview Minford commented that one of the 'interesting things' about the Panel's first ever meeting was that everyone felt that they had to 'make an effort [for] our community of economists, and the community at large'.[40] In Minford's view, the group would only survive and become useful it developed its own 'ethos':

I think that we have all got different views but, at the end of the day, there are important public interest issues to be settled here and we can't afford to let our vanity or whatever it is get in the way of a sensible discussion.[41]

Certainly Minford's own efforts in this direction did not go unnoticed by his colleagues and, by October, some progress was being made in developing this group ethos. Gavyn Davies suggested:

I do think the Panel is showing some signs of developing in ways which are separate from simply the three meetings per annum cycle ... I still think we are kind of groping our way towards a role, but ... I think more of us are buying into the idea that we want to make this thing work.[42]

There was, therefore, a feeling amongst some that, if the Panel was going to be adjudged useful, then it was important to minimize their differences and speak with a single voice. Thus, although they came to the October meeting with a range of different views, they nevertheless reached a consensus because they believed that it was something which they ought to do. In fact, several of the mainstream members made this point quite explicitly in interview, although each stressed slightly different reasons. For example, Andrew Britton highlighted the role of press and public opinion:

I think you are right about seeking consensus. We felt, particularly after the July Report, which got rather a bad press, that people found the arguing in public a bit tedious and that they would prefer to emphasise the agreements rather than the disagreements.[43]

In slightly different vein, Andrew Sentance agreed that there was an effort to reach agreement, but 'not to placate the media'.[44] Rather:

there was a feeling that here was a man we were supposed to be reporting to – the Chancellor of the Exchequer ... and if we couldn't come to some sort of strategy that really came out of the views of the Panel then I think, quite legitimately, he would say 'This is all very well, but it is not helping me a great deal'. [So] it was an attempt by us to do our job – which is to advise the Chancellor.[45]

Finally, the effort towards convergence was also noted by Gavyn Davies:

I think there was more agreement coming out of that [October] meeting than there was going into it, which suggested that there was a willingness to compromise in order to reach a common objective ... I don't want to overstate this. I don't think there was that much disagreement going in, and I don't think there was 100 per cent agreement coming out, but I think there was a tendency to move towards agreement, which I don't think was there in the previous two meetings.[46]

The important point to emphasize is that the Panel actively worked to bring about consensus and hence closure of the debate. The reasons for this, in various ways, related to the perception of others – the media, the Chancellor, other economists and so on. As Gavyn Davies pointed out:

I think that the Treasury has given us a massive opportunity, both as individuals and as representatives of economics outside the Treasury.[47]

It seems that this responsibility is one taken seriously by the Panel and is one of the key factors in explaining why, in October, they were able to work around their differences and speak with a single voice.

5. Economic models and economic policy

This section briefly evaluates the effectiveness of the Panel in shaping economic policy by examining the extent to which the Chancellor can be seen to heed the advice given to him the Panel of Forecasters. The analysis focuses on the way in which (economically) non-controversial reasons can be at odds with the calculations which policy makers must make. The section begins by briefly outlining the policies adopted by the Chancellor in his Budget, which he began by saying that:

My first priority has been to sustain the economic recovery now underway and to create the right climate for growth and jobs. I have been determined to take no risks with inflation. To achieve these objectives, *the task of my first Budget has been to set the governments finances on a sustainable path* for the rest of the decade.[48]

The similarity between the task the Chancellor set himself and the Panel's advice that 'the overriding imperative of policy is to ensure a sustainable fiscal position'[49] is clear enough and is also reflected in the warm reception they gave the Budget, applauding it ' "brave", "skilful" and "an appropriate start" '.[50]

However, it would not be fair to say that the Budget wholly reflected the Panel's priorities, although it clearly did in some respects. For example, direct tax rates were not raised (although most allowances were frozen); tax relief on Mortgage Interest Payments was reduced to 15 per cent; and the tax base was widened through new taxes on air travel and insurance. However, these tax-raising measures were offset by increased expenditures and, of the £5.5bn reduction in the PSBR announced (which was far bigger than anything the Panel considered necessary or even possible) the majority of the saving came from a reduction in the 'contingency reserve' which was halved from £7bn to £3.5bn. Nevertheless, a Budget which reduced the PSBR was definitely what the Panel wanted and to that extent they can be said to have been influential.

On the other hand, when the Budget measures are looked at in more detail it is apparent that several issues identified as important by a number of the Panel were not addressed at all. For example, in their Report the Panel listed, as 'an important caveat', that they would 'caution against anything more that a modest further tightening of the fiscal position for 1994–95 because of the large tax rises already in place'. Clearly the Chancellor did not accept this concern (although he did remove some tax increases proposed by his predecessor). In another departure from their advice that the PSBR be reduced through increases in taxation, the Chancellor achieved most of the reduction in borrowing through reduced public spending.[51] Thus the arguments of members of the Panel such as Gavyn Davies, who recommended that taxes be increased and half the extra revenue be used to 'boost public investment, education and training',[52] were ultimately ignored. A similar point can be made with respect to David Currie's recommendations. Although Currie correctly anticipated that the lower than expected inflation *could* be used by the Chancellor to reduce total public expenditure, he actually counselled against this:

> A preferable alternative would be to maintain the Control Total and redeploy resources within the total from public consumption to public investment. This would allow support of those areas of public spending that help strengthen the long run supply side performance of the UK economy, including education, training and R&D.[53]

There were therefore within the Panel's Report two distinct sets of recommendations concerning fiscal policy. However, only one of them made it onto the Budget speech. The argument that the PSBR was just too big to be reduced by economic growth alone (backed by Congdon, Currie, Davies and Sentance) appears to have been accepted by the Chancellor and was acted upon. However, the argument that the economy was 'out of balance' and resources needed to be re-deployed to reduce consumption and increase investment and net exports (backed by Britton, Currie,

Godley, Davies and Sentance) was not accepted. What therefore is the difference between the two?

One important reason why the Panel were influential in putting fiscal sustain-ability at the heart of the 'Budget judgement' was that they spoke with one voice. Although not everyone agreed that the forecasts for the PSBR suggested it was a problem which required further policy action, everyone did manage to agree that action which further ensured that it did not become a structural deficit could be justified. As noted above, some of the Panel felt that they made a deliberate effort to reach this agreement, others that it just happened due to the nature of the question. In the case of policies which linked government spending to concerns about the 'balance of the economy', however, the debates were much more controversial. Significantly, concerns about the 'balance of the economy' did not bridge the gap between the Classical and the Devaluationist accounts. For example, the main-stream proponents typically included in their justification for more interventionist economic policies reference to the importance of hysteresis in the labour market (something Minford did not accept) and the Balance of Trade and unemployment as legitimate concerns for public policy (something Congdon did not accept). As a result, there was no consensus reached on whether or not the economy really was (likely to be) devoting a disproportionate share of resources to consumption at the expense of net exports and investment and the 'out-of-balance economy' was not collectively accepted as a *potential* problem.

Unlike the sustainability of PSBR, where the Panel could agree a 'safe' strategy whatever the 'true' position of the government finances, the trade deficit and the labour market were not amenable to such compromise. Instead the Panel's eco-nomic models and theories told contradictory stories which challenged the core beliefs of the other Panel members such that differences could not (would not?) be resolved. The contrast between the case of the PSBR and the trade deficit is thus one between a consensus and a contest – the sustainability of the PSBR was (made to be) a consensually agreed problem, the trade deficit had not yet reached that point and the Chancellor and the Treasury had little choice but to choose between the competing accounts.

5.1. Summary

The above discussion has illustrated how, despite the closure accomplished by the Panel over fiscal sustainability, the Chancellor still deviated from their recommen-dations in several important ways. In particular, he did impose a significant tighten-ing of fiscal policy in the first year and he did this by reducing expenditure rather than increasing revenue. Why then did the Chancellor, after accepting the basic premise of the Report, ignore the details? I would argue that part of the reason was that the Panel gave him that choice and he used that discretion. Thus, if economists cannot agree what should be done, then the Chancellor is going to have to choose between them. In such a situation the credibility of economic arguments must surely be related to their resonances outside the economic community.

The point to make here is not that economists should become politicians (or politicians become economists). Rather it is that problems which some of the Panel diagnosed as important for the futures of large numbers of their fellow citizens were simply not addressed in the Budget. The conclusion I draw from this is that if the mainstream members of the Panel want to make their expertise and professionalism count, they need to find ways of communicating it which makes sense to their putative audience – in this case politicians but also the wider publics who vote for and/or lobby the politicians. Of course this does not mean sacrificing their science – after all it is their science which has allowed them to make the diagnosis in the first place. Instead, the point is that before policy measures can be implemented, the problem must be recognized and the context for action created. It may be argued that this is not science, but if scientists cannot make the case for their own science then who can? The alternative, as demonstrated by the mainstream members of the Panel, is at best only a minor influence over events which they believe to be import-ant and at worst irrelevance.

6. Conclusions – creating socio-economic futures

This chapter has shown that, behind the consensus that a prudent Chancellor 'would introduce a package of tax and spending reforms' to ensure control of the PSBR, were views which ranged from the PSBR being cyclical to it being structural; from current policy being sufficient to it being inadequate and an additional argu-ment about whether or not policy intervention was needed to ensure exports and investment were not squeezed by consumption. Moreover, each economist had a wider vision about economic equity and social norms which informed their views about, for example, whether the long-term unemployed should be offered training; how should governments intervene in industry and markets; whether the UK's future should be inside Europe or outside it. The choices facing policy makers (and citizens) when choosing between economic advisers could not be starker or more important.

The problem for policy makers seems to be that although any single economic model seems to have profound implications for policy-making, in offering a unified and quantified theory of how an economic system works and what its future might be, this clarity is lost as other models enter the policy arena. Moreover, ranking or ordering different models is not easy because, as the Panel of Independent Forecast-ers shows, a wide range of models are able to pass accepted forecast and/or econo-metric tests. As a result, the group of economic models as a whole appears to have no clear implication for policy unless someone is able to decide which one to believe. Because of the ambiguity of econometric and other tests, economic mod-ellers have, as yet, been unable to do this and so economic policy decisions remain political in the deepest sense.

Indeed, my own research about the way in which policy makers in the UK used economic models in the early 1990s has suggested that the decisions which policy makers must take about which model(s) to trust must draw on a wide range of other, often non-economic, factors.[54] In addition, if these policies are to work, then policy makers will need to actively enrol, encourage and cajole a whole range of social actors into lending their support. As a result economic policies blend articles of faith with econometrically supported knowledge and power relationships. In this way, my sociological account of economic modelling and policy-making supports a view in which economists can have only a capricious and uncertain influence over economic policy. Although they can make coherent recommendations of their own, and their work can be used as a rhetorical resource in arguments for or against particular economic policies, the basis for these arguments does not rest on convincing empirical proofs. Instead, economic theory and models function as legitimizations (and quantifications) of particular political and moral theories about the world which can be selectively invoked by policy makers and this flexibility, as much as their econometric properties, accounts for the appeal of economic models.

In such a context it is clear that other social interests will also have a powerful influence on the shaping of economic policy. This is not a particularly profound observation, but the sociological perspective does allow a new angle on how to improve it. For example, it is not clear that we need less/more/better economists, or even that the solution lies in making economic models more 'scientific'. Whilst these are no doubt desirable goals for economists, their immediate usefulness for policy makers is less clear, especially as economic policies require for their success the formation of stable social coalitions. Thus, instead of looking to the economics community, the sociological solution to the policy makers' regress is to look outside it and to develop new ways of making economic policies which recognize and build up the consensus needed to sustain policies.

The answer therefore lies not in developing new models (although this might help) but in developing new ways of using economic models. Rather than using models as 'truth machines', successful policy-making in the new context requires decision makers to re-define economic models as a 'discursive space' in which users and economists, through a continuous dialogue, can develop shared understandings.[55] There is some evidence that central banks already use economic models in this way[56] and, this was, I think, the great opportunity presented by the Panel of Forecasters to the UK government. By broadening the information base upon which economic policy decisions were taken through both their own models and their wide range of contacts, consultancies and experiences the Panel brought new voices to the policy debate. The extension of this argument is that a more established Panel would formalize these influences and invite contributions from financial institutions, consumers groups and worker organizations. In this way, situated economic knowledges of different actors could be incorporated into the policy-making and modelling processes and, reciprocally, might also be changed by it. In other words, even though the future is unknown (and unknowable) it is a future which a society, through its policies, institutions and choices, tries to influence and shape. If the Panel of Economic Forecasters, by bringing a sense of the enormous range of economically legitimate views to a wider public, had helped to create a forum which fostered an appreciation of the diversity of economic knowledges and of the opportunities which exist for creating a different society, then this would have been an important achievement.

This critical part of this chapter has shown that, in many cases, taking economic policy decisions will involve choosing *between* economic models. The more positive part has tried to argue that the Panel of Forecasters represented a better way of doing this because it exposed both the Chancellor and the public (if they were interested) to informed debates about a wider range of economic theories, models and policy ideas. Consequently, choices were harder to justify and alternatives more readily available. By effectively creating a controlled forum for economic controversy, the Panel provided an institutional space in which economic expertise was routinely deconstructed and its assumptions, judgements and conventions laid bare.

Let me re-emphasize – this is not a bad thing. In fact, it could have been the beginning of a new style of policy-making in which the social choices implied in different economic futures were actually debated, discussed and agreed upon. Rather than economic policy decisions being taken to meet a government's needs, a more broadly construed Panel could have promoted a more constructive form of economic dialogue in which the social learning needed to articulate and produce the different socio-economic futures could have taken place. However, for this to work, and economic actors to be able take on the roles assigned to them in models, policy makers and modellers will need to re-define the policy-making process as one which begins from the present and tries create the sort of future it citizens want to live in. By presenting the economic choices, and showing that the economic future is still to be decided, the Panel of Economic Forecasters showed that values as well as facts still have an important part to play in economic policy.[57]

7. Postscript

Unfortunately, the New Labour Chancellor, Gordon Brown, didn't see this in quite the same way. On 6 May 1997 the Chancellor announced plans to abandon the Panel and devolve interest rate decisions to the Monetary Policy Committee of the Bank of England. Rather than creating a link between politics and economics this decision would seem, perhaps regrettably, to have the opposite effect. In particular, by taking economic models out of the public domain and back into the privileged expertocracy of economic advisers, it threatens to undo much of (what I consider to be) the Panel's good work.

Acknowledgements

I am grateful to Mary Morgan, Frank den Butter and an anonymous referee for the constructive and helpful comments on earlier versions of this chapter. The chapter has also benefited from discussions with the participants at the Tenth Anniversary Conference of the Tinbergen Institute, 14–16 May 1997 and I thank the participants, particularly Ken Wallis and Simon Wren-Lewis, for the good humour and patience with which they endured what must have seemed very naïve questioning. Any naiveté which remains is of course my own fault.

Notes

1 For an easy introduction to the Sociology of Scientific Knowledge (SSK) see: H. M. Collins and T. J. Pinch (1993), *The Golem: What Everyone Should Know About Science*. Cambridge: Cambridge University Press. For more formal treatments see H. M. Collins ([1985] 1992), *Changing Order: Replication and Induction in Scientific Practice* (rev. ed.). Chicago: Chicago University Press; Bruno Latour and Steve Woolgar (1979), *Laboratory Life: The Social Construction of Scientific Facts*. Beverly Hills, CA: Sage; Barry Barnes and David Edge (1982), *Science in Context: Readings in the Sociology of Science*. Milton Keynes: Open University Press. For SSK applied to economic modelling see Robert Evans (1997), 'Soothsaying or Science? Falsification, Uncertainty and Social Change in Macroeconomic Modelling', *Social Studies of Science*, Vol. 27, No. 3, June 1997, pp. 395–438.

2 Many examples of this interaction are to be found in this volume. See for example O. Bjerkolt, 'Interaction between model builders and policy makers in the Norwegian tradition'; J,. Donders and J. Graafland, 'CPB models and employment policy in the Netherlands; P. Duguay and D. Longworth, 'Macroeconomic models and policy-making at the Bank of Canada'; P. A. G. van Bergeijk and J. van Sinderen, 'Models and macroeconomic policy in the Netherlands' (Chapters 10, 2, 5, and 3 respectively).

3 Cf. Donald A. MacKenzie (1996), *Knowing Machines: Essays on Technical Change*. Cambridge, Mass.; London: MIT Press.

4 In these cases, the models are being used to perform what Ken Wallis refers to as 'if only' analysis.

5 For example, P. J. A. van Els 'Policy-making and model development: The case of the Nederlansche Bank's model MORKMON' (Chapter 6 in this volume)

6 Cf. Sheila Jasanoff (1995), *Science at the Bar: Law, Science and Technology in America*. Cambridge, Mass. and London: Twentieth Century Fund and Harvard University Press.

7 Cf. Collins and Pinch, *The Golem*, op cit., note 1.

8 Robert Evans (1999a). 'Economic models and policy advice', *Science in Context*, Vol. 12, No. 2 (1999), pp. 351–76.

9 For a fuller account see Robert Evans (1999b), *Macroeconomic Forecasting: A Sociological Appraisal*. London: Routledge.

10 For an analysis and graphical illustration see Andrew Burrell and Stephen Hall (1994), 'A comparison of economic forecasts', *Economic Outlook*, Vol. 18, No. 2 (February 1994), pp. 29–35.

11 Alan Budd, Interview, 22 March 1994, p. 8.

12 For example, Andrew Britton, Wynne Godley and Patrick Minford had all previously worked for the Treasury; David Currie and Gavyn Davies had (at different times) close links with the Labour Party; Tim Congdon and, to a lesser extent, Patrick Minford had connections with the Conservative Party in the early 1980s; Andrew Sentance was Chief Economist for the Confederation of British Industry (CBI).

13 Note that this does not imply that economists' understandings of these events have not changed.

14 Wynne Godley (1993). Submission to Report of the Panel of Independent Forecasters, February 1993, para 2.

15 Tim Congdon (1993a). Submission to Report of Panel of Independent Forecasters, February 1993, para 5.

16 Tim Congdon (1993b). Submission to Report of Panel of Independent Forecasters, July 1993, para 2.

17 Patrick Minford (1993a). Submission to Report of Panel of Independent Forecasters, February 1993.

18 See: Patrick Minford (1993b). Submission to Report of Panel of Independent Forecasters, July 1993.

19 H.M. Treasury (1993). Report of Panel of Independent Forecasters, October 1993, para 36.

20 Ibid., para 36.

21 Ibid., paras 36–8, emphasis added.

22 Ibid., para 36.

23 This is not a personal criticism of Godley. Rather, it acknowledges that within Godley's economic thinking, fiscal sustainability, as the rest of the Panel understand it, is much less important. Thus, Andrew Britton suggests that 'if Wynne had been there, there might have been more debate as to whether this was a sensible question to ask'.

24 Tim Congdon (1993c). Submission to Report of Panel of Independent Forecasters, October 1993, para 15.

25 Ibid., para 16.

26 Ibid., para 16.

27 To make things even more complicated, Godley rejects the cyclical-structural dichotomy, arguing that it is an *outcome* of the policy choices made (see note 23).

28 Gavyn Davies (1993). Submission to Report of Panel of Independent Forecasters, October 1993, para 4.

29 Andrew Britton (1993). Submission to Report of Panel of Independent Forecasters, October 1993, para 29.

30 Patrick Minford (1993c). Submission to Report of Panel of Independent Forecasters, October 1993, para 17.

31 David Currie (1993). Submission to Report of Panel of Independent Forecasters, October 1993, para 10.

32 Ibid., para 10.

33 Andrew Sentance (1993). Submission to Report of Panel of Independent Forecasters, October 1993, para 14.

34 Gavyn Davies, op cit., note 26, para 4.

35 Ibid., para 35.

36 Tim Congdon, Interview, 2 June 1994, pp. 1–2.

37 H.M. Treasury, op cit., note 17, para 36.

38 Gavyn Davies, Interview, 27 October 1993, p. 15.

39 Andrew Britton, Interview, 27 October 1993, p. 9.

40 Patrick Minford, Interview 31 March 1993, p. 20.

41 Patrick Minford, Interview July 1993, p. 9.

42 Gavyn Davies, Interview, op cit., note 36, pp. 12–13.

43 Andrew Britton, Interview, op cit., note 37, p. 8.

44 Andrew Sentance, Interview, 29 October 1993, p. 13.

45 Ibid., p. 12.

46 Gavyn Davies, Interview, op cit., note 36, p. 16.

47 Ibid., p. 13.

48 Source: Budget Speech as reported in *The Times*, 1 December 1993, emphasis added.

49 H.M. Treasury, op cit., note 17, para. 36.

50 Lisa Vaughan, 'The Budget: "Wise Men" advise interest rate cut: Economic advisers' verdicts', *The Independent*, 1 December 1993, Budget Page 12.

51 Economists will not need reminding that there is a significant difference between funding a reduction in borrowing through reduced spending rather than through increased taxation.

52 David Currie, op cit., note 29, para 5.

53 Ibid., para 10.

54 Op cit note 9.
55 One example of this sort of process is the way in which 'social partners' use the Central Planning Bureau model in the Netherlands.
56 See: H. J. Edison and J. Marquez, 'U.S. monetary policy and econometric modelling: Tales from the FOMC Transcripts 1984–1991'; M. R. Donihue and J. Kitchen, 'The Troika Process, economic forecasts and macroeconomic policy in the USA' (Chapters 12 and 14 in this volume).
57 Perhaps the one lesson which models do teach us is that anything might be possible. In such circumstances it is surely important to ask: what do we want?

8. Bibliography

Barnes, Barry and Edge, David, 1982. *Science in Context: Readings in the Sociology of Science.* Milton Keynes: Open University Press.

Van Bergeijk, P. A. G. and Van Sinderen, J., 2000. 'Models and macroeconomic policy in the Netherlands' (Chapter 3 in this volume).

Bjerkolt, O., 2000. 'The Interaction between Model Builders and Policy Makers in the Norwegian Tradition' (Chapter 10 in this volume).

Britton, Andrew, 1993. 'Submission to Report of Panel of Independent Forecasters, October 1993.' In: H.M. Treasury (1993c), *Report of Panel of Independent Forecasters, October 1993.* H.M. Treasury: London.

Burrell, Andrew and Hall, Stephen, 1994. 'A Comparison of Economic Forecasts', *Economic Outlook,* Vol. 18, No. 2 (February 1994), pp. 29–35.

Collins, H. M., [1985] 1992. *Changing Order: Replication and Induction in Scientific Practice* (rev. ed.). Chicago: Chicago University Press.

Collins, H. M. and Pinch, T. J., 1993. *The Golem: What Everyone Should Know About Science.* Cambridge: Cambridge University Press.

Congdon, Tim, 1993a. 'Submission to Report of Panel of Independent Forecasters, February 1993.' In: H.M. Treasury (1993a) *Report of Panel of Independent Forecasters, February 1993.* H.M. Treasury: London.

Congdon, Tim, 1993b. 'Submission to Report of Panel of Independent Forecasters, July 1993.' In: H.M. Treasury (1993b), *Report of Panel of Independent Forecasters, July 1993.* H.M. Treasury: London.

Congdon, Tim, 1993c. 'Submission to Report of Panel of Independent Forecasters, October 1993.' In: H.M. Treasury (1993c), *Report of Panel of Independent Forecasters, October 1993.* H.M. Treasury: London.

Currie, David, 1993. 'Submission to Report of Panel of Independent Forecasters, October 1993.' In: H.M. Treasury (1993c), *Report of Panel of Independent Forecasters, October 1993* H.M. Treasury: London.

Davies, Gavyn, 1993. 'Submission to Report of Panel of Independent Forecasters, October 1993.' in H.M. Treasury (1993c), *Report of Panel of Independent Forecasters, October 1993.* H.M. Treasury: London.

Donders, J. and Graafland, J., 2000. 'CPB models and employment policy in the Netherlands' (Chapter 2 in this volume).

Donihue, M. R. and Kitchen, J., 2000. 'The Troika Process, economic forecasts and macroeconomic policy in the USA' (Chapter 14 in this volume).

Duguay, P. and Longworth, D., 2000. 'Macroeconomic models and policy-making at the Bank of Canada' (Chapter 5 in this volume).

Edison, H. J. and Marquez, J., 2000. 'U.S. monetary policy and econometric modelling: Tales from the FOMC Transcripts 1984–1991' (Chapter 12 in this volume).

Van Els, P. J. A., 2000. 'Policy-making and model development: the case of the Nederlansche Bank model MORKMON' (Chapter 6 in this volume).

Evans, Robert, 1997. 'Soothsaying or science? Falsification, uncertainty and social change in macroeconomic modelling', *Social Studies of Science*, Vol. 27, No. 3, June 1997, pp. 395–438.

Evans, Robert, 1999a. 'Economic Models and Policy Advice', *Science in Context*, Vol. 12, No. 2 (1999), pp. 351–76.

Evans, Robert, 1999b. *Macroeconomic Forecasting: A Sociological Appraisal.* London: Routledge.

Godley, Wynne, 1993. 'Submission to Report of the Panel of Independent Forecasters, February 1993.' In: H.M. Treasury (1993a), *Report of Panel of Independent Forecasters, February 1993.* H.M. Treasury: London.

H.M. Treasury, 1993a. *Report of Panel of Independent Forecasters, February 1993.* H.M. Treasury: London.

H.M. Treasury, 1993b. *Report of Panel of Independent Forecasters, July 1993.* H.M. Treasury: London.

H.M. Treasury, 1993c. *Report of Panel of Independent Forecasters, October 1993.* H.M. Treasury: London.

Jasanoff, Sheila, 1995. *Science at the Bar: Law, Science and Technology in America.* Cambridge, Mass. and London: Twentieth Century Fund and Harvard University Press.

Latour, Bruno and Woolgar, Steve, 1979. *Laboratory Life: The Social Construction of Scientific Facts* Beverly Hills, CA: Sage.

MacKenzie, Donald A., 1996. *Knowing Machines: Essays on Technical Change.* Cambridge, Mass; London: MIT Press.

Minford, Patrick, 1993a. 'Submission to Report of Panel of Independent Forecasters, February 1993.' In: H.M. Treasury (1993a), *Report of Panel of Independent Forecasters, February 1993.* H.M. Treasury: London.

Minford, Patrick, 1993b. 'Submission to Report of Panel of Independent Forecasters, July 1993.' In: H.M. Treasury (1993b), *Report of Panel of Independent Forecasters, July 1993.* H.M. Treasury: London.

Minford, Patrick, 1993c. 'Submission to Report of Panel of Independent Forecasters, October 1993.' In: H.M. Treasury (1993c), *Report of Panel of Independent Forecasters, October 1993.* H.M. Treasury: London.

Sentance, Andrew, 1993. 'Submission to Report of Panel of Independent Forecasters, October 1993.' In: H.M. Treasury (1993c), *Report of Panel of Independent Forecasters, October 1993.* H.M. Treasury: London.

Vaughan, Lisa, 'The Budget: "Wise Men" advise interest rate cut: Economic advisers' verdicts', *The Independent*, 1 December 1993, Budget Page 12.

Chapter 14

The Troika process: economic models and macroeconomic policy in the USA

Michael R. Donihue and John Kitchen

In the executive branch of the US Federal government, a group known as the Troika – comprised of senior officials of the President's Council of Economic Advisers, the Department of the Treasury, and the Office of Management and Budget – plays an important role in developing the economic agenda for each Administration. The Troika develops the economic assumptions underlying the Administration's budget proposals including an assessment of current economic conditions and forecasts for key economic indicators. It meets regularly to address a variety of policy issues, to evaluate and modify the Administration's forecasts, and to monitor the current stance of fiscal and monetary policies relative to the business cycle.

Empirical models play an important role in developing forecasts, evaluating alternative policy scenarios, and in on-going analyses of the performance of the economy. Although the models are often used to examine various behavioral responses to policies or shocks, the models also serve to provide a structural framework that guarantees the internal consistency of any forecast and to provide a sound theoretical basis for both short- and long-run forecasts.

This chapter provides an overview of the Troika process and the role of empirical models in the development of the fiscal policies and macroeconomic forecasts of the US government.

JEL classifications: A11, E17, E61

The institutional structure for generating economic forecasts and for evaluating and coordinating macroeconomic policy within the Executive branch of the US government has evolved over the past 40 years into a formal working group known as the Troika. While the Troika membership and scope of responsibilities has changed, the general structure and process have proven remarkably resilient despite the significant changes in Administrations, personnel, and political philosophies which have occurred during this time.

Within the Troika process, economic models play an important role in developing Administration forecasts, in evaluations of alternative policy scenarios, and in on-going analyses of the performance of the economy. Although the models often are used to examine various behavioral responses to policies or shocks, the models also serve to provide a structural framework that guarantees the internal consistency of any forecast and to provide a sound theoretical basis for both short- and long-run forecasts. Various types of models have been used, with the specific application determining the type of model used. Main-stream macroeconomic forecasting models are used to produce the detailed Administration economic forecast that is used for making budget projections, as well as for analyzing the likely performance of the economy in response to a specific policy proposal or economic shock. Growth models and growth accounting frameworks are used to provide a supply-side foundation for making long-term projections. Finally, smaller forecasting models are often produced by staff economists with the gathering of data and the model specification and estimation occurring specifically for addressing a current policy or forecast issue. These smaller, 'in-house' models take various forms, from single equation reduced form specifications, to small multiple equation models, and VAR and VEC specifications.

1. The structure of the Troika

The Troika is made up of representatives from the three Administration groups with primary responsibility for economic and budget issues: The Council of Economic Advisers (CEA); the Office of Management and Budget (OMB); and the Department of the Treasury. Membership in the Troika is divided across three levels, with political appointees in the top two levels and a staff level working group in the third. The cabinet-level principals of each branch of the Troika – Chairman of the CEA, Director of OMB, and Secretary of the Treasury – make up the highest level of the Troika which is commonly referred to as T-1. T-2 generally includes the macroeconomics member of the CEA, the Associate Director for Economic Policy from the OBM, and the Assistant Secretary of the Treasury for Economic Policy. Staff members from the three agencies participate in the T-3 working group. In most Administrations, the Secretary of the Treasury assumes the lead role in directing economic policy and making public statements. The Council of Economic Advisers typically assumes the lead role in developing the economic assumptions underlying the Administration's budget proposals. The CEA also provides an analysis of current economic issues facing the nation and the Administration's economic agenda in its annual *Economic Report of the President*.

For the purposes of both forecasting and policy-making, each of the three branches of the Troika play an important role. Economists at the CEA work with their counterparts at the Department of Treasury to provide background analysis for new policy initiatives while the OMB staff works out the fiscal implications of the proposals. CEA's economic assumptions are used by both the Department of Treasury and the OMB to produce budget revenue and outlay estimates, respectively. And at various times the principals from all three agencies participate in public debates concerning current policy issues.

2. History of the Troika

The President's Council of Economic Advisers was established by the Employment Act of 1946,[1] and shortly thereafter the Troika emerged in the form of informal policy groups which met during several post-WWII Administrations. Raymond Saulnier, chairman of the CEA from 1956 to 1961, referred to an Advisory Board on Economic Growth and Stability (ABEGS) as an important economic advisory group during the Eisenhower Administration.[2] Unlike the Troika of today, ABEGS included the Chairman of the Board of Governors of the Federal Reserve.

The formal beginning of the Troika occurred in 1961, during the first year of the Kennedy Administration. According to the 'Council Activities' section of the 1962 Economic *Report of the President,*

> Of particular importance was the development of new machinery for intera-gency cooperation in formulating fiscal estimates and policies. The Chairman of the Council served with the Secretary of the Treasury and the Director of the Bureau of the Budget on a committee charged with coordinating the eco-nomic, budgetary, and revenue estimates for which the three agencies have primary responsibility, and of reporting on them to the President. The esti-mates are developed with the aid of working groups representing the Council, the Treasury Department, and the Bureau of the Budget.[3]

Former CEA chairmen Walter Heller (1961–64), and Arthur Okun (1968–69) point to a staff member employed by the Bureau of the Budget named Sam Cohn as the 'father' of the Troika.[4] During the Kennedy Administration, the three Troika principals met frequently with the Chairman of the Federal Reserve, and Walter Heller referred to the group as the 'Quadriad'.[5]

The responsibilities of the Troika evolved over time. In the early years, the Troika's focus was primarily on contemporaneous economic behavior and the outlook for economic performance for just the coming year. This focus reflected an era in which the economic and budget outlook was much more short-term in nature than it is today, and a time when economic theory and empirical methods were more rudimentary. The composition of the budget in the early 1960s was also responsible for this short-term focus. In the early 1960s, discretionary outlays accounted for about 70 per cent of total outlays, non-interest mandatory spending accounted for roughly 26 per cent, and Federal budget deficits were less than 1 per cent of GDP. By comparison, in fiscal year (FY) 1997 discretionary outlays had fallen to 34 per cent of total outlays, and non-interest mandatory spending had increased to 54 per cent. The Federal budget deficit, which reached a high of 6.0 per cent of GDP in FY 1983, stood at 0.3 per cent of GDP in FY 1997.

Furthermore, by law the outlook was required to be only short-term in nature. The Budget and Accounting Act of 1921 required publication of the current and following fiscal year budget estimates but made no explicit mention of the under-lying economic assumptions. The Employment Act of 1946 appears to have been the first law that actually required publication of information concerning the eco-nomic outlook. The Employment Act of 1946 required publication of an economic report setting forth, among other things, '. . . current and foreseeable trends in the levels of employment, production, and purchasing power . . .'[6]

As the economy matured, several factors contributed to a lengthening of the temporal horizon for the budget outlook. The increasing importance of international trade and uncertainties regarding its impact on the domestic macroeconomic outlook were one factor. The surge in entitlement spending also weighed heavily on the agenda of policy makers. Thus the forecast window for the economic assumptions underlying the budget widened. The Congressional Budget Act of 1974 extended the requirements of the Budget and Accounting Act of 1921 by requiring five-year budget projections. The Act also specified that:

> Accompanying these estimates shall be the economic and programmatic assumptions underlying the estimated outlays and proposed budget authority, such as the rate of inflation, the rate of real economic growth, the unemployment rate, program caseloads, and pay increases.

This Congressional Budget Act of 1974 brought about a noticeable change in the scope of the Administration's economic assumptions. In 1974, the economic assumptions published with the FY 1975 Budget consisted of one-year-ahead forecasts of gross national product, personal income, and corporate profits. With the publication of the FY 1976 Budget in 1975 (after passage of the Congressional Budget Act of 1974), the economic assumptions became much more complete, showing a table that is very similar in breadth of detail and forecast horizon to the tables presented in current budget documents.

The Full Employment and Balanced Growth Act of 1978 (Humphrey–Hawkins Act) was the most specific piece of legislation regarding required publication of the Administration's economic assumptions. The Humphrey–Hawkins Act required that the President specify '... annual numeric goals for employment and unemployment, production, real income, productivity, and prices ...' and describe the policies and timetable for achieving those goals in the *Economic Report of the President*. Specific goals for the civilian unemployment rate (4 per cent) and the rate of CPI inflation (3 per cent) were established in the Act.[7] The first Administration forecast following the passage of the Humphrey–Hawkins Act complied fully with its requirements. Thereafter, however, there was a steady erosion of compliance, beginning with a delay of the timetable to meet the goals (1980), followed by discussion of the Act's requirements in the *Economic Report of the President* with no explicit timetable for attaining the goals (1981–89), to no specific mention of the Act or its goals (1990–97). The goals of the Humphrey–Hawkins Act steadily faded from the policy-making process as they appeared less and less attainable and as other legislation was passed which imposed other constraints on the efficacy of fiscal policy.[8] Technically, the provisions of the Humphrey–Hawkins Act remain in force today.

3. The Troika process today

Throughout the Bush and Clinton Administrations the Troika has served two main

roles. At the T-2 level, the Troika meets regularly to formulate policy recommendations and construct the Administration's economic agenda on a variety of issues.
General macroeconomic policy issues are typically at the forefront, but the Troika
also has been involved in other issues, including health care reform, welfare reform,
entitlement spending, tax reform, and alternative mechanisms to increase private
saving. The Troika's most important on-going responsibility is to produce the
Administration's economic projections.

The macroeconomic forecasts of any Administration serve two purposes: (i) as a
basis for the determination of the revenue and outlay estimates of the budget; and
(ii) as a policy statement by the Administration. As a basis for the determination of
the budget estimates, there is an implicit requirement for an honest and accurate
assessment of current economic conditions in order to formulate reasonable
assumptions on which to base the forecasts. At the same time however, because
these forecasts are designed to reflect the presumably beneficial economic effects of
the Administration's policy proposals, there is an inherent tension between developing 'politically correct' economic assumptions which suggest a strong economy
moving toward full employment with low inflation versus an honest assessment of
current conditions and the likely impacts of these policies over the forecast horizon.
The weights applied to these sometimes conflicting responsibilities can vary greatly
as membership in the Troika changes.

The Troika forecast is also subjective in nature and this fact historically has led to
the tension between accuracy and political purpose. Various statistical models and
technical and theoretical relationships are used to construct the forecast (as will be
discussed further below), but they do not ultimately determine the final forecast.
This subjective approach isn't very different from the methods used by the vast
majority of macroeconomic forecasters, both public and private, although different
incentives may exist. Judgment on the part of the forecaster typically enters in three
ways: (i) in the specification of the model; (ii) in determining forecast paths for the
exogenous variables; and (iii) in targeting, or 'add-factoring' the near-term forecast
values of the endogenous variables of the model to bring the model predictions in
line with current data.[9] The process of generating a model-based forecast then
becomes an iterative one of specifying alternative paths for the exogenous variables,
fine-tuning the near-term forecasts of the endogenous variables, and checking the
forecast throughout the horizon for reasonableness and consistency.

While the Troika often meets at various times during the year to discuss evolving
policy issues, the process for determining the Administration's economic projections occurs twice a year to coincide with the production of estimates for the
Budget of the United States Government and the Mid-Session Review of the
Budget. The process usually begins about two months before the publication date
for the budget document. After several preliminary meetings within each agency,
consultation with outside experts in the economic and financial community, and
considerable exploratory data analysis, the T-3 staff meet formally to develop a
research agenda for the Troika concerning pertinent economic issues and draft a
memorandum for T-2.

In its final form, the T-3 memorandum typically summarizes the findings pertaining to the research agenda and provides both a current assessment of economic conditions and a forecast of key economic variables over a six-year horizon. The primary purpose of the T-3 memorandum is to provide a 'most-likely' forecast scenario to T-2 under current policies, without political overtones or assumptions about the impact of proposed policy initiatives. Occasionally, the T-3 memorandum will include alternative forecast scenarios under different policy assumptions at the request of T-2. T-2 then examines the staff recommendations and writes a memorandum to the T-1 principals with the T-2 recommendations. Politics often plays a role at this stage of the Troika process as T-2 tries to incorporate the political objectives of the Administration into the economic assumptions. T-1 then specifies (subject to the approval of the President) the forecast paths for the key economic variables.

The set of economic variables for which the Troika determines forecast paths typically have included the following six key indicators: real GDP growth; rate of inflation as measured by the GDP implicit price deflator (now the chain-weighted GDP price index); inflation as measured by the consumer price index; civilian unemployment rate; yield on three-month Treasury bills; and the yield on ten-year Treasury notes.[10] The set of other key variables followed by the Troika has evolved over time but generally includes: the rate of growth of labor productivity for the nonfarm business sector; wage inflation as measured by hourly compensation in the nonfarm business sector; the average workweek; labor force growth; and the percentage shares of GDP for various measures of taxable personal and corporate income.

A detailed macroeconomic forecast, disaggregated across various sectors of the economy comprising over one hundred variables, is then constructed by the T-3 member from CEA in such a way so that the T-1 forecast paths for the six key variables are met precisely, along with more general targets for the other variables of interest. The detailed quarterly forecast paths used internally by the Administration include forecasts of: nominal and real GDP and its components; various labor force, employment, and unemployment variables; various inflation measures and indicators; the various components of national income on a national income and produce accounts (NIPA) basis; and other key variables such as housing starts, motor vehicle sales, and industrial production. This forecast detail is then provided to the Troika members and key staff at the OMB and Department of the Treasury.[11] Both departments then run, independently, their own models of revenue and expenditures based on these economic assumptions to get preliminary estimates of the Budget to report to the President. The Office of Tax Analysis in the Department of the Treasury then produces revenue projections while the OMB works with the various Federal agencies to produce expenditure estimates and together they produce a final estimate of the Budget which is subsequently published.

4. The role of models in the troika process

Economic models play an important role within the Troika process. This section presents various types of models used by the Troika and discusses some examples of how they are used.

Large-scale macroeconometric models Large-scale macroeconometric models are used in several different ways in the Troika process. Such models typically are used to produce the detailed macroeconomic forecast for the budget (as described above) or to examine behavioral responses to specific policies or shocks. Historically, the CEA, Treasury and OMB have subscribed to a variety of commercial macroeconomic forecasts and models. The agencies subscribe to these models rather than face the higher resource cost of estimating and maintaining an in-house large-scale macroeconometric model.[12]

Probably the most important role for these models, in practice, is in the production of the detailed macroeconomic forecast that is used in the budget process as described above. The detailed macroeconomic forecast often is constructed using a so-called 'black box' of accounting identities resident within a dynamic, simultaneous equations, structural macroeconometric model. The so-called 'black box' is a software program of national income and product accounting relationships that allowed for a 'top-down' imposition of the key forecast variables described above on the model, assuring consistency across all the variables of the forecast.[13] The alternative to the 'black box' is to achieve the target forecast paths manually through additive or multiplicative adjustment factors and successive iterations of the macroeconometric model.

Macroeconometric models also are used, in conjunction with internally generated models, to simulate alternative policy scenarios and/or exogenous shocks and their likely effects on key variables such as real GDP growth and unemployment. Specific examples include the examination of potential or actual shocks, such as the oil price increase when Iraq invaded Kuwait; the possible effects of a decline in stock market valuation; and net export shocks from disruptions in international markets. Large-scale macroeconomic models also have been used to examine potential economic benefits from policy proposals. For example, at the beginning of the Clinton Administration in 1993, model simulations of the 'Vision of Change' deficit reduction plan were used to try to project what the long-term interest rate response would be to deficit reduction. The models' predictions for the ultimate effects of the deficit reduction plan on long-term interest rates then served as the basis for a prediction of what the immediate decline could be given the forward-looking nature of financial markets. Later, in 1995, similar simulations examining the response of long-term interest rates to deficit reduction served as a basis for determining what the 'fiscal dividend' might be from proposals to balance the budget.[14]

Smaller macro and policy models Smaller models are often developed internally to address specific issues, and members of the T-3 staff often maintain their own models based on their own research efforts. Examples include Phillips Curve models of the inflation process, Solow-type growth models, and models of the monetary policy process such as Taylor's rule models,[15] among others. By their nature, these models are used to answer specific questions about wage and/or price inflation and unemployment, long-term macroeconomic relationships in the economy and how policy proposals affect such relationships, and projected policy paths for short-term interest rates for alternative paths for real growth and inflation.

The growth accounting framework   During the past two Administrations, medium- and long-term Troika forecasts have focused on properly estimating potential GDP growth. An important part of the philosophy of the Troika has been that the budget forecasts should avoid attempting to predict cyclical turning points in the economy, and instead identify the economy's potential output growth rate as a benchmark for policy recommendations. Hence, the short-run projections are used to return the economy gradually to its long-run growth path. For example, if the level of real GDP was above the estimated level of real potential GDP, the short-run projection would have real GDP growth lower than growth of potential GDP by a sufficient amount and for a sufficient duration to return the level of real GDP to potential. Thereafter, the medium- and long-term projections would follow the path for potential GDP.

Since 1985, the Administration's forecasts have been accompanied in the annual *Economic Report of the President* with a growth accounting table which formed the basis of the official forecasts of medium-term growth and provided a check on the Administration's model-based econometric forecasts. The results presented in Table 14.1, reproduced from the *1998 Economic Report of the President,* are based on a simple accounting identity for real output:

$$\text{Output} \equiv \frac{\text{Output}}{\text{Avg Hours}} \times \frac{\text{Avg Hours}}{\text{Employment}} \times \frac{\text{Employment}}{\text{Labor Force}}$$
$$\times \frac{\text{Labor Force}}{\text{Population}} \times \text{Population},$$

which implies that output can be decomposed as:

$$\text{Output} \equiv \text{Productivity} \times \text{Avg Hours per Worker} \times (1 - \text{Unemployment Rate})$$
$$\times \text{Labor Force Participation Rate} \times \text{Population}.$$

The time periods in Table 14.1 coincide with business cycle peaks in the US macroeconomy. Since 1960, real GDP has grown at an annual rate of 3.2 per cent, according to the Commerce Department's newly-featured chain-weighted measure of real output. As shown in Table 14.1, most of this growth can be attributed to population and average labor productivity (output per hour). By definition,

Table 14.1 Accounting for growth in real GDP (average annual per cent change)

		1960q2 to 1973q4	1973q4 to 1990q3	1990q3 to 1997q3	1997q3 to 2005
	Civilian Population aged 16 & over	1.8	1.5	1.0	1.0
Plus:	Labor force participation rate[1]	0.2	0.5	0.0	0.1
Equals:	Total labor force[1]	2.0	2.0	1.1	1.1
Plus:	Employment rate[1]	0.0	−0.1	0.1	−0.1
Equals:	Total employment[1]	2.0	1.9	1.2	1.0
Plus:	Nonfarm business employment as a share of total employment[1,2]	0.1	0.1	0.2	0.1
Equals:	Nonfarm business employment	2.1	2.0	1.4	1.1
Plus:	Average weekly hours	−0.4	−0.3	0.1	0.0
Equals:	Total hours worked	1.6	1.7	1.5	1.1
Plus:	Output per hour (productivity)	2.8	1.1	1.1	1.3
Equals:	Nonfarm business output	4.5	2.8	2.7	2.4
Minus:	Nonfarm business output as a share of real GDP[3]	0.3	0.1	0.4	0.1
Equals:	**Real GDP**	4.2	2.7	2.3	2.3

Source: 1998 Economic Report of the President, p. 82.
Notes:
Except for 1997, time periods are from business-cycle peak to business-cycle peak to avoid cyclical variation.
Detail may not add to totals because of rounding.
[1] Adjusted for 1994 revision of the Current Population Survey
[2] Translates the civilian employment growth rate into the nonfarm business employment growth rate.
[3] Translates nonfarm business output back into output for all sectors (GDP), which includes the output of farms and general government.

employment rates and average hours worked vary little from one business cycle peak to the next.

As shown in Table 14.1, population growth in the US has slowed during the current expansion, and has led to slower overall employment growth of just 1 per cent, compared with nearly 2 per cent growth during previous expansions. The real puzzle, however, has been the reported slowdown in the growth of nonfarm business productivity despite significant growth in nonresidential fixed investment during the past decade. Much has been written about possible sources of mismeasurement and bias in the reported productivity statistics. And the data on productivity, particularly in the service sectors of the economy, do seem to be much lower than anecdotal and survey evidence would tend to imply. Nonetheless, at the time of this writing and based purely on the reported data, potential output growth in the US seems to be in the neighborhood of 2.3 per cent.

Table 14.1 also provides the current Troika projections for output growth in the medium-term. As such they provide a guide for policy makers seeking to improve the nation's output potential. Among the various categories in Table 14.1, the most likely area in which public policy can have an significant impact is in improving the rate of growth of productivity.

Hits model   Staff members of the Troika from the Office of Management and Budget also maintain a model casually referred to as the 'hits model'. It received this name because it is used to estimate what 'hit' the budget would take from a specific economic assumption change. The hits model is a detailed set of budget accounting identities and relationships that permit a comparison of alternative and base budget estimates. The base scenario typically is the existing Administration budget forecast, and the alternative scenarios account for different, or updated, sets of economic assumptions. For example, if data releases show that real GDP growth is faster and unemployment lower than in the Administration projections, that information can be introduced into the hits model and the likely effect on budget estimates – higher revenues and lower spending – can be predicted.

The hits model allows policy makers and the Troika to understand what the likely budget effects would be on an ongoing basis as new information comes in about changing economic conditions. It also is used during the Troika forecast process, to consider what the likely budget effects would be from changing the Administration's economic assumptions. The hits model allows quick estimates to be made without having to conduct a detailed set of tax and spending estimates – such as occurs for formal budget estimates – that would require a time consuming effort on the part of all agencies and departments.

The hits model also is used to provide rules of thumb to the public about what the likely budget effects would be from changes in economic assumptions. The annual budget submissions contain a table 'Sensitivity of the Budget to Economic Assumptions' showing that information.[16]

Long-term budget model   In recent years, as the budgetary focus of policy makers has become increasingly longer term in nature, efforts have been made to produce long-term budget estimates. The Troika staff from the Office of Management and Budget now maintain a budget model for producing long-term budget estimates based on current policy or new Administration budget proposals:

> Long-run budget projections require long-run demographic and economic forecasts – even though any such forecast is highly uncertain and likely to be at least partly wrong. The forecast used ... extends the Administration's medium-term economic projections ... augmented by the long-run demographic projections from the most recent Social Security Trustees' Report... The economic projections ... are set by assumption and do not automatically

change in response to changes in the budget outlook. This is unrealistic, but it simplifies comparisons of alternative policies. A more responsive (or dynamic) set of assumptions would serve mainly to strengthen the same conclusions reached by the current approach. In their investigations of the long-run outlook, both CBO and GAO have explored such feedback effects and found that they accelerate the destabilizing effects of budget deficits.[17]

Revenue Models   A representative of the staff of the Office of Tax Analysis (OTA) of the Department of the Treasury also participates in the Troika. The OTA is of critical importance in the Troika and budget process because it produces the detailed revenue forecasts for the budget projections. The OTA uses numerous models for estimating revenues from various sources, in the broadly-defined categories of personal income taxes, estate and gift taxes, corporate profits taxes, customs duties, social security and Medicare payroll taxes. The models have to be quite sophisticated, but are proprietary in nature and no details are available for discussion here.

5. Integrity of the Troika forecasts

There are a number of areas in which the integrity of the Troika forecasts can be questioned. The Administration's forecasts are policy forecasts, i.e. the forecasts are made conditional on the adoption of the Administration's policy proposals. As a result, there is a political incentive toward positive bias in the economic projections which would reflect optimistic scenarios regarding productivity and employment objectives. If the Administration's policy proposals are not adopted by Congress, forecast errors can therefore be blamed on implementation failures rather than unrealistic economic assumptions. However, pursuit of policy promotion over accuracy can be a risky political strategy and the credibility of the Administration's forecasts can suffer, incurring costs to both sides of any budget battle as witnessed during both the Bush and Clinton Administrations.

A number of researchers, both inside and outside the government, have followed the accuracy of official government forecasts. The Congressional Budget Office (CBO) regularly provides an evaluation of its forecasts relative to the Administration and a consensus of private-sector forecasts.[18] Kamlet, Mowrey and Su (1987) examined Administration forecasts for the 1962–84 period and CBO forecasts for 1976–84 and found little optimistic bias in Administration short-term forecasts, but substantial optimistic bias in longer-term forecasts. John Kitchen (1993) has examined the informational content of the CBO and Troika forecasts relative to private sector consensus forecasts and identified historical periods of positive biases in the Administration's economic budgetary assumptions.

An interesting difference in the methodologies used by the Administration and the CBO is that the optimal forecast of medium-term growth for CBO rests on the assumption that real output maintains a historical gap below potential, while the Administration assumes medium-term growth at potential. Although the differences in growth projections are often on the order of just 0.1 to 0.2 percentage points per annum, the effects of compounding over a 5 to 7-year budget horizon often have led to significant differences in overall deficit projections.

Table 14.2 shows medium-term Troika projections of real GNP growth, productivity growth, and labor force growth published from 1982 to 1996. Actual historical values are shown for comparison. The forecasts shown tend to be optimistic regarding growth in all three variables, with a positive bias of 0.9 percentage points for real GDP growth. Forecasts of labor force growth, which typically mirror those provided by the Department of Labor, are most accurate, with almost no bias on average among these forecasts. Productivity growth forecasts on average have been 0.6 percentage points above actual and thus account for much of the error for real GNP projections when examined in the context of the growth accounting framework presented earlier.

Table 14.2 Troika medium-term projections

Forecast horizon	Real GNP growth			Productivity growth			Labor force growth		
	Forecast	Actual	Difference	Forecast	Actual	Difference	Forecast	Actual	Difference
1982–87	4.4	3.2	1.2	2.2	1.8	0.4	n.a.	1.7	n.a.
1983–88	3.6	4.0	−0.4	1.8	1.4	0.4	n.a.	1.7	n.a.
1984–89	4.2	3.2	1.0	1.5	0.8	0.7	n.a.	1.7	n.a.
1984q4–90q4	3.9	2.5	1.4	2.0	0.6	1.4	1.6	1.7	−0.1
1985q4–91q4	3.8	2.0	1.8	1.8	0.8	1.0	1.5	1.5	0.0
1986q4–92q4	3.5	2.2	1.3	1.9	1.1	0.8	1.5	1.3	0.2
1987q4–93q4	3.2	2.2	1.0	1.9	1.1	0.8	1.4	1.3	0.1
1988q4–94q4	3.2	2.2	1.0	1.9	1.3	0.6	1.4	1.3	0.1
1989q4–95q4	3.0	2.2	0.8	1.8	1.9	−0.1	1.3	1.1	0.2
1990q4–96q4	2.6	2.5	0.1	1.8	1.8	0.0	1.3	1.1	0.2
Average	3.5	2.6	0.9	1.9	1.3	0.6	1.4	1.3	0.1

Notes:
Actual data for real GNP growth for 1982q1–1995q2 are calculated using constant 1982 dollars. Actual data for real GNP growth for 1995q3–1996q4 are calculated using constant 1992 dollars.
Actual data for productivity growth for 1982q1–1995q3 are calculated based on an index of 1982 = 100. Actual data for productivity growth for 1995q4 – 1996q4 are calculated using the revised 1992 = 100 index values.

Stephen K. McNees (1995) has examined the historical accuracy of economic projections through 1994 made by the Council of Economic Advisers beginning in 1962; the CBO beginning in 1976; and the Federal Reserve Board dating back to 1980. McNees looked at forecast errors for inflation and output projections made by each agency relative to each other and a variety of private-sector forecasts. As expected, his results vary depending on the time period in which the forecasts were generated, the economic variable analyzed, and the length of the forecast horizon. He does, however, confirm the significant positive biases in the Administration's multiyear output growth forecasts and notes that the private-sector and CBO output growth forecasts were noticeably more accurate. Of these agencies, however, McNees concludes that the Federal Reserve Board forecasts were, in general, more accurate than other 'official' forecasts and slightly more accurate than private-sector forecasts.

Partly in response to criticisms that Administration forecasts had become too optimistic during the later 1980s and early 1990s, there was an effort which began during the Bush Administration and has continued through the Clinton Administration to re-establish credibility in the Troika process by placing greater emphasis on the accuracy and credibility of economic and budget projections.

6. Conclusion

Over the past three decades the Administration Troika has played an important role in evaluating economic policy and coordinating the development of the Administration's economic outlook and projections. It is hard to imagine how an Administration could function properly on macroeconomic policy and outlook issues in the absence of a formal structure and process such as that provided by the Troika.

The issue of forecast accuracy and possible biases will continue to influence the Troika process as the conflicting objectives of policy promotion versus credibility weigh on the inherently political nature of the process. Ultimately, the success of the Troika will rest on the accuracy and credibility of the forecasts and soundness of the advice it presents to the President and Administration policy makers.

Authors' Note

Michael Donihue was the senior economist responsible for macroeconomics and forecasting at the Council of Economic Advisers during 1994 and 1995. John Kitchen held the same position from 1991–93 and currently represents the Department of Treasury as a T-3 member of the Troika. The conclusions and results presented in this chapter are the authors and do not necessarily represent the opinions of the US Department of Treasury or the Executive Office of the President.

Notes

1 See the three articles by J. Bradford De Long, Charles L. Schultze, and Herbert Stein published in the Summer 1996 issue of *The Journal of Economic Perspectives* commemorating the fiftieth anniversary of the Council of Economic Advisers.
2 See Hargrove and Marley (1984), p. 135.
3 *Economic Report of the President 1962*, p. 197.
4 See the interviews published in Hargrove and Morley (1984), pp. 6, 190, and 286.
5 Hargrove and Morley (1984), p. 190.
6 Bailey (1950) provides a good overview of the Employment Act of 1946.
7 The act explicitly stated, however, that the unemployment rate goal took precedence over the inflation goal (Sec. 4. (b) (2)): '. . . policies and programs for reducing the rate of inflation shall be designated so as not to impede achievement of the goals and timetables specified in clause (1) of this subsection for the reduction of unemployment.'
8 Examples include the Balanced Budget and Emergency Deficit Control Act of 1985 (Gramm–Rudman–Hollings), and the Omnibus Budget Reconciliation Acts of 1990 and 1993.

9 See Donihue (1993) for an analysis of the role judgment plays in producing macroeconomic forecasts.

10 The yield on ten-year Treasury notes first appeared as part of the official Troika forecasts in 1983.

11 OMB circulates an edited version of the disaggregated economic assumptions to various agencies of the Federal government for use in determining their agencys' budget projections.

12 This contrasts with the Federal Reserve, for example, where resources are devoted to a large staff of research economists to maintain forecasting models and undertake specific research projects.

13 The 'black-box' and accompanying structural macroeconometric model, were developed by Laurence H. Meyer & Associates (now known as Macroeconomic Advisers, LLC) of St. Louis.

14 The 'fiscal dividend' was generally defined as the beneficial economic effects that would result from deficit reduction, but typically focused on the lower real interest rates and higher real GDP growth rates. The Congressional Budget Office (CBO) conducted similar simulations (see Congressional Budget Office, April 1995).

15 See Taylor (1993).

16 See, for example, *Analytical Perspectives, Budget of the United States Government, Fiscal Year 1999*, p. 14.

17 *Analytical Perspectives, Budget of the United States Government, Fiscal Year 1999*, pp. 24–5.

18 See, for example, *The Economic and Budget Outlook: Fiscal Years 1996–2000*, p. 20.

References

Bailey, Stephen, 1950. *Congress Makes a Law: The Story Behind the Employment Act of 1946*. New York: Columbia University Press.

Congressional Budget Office, April 1995. *An Analysis of the President's Budgetary Proposals for Fiscal Year 1996*. Washington, D.C.: Government Printing Office.

Congressional Budget Office, 1997. *Analytical Perspectives, Budget of the United States Government, Fiscal Year 1999*, Washington, D.C.: Government Printing Office.

Congressional Budget Office, 1997. *Budget of the United States Government, Fiscal Year 1998*. Washington, D.C.: Government Printing Office.

Congressional Budget Office, January 1995. *The Economic and Budget Outlook: Fiscal Years 1996–2000*. Washington, D.C.: Government Printing Office.

Council of Economic Advisers, 1962, 1997. *Economic Report of the President*. Washington, D.C.: Government Printing Office.

De Long, J. Bradford, Summer 1996. 'Keynesianism, Pennsylvania Avenue style: some economic consequences of the Employment Act of 1946', *The Journal of Economic Perspectives*, Vol. 10, No. 3, pp. 41–54.

Donihue, Michael R., February 1993. 'Evaluating the role judgment plays in forecast accuracy', *Journal of Forecasting*, Vol. 12, No. 2, pp. 81–92.

Hargrove, Erwin C. and Samuel A. Morley, 1984. *The President and the Council of Economic Advisers: Interviews with CEA Chairmen*. Boulder, Colorado: Westview Press.

Kamlet, Mark S., David D. Mowrey and Tsai-Tsu Su, 'Whom Do You Trust? An Analysis of Executive and Congressional Economic Forecasts', *Journal of Policy Analysis and Management*, Vol. 6, No. 3, pp. 365–84.

Kitchen, John, 1994. 'Relative Information in Public and Private Sector Macroeconomic Forecasts', *Federal Forecasters Conference – 1993: Chapters and Proceedings*, pp. 171–80.

Schultze, Charles L., Summer 1996. 'The CEA: An Inside Voice for Mainstream Economics', *The Journal of Economic Perspectives,* Vol. 10, No. 3, pp. 23–40.

Stein, Herbert, Summer 1996. 'A Successful Accident: Recollections and Speculations about the CEA', *The Journal of Economic Perspectives,* Vol. 10, No. 3, pp. 3–22.

Taylor, John, 1993. 'Discretion versus Policy Rules in Practice', *Carnegie Rochester Series on Public Policy,* pp. 195–214.

United States Government, 1985. *Balanced Budget and Emergency Deficit Control Act of 1985, 99th Congress, 1st Session, Dec. 12, 1985.* Washington, D.C.: Government Printing Office.

United States Government, 1978. *The Full Employment and Balanced Growth Act of 1978, 95th Congress, 2nd Session, Oct. 27, 1878.* Washington, D.C.: Government Printing Office.

United States Government, 1990. *Omnibus Budget Reconciliation Act of 1990, 101st Congress, 2nd Session, Nov. 5, 1990.* Washington, D.C.: Government Printing Office.

United States Government, 1993. *Omnibus Budget Reconciliation Act of 1993, 103rd Congress, 1st Session, Aug. 4, 1993.* Washington, D.C.: Government Printing Office.

United States Government, 1946. *Public Law 304 [Employment Act of 1946], 79th Congress, 2nd Session, Feb. 20, 1946.* Washington, D.C.: Government Printing Office.

Chapter 15

Emergent policy-making with macroeconometric models*

Ron Smith

Despite extensive criticism from academic economists, large macroeconometric models have thrived in government. This chapter considers why they have been found useful. It argues that the way economists describe the forecasting and policy process can be misleading and the actual process by which policy emerges is quite different. It then uses accounts by UK government economic advisers and politicians to describe the role of models in this 'emergent' policy-making process.

JEL classifications: C53, E17, E61

1. Introduction

Large macroeconometric models have been widely used by government and business for about 25 years and the number and types of model in use is still increasing.[1] Their ability to survive and breed is something of a puzzle. Given the widespread criticism to which they have been subjected, one might have expected them to be heading for extinction. The models have been subject to repeated attacks by theorists who argue that they do not represent best practice understanding of the economy and econometricians who argue that they do not represent the data, particularly as systems. In addition, their poor record at ex ante forecasting has been the subject of general scorn. These criticisms are not new. Pesaran and Smith (1985, 1995) discuss how they arose, and they have continued. On the basis of these criticisms many have concluded that the whole enterprise of macroeconometric modelling is inherently flawed, since as the Bank of England (February 1996 Inflation Report, p. 46) put it 'the economy is too complex and rapidly changing for its behaviour to be captured in any fixed set of equations or "model" of the economy'.

In this chapter, I do not want to examine these criticisms, they have been extensively discussed elsewhere.[2] Nor do I want to discuss the scope for improving the econometrics, economic theory or forecasting performance of these models. The question I want to consider is why have they thrived in the competition for

---

*Reprinted from *Economic Modelling*, 15, Ron Smith, 'Emergent policy-making with macroeconometric models', pp. 429–42, Copyright (1998), with permission from Elsevier Science.

resources, given the prevalence of these criticisms? What ecological niche do they inhabit and what is their function in that niche? The discussion focuses on their use in UK macroeconomic policy-making – more general features of the international macromodelling industry are discussed in Smith (1994).

I will argue that the way we economists teach forecasting and policy-making, though pedagogically and analytically useful, does not represent the reality of the policy-making process. Correspondingly, the models do not fulfil the functions that we would impute to them in that process. Thus the academic criticisms that the models are unable to fulfil those particular functions is beside the point, that is not how they are used. It is quite easy to document the fact that models are not used in the text book way, it is more difficult to describe the way in which they are used, and are found useful. For policy makers, models seem to have a similar role to economists in the old joke that 'bankers regard economists like their ties: they don't know what their function is, but they would not go to work without one'.

To understand why macroeconometric models have survived and prospered, despite their manifest deficiencies, we have to understand their latent function within the actual policy-making and forecasting process. Before trying to examine what that function is, we need to briefly consider the alternative explanation. It is possible that the models do not have a latent function at all but really are like banker's ties; a low-cost piece of adornment which provides a useful indicator of conformity and status. I find this explanation implausible. The models are not low cost. A large amount of public funds are spent on the Treasury and Bank of England model teams and the ESRC macromodelling consortium funding of academic model development. The Treasury Bank and ESRC have continued to spend on them despite the fact that in all three cases support for models have been subject to hostile reviews, where other important activities of the organizations were cut.[3] In the Treasury the model survived continual hostility from politicians. Lawson (1992, p. 49), who was Financial Secretary in 1979 when the Conservatives came to power says, 'As soon as we took office, I urged Geoffrey Howe to repeal the Industry Act in its entirety, or failing that, at least the Bray Amendment itself and the obligation to maintain, and publish the results of a computer model of the economy.' He also comments on the 'deep in-house commitment not merely to the Treasury forecasts but to the Treasury model as a central tool of analysis and policy evaluations'.

The argument I will use is very similar to one common in the management literature, which focuses on emergent strategy, hence my title. Barwise (1996) summarizes the main argument, which I paraphrase. The argument is that the formal top-down Analysis, Planning, Implementation and Control model taught in management textbooks is a useful abstraction rather than an accurate description of what managers actually do. Mintzberg (1994) discusses the evolution of these formal methods and why they failed. The reality of management is very different from the textbook model and despite the success of analytical techniques in certain well-defined areas, the core processes of strategy and line management have not moved towards this textbook pattern. Instead, much of the intended strategy is not realized, and much of the realized strategy emerges from a set of less formal, interactive relationships as the agents respond to events. In this process, formal structures such as Capital Budgeting systems with their Discounted Cash Flow projections and the like are not operated in anything like the textbook way (Marsh *et al.*, 1988). However, the conclusion of the literature is that while the formal systems are ritualistic, they are nevertheless a necessary framework for developing the emergent strategy. They force players to be more specific about their key assumptions and options, set deadlines, facilitate the movement of information up and down and sideways and generate commitment to projects.

My argument is that much macroeconomic policy is emergent in this sense, bubbling up from a variety of sources and often primarily driven by events. The movement in the UK between 1986 and 1992 from targeting money stock, to targeting the exchange rate to targeting inflation directly, is a case in point. Smith (1992, p. 206) reviewing the boom–bust of the 1980s comments, 'politicians claimed foresight and intent for situations that they had blundered into by accident'. In these circumstances, the model provides a formal structure, like capital budgeting systems, within which to debate the policy proposals, quantify judgements, ensure consistency, identify the uncertainties, collate information and provide propaganda for successful proposals. Even if its use is often ritualistic, the model plays an important part in providing some discipline to the informal learning and decision process by which policy options are evaluated.

While there is a substantial amount of case study evidence for the emergent strategy account in management, it cannot simply be transferred to macro policy. There are obvious similarities between strategic decision-making in large corporations and macro-policy-making, but there are also obvious differences. Unlike the management literature, where strategy determination has been extensively studied, there is relatively little evidence on the details of internal process by which UK macro policy is determined and the role that models play in this process.[4] The main sources that I have used are published statements by UK modelling teams (particularly the memoranda submitted to the Treasury and Civil Service Committee investigation into official forecasting, TCSC, 1991), economic advisers and politicians. While these may be partly self-serving, they are at least based on experience.

While some aspects of this account of the UK process may apply elsewhere, some may not because of different institutional structures. Until 1997, when the Bank of England was given independent control of monetary policy, UK economic policy-making was highly concentrated in the Treasury, who conducted its own modelling in house. The process is different when there is an independent Central Bank, particularly where there are transparent contractual arrangements as in New Zealand, discussed by Mayes and Razzack (1998, Chapter 7 in this volume). The process is also different when there is an independent source of modelling and analysis as in the case of the CPB in the Netherlands, discussed by Donders and Graafland (1998, Chapter 2 in this volume), or in Norway, discussed by Bjerkholt (1998, Chapter 10 in this volume).

Section 2 sets out the standard academic account of the use of models in forecasting and policy and discusses why this account is inadequate. Section 3 summarizes what UK economic advisers and politicians have said about the use of models. Section 4 discusses how the Treasury currently uses models and forecasts. Section 5 contains some tentative conclusions.

2. The standard account[5]

A macro model describes how sets of exogenous variables determined outside the model, policy instruments and disturbances determine a set of endogenous variables. It is estimated over the sample period, using data up to the present. The Government is assumed to have some objective function defined over current and discounted future values of endogenous target variables (like unemployment and inflation) and instruments (e.g. fiscal and monetary policy variables). The policy problem is then to choose optimal settings for the instruments, by minimizing the objective function, subject to the model, conditional on forecasts of the exogenous variables and disturbances. The forecasts of the disturbances are known as residual adjustments and are almost universal in forecasting models. The model then provides a consistent set of policy settings and forecasts which the Chancellor can present to Parliament in his budget.

This account so far neglects uncertainty and there are a number of ways that the model can be used to investigate uncertainty. Confidence intervals for the forecasts can be obtained by stochastic simulation. The model can be used for scenario analysis to investigate the implications for policy and performance of a different set of exogenous events and error terms. The robustness of a particular policy can be evaluated by running it on another model and hedging strategies could be developed. The scenario analysis can be used to prepare contingency plans, which would enable the policy maker to respond rapidly if one of the central exogenous assumptions (e.g. staying in the European Exchange Rate Mechanism prior to 16 September 1992) were not to be realized. Full stochastic optimization would involve minimizing the expectation of the objective function, where the expectation is taken by averaging over simulated realizations of the exogenous variables and the disturbances generated randomly from some distribution.

This account also abstracts from forward-looking behaviour. But it is now relatively straightforward to allow for rational expectations in large models, and there is a substantial literature on the appropriate solution concepts for the dynamic game between a government and a forward-looking private sector. In addition, since countries are interdependent, there is potential for international policy co-ordination, e.g. on the emission of greenhouse gases. Model simulations can be used to clarify the issues and alternatives under negotiation.

Although such a process could be implemented, and there is a large academic literature which does implement elements of this process (e.g. see Bray *et al.*, 1995); it is not how models are used in the formation of real policy decisions. Many of the arguments of the Ball (1978) Committee on Policy Optimization remain valid as does their general conclusion that while optimal control is a useful tool in model evaluation, it is of limited applicability to policy formation. Bray *et al.* (1995,

p. 997) comment, 'In practice, what tends to happen with an empirical macro-model is that there will be some odd quirk in the model, an odd non-linearity, a corner solution or even an extreme assumption, such as rational expectations which the optimal policy rule is able to exploit . . . Rather we must use our understanding of the model . . . and to deemphasize the less reliable elements of the models structure.'

There are a variety of reasons that the models are not used in the textbook way. They represent the instruments of policy in an over-simple manner, real tax and expenditure decisions are more complex. There is scepticism about the effectiveness of the short-term adjustment of policies. Real political objectives and constraints are far too complicated to be summarized in a loss function, since they involve multiple changing values and sequential attention to goals. The models cannot capture the swings in sentiment, particularly of financial markets, which are crucial to policy and not well presented by the usual models of expectations.

The models are certainly used to produce forecasts, though a substantial amount of judgement is used in setting the exogenous variables and residual adjustments. Dicks and Burrell (1994) provide a detailed account of the practice of forecasting with a model. They point out that the differences between forecasts is usually small relative to the difference between forecasts and actuals. Forecast performance has been extensively analysed, e.g. see Wallis (1989) and Lamont (1995). However, most of the macroeconomic forecast evaluation literature cannot answer the fundamental question: would policy have been better or worse without the forecasts. In financial markets, where there is a clear criterion, money, one can ask whether using forecasts leads to more profitable decisions, e.g. Leitch and Tanner (1991); Pesaran and Timmerman (1994). In macro policy, there is no unambiguous criterion, since we lack an agreed loss-function, thus one cannot judge the value added in policy terms of these forecasts.

The text book account treats forecasting and policy-making as complementary activities, there is now increasing concern that they may be competitive. This may be because the best model for forecasting may not be the best model for policy formation, or because the constraints of short-term forecasting, establishing a best guess, may distract attention from the central policy issues, which require consideration of a range of alternatives; see Wren-Lewis (1997). In principle, scenario analysis can be used to investigate alternatives, in practice there are difficulties. Scenario analysis has been most useful in business, where the uncertainty is about a single variable (e.g. the price of oil in the case of Shell, one of the main proponents of scenario analysis). In macro policy there is rarely a single uncertainty. Of the many possible shocks, the one that actually hits you is unlikely to have been considered.[6] When there is a single uncertainty, e.g. ERM membership, it is often about policy. Commitment to the policy within the organization then makes it very difficult to use scenario analysis to produce contingency plans. Unlike decision-making in financial markets, it is very difficult to construct hedging strategies for macro policy.

3. Users' views

It is very clear from published material that policy makers use models with a degree of scepticism that is not captured by the standard account. But despite this scepticism they find them useful nonetheless. The producers of forecasts and users of models are if anything more familiar with their deficiencies and the fragility of their outputs than academic economists. The Treasury publishes average errors for the variables it forecasts. The average error for the year ahead GDP growth forecast given in the 1995 Budget is 1.5 per cent. Thus a 3 per cent prediction for growth would suggest a 95 per cent confidence interval between 0 per cent and 6 per cent growth. Comments by the Chancellor's and Treasury economists suggest that they recognize similar margins of error. The presentation of the Bank of England's inflation forecast, with its brightly coloured fan of a confidence interval, also emphasizes the uncertainty. The February 1997 forecast for the inflation rate in 1999 covers a range from below 1 per cent to above 5 per cent.

A quote by Healey (1990, p. 381) when he was Chancellor in 1974, before he suffered the consequences of the major forecasting errors of his time, is well known: 'after only 8 months in the Treasury, I decided to do for forecasters what the Boston Strangler did for door to door salesmen – to make them distrusted for ever. So I summed up my misgivings about economic forecasts in my November Statement. "Like long-term weather forecasts they are better than nothing . . . but their origin lies in the extrapolation from a partially known past, through an unknown present, to an unknowable future according to theories about the causal relationships between certain economic variables which are hotly disputed by academic economists and may in fact change from country to country or from decade to decade." '

Burns (1986, p. 118), then Chief Economic Adviser and subsequently Permanent Secretary at the Treasury, emphasizes that predictions are an unreliable basis to determine the operation of policy and that the size of the forecast errors means that it is dangerous to place excessive reliance on one approach. 'This suggests the need to monitor a range of forecasts and policy simulations based upon different views of the way economies function and respond.' He then goes on to say that this means that the scope for discretionary stabilisation is limited, 'the design of policy must pay full regard to the limitations of predictions. If excessive demands are made for forecast accuracy this can only lead to increasing frustration with the forecasters' (p. 120). Rather the Treasury tries to develop policies which are robust to outcomes different from the central predictions, though such policies can be difficult to design.

The tendency of econometric relationships to break down when used for policy-making (Goodhart's Law) is also widely recognized. Lawson (1992, p. 55), Financial Secretary and Chancellor, says of the early 1980s, 'The long-standing relationship between output and jobs, used in Treasury forecasting, was shattered (as most forecasts and relationships tend to be when they are really needed by policy makers).' Nonetheless, Lawson (1992) and Healey (1990), for all their scepticism, relied heavily on forecasts, projections and model analyses. In both their memoirs, they repeatedly refer to model outputs as important inputs to policy formation. Lawson (1992, p. 56), 'conceded that projections could raise useful questions about the coherence of policy'. In many cases one requires a quantitative, rather than a qualitative basis for policy, e.g. to judge exactly how much interest rates should rise. Such quantification can only be provided by a model, particularly when the final outcome is the net result of many interacting mechanisms and qualitative results are parameter dependent.

As an example of such quantification surrounded by scepticism, Lawson (1992, p. 838), discusses the rule of thumb that emerged from the model that a 4 per cent rise in the exchange rate was roughly equivalent in terms of its restrictive effect on demand and inflation to a 1 per cent rise in base rates. 'I myself never went overboard for the 4-to-1 rule. Interest rate and exchange rate changes worked their way through the economy by such different channels and through such different sectors that to treat them as equivalent with this degree of quantification was too great a violation of reality even for macroeconomic policy.' Of course this is the politician's presentation of events. Economic advisers are more likely to see the world as full of policy makers who insist on having answers to damn-fool and ill-specified questions where the present state of knowledge is grossly inadequate, and who then dump on the analysis when either it proves wrong ex post, or when they or events in general have moved the goal posts.[7]

Whatever their scepticism, users recognize that one has to make some judgement about the future in order to determine policy. As Burns (1986, p. 117–18) says: 'Some kind of forward look is therefore essential and it is best to do this in a consistent way ... The discipline of recording predictions along with the logic involved in their preparation is an essential part of the learning process, along with regular postmortems of the results. The model itself provides a description of how the economy works, and a benchmark against which to set out judgements.' 'The conduct of monetary and fiscal policy would have been considerably more difficult if we had not set out for our own use an articulate, coherent set of projections for the main variables' (p. 121).

Burns (1986) emphasizes the role of the model as a framework: an efficient way of storing information and ensuring consistency coherence and attention to detail and most of the responses to the questions of the TCSC also emphasize this function: 'The framework for bringing all the relevant information together is the Treasury's econometric model of the economy' (TCSC, 1991, p. 3) and within this framework, forecasts 'are a good way of collating the wide range of information' (TCSC, 1991, p. 6). The Bank of England: a model 'provides a coherent framework for organising research and forming policy advice' (TCSC, 1991, p. 54). The model stores a variety of different types of information. At the simplest it is a data bank, which allows one to evaluate the forecast in an historical perspective. It is also a library which embodies the received wisdom about economic relationships in its equations. It helps pull together a wide range of disparate indicators about the current conjuncture, helping you determine where the economy is at the moment.

Dicks and Burrell (1994, p. 130) say, 'On a daily basis there is a barrage of new information, which needs to be processed ... Of course, there is a great deal of "noise", especially in the market data, but repeatedly the forecaster has to ask what information is there in the latest data, to assess whether his or her analysis of the conjuncture is correct and if not why not. This applies not just to the big picture but also to the small detail of the computer print-out.' At times, large model residuals may throw doubt on data for the recent past, which is usually unreliable, and prompt further investigation and revision of the data.[8]

The model ensures consistency not only by making the identities hold but by making sure that assumptions (e.g. about exogenous variables and theoretical relationships) in different parts of the policy-making organization are non-contradictory. When economists are distributed over many departments and each economist has a different small analytical model in the back of their brains, using a common model can reduce contradictions. As is discussed in the next section, the UK Treasury model is used in this way to ensure that macro policy, revenue and spending departments work with the same assumptions. The model also provides coherence, by providing a fully articulated story about the process by which the policy is supposed to work. It is an advantage if the story is right, but the coherence and consistency are themselves valuable, even if the story is wrong.

Godley, who had been in the Treasury, emphasizes not only the framework role, but also the need to 'tolerate and handle the confusion which is truly there' (TCSC, 1991, p. 62). Handling the confusion involves: (1) judging where the economy is now (starting in the right place and facing in the right direction); (2) judging whether the proposed policy is sustainable in the medium-term; and (3) trying to quantify the uncertainties and identify risks. As Hughes describes, this involves a 'two tier approach to forecasting, focusing on overall economic strategy on one side and a regular assessment of economic risks on the other' (TCSC, 1991, p. 78). Within this two-tier approach, medium-term forecasts are more a way of judging the sustainability and thus the credibility of policy than a judgement about what is likely to happen. On p. 58 the Bank says: 'The longer-term is not usually taken very seriously as a forecast because unforeseeable events or policy changes are likely to render it obsolete well before that time arrives. But it can have an important role in considering the sustainability of policies.' The Treasury (TCSC, 1991, p. 6) said that 'The Chancellor needs forecasts before he can judge whether the outlook for public finances in a particular year is consistent with his medium-term objective.'

In the process of dialogue determining policy, alternative scenarios can play as important a role as the central forecast. Lawson (1992, p. 875) says: 'The usual pre-budget economic chapter warned that the struggle (against inflation) could be harder and longer than the official forecasts envisaged.' After setting out the alternative scenario, Lawson (1992) comments that it was more or less what happened. In the discussion of Burns (1986) Sir John Mason (a weather forecaster) suggests that in their present state of development it would be wrong to judge the value of models solely in terms of the accuracy of their forecasts, rather 'they probably have even greater value in the synthesis, diagnosis and simulation of the major components of the economy and for experimentation designed to improve understanding of how the economy works and its sensitivity to various uncertainties introduced by deficiencies in the input data or in the model itself. Burns replies that in the Treasury at least as much time is devoted to such model-based policy and analytical studies as to forecasting.

The Bank of England's description of its then use of the model and forecasts (TCSC, 1991, p. 54) summarizes a lot of these elements. 'The purpose of our forecasts is to understand the economic processes at work and to apply this understanding to an analysis of policy options. We also attach importance to identifying the margins of error of the modelling and forecasting process and its sensitivity to shocks. The process of forecasting in the Bank is therefore one in which a base case is calculated, around which variants are run to suggest a range of uncertainty ... Thus the idea that the Bank forms a central view of the most likely course of the economy at discrete points which could fairly be compared with other forecasts or the outturn does not properly reflect what the Bank actually does.' Since then, of course, the Bank has started to publish inflation forecasts, with confidence intervals.

Clearly, whatever the uncertainties, the published Treasury forecast has an important political function and propaganda role. It provides a coherent vision of the path of the economy which can be defended in Parliament and the media. As the Treasury make clear (TCSC, 1991, p. 6), the forecast is political. 'Ministers are responsible for all material published by the Treasury. The economic forecasts published as an integral part of the Government's twice yearly statement of economic policy, are no exception to this. The forecasts are the Government's forecasts, and have been described as such. They are published after taking advice from Treasury officials, but it is for ministers to decide how far to accept official's advice. This has been the case for many years.' Lawson (1992, p. 50) describes the political process of the revision of the forecast for the 1980 Budget.

Model simulations can be used to persuade and attempt to change attitudes. Lawson (p. 427) is clear that this was the function of the numerical model estimates published in January 1985 in the Treasury Chapter entitled: The Relationship between Employment and Wages: Empirical Evidence for the UK. In the academic community, these particular estimates backfired on the Government, since they involved unexplained changes to an endogenous variable of the model; what Ken Wallis labelled 'if only' rather than 'what if' simulations. It remains the case that groups who wish to argue for policy change are in a much stronger position if they can validate them on an economic model. As Dicks and Burrell (1994) argue, most of the model proprietors were motivated more by belief in policies they wished to propose than by a desire to forecast. The models were constructed to give their theoretical analysis and policy recommendations more coherence and credibility.

4. Current use in the treasury

There is a recent source of information about the extent to which models are used in the UK Treasury. While this document sheds little light on how policy emerges, it does bring out how pervasive the model is as a formal structure. In the UK as part of a series of policy initiatives, various government functions are 'market tested', in-house and outside organizations are asked to bid to carry out the function and subject to certain quality controls, the lowest bidder, private or public wins. At various stages there has been discussion of market testing the Treasury modelling and forecasting function. Prior to any market testing, consultants are hired to assess the feasibility and design of the proposed market test. In January 1997, the Treasury issued an invitation to tender for consultants to assess the feasibility of, and to undertake a scoping study for, a proposed market test of all or part of the Treasury's macroeconomic and public finances forecasting and monitoring function.

If the market test is thought to be feasible, the scoping study sets out the definition of the activity to be subject to market test: the outputs that will be included in the market test specification; the type of service provider best equipped to perform the service; the structure of the remuneration; any possible need to specify production processes; and the evaluation of bids. This would inform the contract specification for the market test. Of course, the consultants who do the feasibility study are not allowed to bid in the market test.

The summary of the services to be considered for market testing include: macroeconomic forecasting; forecasting of public finances; providing advice on medium-term economic assumptions for public expenditure planning and fiscal projections for fiscal policy decisions; monitoring and analysis of macroeconomic and public finance out-turns against the forecast; and assessment of the current economic position. Most of these services could not be provided without a model. As annexes to the invitation to tender, the main tasks and coverage of the activity and the issues to be considered as part of the scoping study are set out. The specification of the tasks covers the very large number of forecasts that are required, the scenario analysis, the monitoring and assessment of the state of the economy, and the regular briefing on the 20 or so key releases a month of new economic statistics. It indicates a very substantial amount of model-based activity since even briefing on new economic statistics is likely to be filtered through the model.

The first issue the document raises is whether the whole, or some part, of the forecasting and monitoring activity can be distinguished from the Treasury's policy advice work, in a way that will allow it to be market tested. This 'boundary' issue recurs in various guises, e.g. the problem of confidentiality and possible conflicts of interest by the service provider. What is clear in the discussion of the boundary issue is how many groups within the Treasury, Inland Revenue and Customs and Excise are involved in the production or use of forecasts and other model outputs. Thus the central question in the scoping study has to answer is whether policy-making and modelling can be separated, and if so where the line should be drawn.[9]

There is an obvious difficulty, noted in the issues, that on the one hand the Treasury wants to be able to set clear contractual performance standards for an independent contractor, yet on the other hand wants to be flexible enough to change its demands dependent on circumstances. In general terms the Treasury wants the forecast to be accurate, timely, internally consistent, well thought through, set out in the required level of detail, well presented, and readily explicable to all necessary audiences. Designing performance indicators for some of these is straightforward, but for others it would not have been easy had modelling been sub-contracted. It notes that the size of errors between forecasts and out-turns would be an imperfect performance yardstick for several obvious reasons which are listed. The fourth of these is that the objective is not simply to produce the best possible point forecasts but also to present a clear and coherent analysis of economic prospects and an assessment of the balance of risks involved.

What comes through in the invitation to tender is the pervasive role of model outputs rather than the importance of the model itself. Forecasts and simulations are used extensively and there is no other way that this large amount of information could be generated and updated in real policy time except through the use of a model. The questions that an academic economist might want to ask – should the model be monetarist or Keynesian, structural or a VAR, real business cycle or computable general equilibrium? – are secondary to the important question: will it produce the required outputs that are needed as inputs into the decision process easily in real time? While most organizations will, quite rightly, use different models for different types of question, there is almost certainly going to be a role for models that look like traditional econometric models, because their outputs are tailored to the policy process in the way that most alternatives, e.g. ARIMA models, are not. Firstly the outputs, forecasts or simulations, embody an economic story. When an adviser presents a forecast and is asked by the Minister to explain it, they can go through the linkages and the plausibility of the story can be judged. This is not the case with ARIMA type models. Secondly, they allow 'what if?' investigations, which unconditional forecasting models, like ARIMA, do not. Thirdly, decision maker's beliefs and judgements can be easily integrated into the model outputs.

5. Conclusion

Macroeconomic policy emerges in many different ways from a variety of sources, not least the pressure of events. The announced policy is the product of an organization and that organization must ensure that all the interconnecting details mesh. In these circumstances, a formal model has advantages. The quotes suggest that a model can help the organization in storing and sharing information, provide structure and discipline to the policy evaluation process, provide a focus for dialogue about particular issues under dispute, ensure coherence and consistency and aid the learning process. The outputs of the model are a useful input into the policy-making process. Policy-making is an inherently quantitative process and needs numbers. A model is the most efficient way of producing coherent and consistent numbers quickly. It is also a flexible way, allowing the input of judgement and the exploration of alternatives.

The practitioners' accounts suggest that the model operates as an aid to the political and bureaucratic process by which policy is determined rather than a mechanical substitute for the process as the standard academic account tends to suggest. The model provides information that helps answer the questions, it does not provide answers. But if you are going to need a comprehensive consistent set of numbers that satisfy past economic relationships, and are going to want to look at alternative policy scenarios and input your judgements about the future, you are going to end up with something that looks like a traditional macro model.

Acknowledgements

This chapter was prepared for the meeting on Empirical Models and Policy-Making, Amsterdam, May 1997. An earlier version of this chapter was presented at the ESRC Macroeconomic Modelling Bureau Conference, July 1996. I am very grateful for comments from participants at both conferences.

Notes

1 Kenway (1994) provides a history of the development of UK models.
2 The *Economic Journal* Policy Forum, edited by Greenaway (1995) is a good introduction.
3 In 1998, the ESRC did abolish the macromodelling consortium.
4 Edison and Marquez (1998, Chapter 12 in this volume) and Duguay and Longworth (1998, Chapter 5 in this volume) provide accounts of the internal process at the US Federal Reserve and the Bank of Canada, respectively.
5 Whitley (1994) and the chapters in Hall (1994) provide detailed discussion of the issues in this section. Blinder (1997) uses the targets-instruments framework to organize a fascinating discussion of the economics of real policy-making.
6 In principle stochastic simulation can cover a very wide range of shocks, but the historical distribution on which the simulation is based may not be a good guide to the future.
7 I am grateful to an anonymous referee for this characterization.
8 Higgins (1986) comments: 'A related, often less recognised imperative for the use of a macroeconometric model is the assistance it can afford in appraising data revisions. Recent economic history is often rewritten by the process of data revision. If the latest published data are passed through the filter of an econometric model, much can be learned about the appropriate weight to be placed on the various pieces of those data.'
9 In fact, it was decided that they could not be separated, so no line was drawn.

References

Ball J. (Chairman), 1978. Report of the Committee on Policy Optimisation. Cmnd 7148, HMSO.

Barwise, P., 1996. Strategic Investment Decisions and Emergent Strategy. Mastering Management, Part 15, *Financial Times*.

Bjerkholt, O., 1998. 'Interaction between model builders and policy makers in the Norwegian tradition', *Econ. Model.* 15, 317–39 (Chapter 10 in this volume).

Blinder, A. S., 1997. 'What Central Bankers could learn from academics – and vice versa', *J. Econ. Perspect.* 11, 3–20.

Bray, J., Hall, S., Kuleshov, A., Nixon, J. and Westaway, P., 1995. 'The Interfaces between policy makers, markets and modellers', *Econ. J.* 105, 989–1000.

Burns, S. T., 1986. The interpretation and use of economic predictions. Predictability in science and society. *Proc. R. Soc. A.*, 407, 103–25.

Dicks, G. and Burrell, A., 1994. *Forecasting in Practice*. Hall.

Donders, J. and Graafland, J., 1998. 'CPB Models and employment policy in the Netherlands', *Econ. Model.* 15, 341–56 (Chapter 2 in this volume).

Duguay, P. and Longworth, D., 1998. 'Macroeconomic models and policy-making at the Bank of Canada', *Econ. Model.* 15, 357–75 (Chapter 5 in this volume).

Edison, H. J. and Marquez, J., 1998. 'US monetary policy and econometric modelling: tales from the FOMC Transcripts 1984–91', *Econ. Model.* 15, 411–28 (Chapter 12 in this volume).

Greenaway, D. (ed.), 1995. 'Policy forum: macroeconomic modelling. Forecasting and policy', *Econ. J.*, 105 (431), 972–1031.

Hall, S. (ed.), 1994. *Applied Economic Forecasting Techniques*. Harvester Wheatsheaf, London.

Healey, D., 1990. *The Time of My Life*. Penguin.

Higgins, C. I., 1986. Coming of Age in the 1970s: Reflections of a Practical Macroeconomist in Foreign Macroeconomic Experience: A Symposium (J. Sargent, research Coordinator). Royal Commission on the Economic Union and Development Prospects for Canada, *Collected Research Studies*, vol. 24. University of Toronto Press, Toronto.

Kenway, P., 1994. *From Keynesianism to Monetarism. The Evolution of UK Macroeconometric Models*. Routledge.

Lamont, O., 1995. Macroeconomic Forecasts and Microeconomic Forecasters. NBER Working Paper 5284.

Lawson, N., 1992. *The View from No. 11*. Corgi Books.

Leitch, G. and Tanner, J. E., 1991. 'Economic forecast evaluation, profits versus the conventional error measures', *Am. Econ. Rev.* 81, 580–90.

Marsh, P., Barwise, P., Thomas, K. and Wensley, R., 1988. Managing Strategic Investment Decisions in Large Diversified Companies. Centre for Business Strategy Report Series, London Business School.

Mayes, D. G. and Razzack, W. A., 1998. Transparency and accountability: empirical models and policy-making at the Reserve Bank of New Zealand. *Econ. Model.* 15, 377–94 (Chapter 7 in this volume).

Mintzberg, H., 1994. *The Rise and Fall of Strategic Planning*. Prentice Hall.

Pesaran, M. H. and Smith, R. P., 1985. 'Evaluation of macroeconometric models', *Econ. Model.* 2, 125–34.

Pesaran, M. H. and Smith, R. P., 1995. 'The role of theory in econometrics', *J. Econom.* 67, 61–79.

Pesaran, M. H. and Timmerman, A., 1994. 'Forecasting stock returns', *J. Forecast.* 13, 335–67.

Smith, D., 1992. *From Boom to Bust: Trial and Error in British Economic Policy*. Penguin.

Smith, R. P., 1994. *The Macromodelling Industry: Structure, Conduct and Performance*. Hall.

TCSC, 1991. Memoranda on Official Forecasting. House of Commons Treasury and Civil Service Committee, HMSO 532-i.

Wallis, K. F., 1989. 'Macroeconomic forecasting: a survey', *Econ. J.* 99, 28–61.

Whitley, J., 1994. *A Course in Macroeconomic Modelling and Forecasting*. Harvester Wheatsheaf.

Wren-Lewis, S., 1997. Conflicts between macroeconomic forecasting and policy analysis. Paper presented at the conference on Empirical Models and Policy-Making, Amsterdam (Chapter 11 in this volume).

Part V

Empirical models and policy-making

Chapter 16

The relevance of economic modelling for policy-making: a panel discussion

Edited by Mary S. Morgan

The essays on empirical models and policy-making contained in this volume were presented at the 10th Anniversary Conference, in Amsterdam, of the foundation of the Tinbergen Institute. As part of the final day of the conference, we (the conference organisers and editors of this volume) arranged a panel discussion to explore policy makers' perspectives on their experiences of the modelling-policy interaction. Our three panellists and chairperson were all invited because they have experience of public policy-making from very high up inside governmental organizations but are also academic economists. We provided four questions in advance to our panellists, with the idea that this would help them to focus on the issues which formed our conference agenda, namely the nature of the two-way interaction between empirical models and policy-making. Our four questions were as follows:

1   There is a wide difference between countries in the experience of using empirical models in the policy process. What, in your experience, is the main way in which economic policy makers use empirical economic models?
2   It is apparent that there are often big gaps between intentions (or expectations) and outcomes in policy makers' usage of empirical models. How do these gaps arise? For example, do they arise through differences in knowledge and experience by modellers and by policy makers or through differences between the kind of questions policy makers ask and the ability of the models to provide answers? How are they resolved through interaction between the groups?
3   The structure of the modelling industry varies considerably. What is the structure of the modelling industry in your country and what are the particular advantages and disadvantages of such a structure in your own experience?
4   The usefulness of economic models in policy-making has recently been called into question. Is there in fact any consensus that empirical economic models are useful in economic policy-making? What would be the best way to improve their usefulness in the future?

These four questions were introduced by the chair of the panel, and each panellist had the opportunity to respond to the question, and to each other's comments, in their replies. We present here an edited transcript of the panel discussions.

Mary Morgan

I'm delighted to welcome our three panel members and chairman for the discussion:

First, I welcome Professor Lisa Lynch, from the Fletcher School of Law and Diplomacy at Tufts University, who is an academic labour economist and editor of the *Journal of Labour Economics*. Professor Lynch has also been involved in public policy-making, serving on a number of advisory committees before becoming, in October 1995, Chief Economist at the US Department of Labour. She resigned in January 1997 to return to academic life. We are particularly pleased that we have been able to secure Professor Lynch's participation because her work focuses on microeconomic issues and so will redress the balance compared to the macroeconomic dimension which has dominated most of our workshop papers.

We also are very pleased to welcome Professor Henk Don, an econometrician primarily involved in public policy analysis and in model-building at the Central Planning Bureau (or, as it should be called in English: the Netherlands Bureau of Economic Policy Analysis). Professor Don became deputy director in 1989 and director of that Bureau in 1994. He has been a visiting professor at the University of Pennsylvania and is now a member of the economics faculty at the University of Amsterdam.

For the third member of the panel, I welcome Professor Edmond Malinvaud who has a very, very distinguished career both domestically in France and of course internationally. When I came to look up the biographical details of Professor Malinvaud there were many, many lines of experience that I might mention. Perhaps the most important and relevant for our purposes is his association with INSEE (Institute National des Statistiques et des Etudes Economiques), where he has worked for many years and was director-general between 1974 and 1987. The INSEE is a rather unusual institution as it incorporates both some of the responsibility taken by the Central Bureau of Statistics in other countries and some of the more general responsibilities of a policy analysis bureau like NIESR in Great Britain, but it is also the '*grand école*' institute responsible for advanced training in economics and statistics. Professor Malinvaud is recognized internationally for his work in econometrics and has twice held a visiting professorship in the United States. Last but not least, as far as we are concerned, he is chairman of the Scientific Council of the Tinbergen Institute.

Lastly, I welcome our Chairman – Professor Ruud Lubbers. It would be difficult to find someone with more policy-making experience here in the Netherlands. Ruud Lubbers, who was Minister of Economic Affairs between 1973 and 1977 and then Prime Minister thereafter from 1982 to 1994, is now Professor of Economics at Tilburg University and is chairman of the Tinbergen Institute Advisory Committee. Professor Lubbers is the chairman of our panel and I now hand over responsibility for the panel discussion to him. Thank you.

Ruud Lubbers

Thank you so much! The idea for this panel is that the three other people here, who are really the experts, will answer four pre-cooked questions. They do not know the answers of the other people so we hope their answers will create interesting contrasts.

The first question relates to the fact that there is a wide difference between countries in the experience of using empirical models in the policy process. 'What is the panel's experience of the ways in which economic policy makers use empirical economic models?' I suggest that Professor Malinvaud starts.

Edmond Malinvaud

Of course the way in which policy makers use empirical economic models has much changed in my experience, as well as in that of others, and was the main theme of our discussions during these past two days. Policy makers have largely revised their conception about what economic policies have to achieve. Although I agree with the message of Ron Smith's chapter, I am tempted to dramatize the implication of this change in objectives. In the 1960s and 1970s policy makers were aiming at macroeconomic fine-tuning. They naturally turned to policy engineers who could tell them how much to press on each instrument at their disposal. This conception fitted perfectly well with the methodology taught by Jan Tinbergen and with the use of macroeconometric models that were set up in this country and elsewhere.

Nowadays a wholly different conception of the main aim of economic policy dominates, at least in two respects. First, a macroeconomic policy line is defined and this line is meant to be implemented over a long period. The main role of policy makers is to attend to implementation, not to discuss the policy line, which is considered to be directly given by sound principles of economic management. Secondly, structural reforms and structural policies are needed: one example of such a policy is the need to lower the cost of unskilled labour for employers, a policy recommendation that is held both in the Netherlands and in France. (Many other examples could as well have been chosen.)

The demand of policy makers for empirical economic knowledge has correspondingly changed. The requirement now is to evaluate the direct and the indirect costs and effects of various actions intended to implement the policy line, or to achieve the objectives of structural changes. So there are two significant differences in language with respect to older times: we now more often speak of evaluating policies rather than proposing policies, we now more often speak of empirical knowledge rather than empirical models. Of course this knowledge is based on underlying models, required for a clear definition of what is known and also for the efficient use of data. The change of words is, however, significant. It means that a wide variety of models can be used depending on the matter at stake and indeed we have seen in the conference papers that a range of models is being considered now.

I believe, however, that this major change with respect to older times in the purpose of policies is of secondary importance when we consider the fundamental difficulty in the collaboration between policy makers and experts in economic knowledge and economic research. The difficulty was in the past – and still is now – the tension between the need to act and the need to know. In other words: the tension between the natural self-confidence of policy makers – who have to act – and the natural diffidence or cautiousness of scientists – who have to guarantee the solidity of knowledge.

I shall quote a revealing case that concerned me in the middle of the year 1974 when we experts, I mean French experts, had correctly diagnosed a serious future stagflation. I was explaining to a minister in charge that I did not know of any policy that could permit us to maintain both the inflation rate and the unemployment rate at the levels that they had at that time. I was explaining that the times had changed, and that there were such things as the collapse of Bretton Woods, oil shocks, and the like. Then the minister, after some time smiled at me and this smile meant something quite clear. 'You do not know of any such policy that would maintain the inflation rate, and the unemployment rate at the level where they are now. You do not know, you smart theorists. But I know!'

Since I was aware of the uncertainties of economics and econometrics, I could not insist. Remembering, in retrospect, what happened to French stagflation in the following years, . . . I am smiling!

Ruud Lubbers

One thing is clear: sometimes it is better to wait and see and then to decide either to smile or not to smile. So far so good! This is an excellent beginning, I think, and we move now to my left, to Professor Lynch.

Lisa Lynch

My role on this panel is to talk about my experience and more generally my perception of the use of empirical models in areas outside of macroeconomic forecasting.

One of the reasons why policy makers smile (or perhaps more worryingly grimace) when we economists begin to speak, is because they are convinced that we are out of touch with the kinds of questions that they have to answer and cannot produce for them the type of information that they need for the policy questions that they face on a daily basis. Of course, the large macro models are quite important in budgetary decisions and in how budget policies are actually implemented. But when you look at many of the current policy debates within the United States (and I think also in Europe), you realize right away why large macro models don't give policy makers the kind of information that they are interested in.

What are some of these issues? First, in the United States, the issue of widening wage and income inequalities is a crucial issue that is not really explicitly addressed by the macroeconomic models. Second, welfare reform, specifically how one moves individuals off welfare into work, is another critical issue where the large macroeconomic models don't provide us with the empirical basis for doing much policy evaluation. In fact a lot of the debate on welfare reform has been informed by microeconometric analysis of longitudinal data, using data sets that have been going sufficiently long that we can follow the transition behaviour of individuals in and out of social welfare programmes, or perhaps more worryingly, constantly remaining in welfare programmes.

A third issue where there has been a lot of interaction between empirical models and policy makers is the minimum wage question. I will return to this issue in more detail in a moment. The fourth issue is social security and pension reform. There was some discussion earlier today in the conference about introducing age and demographic components into macro modelling. Certainly within the United States and in Europe (countries like Italy etc.), these are important dimensions that need to be incorporated in macro models. But the policy debate in the US on pension reform has not been limited by the fact that the macro models do not incorporate these characteristics. Instead there has been substantial input from the micro-front that has been extraordinarily helpful in moving this discussion forward.

The two areas where I think microeconometrics has been particularly helpful in the policy debate is the study of unemployment and the role of investments in education and training. In the area of unemployment, empirical work on the determinants of unemployment durations, the role of unemployment benefits and benefit structures in influencing the transition probabilities out of unemployment, etc. . . . has been crucial for reform of unemployment benefits. In the area of human capital investment, microeconometric studies have informed our understanding of the impact of human capital on wages, wage inequality, labour mobility and productivity.

The minimum wage debate in the early to mid 1990s in the United States, is a good example of a combination of microeconometric and macro analysis of the impact of changing the minimum wage. It highlights some of the issues that have been raised at the conference. The debate in the United States was informed by a great deal of recent micro work that used 'natural experiments' to re-examine the impact of increases in the minimum wage on the labour market. There was a series of studies that suggested that, at the levels of the minimum wage that we had in the early 1990s, a modest increase in the minimum wage (say by 10 per cent or 20 per cent) would have a minimal impact on disemployment or unemployment. This body of empirical literature was produced outside of the policy environment by independent labour economists. Although the research was not undertaken for policy purposes, the researchers and their findings immediately got sucked into the policy debate and the minimum wage became one of the platform issues in the 1992 Presidential election campaign.

The minimum wage literature was not and is not a literature of congruence. There were a lot of contradictory studies and in fact we got into a somewhat embarrassing state of affairs where people were literally throwing down studies on tables and counting up how many studies showed one effect versus how many showed another effect. We had a range of empirical estimates of the disemployment effects associated with a 20 per cent increase of the minimum wage (on the level as it was set in 1995), running from positive employment growth to job loss of up to 600,000 people. This became a considerable challenge (when you are sitting as Chief Economist in an administration) to explain how the 'dismal' science could come up with such a range of estimates from positive employment growth to over half a million individuals losing their jobs!

One interesting feature in the minimum wage discussion (apart from the rather ferocious personal debate that ensued between different researchers at the micro level on studies of the impact of increases in the minimum wage) was that the macroeconomists got into the game as well. Large private forecasting companies, such as DRI and Wharton, ran the proposed minimum wage increases through their macro models, to generate what would be the impact on the unemployment rate. And perhaps more important, during 1995 and 1996, were Federal Reserve bank discussions (in the context of interest-rate policy) about what the impact of the minimum wage would be on inflation. The macro models produced rather small effects of the increase of minimum wages on the price index, a finding which was quite critical in the policy debate. There was a complex interaction here: findings of empirical micro models being picked up by policy makers, policy proposals being put forward, macro modellers modelling the proposed increases in their models, their findings being picked up as well in the policy debate in the view that: 'well, this is not going to have a large inflationary effect, perhaps we should go forward', and then finally the policy debate shifting back to what would be the distributional consequences of an increase of the minimum wage both on demographic groups and on companies.

This is one good example where there was a lot of use of micro and macro empirical models. I personally believe the right decision was made from a public policy point of view, but I think all of the players learned from this interaction between the micro, the macro and the policy makers.

Henk Don

How do policy makers use economic models? I mainly refer to my experience of the Dutch situation, where there is a range of uses that policy makers make of economic models. Perhaps the most important one is to use models as an information processing device: to monitor the economy, to monitor the budget outlook in particular, and to provide information about different scenarios that the near future might bring.

Of course a much more interesting use of models, which attracts a lot more attention, is to test various ideas and proposals for policy or even to test full election programmes of the political parties (or at least the financial economic parts of them), as we attempt to do in the Netherlands. Specific proposals or ideas might be those that have been put forward by different groups in the area of tax shifting (for example shifting from labour to the environment, or shifting from labour to other sources of taxable income), as well as studies on a negative income tax and all kinds of variants of that. There has also been a minimum wage debate which was conducted in part using the analysis that models could bring to bear. What we attempted there in the end was to try to come up with an assessment which we hoped to be encompassing in the sense of bringing together all main factors from both the demand and the supply side relevant for the minimum wage debate. But of course, this took a long time, and by the time that model was ready the minimum wage debate had more or less passed! We made a quick and somewhat dirtier analysis at the time that the minimum wage debate was going on, and I still feel there were many good elements in that quick assessment; I won't try to judge the end of debate.

Another use of economic models is to study the past performance of the economy. One question that has been put to us quite forcibly was 'Why did employment growth pick up in the Netherlands so strongly in the second half of the eighties? What were the main factors behind that performance and may be we can learn from that analysis for the future?' Our model was used to try to answer that main question and we are using different models now to answer basically the same question: 'What explains this Dutch miracle that everyone talks about?' (If there is one!)

In Dutch policy-making there is still another use of economic models, which is to use it as a tool in consensus building. This use may attract less attention, but it might be more important than the more spectacular uses on policy proposals. The model and the expert information that it embodies – I agree with Professor Malinvaud that it is not really the economic model (the empirical model), but the empirical knowledge that you try to encode, and a lot more goes into that than just a model: all that is used to find some common ground in the political debate and to try to find some basis for consensus. Using the model may help to locate exactly where the political differences are and whether these are differences of preferences in what people would like the economy to produce or whether these are differences in analysis of what the economic trade-offs really are. The model helps very much in assessing all these differences and in getting as much common ground as you can get. That is an important use of models, or of the empirical knowledge encoded into models, in the Netherlands as we have a tradition of coalition building and consensus formation in our political process.

In these cases of model usage, I would say that the model is used as a partner in the debates, a partner with a remarkably good memory, with much patience, but with no fantasy whatsoever. That's where you need experts to handle the model and where you need politicians to come up with some wild ideas, or possible policies, that you might want to test on the model.

There are also misuses and I want to end my remarks with some examples of misuses of models that we have witnessed. The main reason for misuse, I guess, is to ignore the uncertainty which is always there in the model, in the forecast and in the policy analysis. Often policy makers, consciously or unconsciously, I think most of the time consciously, attach far too much precision to the outcomes of the modelling analysis.

There is still some tendency towards the engineering usage of models that was suggested as being part of an earlier tradition. I will give you two examples. One is the small differences in employment effects that came out of the analysis of election programmes for different parties a couple of years ago. These differences were magnified in the political discussion, though they were hardly significant in some cases. Now I think this was a conscious misuse and not an unconscious misuse. On the other example I would tend to the same conclusion. This is an example that was a very interesting experience for me, and one which our Chairman may remember. I attended meetings with negotiators to form a cabinet in 1989 under the Presidency of our present Chairman. We had debates with the negotiators on what the economic effects of different policy options would be; there were draft programmes and we were asked to assess exactly what would be the impact on the deficit and the burden of taxes and premiums on the economy. At one point, a fairly late point in the negotiations I should say, they asked us: 'Now please give us the second decimal of this burden of taxes and premiums on the economy!' (I tend to have a happy recollection of my reaction to that question, which I won't give to you. I don't know if the Chairman has the same recollection of that particular event?) The event stands out in my memory quite vividly, and I would explain it as a sign of giving too much precision to these outcomes. Now of course this was for a reason. There was a political tension between the negotiating parties. They had a particular target and wanted to know the rounding error for the assessment on the particular data. Maybe the Chairman will react to this point?

Ruud Lubbers

Certainly I will. Exactly for your answer you were selected for the job you are doing: it was more a test-question to you!

Thank you to all three of you. Let me add a few points myself in the context of this question. I very much agree with what Professor Malinvaud said about the development over time in making use of these empirical models. In my own experience, I remember vividly in the sixties, when my life started as a policy maker but while I was still in industry, we had the macroeconomic model and we had all the figures of the famous Centraal Planbureau (as I still call them) taken as a given fact. We were really fascinated by the consequences, in that growth decade, for the several segments of industry and the several regions in the Netherlands. In the seventies the climate changed because there was a more heated debate about the need for structurally sound policies and the need to get rid of the Keynesian interpretation of what was considered to be good economic policies. I think the OECD played quite a role in the way the picture shifted.

The next shift, in my recollection, was in the eighties when two things happened. First, as was suggested in the American explanation of what happened, we have seen a change to become more interested in more specific questions: not only sound macroeconomic policies but specific micro or segment questions. That was quite a change. This was really needed because the empirical models which were used predicted results that as politicians we found totally unacceptable. We could not use them to formulate a sound economic policy which would do the job we wanted to do in a proper way. Therefore you had to be imaginative and so you started to ask questions like: 'Can we do it differently?' I remember from that time that, as Prime Minister, I used to say to Henk Don's predecessor, Van der Beld: 'If we do it as you predict it will happen in the Netherlands, we are lost! We simply have to do better!' This seems a little bit arrogant but I don't regret that. Not that the models were not good, the empirical models were OK to that extent. But there is a margin, a possibility, to change the behaviour of people and institutions and it is exactly that margin which is the interesting point for politicians. So you cannot ask those who are active in empirical models to predict that change, but at least you can try to find the limits of what is sound economic policies and then take that as a fact of life and see what you can add in terms of policy.

The second experience I want to mention was basically Dutch, but it may be not only Dutch. We were doing our job, trying to do better in the Netherlands, and today it is called the Dutch miracle, but that was not a miracle at all. It was hard work changing the attitude of the population and that is what we were doing. It took quite a period before we were successful and at that same time the budget deficit and cumulative debt were not OK. So at the end of the eighties, although there had already been a lot of progress and improvement in the situation in terms of the behaviour of people and systems, we were running out of oxygen. Then the Centraal Planbureau and the political parties agreed to be more serious, more conservative in their estimates of economic growth and not to take any risks any longer with the budget deficit. In fact what happened was that several scenarios were developed of possible economic growth, we selected the most pessimistic one, the most conservative one, and we tried to formulate budget policies to control ourselves. This was deliberately done but in the beginning we experienced a very negative side-effect, namely that people really believed that the conservative estimate of the Centraal Planbureau was the prognoses for the future. It took us some time to find our way, because people really thought for a while that unemployment would grow fantastically (because it was based on the very conservative estimate). But after all, there was enough trust in the system and we overcame that situation. So that is part of the past. What remains is still an increased interest in micro questions and that is, I think, part of the answer to how policy makers make use of empirical models these days, and what sort of questions they put to the experts.

This brings me to the second question. We talked already a bit about it, but let's try to get more specific answers. The question is as follows: 'It is apparent that big gaps often arise between intentions and outcomes in policy makers' usage of empirical models. How do these gaps arise? How are they resolved through the interaction between the groups?' Let's start for a change with Henk Don.

Henk Don

In this 'gaps' question, concerning the gaps between economists and policy makers, there are two types of gaps. One is the possible gap on the issue of skills and understanding. Do the politicians understand the model analysis? Do the modellers understand the policy questions? There is a language barrier, if you like, between the two. But what helps, at least in the Netherlands' case, is that on the long line that Ralph Bryant drew, in his discussion,[1] between the analysts and the policy makers where there was nothing in between – we are lucky in the Netherlands to have many people on that line in between.

There is a lot of interchange especially between the modellers (the outside analysts) and the staff in policy-making institutions. In fact we have the Central Economic Committee which is a major group of civil servants, including myself, discussing the outcomes of models in a quite informed way, and on the basis of that, drafting advice to the Cabinet. The Social Economic Council has quite a large staff of experienced economists who know what we modellers do, who can understand our reports and who draft advice and discuss issues with employers' organizations, with the unions and with outside experts. Also, inside the Bureau [CPB], we put a lot of text in our reports explaining the results of the model, and in fact when we communicate the results of the policy analysis, you will almost never see a very technical report. We try to make these reports as transparent and as clear-cut to the policy makers as we can, but still there is a need for some intermediation on that route.

The other type of gap relates to the obvious problem that the model cannot answer all questions. What do we do about that? The first thing is that some questions that you cannot answer nevertheless do define the agenda for research. One example: the unemployment problem in the early seventies lead to the construction of the VINTAF model which helped very much in analysing the unemployment problem throughout the seventies. I recognize the feeling of Professor Malinvaud that in the mid-seventies there was a fairly good analysis of what was going on, but it was very hard to find the right policy response. Perhaps it was possible to find the policy response on the technical level, but the politicians were not really prepared to pay the price (suggested by the technical analysis) to reduce unemployment at that time.

A second example on the issue setting the agenda for research was the debate about institutions that emerged in the early eighties. This was the debate on *how do we best reform our institutions, in particular to encourage a better response from the labour market*. Those issues lead to the construction of the MIMIC model on inter-relations between the social security system, the tax system and labour market performance.

Of course it is still better to try and lead in modelling exercises, and to have the models ready when the policy questions come to the floor. The examples I just gave were where the model development was lagging, but I think we have been successful in leading in some sense on at least two issues. One is the study that we made called *Scanning the Future*. This was intended to be a modelling exercise, though the model came after the publication. Still, the publication was very useful in studying four different major scenarios for the world economy and they were subsequently translated into three different scenarios for the Dutch economy, focusing again on institutional issues rather than on growth as such. A second, more recent example, where a smaller model is involved, is that we took up generational accounting over a year ago because we anticipated that the issue of what the fiscal deficit should be in the long run would come up around this time, as indeed it has in preparation for the next cabinet period. This generational accounting analysis, which is now available for the Netherlands, is very helpful in discussing the issues that are relevant in this field and tackling some of the demography questions that have recently been put on the agenda.

Now, finally one other reason why the model cannot answer all questions is that sometimes you get the wrong questions. An example of this is that politicians tend to want to know the employment effect of everything, and are hardly interested in any of the other effects on the economy. I think we should try harder to educate them, so that they ask not for the employment effects but for the welfare effects on the economy. We have not yet succeeded in changing those questions, but I hope we are making some progress there.

Lisa Lynch

I am going to use this 'gap' question to talk about one way, at least in the United States, in which we have tried to bridge the gap between policy makers and empirical economists, to inform *both* sides better so that this gap is bridged.

In the context of this gap, academic economists are often viewed by policy makers as being from a different world. I was certainly accused of coming from another planet from time to time in my last job. One of the things that the Clinton Administration (and previous administrations as well) did was to take people from the academic world, and place them either into staff positions in policy-making institutions or even more 'front-line' policy-making positions such as at the Assistant Secretary level, or Deputy Secretary of Treasury. Placing economists right in the thick of the policy discussion forces us to translate the work that we have done and that our colleagues are doing and make it relevant in the policy world. The translation process, speaking from personal experience, is a useful one because it makes you think more crisply about what is actually being done in a variety of empirical studies and to try to focus on what the bottom line of different studies actually is. As one of the previous speakers mentioned: as economists we tend to make our reputation by the third, or fourth decimal point of some empirical estimates or by coming up with specific properties of some new estimator. These are important contributions, but are rather irrelevant from the point of view of a policy maker. In the sense that they are policy irrelevant, you cannot waste time explaining it to them, you have to tell what the bottom line of the finding is for the particular question that they are looking at.

The other thing what the Clinton Administration has done is not just to take academics into policy-making positions, but to throw us out as well. People are thrown back in to academia – some people go back faster than others. If they cannot do the translation, they are thrown out quite quickly; if they can do the translation they are usually asked to stay. I think that the turnover process is good: it is probably a good idea to refresh the basket of policy makers and at the same time economists go back into the academic environment with a different appreciation of the sense of timing and needs of the policy world, the kind of questions that come up and the ability to respond quickly to those questions.

Edmond Malinvaud

I would like to make two points on these questions of gaps, big gaps, between intention and outcomes in policy makers' usage of empirical models. The first is that the relationship between policy-making and the economic models is hardly ever direct. In actual fact, there are mediations, various mediations: the channel of influence may be through public information and changes in public views about economic policies, as was pointed out a moment ago by Professor Don, and which indeed is an important aspect. When the economist in charge of an empirical model is not directly heard by the policy maker, he may wait, and perhaps later he will find it rewarding that his analysis went through public opinion and emerged in the formation of a different consensus.

My second point is that maybe empirical modellers are responsible for the gaps, and this is going in the direction of what our Chairman said a few moments ago. Models may be too slow in reacting to major changes in policy needs. The modellers are the people who know, in principle, so they should know what the changes in the policy needs are. I think that since there are more modellers than policy makers in the room, I can challenge in particular you modellers of Western Europe: Did we (you and me) provide quickly enough, in the late 1970s, the appropriate models for policy makers to cope with the sharp deterioration of profitability and competitiveness in our countries? Did we provide quickly enough, in the early nineties, the appropriate empirical models for policy makers to cope with the debt deflation that was occurring then? Now Ralph Bryant told us earlier that in the US at least, modellers did respond to progress in economic theory and changes in economic problems. But all his examples had to do with pleasing the theory people (so that they find in the model what they liked to see in their theory) and the examples did not really deal with the problems close to the policy makers' needs. Of course it may be that Europe is different from the US; we are perhaps less academically conscious.

Ruud Lubbers

Thank you, that was great! I will add just two remarks. I would say most of the 'gaps' problem is related to the definition of empirical models. The word itself says it already: it is about empirical facts and some things that happen you cannot read in empirical models.

I restrict myself to two examples. One is the behaviour of people in relation to regulations. It is very difficult to predict, on the basis of empirical models, any gradual development in human behaviour. Yet I could tell you a long story about the change that the welfare state has brought about, and its more recent reversion in Europe, in terms of the behaviour of people. The other example is, for me, even more intriguing. It is about technology and entails two distinct questions. One is about estimating the increase in productivity and the way technology drives productivity. Maybe this is do-able? But there are other consequences of changes in technology, especially in the last five to seven years, which are very difficult to translate into empirical economic models. I think most of the gaps we experience are a consequence of these very basic points. We have to live with the gaps. It is not a question of misunderstanding. You can't solve all the problems by expertise so maybe we should be more modest, as Professor Malinvaud urged us to be.

Now, for the third question, to turn to Professor Lynch. The structure of the modelling industry indeed varies considerably between countries. 'What is the structure of the modelling industry in your country? And what are the particular advantages and disadvantages of such a structure in your own experience?'

Lisa Lynch

One of the ways of talking about the structure of empirical modelling in the United States is to talk about it in the specific context of the budget debates over the last few years. In the budget debate between the Democratic Administration, the Democratic President and the Republicans who controlled Congress, different empirical models have played quite an important role in how the negotiations on the budget unfolded. Over the years 1995–96 we saw quite different results, depending on what the models generated. These results ranged from a government shut-down in 1995 that was the longest and most sustained government shut-down that ever occurred in the United States (something that I thought I would never see: civil servants out for extended periods of time, in total for more than a month) to a budget deal in 1996 being agreed in principle between parties who seemed so very far apart only a year before.

I think a lot of that difference in experience in the budget negotiations was in part driven by what the macro models told us in predicting 'Where the economy is going to be in five years?' and 'What does it take to get to a balanced budget?' In the budget negotiations that unfolded in 1995 and early 1996, we had a large discrepancy in the forecasts produced by the Administration and those produced by the Congressional Budget Office (CBO), which is funded by the Congress. (At that stage, after the 1994 elections, it was a Republican controlled Congress.) There were large differences in what was predicted as you ran the Administration's budget proposals through the CBO model: you would not get balance five or six years out; yet, if you looked at the specific macro variables – the inflation rate, GDP growth figures – there were not large differences in the forecast values across the two models (from the Administration and from Congress). Neither of these models, from a statistical point of view, were very different from one another in terms of the estimates that they were predicting, yet small differences in the inflation rate, given the compounding effects of that, had a profound impact on whether or not any one political party's policy proposal was predicted to reach a balance in 2000 or in 2005, or whatever year people were looking at. The fact that the two political parties were able to reach an agreement later on comes from the fact that the CBO upped its forecast for GDP growth on the basis of the (then) most recent information on the strength of the economy, and so a $200 billion plus difference between the Administration and the CBO miraculously disappeared overnight by some slight changes in the decimal point values of GDP growth!

This generates a certain degree of cynicism amongst some people in terms of the power of macro models and there is certainly a discussion about how these point estimates are derived by the respective parties and the role of the politics in this. That is one area where I think the modelling industry, certainly the way that it is structured in the United States, at a minimum generates interesting negotiation dynamics between the respective political parties.

Secondly, what I think is interesting in the United States is that, as part of a process to downsize the Federal Government, increasingly the funding for policy research is subcontracted. So, for example, in the Department of Labour, the office of policy evaluation, which would have in the past hired 60 economists to do policy evaluation within the Department, is now down to a staff of about 10 and they subcontract those evaluations. I think this has been important to bridge the gap between policy makers and economic modellers because now there is more direct funding to economists to look at policy issues.

Henk Don

For the market structure in the Netherlands, it is fair to say that the models of the Planning Bureau (I should say the CPB Netherlands Bureau for Economic Policy Analysis) dominate the scene. There is one monopoly, I would say, which is the information processing for the government, and I think it is a natural monopoly. There is a check on the work that we do there by the Ministries that are involved; they scrutinize our figures. But the confidential information on contemplated policies makes it very difficult to have a competitive market on this information processing task.

The other two tasks though, forecasting and policy analysis, are much more open to competitors. It is fair to say that there are no major large models out there that do compete with the models of the Planning Bureau though there are plenty of institutes that do offer competing forecasts and do policy analysis on a lot of issues. There are some large rival models: one is the Central Bank's, that is about the same size as the main macro model at the CPB (the main workhorse of much of what we do). There is a similar model, a joint venture of different universities, located in Groningen and there is a lot of modelling work in particular at the Department of Economic Affairs. There are also other institutes with several smaller or specialized models which focus on different issues.

In the past, particularly in the late seventies and early eighties, more large models were around on the scene in Holland. They were developed by commission of the government or the Scientific Council for Government Policy, but we have seen that these models could not survive over time. The main reason for this being, in my assessment, the large costs that go with these models in terms of maintenance of the model itself and of the database and the required expertise to run and use the model. At the same time, and probably adding to this cost, there was a strong tendency for the different models to converge and I notice a similar observation in one of the papers at this conference: there seems to be a tendency that modelling groups basically come up with more or less the same model. It's also true that the model of the Central Bank and the model that we use at the CPB come up with basically the same assessment for the current state of affairs and forecasts for the near future, according to my experience twice a year when we debate the forecasts in the Council for Economic Affairs of the Ministerial Council. The President of the Bank gives his views and he also tells us what his model puts forward, and it tends to be always in line with our own analysis, except perhaps for one or two variables – and then there is usually a good reason why the forecast is different on that issue.

Now this sort of monopoly, or at least dominant position, does have some disadvantages. The main disadvantage being: What controls the quality? What gives us the right incentive to work hard and do the right analysis? In the absence of competition on these issues, we try to organize the quality control ourselves. We try to be as open as possible to outside scrutiny, to be open to the public and to scientific debates. All the information that we can make available is made available, and we only leave out some confidential stuff which is really not important if you want to study our published documents. On top of that we organize – and this is a very recent thing – peer reviews on the modelling exercises that we do, in particular on the models themselves. Recently we also had a review on the full scope of the work of the Bureau. The main asset that we have to guard, I am convinced, is our independence (and I understand that our independence from at least the Ministry of Economic Affairs was amply demonstrated earlier in this conference).

What is the impact of the market structure on the interaction between policy makers and model builders? This particular structure creates some tension in that relation: a tension of love and hatred. Is the model a flexible friend of the policy maker, to paraphrase one of the paper titles of this conference, or is it actually a flexible enemy? Sometimes politicians do feel that they are at the mercy of those technocrats at the Central Planning Bureau (in the words of some: 'those capitalist technocrats'). But I was very happy that even the Green Left Party several years ago decided to ask for a CPB analysis of their policy programme and I think this exercise was very useful, both for the Green Left Party and for the Planning Bureau, in improving our analysis on many of the environment issues and in improving their analysis on what policy options would be feasible and what would not be.

The last part of the question, why the market structure may help the policy makers, is that the politicians are not faced with the problem of an embarrassment of choices; there is only one answer that the economics profession gives to them, at least through the Planning Bureau, and some of the other answers they get they can safely ignore because they don't play a very major role in the public debate. Occasionally they do and that stirs things up, which may be good for the relation between policy makers and modellers, but of course it may be bad for quality, and I discussed quality just a second ago. Another good side is the consistency of the analysis that is given. The models in particular help us to be consistent in the analysis and in the reactions that we give to different policy questions that are put to us.

Finally, this love relation may also mean that the politicians actually hide behind the results of the policy analysis. They may feel too comfortable! And that relates back to the question of 'How do we communicate as effectively as possible the uncertainty that surrounds both the analysis and the forecast?'

Ruud Lubbers

It was a pleasure to listen to this specifically Dutch story. I only want to add that the audience should know that our Ministry for Economic Affairs in the Netherlands, in line with the general feeling, is trying to 'marketize' all Dutch things: everything has to be brought onto the market and that will improve the quality. The last bastion, I think, is the Centraal Planbureau. So the Centraal Planbureau does its utmost to make it clear that the quality is good and the price is okay, so that they can continue! They are right because they have an outstanding quality, and this brings me to my second remark. We have, as politicians, always survived, notwithstanding the outstanding quality – that was quite a handicap. Maybe that is the true Dutch miracle.

Edmond Malinvaud

I may be very short because, in France, the modelling industry is a new industry. For a long time we had no serious model, no econometric model. That doesn't mean that there was no macroeconomic forecasting or policy analysis. From the end of the last war we had this economic information provided and publicized, but no one precisely knew how the figures in those forecasts and policy analyses were cooked. So a first step, in the 1960s, was to write models that would make explicit how all those figures were produced. Those models were quite *ad hoc*, with only calibration, not econometrics, used to give the parameters of the relationships. (This means that the French model builders were unrecognized forerunners of the development that invaded the world only recently.) In any case, during the seventies, macroeconometric models were actively built and used. But those models were built only within the public administration. (I use this broad term because it would take too long to explain how our public administration is divided, and there were several models done by different groups, but groups that were closely connected to one another.) Economic assessments coming from these models were regarded, by the French public and French intelligentsia, with some suspicion as being subject to political influence. It was realized that outside assessments, with objectivity and good technical quality, were needed. Then in the 1980s, with the help of Minister Barre, who was particularly active in launching these developments, and with the help of public money, we set up some competing institutes, able to do modelling work and policy analysis. This worked well to the extent that they provided competition to the teams within the public administration and at the same time they showed to the French public that the results were not so different.

Ruud Lubbers

Thank you so much for this French experience, Professor Malinvaud.

We turn now to the general picture about economic models in our last question: 'What will be the best way to improve the usefulness of these economic models in the future?'

Edmond Malinvaud

There were two questions raised. Is there any consensus that empirical economic models are useful in economic policy-making? In France, yes, there is a better consensus than there ever was before. Now that maybe surprising to hear, even for French people who are exposed to statements of criticism against the models and the work of economists more generally. But actually, today, ministers request policy evaluations from a team of economists using empirical material and econometric methods on many more policies than they did before. They take the results seriously. The results often make the headlines in the press and are quoted as if they were fully reliable, a feature which often makes me feel somewhat uneasy.

The last question is the question you asked: 'How can we do better?' This is a hard question, and I have a long answer to that, but it is not appropriate given the time so I will give a short answer. No, I don't know of any better research policy than the one we tried to apply in the past decade. Please don't smile!

Ruud Lubbers

This was really very nice, so nice that I cannot resist repeating it. First you were really worried that you were applauded and now you are convinced that you cannot do better!

Professor Lynch, about these two last questions?

Lisa Lynch

It is always a hard act following Professor Malinvaud. I thought that in answering these questions I should try to come up with a specific example, again from a more micro point of view. I will talk about an interesting development in the policy evaluation area in the United States which is certainly being picked up by some European countries. It is the use of random assignment for evaluating government training programmes: to take people as they are coming through a door and say 'First person in, you are in the programme, second person in, you are in the control group'. In other words, to pretend that we are in the lab and creating scientific experiments and are looking at the impact of treatment compared with the control.

This movement to do a random assignment evaluation of programmes, from a funding point of view, is extremely costly. But it is being used increasingly in the United States, primarily I think because policy makers have had a hard time wrapping their minds around some of the empirical evaluation studies that have been done, and particularly the debate that we economists have had about the appropriate treatment of selection issues, etc., in those studies. In my personal experience with policy makers, I had three rules of thumb in terms of presenting results of our evaluation studies: Could I put it on a simple line on a chart? Could I do a bar-graph with it or, at most, could I do a two-way cross tab? That's as far as I could go in terms of being able to make sure that the audience could understand what I was presenting. And the beauty of a random assignment (treatment versus control) experiment is that you can produce a two-by-two cross tabulation. You can have a column that says treatments, you can have a column that says controls, and you can write across what were their earnings, what was their unemployment experience, what was their re-employment experience. A policy maker can look at that and say 'Oh look, the number is bigger or smaller for the treatment'; that means the program worked or didn't work.

The problem that we have in the United States, and I think we are only just beginning to appreciate this, is that it is not always possible to create the lab environment for doing this random assignment process. In particular, some recent work by Jim Heckman has shown that social workers that were involved in the random assignment were so offended by it that they actually interfered in the random assignment process and tried to change the ordering so that they could get certain people, that they viewed as being in more difficulty, into the government treatment program, rather than in the control group. In doing so, they totally tainted the evaluation process. But I think that the commitment by Congress to do random assignment evaluations reflects some of the frustration that policy makers have had with some of the empirical evaluation studies that have been produced.

So I think there is a challenge for us to do better. I think that I would go one step further than Professor Malinvaud: I think one of the things that can be done to improve the use of models is to collect better data, and in a more timely fashion, so that it can be used in policy analysis. In particular from a micro labour point of view, I think the establishment of longitudinal data bases, of workers matched with firms and characteristics of the firms, will go a long way in providing information that can be used to address some of those problems that I mentioned in the beginning of my comments this afternoon.

Ruud Lubbers

Thank you so much. Finally, Professor Don.

Henk Don

At this point I'll try to respond to your earlier remarks, Mr Chairman, concerning the unanswerable questions that you raised on technology and human behaviour. I would tend to go along with you on the technology issue: maybe we don't know how to predict productivity growth in the longer run; we don't know how to analyse what goes on in technological innovation and its implementation and diffusion. I do think we can move ahead and get a better grasp of what is going on there, but the ultimate goal of putting it all in a model and doing policy analysis on those issues seems to be a very hard nut to crack.

I am more optimistic on the behaviour side, and I think we have already made some progress there. It is possible, but not with the standard traditional macro type of model, but with different types of models to study human behaviour, consumers' behaviour, household behaviour. But you also need different data for that. There I go along with Professor Lynch very much: we need a lot more data than is available right now (although a lot more is available now than 20 years ago). But still, if it is possible and feasible to get a lot more data with information on those issues, and with modern computing technology to manage the data, then we can also expand the range of models that we have now. We already have a much broader range than the focus on macro-type models discussed in this conference. We have models for special issues, for labour market issues, for market structure issues, etc. To give two examples: we made special purpose models for the issue of shop-opening hours and for the issue of the regulation of the broadcasting industry in the Netherlands. These are very small models, especially made for a specific policy question. But we have also developed the larger ones like the MIMIC model, which tries to model household behaviour in the context of the social security and tax system. This is a very good example of how we try to get a better grip on behaviour, but to get more data, especially micro data, would help to improve that further.

Ruud Lubbers

I don't think I should comment at any length myself on the last question. The point made by Professor Don, in fact as well by Professor Lynch (and rather different from that by Professor Malinvaud) is that maybe improvement of modelling is possible, by taking into account the questions and then asking what are the possibilities to go into more specific tailor-made modelling for those questions. This is in fact the beginning of modesty of course, that we think we can do better! So I applaud that!

Thank you all so much. These were the four questions and the answers to them. I have found the discussion very fascinating. I regret only one thing, that Professor Tinbergen was not able to be here this afternoon. I remember him as one of my professors at the end of the fifties in Rotterdam when he quite unexpectedly joined the team of professors and became instrumental at the end of my studies in awarding me a 'cum laude'. In the years thereafter, in academic meetings as well as in policy meetings as a Minister of Economic Affairs, I had the privilege often to meet Professor Tinbergen. He was – as you all know – a famous man as a scientist, but he was also a gentle man and he would have loved the discussions here. I do hope that his attitude: to be convinced that models can help policy makers but at the same time that they can't produce all the answers to improve the quality of life, might be a guideline for all who are working in this area to do better. Even when we are doing better, there is always a margin for policy makers to go beyond, which is a question of awareness, imagination and creative thinking.

Mary Morgan

I thank the members of our panel and the Chairman very much for their informed responses to the questions that we posed to them. The discussion was most fruitful and full of insights into the process of interaction between empirical modellers and policy makers: thank you all.

It is appropriate – as everyone else has had the opportunity – for me to add a few words about the Tinbergen tradition which is so important for practical economics. I gained tremendous admiration for Tinbergen from my work on the history of econometrics: my PhD thesis contained, not surprisingly, a chapter on the development of Tinbergen's macroeconometric models. As I worked on the other chapters, Tinbergen's name kept popping up again and again as the originator of critical examples which were often small empirical models, both micro and macro. I was very pleased to hear Jacques Polak refer to the qualities of his little model this morning as being part of this Tinbergen tradition. So the Tinbergen tradition includes not only the large macro model of the CPB and other public administrations, but also these small models that have become the mainstay in empirical modelling. It is easy to write down a simple model, but it is not easy to make a useful simple empirical model and that's where Tinbergen's elegance and skill really came in.

It is difficult to appreciate now how one could ever do anything in practical economics, or how one could apply economic ideas or do policy analysis without such empirical models; and the idea and accepted qualities of a good empirical model in economics are primarily due to Tinbergen: he put the notion on the map. So, though I did not grow up in the Tinbergen tradition, I am proud to be able to call myself a Fellow of the Tinbergen Institute. On behalf of Frank den Butter and myself, and our assistants Udo Kock and Edwin van Gameren and on behalf of the Tinbergen Institute directors, we thank all participants of this 10th Anniversary Congress of the Tinbergen Institute and look forward to the success of the next 10 years.

Note

1 Henk Don refers to a previous commentary at the conference by Ralph Bryant in which he reviewed the chapters at the workshop. His comments and parallel ones by Ken Wallis are not published in the present volume.

Chapter 17

What makes the models–policy interaction successful?*

Frank A. G. den Butter and Mary S. Morgan

The interaction between empirical modellers and policy makers is analysed in terms of the structure of the industry, the products involved, the value chain and its working arrangements. Our account of successful interaction focuses on models as the site for knowledge creation and consensus building in both fore-casting and policy analysis. The application of network analysis and ideas from knowledge management enable us to interpret the structures and the institutional arrangements described in a range of case studies. We explain why some institutional arrangements may lead to helpful interaction, but our analysis suggests that the way a structure is used is more critical than the nature of the structure in determining the success of interaction between modellers and policy makers.

JEL classifications: A11, C5, E17, E61

1. Introduction

Economics has two faces. Its first face is that of a positive science where scholars as mere observers try to give an adequate and unbiased description of economic reality and of the mechanisms which govern economic behaviour. Its second face is that of a normative science. Here insights into the working of economic mechanisms are used for policy advice. The idea is that, in one way or another, economic knowledge can be helpful in the design of policy measures which are to enhance individual or social welfare, or which are instrumental in avoiding unwarranted developments. Our interest lies in the second face of economics. More specifically we are interested in the role that empirical models play in economic advice and in the use of that advice by policy makers. That is because, in our opinion, empirical models have become the main link between the positive and normative faces of economics. To put it more directly: empirical models are the bridge between positive theory and normative practice.

A common feature of most bridges is that they enable traffic in two directions.

*Reprinted from *Economic Modelling*, 15, Frank A. G. den Butter and Mary S. Morgan, 'What makes the models–policy interaction successful?', pp. 443–75, Copyright (1998), with permission from Elsevier Science.

This interaction between policy makers and economists in the design and usage of empirical models was the theme of the 10th Anniversary Conference of the Tinbergen Institute and hence of this volume of papers. This two-way interaction between economic models and policy-making is almost certainly widespread, and recognized by those participating in policy work, but has been subject to very little systematic research and analysis. Our research asks pertinent questions about the interactions: How do such interactions work? What constitutes successful interaction? Upon which factors does successful interaction depend? In order to make sense of both questions and answers, an analytical framework is also needed to help us interpret the cases we have assembled here and systematize our knowledge about the ways empirical models (both large- and small-scale) are used. The ultimate aim of researching these questions is to investigate within which institutional framework such interaction between model makers and model users is likely to be most fruitful.

2. The framework

There is a very considerable body of literature which has studied various aspects of econometric models. Almost from the beginning, academic model builders have assessed their macroeconometric models by forecasting tests as in the pioneering work by Tinbergen and Klein. Starting in the Netherlands, they also used their models to simulate policy options – the classic example being the first macroeconometric model ever built, which Tinbergen used to simulate various options facing Dutch policy makers in 1936 [see Tinbergen (1936, 1937) and commentary by Morgan (1990)].[1] This tradition has evolved into a comparison of policy analysis with different models (see, for example, Bryant et al., 1988; D'Alcantara, 1988; Van Els, 1990; Henderson, 1991), but this is a difficult matter as a recent survey paper by Bray et al. (1995) shows (see also Bryant et al., 1993). Academic assessment of these models has mainly been concerned with statistical adequacy and consistency with economic theories, and, more rarely, with historical performance of the model (see Fisher and Wallis, 1990).

At the same time, economic policy actions have independently generated a considerable literature assessing both successes and, more often, the failures of policies. These assessments have, in turn, more often been used to cast doubt on the broader theories such as Keynesianism or monetarism than on the specific empirical models involved, although it is also clear that economic events have led to the revision of models (see Wallis, 1989).

The question of how models are actually used in policy work, however, is a very different matter. Here the literature is much thinner (see, for example, Llewellyn et al., 1985; Martens, 1986; Don and Van den Berg, 1990; Westaway, 1995).[2] We know that empirical models, both large macroeconometric models and small-scale, single-question models, are widely used in the policy process. However, we know comparatively little about how they are used. We have chosen to concentrate on three linking issues.

2.1. Structure of the industry

Smith (1994) has recently used a structure of industry approach to discuss the organization of the macroeconometric model-building industry in Britain (government funded, but independent and separate models) and compares it (very briefly) with those of the US (mainly commercial) and France (centralized and nationalized). He makes a number of perceptive observations about the different arrangements (e.g. about their effect on incentives to innovate), and his suggestive comments provide a useful analytical starting point for our question: How does the structure of the model-building industry affect the interaction with policy users? However, in many respects, the structure of this industry does not fit the standard type assumed in the economics of the firm, in which there are clearly labelled producers, products and consumers linked via a market mechanism. Because it is not necessarily clear what the market is in this case; because the model builders and users may lie in closely adjacent or connected organizations; and because the input organizations co-operate to produce outputs – we make use of the network approach as developed in management theory (see, e.g., Miles and Snow, 1992). This approach may be more useful to illuminate and categorize the process of joint production, for network analysis looks at the structural arrangements of the parties to the value chain, the type of ownership involved and the methods by which exchange takes place.

2.2. The value chain

By concentrating our attention on the interaction of model builders and policy users we are suggesting that there is no simple 'value chain' going from builders to users. Rather, as Smith (1994) also realizes and is implicit in network analysis, both parties may be gaining value created from the interactions. Relevant questions in this respect are: What are the costs and benefits to both parties from interaction and do certain forms of market structure (Section 2.1) and organizational relations (Section 2.3) create more or better value for both parties than others? Here we could draw on long-standing economic approaches using cost–benefit analysis (broadly conceived) and the notions of gains through trade as well as co-operative game theory. However, since we are dealing with the creation of knowledge rather than trade in goods, answering questions on the appropriate models–policy interaction may benefit from adopting newly developed ideas of how knowledge is created, stored and transmitted in organizations (see Nonaka, 1991).[3]

So far we have, on purpose, left open the question of what constitutes 'successful' interaction. We stress again that our aim is not to assess independently either the models or the policies: we do not aim to put any kind of 'objective value' on either aspect. Our definition of 'successful' is: that the interaction is useful for both parties – i.e. it creates value for both parties. If governments continue to fund model-building and use them for policy analysis, and so long as model builders continue to find it rewarding to work with policy makers, then we might assume that both groups get some value from the interaction. If the interaction is subject to commercial considerations, then we also have an economic valuation to rely on. We note that Faulhaber and Baumol (1988) consider macroeconometric forecasting a major practical innovation of economics because of its (commercial) success in policy preparation.

2.3. Organization

By 'organization' we mean all that is involved in the working arrangements between model builders and policy users. Here questions that emerge from the chapters and discussions of our conference are: Are they the same individuals, or do the two groups work together in teams, or are they in separate organizations? Does the work flow begin with the model builders or the policy questions or is there an iteration back and forth? How are results of policy simulations on the model reported and how are they used? For example, we know that in making forecasts from a model, the academic/commercial proprietors of the models habitually add on an extra element of judgement which appears to improve their forecasts (see McNees, 1990; and also Fair and Shiller, 1989, 1990; Den Butter, 1992; Mourik and Boeschoten, 1994). Is there a similar habitual additional element of judgement added on to a model simulation by the policy user? Despite this interesting work on the role of judgement, many details of this interactive process and its organization remain inside a black box.

Questions of organization, as we shall see, can rarely be separated clearly from those of structure and the value chain. Thus the ideas outlined above also help to frame the issues here. Since it seems likely that different structures and organizations of work are likely to be associated with different costs and benefits, some might create more value than others overall. Therefore, in line with the seminal work by Coase (1937), whose understanding of the 'organization' encompassed the whole contractual relationship both formal and informal, our questions are designed to help us analyse what kind of institutional arrangements are associated with differences in the creation of values for both parties in the interaction.

As can be seen from the above, we have chosen to focus on aspects of the interrelationship of model builders and policy makers which can be treated largely within the frameworks of the theory of industrial organization and of the theory of the firm (broadly conceived to include management theories). We are aware that there are many aspects of our question which would be better treated by organization specialists or sociologists of science (for example). While not ignoring their approaches, we wish to make use of our comparative advantage as economists in posing the questions in a broadly economic way.

Our aim here is to explore the case materials we have assembled and the literature in the field using a number of simple economic ideas to guide the research. We are not seeking to model the policy-making process. Nor are we expecting to come up with definitive structures and organizational designs. Rather, our aim is to use these economic ideas in an informal way to understand and interpret the characteristics of observed interactions between empirical model builders and policy users.

The remainder of our chapter is organized according to the three linking issues referred to above. The next section discusses the structure of the industry and the differences in organization between various countries mainly, but not exclusively, in the use of empirical models in macroeconomic policy-making. The different role of models in forecasting and policy analysis which was discussed in a number of papers at the conference and which is closely connected to the structure of the industry, is also considered in this section. Section 4 is on the value chain. We illustrate it by means of historical evidence, by some appealing cases from the chapters of this volume and by our own experience with the model-policy interaction. Section 5 is on the organizational and institutional aspects of this interaction. In our opinion the formal and informal structure in which modellers and policy makers interact is essential for the success or failure of the use of models in policy-making. Finally Section 6 concludes.

3. The structure of the industry

The standard account of the structure of industry pictures organizations (or firms) that produce and supply products (models and model products) and other, separate, organizations who consume those products (policy-making offices). The characteristics of the supply side – with a continuum of labels from single monopolist to atomistic competition – determine the market structure label, and this suggests how the particular industry will perform. This analysis involves an idealized kind of picture which is useful in certain respects. Smith's (1994) discussion of the market for models is most helpful as a starting point and we shall refer to it below, particularly in relation to the apparent monopoly case in the Netherlands and the case of competition in the UK. As noted in Section 2.1, the modelling industry in many countries does not fit easily into these idealized boxes of the conventional paradigm, so we also draw on recently developed theories about network structures. Network analysis offers an alternative way to portray the links between the various institutions involved in empirical models and policy-making.

Seen through the network lens, it becomes clear that units in this industry are not isolated and competing, but rather closely joined in complex networks of relationships. The characteristics associated with such 'networked firms' can be made relevant in terms of the modelling industry. First, although there are many possible arrangements of a network, the relations between the units are characterized by contracts and exchange agreements (even where the units are co-owned), rather than by either controls and instructions (as within hierarchical firms) or by market transactions (as between firms). This suggests that we can consider the relations between statistical offices and planning or modelling offices, or between modellers and policy makers, in terms of units in a networked arrangement. Second, the assets of several units may be utilized at many points along the value chain and here we might consider data and models, and even modellers, as assets. Third, there will be a (market) mechanism of co-ordination between the units on the basis of shared information, co-operation and customization of product. The units are voluntarily linked and tend to be pro-active and co-operative in improving the product. Here we might consider the way in which different agencies and people have to co-operate and share information in model making and policy analysis and even in the process of model improvement.

Because of these characteristics, Miles and Snow (1992) claim that networked organizations can be both more efficient and more innovative than market or hier-archical arrangements. (They may also be less subject to internal political threats – in this case, for example, to their independence or objectivity – than when all parts are integrated into one firm.) The importance of the network form in the value chain is made evident in the discussion of Section 4.1. In large part, the rest of this section offers descriptions of some of the network relations we find in the cases in this volume, to illustrate the range of such structures and to provide material for the analysis in the following two sections.

3.1. Market structures

Obviously the two pioneering countries in model-based policy analysis were the Netherlands and Norway. This was due to the two protagonists of empirical econo-metrics and first Nobel-prize winners in economics, Tinbergen and Frisch.

3.1.1. The Netherlands

Tinbergen was the first managing director of the Dutch Central Planning Bureau. According to the establishing law of 1947, the Central Planning Bureau should prepare each year a so-called 'Central Economic Plan' (CEP) containing estimates and guidelines for the national economy (see CPB Netherlands Bureau for Eco-nomic Policy Analysis, 1997; see also Donders and Graafland, 1998, Chapter 2 in this volume). In fact the Central Economic Plan never contained guidelines but only projections and alternative policy scenarios to help the decision-making process of the government. So in spite of its name, the CPB has never been involved in 'central planning', but is, in the interpretation of the law, strictly an advisory board.[4] In addition to the CEP the CPB publishes each year in September the Macroeconomic Outlook simultaneously with the Budget Memorandum of the Cabinet. The Government budget for the year to come is based on the forecasts of the CPB in the Macroeconomic Outlook. So these constitute official government forecasts, which provide the CPB with a monopoly position in the Netherlands in this respect. In line with Tinbergen's research agenda, from the 1950s, these esti-mates, projections, scenarios and forecasts have been model-based figures. The CPB's 'model' early acquired a high status in academic circles and has come to be regarded in Dutch society as an objective piece of economic science. Although the CPB is independent, its forecasts and scenarios are discussed with experts at various ministries and at the Central Bank. The analysis of the CPB is also a major input for the so-called Central Economic Commission, which consists of high-ranking officials from the Ministries and which prepares the macroeconomic policy of the government. The managing director of the CPB is a member of this Commission which also has a director of the Central Bank as its permanent adviser. The Dutch structure and its development are discussed in, e.g., Barten (1988), Siebrand (1988), Den Butter (1991) and Van den Bogaard (1998).

This description of the institutional setting of policy preparation in the Netherlands illustrates the central role of model-based economic policy analysis by the CPB. In contrast to the situation in Norway (see Bjerkholt, 1998, Chapter 10 in this volume) and more or less also in France, the analytical tasks of the CPB are clearly distinguished from the data collection which is done by Statistics Netherlands (CBS) and the Dutch Central Bank. This formal separation between data collection on the one hand, and analysis and forecasting on the other hand is even established by law, which prohibits the CBS from making forecasts other than in the field of demographics. It does not mean, however, that the CPB has a formal monopoly of model-based policy analysis. Some Ministries have their own research teams employing empirical models in policy analysis (see Van Bergeijk and Van Sinderen, 1997, Chapter 3 in this volume), and the Dutch Central Bank has also built up a tradition in the use of models for its macroeconomic policy analysis and forecasting (see Van Els, 1997, Chapter 6 in this volume).

3.1.2. Norway

It is of course most interesting to compare the institutional setting of the modelling industry in the Netherlands with that in Norway, where the organization of model-based policy analysis has been much influenced by the ideas of Ragnar Frisch. Bjerkholt (1998, Chapter 10 in this volume) illustrates that in Norway, even more so than in the Netherlands, the idea was that economic policy should be based upon a programme of comprehensive macroeconomic planning. This was conceived 'as the coordination of decisions taken within a large administrative system' where 'models used for policy-making became institutionalized ... i.e. embedded in the administrative structure of policy-making' (Bjerkholt, 1998, Chapter 10 in this volume). As noted above, a difference as compared to the Netherlands was that the modelling unit was not established as an independent bureau but was located within the central statistical institution.

The products of the modelling industry in Norway and in the Netherlands are also somewhat different. This is mainly caused by a difference in orientation and philosophy of model-building between Frisch and Tinbergen. Whereas Tinbergen, in his first modelling exercise for the Netherlands in 1936, was already very concerned with the analysis of policy measures, Frisch focused more on the help of models in optimal decision-making. Hence, the first models used in Norway for policy preparation were large input/output models closely connected to the system of national accounts. On the other hand, the first generation of Dutch models of the CPB were relatively small Keynesian demand models used for cyclical analysis.

3.1.3. United States

Model-based policy analysis seems to be subject to more competition in the Anglo-Saxon world (US, UK) than in the Netherlands or Norway. In the American institutional setting the preparation of budgetary and monetary policy is quite separated. Donihue and Kitchen (1997, Chapter 14 in this volume) describe how the 'Troika' in the US Administration, which comprises senior officials of the President's Council of Economic Advisors, the Department of the Treasury and the Office of Management and Budget, comes to some kind of consensus about the forecast for the economy which acts as an input to policy-making of the US Government. Meanwhile, the staff of the Federal Reserve Board uses its own models and has its own philosophy on model-based policy analysis. Edison and Marquez (1998, Chapter 12 in this volume) provide a unique insight into the models–policy interaction in the decision-making process at the Federal Reserve System. A special feature of the American model industry is that, much more than in continental Europe, model-based economic forecasts are made by private and commercial institutes and agencies aimed at the commercial sector.

3.1.4. United Kingdom

As in the USA, there is no monopoly of empirical models in any one UK government agency. For example, both the Treasury and the Bank of England have a tradition in using models in policy analysis that goes back to the early 1970s. From 1976, the Treasury has been obliged to publish economic forecasts produced with the aid of a model at least twice per year. In addition, the Treasury model is in the public domain, though the assumptions and judgements used in its forecasts are not.[5] There exist several other large empirical models, all funded by public money (via the science research budget), one at the independent National Institute of Economic and Social Research and others in the academic sector. These are used by their proprietors for policy analysis and though they do not contribute directly to policy formation, their analyses inform the policy debates. There has been considerable interaction between these models in the sense that both model designs, practices and personnel have moved between the sectors [the best history of these interactions is Kenway (1994)]. For example, the Bank of England acquired its first model from the London Business School modellers in the 1970s, and this move was supported by the Treasury (to which the Bank reported at the time) on the grounds that the Bank should have an independent source of advice (see Latter, 1979). However, at the same time, and despite these family connections between models and modellers, the models are regarded as 'competitors' (on which we comment later). Most recently, and for a very short period 1993–97, the UK government constituted a panel of advisers to the Treasury drawn from these modellers and from forecasters in the commercial and financial sectors (see Evans, 1997, Chapter 13 in this volume; Evans, 1999).

3.1.5. Other countries

There is obviously no one kind of arrangement for modelling. The organization of the modelling industry in France is, like that in Norway and the Netherlands, centralized, but the industry developed much later than in the two pioneering countries because indicative planning has played a major role in the state-oriented policy-making of the French government. The economic forecasting is done by two agencies which are part of the Ministry of Finance, namely L'Institute Nationale de la Statistique et des Études Économiques (INSEE) and La Direction de la Prévision (DP). As INSEE combines its function of collecting data with this forecasting function, it can be compared, to some extent, with Statistics Norway. On the other hand, indicative planning in France is the task of the Commissariat Général du Plan (CGP), which is an independent agency but has no executive power. In Germany the major body for economic policy advice is the 'Sachverständigenrat zur Begutachtung der Gesamtwirtschaftlichen Entwicklung (SGR)'. This Council consists of five members, most of them are university professors, referred to as the 'Five Wise Men'. In contrast to the Council of Economic Advisers in the US, the Sachverständigenrat is politically independent. Another major role in economic policy advice in Germany is played by six independent research institutes. They all study the national and international economic developments but they are quite diverse in their fields of specialization and economic perspective. Although the use of models by the research institutes is not documented and seems to play a minor role only, obviously in Germany there is no monopoly in the modelling industry. Models from universities, like the 'Bonner model' and the SYSIFO model of the universities of Hamburg and Frankfurt, have in the past been used occasionally for actual policy analysis. However, it must be said that the influence of model-based analysis on the formation of policy in Germany is small compared to other major OECD countries. This is especially true for the 'Bundesbank': its policy advice carries a large weight in Germany, but its model seldom seems to be used to help formulate this advice. By comparison, in Denmark, empirical models became part of economic policy-making in the 1970s, when both the Danish Central Statistical Office (for the Ministry of Finance) and the Danish Economic Council began to use models in policy preparation and debate (see Kægård, 1997).

In a number of other industrialized countries, macroeconomic modelling and model-based policy analysis is most actively practised at central banks: for example in Italy and Canada. Although the Banca d'Italia has been one of the forerunners amongst central banks in model-based policy analysis, the role of models in today's Italian economic policy seems to be less pronounced (see Siviero et al., 1997). On the other hand, as witnessed by Duguay and Longworth (1998, Chapter 5 in this volume), the Bank of Canada has retained its prominent role in the models-policy interaction and the preparation of Canadian economic policy after their pioneering work in the mid 1960s.

3.2. Products and product differentiation: forecasting vs. policy analysis

The previous discussion on the economic modelling industry has focused on what we may call the market structure and network of the industry, and has assumed that the nature of the product is straightforward. It might also be useful to consider competition by product and the nature of product differentiation. The most prominently differentiated products from the industry are forecasts and analyses of the effects of policy measures ('what if' analyses, scenario analyses[6]). In some countries, as in the Netherlands, the law delegates the production of forecasting to one specific agency. In that case a monopolistic situation may easily arise, the more so as large sunk costs are involved in producing forecasts. Moreover, the producer of such 'official' forecasts may have access to information which is not publicly available. In other countries, as in the UK, in Germany and in the US, there is much more competition in forecasting and it spans public and private sector organizations. In some of these countries a forum for discussion and judgement on the various forecasts has been organized in order to come to a common view on future developments on which government policy can be based [for example, the Troika process in the US (see Donihue and Kitchen (1997, Chapter 14 in this volume), the so-called Five Wise Men in Germany and the Panel of Independent Forecasters in the UK (see Evans, 1997, Chapter 13 in this volume)]. (In Section 4 we will pay more attention to the role of model-based analysis in arriving at a consensus advice on both forecasts and adequate policy measures.)

Based on the UK case, we can start with the distinction made between what were apparently the two tasks of the UK Panel of Independent Forecasters (in spite of its name), namely to provide *forecasts* of economic development in the UK and to formulate *policy prescriptions* (see Evans, 1997, Chapter 13 in this volume). With respect to the use of models in the forecasting process the discussions of the Panel appear to focus on the role of judgement in the forecasts. On the issue of model-based policy analysis, their discussions involved the differences in opinion on the working of economic mechanisms, or the type of theories incorporated into the models. In the case of policy prescriptions, the statement of Patrick Minford in the discussions in the Panel (see Evans, 1997, Chapter 13 in this volume) makes it clear that here there is a third distinction, namely between policy analysis, based on mechanisms at work in the economy, and recommendations based on *policy preferences* (e.g. about the allowable size of the sacrifice ratio). An even clearer example of this distinction is the use of the Dutch CPB model in calculating the economic programmes of the political parties at election time. Here the same model is used so that the assumed mechanisms are constant, but the policy preferences are those expressed in party programmes.

Rather provocatively Wren-Lewis (1997, Chapter 11 in this volume) argues that the production *methods* of forecasts and of other model-based policy analyses should be differentiated as well as the products in the sense that different models should be used for each. Yet in practice there is not much evidence that sheer mechanical forecasting methods have been used in the preparation of government policy. Of course mechanical methods, like ARIMA- and VAR-models, are used for short-term forecasting of a large number of disaggregated time series, or they are used as benchmarks for the quantification of the propagation of shocks, but most macroeconomic variables which play a role in the policy discussions, are predicted using structural models. There are two reasons. First, structural models allow for inclusion of judgemental elements into the forecast. Secondly, when publishing the forecast, the forecasting agency should be able to tell a story to go with the forecasts. The economic mechanisms, which constitute the framework of this story, will not be very different from the mechanisms that govern the calculations of the effects of policy measures. Therefore agencies that produce both types of products will tend to use the same kinds of (structural) models.

Nevertheless, there is, of course, a major difference in the way a model is used between model-based forecasting and model-based policy analysis. It is, by definition, impossible to foresee (and thus forecast) an unexpected shock, whereas scenario analysis using an empirical model may give a clue about the propagation of a supposed shock through the economy, and may enable an analysis of the policy measures required to sterilize the adverse effects of the shock. From a historical point of view, we might note that Tinbergen designed his first model (Tinbergen, 1936, 1937) for the Dutch economy in order to calculate the effects of various policy measures (and the model was not used for forecasting), whereas his US model (Tinbergen, 1939) was used for forecasting and policy analysis: but they were both the same kind of structural model. The first models of the Dutch CPB in the fifties were mainly used for forecasting whereas nowadays there is a strong tendency to use the same type of models mainly for policy analysis. The MIMIC model is specially designed for that, and is not used for forecasting. This somewhat corroborates the experience at the Bank of Canada. Duguay and Longworth (1998, Chapter 5 in this volume) recollect that model-based projections occurred at the Bank of Canada only 10 years after publication of the RDX1 model was introduced for policy analysis. It suggests that indeed there has been in the past a clear distinction between the use of models for forecasting and for policy analysis – but not using essentially different models.

It seems that nowadays the differentiation of the production methods proceeds in a somewhat different direction than between forecasting and policy analysis. There is currently a proliferation of models, each of which might be used for specific types of forecasts and various policy analyses, often within the same agency. The result is that the models used in short-term forecasting and cyclical analysis also differ from those producing long-term scenarios. In the first type of models, the emphasis is on adjustment lags and the propagation mechanisms of shocks, whereas the latter type of models focuses on long-term equilibrating mechanisms and on endogenizing structural developments. Thus, in this trend to proliferation of models, some model specialization between forecasting and analysis of policy effects also takes place, along with the use of different types of models to answer different policy questions. There is also a tendency towards the use of small models: the large 'multipurpose' policy models are replaced by a more modular approach with a core model and special modules connected to that core depending on the occasion. A case which neatly illustrates this last point is that of the recent changes at the Bank of England. Whitley (1997) explains how this involved the move from one large macro model supposed to be able to answer all sorts of questions to a suite of small complementary models, each designed for different purposes. Apparently, one of the reasons for the change was that 'policy makers require a framework that gives them a stable and consistent way of interpreting an economic system subject to many and varied shocks' and 'Large macroeconometric models were perceived by their users to have failed to meet this need' (both quotes p. 165) perhaps because their very size hid the large amount of uncertainty about what was really known about the economy. Some of these small models are used only for forecasting, whereas those designed for analysis might also be used for forecasting. He notes the importance of 'some basic consistency in economic paradigm across the various models' (Whitley, 1997, p. 168) which enables the models to be used in conjunction with each other.

4. The value chain

By concentrating our description above on the market structure, the goods produced, and the links between institutions, we have temporarily lost sight of our main topic. When we selected the theme of our conference and of this volume, it was at the outset clear to us that interaction between modellers and policy makers *does* take place. It was not our aim to gather evidence to test the hypothesis whether there is a two-way interaction: it is obvious that such two-way interaction exists. Our purpose was to highlight how the interaction takes place, and to compare experience from different countries and institutions.

The technocratic (in the terminology of Habermas, 1968) methodology of mainstream economics may suggest that the design of testable economic theories and the building of scientifically sound economic models is purely an academic question. Accordingly there should be information flows in only one direction, namely from the models to the policy makers. In this view models add value to the policy-making process as they are the results of (public) investments in scientific research. Indeed it is true that the modelling exercises have been helpful in the design and implementation of policy measures. However, as the chapters of our volume and of the history of model-building and use in various institutions show, there has in practice been a continuous interaction between both groups involved. Sometimes they were the same people and quite often there has been mobility from one group to the other [see the introduction by Zalm (1998, Chapter 1 in this volume)]. Experience strongly suggests that without the second value flow, from policy makers back to model builders, economic models would not have been found valuable in policy practice. Thus we are invited to think about the question of the value chain not as a case of model builders producing outputs used by policy makers (as in the standard economic paradigm), but rather as a case of a networked organization in which modellers and policy makers both contribute to the creation of value by sharing information and by co-ordinating their activities as implied in the network approach.

4.1. Models in policy evaluation: the value chain at work

In the early 1930s there was a lively academic and policy debate in the Netherlands on exchange rate policy. Although the UK had left the gold standard in 1931, the Dutch government was greatly in favour of having the guilder remain fixed to the gold standard. Those opposed argued that leaving the gold standard would mean devaluation which would enhance the competitive position of the country and would therefore be beneficial to employment. Tinbergen's model (1936) was especially built to investigate these policy questions. So even at the dawn of model-building there was interaction from policy questions to model formulation and usage. Since then, one of the most obvious ways in which model and policy interaction goes on is in the use of models to analyse the effects of possible policy actions and thus act as a substitute for natural experiments (or even the controlled experiments available in some natural sciences).

A somewhat revealing and recent example of this aspect of how the interactive value chain works is the discussion in the Netherlands about the so-called Plan of Van Elswijk (1996). Van Elswijk is a business economist who has designed a new structure and financing system for social security. In this system, social security premiums are to be levied on value added instead of on wages, and there would be a large employment subsidy for each employee. Van Elswijk has found some political support for his plan, mainly because his presentation of the plan suggests that the proposed policy change would provide a free lunch for enhancing labour participation and labour market efficiency. The CPB, however, was reluctant to calculate the effects of this plan, as it seemed too risky, i.e. it might provoke behavioural change in elements not included in the models. So the advice of the CPB was negative in spite of the fact that, according to the model simulations by the CPB, some favourable results were found for *parts* of the plan (see Centraal Planbureau, 1995). Given these favourable results, the Minister of Social Affairs and Employment was asked by members of Parliament why he did not implement (parts) of the plan. In his letter of response to Parliament, the Minister included the advice of two independent experts not to implement the plan. Yet even after a hearing of the experts in a Parliamentary Commission, some members of Parliament are still not convinced of the risks of introducing the plan.

This episode shows an interesting and somewhat unexpected aspect of the value chain. The high esteem for the model-based calculations by the CPB in the Netherlands in policy-making causes an almost unconditional belief in the outcome of *the models*, more especially when the policy plans look politically attractive and seemingly lead to win–win situations. Non-CPB-model-based objections against such plans from a theoretical perspective, by both experts and even by the modellers of the CPB themselves, namely that a shift in the tax base may not automatically be more efficient and that the proposed labour subsidies may yield large deadweight losses, are easily disregarded by the politicians. It seems that the credibility of the model outcomes is much higher than the credibility of advice from the CPB modellers, and other experts. This example also illustrates another problem of tension in the value chain created by using the model. In order for the results of the model-based analyses to gain weight in the process of policy-making, some reputation for usefulness and reliability with respect to this method of analysis has to be built up. Yet frequent changes in the working of the model, or remarks that the model is not suited for the specific question at hand, destroy that reputation.

We have concentrated on the Dutch case here, not just because we know a lot about it, but because in no other country does the modelling agency and the model have such a public, important collaborative and open role in economic policy analysis. The interactions between modellers and policy makers starts early on: there are ample discussions between the economic experts of the political parties and the CPB officers when the Bureau is to make an assessment of the effects of the economic policy measures proposed in the election programmes of each political party. These discussions may even lead to changes in the formulation of the final draft of the parties' programmes.

Another good example of the value chain at work involves the issue of transparency. It is fairly generally accepted that models can be useful in making economic argumentation transparent. This transparency is, as Mayes and Razzak (1998, Chapter 7 in this volume) illuminate, one of the most valuable elements in the use of empirical models in policy-making at the Reserve Bank of New Zealand. The performance contract for the management of the Reserve Bank of New Zealand (officially called the Reserve Bank Act and the Policy Targets Agreement) can be regarded as the principal-agent solution to the time inconsistency problem. This really forces the decision makers and the policy analysts at the Bank to join hands and it urges the analysts to be practical and the policy makers to make their decisions transparent via the model. But why is this transparency needed in the framework of the principal-agent solution? One could argue that, when the management of the Bank is judged on their performance on reaching prespecified policy goals, there is not much need for them to show how they achieved these policy goals. Then they have no reason to be transparent. Mayes and Razzak explain that the transparency is necessary to induce the market to react consistently with the policy targets represented in the model and thus ensure that the performance contract is met. Here, one could say, the value from the models–policy interaction is optimized, because the salaries, if not the jobs, of these officials depend on the reaction of the market to the Bank's view on the working of the economy. Here the network seems to extend from the Government, via the decision makers and modellers at the Bank to the financial markets: all collaborate in making the model–policy analysis succeed.

We can regard both the Dutch examples and the New Zealand one as providing strong cases indicative of how the co-ordination and asset sharing of network organizations can be effective in the value chain. (Indeed, one might say that the Dutch case is an embarrassingly strong one.) In equal support, the next example reveals clearly how the value chain may fail because of inadequate network arrangements. This case is recollected in Bradley's (1997, Chapter 9 in this volume) account of the use of models to assess the fairly erratic policy with respect to the regional aid programmes of the European Union. It describes how the effectiveness of these programmes in the so-called Community Support Framework (CSF) were only evaluated after their implementation in the relatively poor regions (or countries) of the European Union. It appears that there was no clear theoretical backing for the policy proposals when they were implemented, so that the theoretical arguments for the assignment of the CSF programmes to the poor regions were only developed after selection, approval and execution of the plans. Consequently, the interaction between policy makers and modellers appears mainly to consist of the fact that the policy makers wanted to derive *ex post* arguments for their plans, whereas the modellers were forced to think about an appropriate modelling framework for evaluating the effectiveness of the plans at the macro level. This seems a clear example of failure to create value due to a lack of appropriate contracts and connections between the various groups involved and a total failure to share information and products before the policy had been carried out.

4.2. Models as information systems and knowledge creators

So far, our account has considered the industry, the product and the value chain. However, inherent to our case is that this industry is a knowledge-creating industry: above all, the models–policy interaction is about knowledge, its creation and its transmission. What is special about this? Nonaka (1991), writing in the management literature on the characteristics of Japanese 'knowledge creating companies', has made a number of points which seem relevant to our investigations. First, he contrasts the old (Western) view of organizations as 'a machine for information processing' in which the only useful knowledge is 'quantifiable' with his new view (based on study of Japanese knowledge-based industries) which pictures the organization as a 'living organism' whose ability to 'create new knowledge' depends on a process of turning 'personal' knowledge into usable knowledge shared across the organization (all quotes from Nonaka, 1991, pp. 96–7). Nonaka draws on Polanyi's notion of 'personal knowledge' more often now known as 'tacit' knowledge, for the basis of his account (see Polanyi, 1958, 1966). Personal knowledge involves craft-type skills or 'know-how' of a technical nature (which is not articulated) as well as a cognitive dimension: a mental perspective about how the world is, how things work, etc. As Nonaka points out, the organization learns little from the exchange of either tacit knowledge between two individuals, or the processing of explicit (i.e. already articulated) knowledge. Useful though both actions might be to the organization, they do not create new knowledge. (If we apply these ideas to our case, we might note, for example, that most modellers learn their work through some kind of apprenticeship training, and although this is useful, it doesn't have implications for the creation of new models or the interactions between policy makers and empirical modellers.) In contrast, Nonaka claims that the ways in which the organization increases its knowledge base is through the process of 'articulation': the conversion of tacit to explicit knowledge and 'internalization': the conversion of explicit to internalized personal knowledge.

How is this process of articulation achieved? Two points are particularly relevant to our case. One is that the articulation of tacit knowledge often involves some kind of analogical thinking or modelling. We can regard the empirical model as a paradigm case for Nonaka's knowledge management approach: the empirical models of economics embody much tacit knowledge: craft econometrics skill, modelling skills, etc.,[7] as well as cognitive elements: the mental perspectives inherent in economic theories about the working of the economy. (Interestingly, empirical models are also exemplars of the information processing role, creating hard quantitative information, pictured for the role of organizations in the older paradigm.) By putting these things together, the modellers are able to convert their combined personal knowledge and create an articulated knowledge of the economy embodied in the model, forecasts, policy scenarios, etc. The problem of fully articulating the knowledge in the model into explicit knowledge amounts to explaining the model and its forecasts and scenarios so that it can be shared by others – especially policy makers – in the organization. In this light, the difficulties of satisfactorily explaining large models and sharing the information given in their outputs emerges as one cogent reason why large models fail to convert personal into organizational knowledge. This in turn helps to explain the move to smaller, more easily comprehended models which can be articulated and shared.

The second point that emerges of relevance is the principle of redundancy. The knowledge approach argues for a 'conscious overlapping of ... information ... activities and ... responsibilities' (Nonaka, 1991, p. 102). This is not a sign of waste, rather a necessary condition for the organization to encourage a favourable transfer of tacit knowledge into explicit knowledge, particularly important in 'product development'. Under conditions of free access to information and shared responsibilities for creating explicit knowledge, innovation will flourish. This of course is contrary to much standard wisdom about economic efficiency in the theory of the firm based on specialization of tasks, division of labour, etc. It is applicable to our case for it tells against the received view that theoretical economists, or perhaps academic economists, are responsible for innovation, and policy makers decide policy, leaving modellers in a mechanical information-processing zone in the middle. In this view, it seems there is no normative science! It may be helpful to the argument to note here that Nonaka's idea of knowledge creation is closer to a Schumpeterian innovation (the development of new ways of doing things, new combinations, new specific applications, etc.) than to the idealized notions of either a scientific 'discovery' or 'proof' which hold in the realm of positive science. It is in this Nonaka–Schumpeterian sense, that the normative part of economic study involves the creation of knowledge, not only about how to do applied analysis, but because it undertakes a type of analysis relevant for creating knowledge about the specific case and what would constitute a good policy for that case. In this normative part of economics, if Nonaka is correct, good conditions for such knowledge creation will prevail where academics, modellers and policy makers share information and responsibilities freely and where the tacit knowledge of both the modellers and policy makers is combined.

We focus our discussions here on the academic critique of empirical modelling activity as one way of bringing out the positive insights we can gain with the help of Nonaka's ideas and analysis of knowledge creation. In this light, it appears much of the academic critique is misplaced.

4.3. Creating and transmitting knowledge: the difference between the perceptions of policy modellers and academic researchers

One of the apparent weak links in the value chain is the growing gap between the academic perspective on economic modelling and the use made of empirical models in policy practice. This has several aspects, and we use these to understand how the modelling interaction can create knowledge and so value.

Smith (1998, Chapter 15 in this volume) lucidly describes how the extensive criticism from academic economists on large macroeconometric models used in policy agencies relates to the academic concerns about the status and qualities of these models, and not to the actual use of these models in policy practice, which is quite different from the academic preoccupation. The knowledge created in the models–policy interaction is not that the policy makers become convinced that the models yield a perfect image of the various mechanisms at work in the economy. The major value of the models–policy interaction is just that models bring both information and consistency into the policy debate. Without the model there is, as Smith remarks, no way that the large amount of information on economic developments could be generated, and updated, and put together rapidly enough to be used in policy-making.[8] Modelling, and its data requirements, create the kind of information systems that policy makers need and use. Smith's illustration of these requirements, by referring to the invitation to tender issued by the UK Treasury for the proposed market test of all parts of the Treasury's macroeconomic and public finance forecasting and monitoring functions, is quite revealing in this respect.

A second difference in perspective between academic economists and modellers involved in the policy process has to do with the gap between the positive use of models where academic scholars feel comfortable, and the normative use warranted by the policy makers. Against this background, in his summary of the papers presented at the conference, Ralph Bryant mentioned the issue of model selection. The positive and academic attitude towards the choice of models may lead to the conviction that model evaluation and model improvement would get us eventually towards the best encompassing model. Estimation of encompassing models which can discriminate between the various theories is still a faraway idea. The UK experience of academic assessment of the properties of various models in policy analysis suggests that there are as many different sets of advice as there are models to choose from (see, for example, Wallis, 1984; Turner et al., 1989; Fisher et al., 1990). In policy practice, the choice of the model, and of the mechanisms contained in the model, is conducted in a much more intuitive and informal manner, involving both technical and non-technical expertise. This is also true of model usage. The implementation of proposed policy measures in the models and conduction 'what if' simulations, requires a lot of judgement. That judgement may come from experienced policy makers as much as from the modellers (see Martens, 1986). It is by using judgement in conjunction with the models that modellers and policy makers come to share their information and expertise. The chapter by Edison and Marquez (1998, Chapter 12 in this volume) illustrates this process of creating shared knowledge from two sorts of tacit expertise: from modellers and from the various Governors of the US Federal Reserve System.

A similar misunderstanding surrounds the use of optimal control theory. Westaway (1995) comments, in a nicely understated way, on the twofold gap between the theory of policy design and its practice in the context of using optimal control analysis on the National Institute model of the UK economy. On the one hand, he notes, theory suggests that such policy analysis is merely a technical problem; but this is so only because such theory assumes that the Government can state its relative priorities explicitly and that it knows 'which model of the economy is the most accurate' (two large assumptions which create problems in practical design – see Westaway, 1995, p. 54). On the other hand, theory starts with idealized models and elements (such as 'utility'), whereas practice must use those variables for which we have measurements and this creates difficulties of translation not only from the theoretical to the empirical model but in delimiting final from intermediate policy objectives. Optimal control theory may be useful in policy analysis not so much as a process of solving technical problems (i.e. a mechanical answer to the policy question), but for exploring the tacit knowledge contained in models via a systematic simulation of their policy outcomes.

A third element in the academic critique is that academic research has also shown a tendency to move away from quantitative analysis using models and concentrate on theoretical models which highlight one major mechanism to explain observed stylized facts. But obviously the demand from the policy makers requires an assessment of the overall effects of policy proposals which result from interaction between various mechanisms involved. More general empirical models provide a consistent and quantitative indication of the *net outcome* of the various principle mechanisms thought to be at work *based on the particular case* (not the stylized facts) and which might be affected by the policies proposed. Empirical models are needed just because the qualitative analysis of stylized facts is indistinct. Polak (1998, Chapter 4 in this volume) stresses the importance of considering the interaction of various mechanisms and the need for specific quantitative outcomes. He remarks, based on long experience using a small simple simultaneous equations model in policy analysis for the IMF, in a variety of different countries and times, that the outcomes of a simultaneous macro model can be quite different from first-round effects of a single equation model to which policy makers sometimes like to adhere, especially if these first-round effects are favourable and second-round ones unfavourable. This is a major practical advantage of model-based policy analysis as compared to partial studies which concentrate on a specific behavioural relationship in isolation from feedback mechanisms at the macro level.

Another point of departure between academic and policy modellers is in the use of calibrated vs. econometric estimated models. Academic economists (or even more so econometricians) may favour the use of estimated models, whereas in the more practical application of models, calibration seems unavoidable [see, e.g., Duguay and Longworth (1998, Chapter 5 in this volume) on the calibration of the QPM model for the Canadian economy]. In case of macroeconometric models, the information content of single time series is sometimes too poor to be relied upon completely when specifying and estimating the model. For well-established macroeconomic relationships, much information on specification and parameter values is commonly available from previous empirical research. Therefore, in practice, a lot of additional local tacit knowledge and information is used by the model builders, especially when there is a proliferation of models in the same agency and when consistency in the working of these various models is required in the presentation of policy advice by the agency. In that case some formal or informal calibration is needed in the construction of the model in addition to the use of estimation techniques. (One could argue that in this way the model builders follow a kind of informal Bayesian procedure in specifying and estimating their model.) This illustrates another of the ways in which individual modellers' tacit knowledge of their part of the model or equation is made explicit and shared in the modelling activity as a whole (see Kenway, 1994).

Smith (1998, Chapter 15 in this volume) and Westaway (1995) have both illuminated the distinction between the formal idea of using models in policy preparation to which the academic profession adheres, and the actual usefulness of models for policy analysis. From this perspective the question arises why the academic criticism against the use of models from the formal perspective is still taken seriously for, as Smith argues, these critics fight on the wrong battlefield. Is there an element of cognitive dissonance both for the academics who criticize, and for the modellers who try to defend themselves against these kinds of criticism? Why do the modellers still care? The reasons are twofold: modellers still consider elements of the academic criticism valuable for improving their model and analysis; and, academic reputation of the models can be helpful in obtaining acceptance for the outcomes in policy preparation (and the scientific credibility of the modellers in the academic world). For example, one problem is the fact that traditional policy models have been rather eclectic and did not always provide a theoretically consistent description of the interaction between the various mechanisms. As reaction to this criticism the present trend is to use models which are theoretically consistent.

The distrust between academics and policy makers is also a dual one. There may be good reason for academics to distrust the scientific credentials of model outputs, given that these outputs rely on judgements which may involve pressure and preferences from political masters rather than 'purely scientific' judgements. But one must be careful not to misjudge the expertise of policy makers. Their expertise is more likely to be tacit and personal than academic and formal, but it may be just as important for policy analysis as the dual tacit and formal knowledge base of the modeller [again, see the Edison and Marquez chapter (1998, Chapter 12 in this volume)]. There might be equally good reasons for the policy makers to distrust 'academic' innovations – for these may appear both impractical and not yet empirically validated (i.e. 'academic' in the derogatory sense sometimes used). But of course the application of new developments from academic research in model-based policy-making also adds value and, therefore, constitutes an important element of the models–policy interaction and the creation of knowledge at the normative level. In the context of an implicit comparison between the situation in the UK and in Australia in 1993, Wallis noted that Mankiw's view of the failure of applied economists to change along with changes in academic (theoretical) macroeconomists was a caricature, which could not be exported from the US to other countries. Thus, in contrast, in the UK and Australia (the context of Wallis' discussion): 'there has been a wide range of modelling activity over the same period, often with a strong academic base yet representing a fruitful interaction between theoretical developments and policy concerns' (Wallis, 1993, p. 114).

The most prominent example of the successful interaction between theoretical developments and empirical modelling which emerged from the conference discussions is the inclusion of forward-looking expectations (or model-consistent expectations) in empirical models. For instance, the citations in the chapter by Edison and Marquez (1998, Chapter 12 in this volume) clearly show that there was an urge from the policy makers to include this feature in the models. In this respect, Ralph Bryant remarked that we need to reach a position where we can treat expectations as the halfway-house between the two extremes of adaptive backward-looking expectations (the old-fashioned way), which we know are completely inadequate, and the other extreme of model consistent, fully rational expectations, which in their own way are very much a straitjacket too. We may regard the content of this remark as a nice illustration of the learning process in the two-way interaction between modellers and policy makers and of the importance of collaboration between academics, modellers and policy makers in pooling their knowledge. (We discuss further examples of collaboration in Section 5 below.)

4.4. Role of models in consensus building

Our last sub-section here uses the knowledge management approach to give some understanding of how explicit knowledge is transformed back to implicit knowledge. To work effectively, the knowledge creating organization needs to turn its shared explicit knowledge into personal knowledge in the sense of reforming the shared mental map (the cognitive level). This consists of a process of converting the new knowledge so that it is no longer seen as new, and since there is usually some level of disagreement to overcome, it involves some work to create a new consensus. The notion of team working is critical here, since that is the place where this conversion and consensus formation goes on. Nonaka (1991) takes teamwork for granted, as part of a well-established set of characteristics of Japanese work patterns; here we interpret the notion of team-working more broadly.

In our particular case, one of the major gains in value from the interaction between modellers and policy makers is that the models may be instrumental in bringing consensus about policy measures. This is especially true in countries where model-based policy analysis is conducted at various different institutes and agencies. For instance, Donihue and Kitchen (1997) and Evans (1997) (Chapters 14 and 13 in this volume) show for the US and UK, respectively, that this competitive structure of the industry creates the need for co-ordination of the forecasting efforts. Both cases, the Troika process and the UK's Government's Panel of Independent Forecasters, show that there is a remarkable desire among the competing experts to come to a consensus. The major reason behind this is probably that the experts know that the model-based policy advice will be much more influential when the advice is unanimous than when the policy makers are allowed to make their own choice from a set of conflicting experts' opinions. However, this does not overcome the problem that where advice comes from many modellers, each may have a different model based on a different theory. In such cases, this means that, in order to come to a consensus policy advice, a kind of colligation is needed. The relative relevance of the various theories has to be judged and the difference outcomes have to be framed in one encompassing story, which is different from an encompassing model. Evans' (1997, Chapter 13 in this volume) account of the UK Panel of Independent Forecasters provides a good example of this type of consensus formation.

The account given by Edison and Marquez (1998, Chapter 12 in this volume) on the discussions in the FOMC provides another neat illustration of how a committee system contributes to consensus formation on the assessment of the relevance of different economic mechanisms for policy purposes. Here the model exercises provide an idea about the systematic component of the economy so that the focus in the discussion is directed at evaluation of, and the policy response to, the unsystematic component of actual economic developments. The desire to be unanimous in FOMC meetings is very interesting from the point of view of how the interaction works. May be some part of this consensus is already achieved in the preparation prior to the FOMC meeting (as is, for example, the case in the meetings of the Social Economic Council in the Netherlands, when major policy advices are to be established). Is it actually at the FOMC meetings that the big decisions are made, or is some consensus on the decisions already achieved in informal consultations before the meeting? Unfortunately the records do not tell us how prominent the influence of model-based analysis is in those informal circuits. Most probably, in preparing the text for the *Greenbook* and the *Bluebook*, the discussions and the policy stand in the meeting of the FOMC will be somehow anticipated. The same applies when model simulation results are presented to the FOMC meeting: the staff of the Fed must have some *a priori* notion of how these exercises will be appreciated by the FOMC members. Most probably part of the interaction between models and policy has already taken place before the meeting.

In contrast, in the Bank of England case, it is considered important that a shared consensus forecast be obtained which integrates the implicit knowledge from policy makers with modellers' explicit model knowledge. According to Whitley's (1997) account, the committee structure is the mechanism chosen to ensure input from all levels of policy maker (including the most senior policy officials) into the qualitative judgements and analysis of events which feed into the quantitative forecasts made by modellers using the models. Over time, ideally, 'both [directors/governor and forecasters] will tend to share the same analytical framework' (Whitley, 1997, p. 170) and thus justify the claim made by the Bank of England's Governor that the forecasts are 'the Bank's' whereas at the Treasury, the forecasts are those of its 'officials'. This provides a clear example of the modellers–policy makers interaction based on sharing responsibility for forecasting and in the process of their committee work, making a new mental picture of how the world is likely to change.

The contribution of model analysis (rather than forecasting) to consensus formation is, in a somewhat different perspective, also apparent in the different institutional settings of both Norway and the Netherlands. A nice example is given by Bjerkholt (1982), who describes how the Norwegian input–output model can be used at different levels of aggregation. The role of the input–output model seems to have been critical in helping to form consensus on policy at both the national and sectoral level – it created a constraint on negotiation, but also a picture of the interrelations in the economy within which economic actions had to add up at sector level and in the aggregate. In the Netherlands, it almost appears as if consensus about the quality of the policy measures can only be reached when these measures have obtained the CPB's 'stamp of approval' by a successful model experiment. For that reason, amongst others, the analyses of the CPB also play a dominant role in discussions with the employers' organizations, trade unions and independent experts in the Social Economic Council (see Review Committee CPB, 1997). Here the common attitude of policy makers towards economic problems as influenced by the model-based analysis of the CPB may, 'hypothetically', bring about a consensus on 'wrong' policy measures [as was remarked during the interviews conducted by the Review Committee CPB (1997)]. In this respect the comment by Smith (1998, Chapter 15 in this volume) that optimal policy rules can exploit the odd quirks in the model reminds us of the discussion in the Netherlands on the benefits from the Robin Hood policy, which is a typical feature of the MIMIC model. In the interaction process between the political parties and the CPB in the assessment of the economic effects of the election programmes, the political parties were eager to include those policy options into their programmes, which proved most beneficial according to the MIMIC model [see also Zalm (1998, Chapter 1 in this volume) and Van Bergeijk and Van Sinderen (1997, Chapter 3 in this volume)].[9]

We have been treating consensus formation as an example of knowledge creation (within the Nonaka framework), and yet, perhaps as a first step in discussions, it is equally important that the models can clarify where analysts disagree. Here the case of the UK may be relevant, for the work of the Macroeconomic Modelling Bureau made it clear to policy makers that there were as many policy advices as there were models; but their literature comparing models suggests that, indeed, it is possible to clarify where disagreement stems from differences in the model elements, or in the judgements used in conjunction with them, whether by modellers or policy makers (see Wallis and Whitley, 1991a).

5. Organization

A major hypothesis, that we did want to examine by means of the case studies presented at the conference, is how and in what respects the models–policy interaction depends upon the institutional arrangements? This involves both organizational design and communication channels between modelling economists on the one hand and policy makers on the other hand. Essentially this is the background of our question 'What makes the models–policy interaction successful?' Here we draw on the ideas already outlined above on networked organizations, and the process of transforming tacit into explicit knowledge.

From the case studies presented in the conference, and in the literature, it is obvious that there are large differences between the various countries in their organizational set-up and scientific underpinning of economic policy-making. The description of the structure of the industry in Section 3 highlights some of these differences. Yet, in spite of these differences, it seems hard to give an operational interpretation to what we call 'successful interaction'. We might say that the interaction is successful in cases where there is a quick diffusion and adoption of new, useful knowledge and techniques resulting from academic research in the practical process of policy-making. On the other hand, interaction is also successful when there are no long recognition lags from new policy questions and events in the world to the answers on these questions that empirical models can give. A major gain in value could result from an adequate institutional set-up of the models–policy interaction, when, in the taxonomy introduced by Edison and Marquez (1998, Chapter 12 in this volume), direct requests, persuasive requests and idiosyncratic requests, would be as much as possible anticipated by the model builders. The cases presented in this volume suggest that the relationship between the success of the models–policy interaction and the institutional setting is very much country specific. Institutions that lead to a successful interaction in one country are not necessarily adequate for another country. Therefore we will refrain from giving specific guidelines for a successful interaction and only mention some striking aspects in the organization of the diffusion of the knowledge into and within the economic modelling-policy-making interaction.

The first aspect influenced by the institutional set-up is the speed with which new developments in the economy (e.g. the transition from a command to a market economy in Eastern Europe, proposals for tax reforms and reforms of the social security system, the role of institutions itself, policy measures to enhance competition) are incorporated in the models. Good communication channels between modellers and policy makers, and frequent interchanges of personnel between model builders and model users appear to contribute to the anticipation of these developments by the model builders. However, even in the Netherlands, where these lines of communication seem to be relatively open and intense, some major policy questions have not been anticipated by the CPB, as Van Bergeijk and Van Sinderen (1997, Chapter 3 in this volume) complain in their contribution to the conference.

There is an element of physical arrangement here which can be illustrated by a difference between the Netherlands and Norway. In Norway the Research Department of Statistics Norway (RDSN) is only involved in model-building whereas the use of the models for policy preparation is made at the Ministry of Finance (see Bjerkholt, 1998, Chapter 10 in this volume). On the other hand, in the Netherlands, as in most other countries, model-building and model use is located at the same agency (CPB), although within the agency, model builders and model users are sometimes in different departments. A strict separation of the model-building function and the policy preparation function may seriously hamper communication in the model–policy interaction. In Norway this problem seems to be partly solved by a considerable mobility of personnel from the RDSN to the Ministry [see also the situation in the Netherlands as described by Zalm (1998, Chapter 1 in this volume)].

A second aspect is how to ensure that new developments in scientific economics are taken up in modelling agencies. This may be thought to be unproblematic, since modellers are also part of the scientific community.[10] Smith (1994) has some pertinent remarks on the speed of innovation from academic innovation into the models in the case of the UK, where the structure is somewhat competitive which we can contrast with the rather more monopolistic case in the Netherlands. But he also points out that the optimal rate of technical diffusion is unclear. There may be good reasons for delays, academic innovation may be a fashion not worth following immediately given there are known difficulties of reforming just one part of a large complicated empirical model. The case of integrating forward-looking expectations came up as a frequent example during the conference discussions.

One organizational device to encourage interaction on model-based policy analysis between model builders and academic professionals is provided by scientific committees and peer review procedures. The establishment of the Modelling Committee in Norway (see Bjerkholt, 1998, Chapter 10 in this volume) is one example. In the Netherlands the so-called Central Planning Commission, which after a large restructuring of advisory bodies in 1996 consists of members from universities, international organizations, industry and trade unions, has a somewhat similar role with respect to the work of the CPB. In contrast to Norway, no officers from Ministries or from the Central Bank are members of the Central Planning Commission; these interests discuss the work programme of the CPB in the Central Economic Committee. The best example of a peer review system comes from the UK. In the UK, models have been subject to peer review as a consequence of the fact that there has been, over the past 30 years, considerable competition between empirical macroeconomic models built in the academic, quasi-official and official sectors in the UK. The nature of the 'competition' between models (treated as products) has been reviewed since 1983 by the Macroeconomic Modelling Bureau (established by the UK government science funding agency at the University of Warwick). The Bureau (and associated academics) has carried out a series of assessments of the models, including those of the Treasury and the Bank of England, and particularly compared their properties as instruments for policy analysis. This has involved many comparisons of forecasts, various kinds of scenario analysis, and optimal control policy outcomes (see, for example, Wallis, 1984, 1987; Fisher and Wallis, 1990).

During the period of the Bureau's work, several models have either arrived or disappeared, and those remaining have been modified considerably in response to changes in the economic world, changes in economic ideas and changes in the policy stance of governments (for a survey, see Wallis and Whitley, 1991b) and perhaps even in response to the work of the Bureau. It is sometimes rather difficult to disentangle the causes of these changes: for example in a 1990 report (see Fisher et al., 1990), the Bureau's staff referred to the introduction of supply-side economics and improved modelling of inflation in response both to concerns of policy makers and competition from other empirical models with alternative theoretical paradigms. A report of 1995 (see Church et al., 1995) noted changes to models in response to the requirement of the Maastricht treaty, leading to the incorporation of new feedback loops and the endogenization of income tax rates and interest rates as policy instruments.[11]

The third aspect which is connected to the organization of the models–policy interaction relates to the type and particularly the size of models that are used. Traditionally and following the pioneering work of Tinbergen and Klein, rather large and eclectic models were used for policy analysis at the macro level. One can regard these as 'multipurpose' models, which means that they are used to simulate the effects of a variety of policy measures. Some of these models contain thousands of equations (e.g. the Brookings Model constructed in the 1960s) and this size may obscure the working of the model in such a way that it becomes difficult to implement policy measures in the model when a change in specification and the structure of the model is needed. As we noted already, there is new tendency towards use of a smaller and more flexible models which are directed at specific policy questions. Against this background the long history of usage of the Polak model at the IMF provides a very remarkable contrast (see Polak, 1998, Chapter 4 in this volume). This model was developed to be usable in every country. It is therefore very small, with minimum data requirements; it can be flexibly applied and explained with relative ease to policy makers with no experience of empirical modelling.[12] Whitley's account (1997) of the Bank of England's experience emphasizes that their new models also have the advantage of smallness. Smallness makes a model easier to understand and explain – it is more transparent. The tacit knowledge of such models can more easily be made explicit and the tacit-knowledge judgements of policy makers can more easily be integrated into the usage of small models. But the switch to such models also seems to have been the result of an effort (by modellers?) to rebuild confidence in the use of models amongst the Bank's policy makers.[13] Whatever the reasons, the switch to small models seems to have achieved a greater integration of tacit knowledge from empirical modellers and policy makers into the policy-making process.

The tendency to design specific models for different purposes has, as also mentioned above, been another factor causing a proliferation of models even within the same agency. For instance, in the Netherlands three models of major size have to be maintained by the CPB's staff. As this is rather costly in terms of personnel, the Review Committee CPB (1997) advises that an alternative approach is to be considered in future, namely to construct empirical models in a more modular fashion. A small, theoretically sound equilibrium model with appropriate long-term properties could be extended with especially designed modules which would provide sufficient detail on that sector of the economy on which the policy question focuses. This suggestion of the Committee also concords with the tendency in model-building to make small maquettes of large models (MINIMOD at IMF, SAM at the Bank of Canada) in order to get a better insight into the major mechanisms at work in the model. It emerged, with surprising unanimity during the conference, that it always takes approximately four years before a new model is operational. (It almost looks like an empirical law!)

A fourth aspect in the models–policy interaction regards the way in which models are designed. The extremes are bottom-up (modellers) vs. top-down (policy makers) design inputs to the models. The question is whether the model builders are trying to convince the policy makers that their ideas on the working of the economy implemented in the model are correct or, the other way around, that the policy makers explain their intuition of the major mechanisms at work in the economy to the model builders and request that these mechanisms are included in the model in that fashion. There are two sorts of tacit knowledge involved here, and both, in some form of balance, are likely to be incorporated into the empirical model. It appears that a good balance between the top-down and the bottom-up approach to design will be most valuable to the successful interactive usage of the model in subsequent policy analysis. This would indeed be the prediction from both Miles and Snow's view of the effectiveness of networked organizations in shared product development and from Nonaka's view of the role of shared mental maps in knowledge creation.

The success of the models–policy interaction seems to be enhanced when policy makers have also been modellers or are at least familiar with the broad outlines of the contents of the model and may even have some say in design. In such cases, the policy makers seem more likely to take the modelling analyses seriously. According to Duguay and Longworth (1998, Chapter 5 in this volume) at the Bank of Canada the Governor and Senior Deputy Governor valued the projection with the RDXF model as a consensus view of the staff. Of course the question remains whether this forecast was really made independently by the staff with no hindsight to the experience and expertise embodied in the views of the Governor and Deputy Governor. Reading between the lines the impression is that top-down influence on model design has been rather important at the Bank of Canada. In contrast, Smith (1998, Chapter 15 in this volume) quotes a number of sweeping misgivings against model-based policy advice of high-ranked UK policy makers who were unfamiliar with the models and how they work in analysing policy. There seems to be a marked difference in this respect between the UK and countries like Canada, Norway and the Netherlands, where members of the government, and even of Parliament, are quite knowledgeable about the possibilities and reservations of model-based policy analysis. Some of them even have a background in the industry.

A fifth point, symmetric to this, also concerns model usage. That is, it also seems to be the case that modellers take policy problems and questions more seriously when they themselves form part of the policy-analysis process and may even have some responsibility for explaining policy [as in the case described by Mayes and Razzak (1998, Chapter 7 in this volume)] rather than being kept in the back-room, at arm's length from policy makers and those affected by the policy. The very close-ness of the modellers to the policy process at the Reserve Bank of New Zealand seems to have enhanced the speed and quality of modellers' design responsiveness to policy problems compared to the speed of reaction of model builders at the independent and rather more remote Dutch CPB. Whitley (1997), from the Bank of England, also notes that their change to small-scale models and a committee structure for forecasting was related to the introduction of a new monetary policy requiring transparency in inflation targeting and forecasting. The effect of adopting new and open contracts between the Treasury and the Bank in the UK parallels the case of New Zealand and reminds us also that the success of networked organ-izations is thought to be partly dependent on visible contractual arrangements.

A final aspect of the models–policy interaction concerns the question whether state monopoly or a free entry and competition for model-based policy advice affects the success of the interaction. This brings us back to our starting point of market structure in Section 3. In this respect there seem to be large differences between the countries considered in the case studies of this volume. Yet no clear recipe emerges which market structure yields the most successful interaction. The Dutch model of monopoly seems to work well in the Netherlands as it guarantees an independent position for the CPB. On the other hand, the lack of competition may have a negative influence on the quality of the analyses of the monopolist. The assessment of the Review Committee of the CPB is that traditionally the CPB could be characterized as a rather inward-looking institute. Yet, as is also shown by a number of papers of the conference (Van Bergeijk and Van Sinderen, 1997; Van Els, 1997; Chapters 3 and 6 in this volume), the CPB is nowadays not completely free from competition in the field of model-based macroeconomic policy analysis and forecasting. The Netherlands' Bank produces its own forecasts and so does the research institute NYFER from Nijenrode University. However, an open contro-versy about policy analyses or forecasts is avoided by the Central Bank, and for the time being the informational backlog of NYFER is so large that its forecasts do not really compete with those of the CPB.

Competition between agencies who perform model-based policy analysis, as in the UK and the US, also has its advantages and disadvantages. The various agencies may become too easily associated with specific political interests which endanger their credibility and independence. In this respect Smith (1998, Chapter 15 in this volume) records that in the UK the Treasury forecasts are regarded as 'political'. (Counter-intuitively, the strength of the CPB forecasts in the Netherlands is that politicians, and even the social partners, will consider the forecast to be apolitical, as a result of the reputation of independence cherished by the CPB.) On the other hand, competition of models in the UK has (also counter-intuitively) created a great deal of openness about the content of models. The role of the macro-modelling review Bureau and its investigations have helped to make public and transparent the differences between the models and their powers. In this way, the work of the Bureau and its analyses are believed to have contributed to the economic policy debates, via the publications emanating from the Bureau staff and their annual conferences. The contribution of competitive models and the assessment Bureau are both difficult to assess, but probably the impact of both have been in an informal way and at the level of experts inside and close to government, political circles and amongst their academic supporters and critics. [For an assessment of the Bureau's work, see Smith (1990).] Wallis (director of the Bureau) argued in 1993 for 'model-building and model-using' to be 'fully documented and completely open' and pointed to the fact that the publication of official models in the UK has not created problems, rather that the publication and access to such models 'makes them less likely to be used as political footballs'. Particularly in policy analysis, Wallis argues the need for maximum transparency is critical, since not only the models, but 'off-model calculations' or judgemental inputs, can be assessed by all involved (all quotes, Wallis, 1993, p. 127).

6. Conclusion

This extended review of the interaction between empirical models and policy-making has demonstrated the difficulties of making general claims about their interaction given the very wide variety of experiences reported in the chapters of this volume and the literature surveyed. We trust that our analysis has, at least, focused attention on the critical (but hitherto neglected) question: How is value created in the interaction between modellers and policy makers? It is perhaps no surprise, given the recent turn of much economics, to find that the institutional arrangements governing interactions, and the specifics of contracts and organizational design, have proved as important, if not more so, than the question of market structure. Although this chapter has not undertaken formal application of either theories about network organizations and the value chain or theories about the creation and transmission of knowledge, both these frameworks have proved useful. To a considerable extent, these frameworks have helped us to provide insights into the mechanisms of interaction and to understand the range of outcomes reported in the case study material.

The ideas of network analysis have helped us to see more clearly the importance of examining the full scope of the network; of analyzing non-market based exchange arrangements and of understanding the role of sharing information. We conclude that to understand the full extent and impact of the model–policy-making interactions, the elements of the network should be conceived in very broad terms, to extend from academics, statistical offices and model builders, to model users, policy makers and the public. We also conclude that although institutional arrangements do play a considerable role in the successfulness of the interaction between empirical modellers and policy makers, there is no one institutional arrangement which can be judged optimal from our case studies. These institutional factors include on the one hand the physical connections between modellers and policy makers in terms of location, but also the extent to which personnel cross the divide. It seems that the success of this interaction can be enhanced when the institutional arrangements provide career incentives for job mobility between model builders, model users and policy makers. On the other hand, successful interaction also relies on the nature of contractual arrangements between groups, and here the extent to which information and tasks are shared between the groups appears to be critical to the value gained by both modellers and policy makers from the interaction.

Characterizing the process of interaction and the creation of value in terms of the articulation of tacit knowledge or personal expertise from both modellers and policy makers has helped us to examine the knowledge-creation process that goes on in using models in policy-making. Here we conclude that the successful interaction depends on the ability of the two main groups involved – modellers and policy makers – to share their expertise and make it explicit, both in models and model products such as forecasts and policy evaluations. If neither side takes the expertise of the other side seriously, if neither side can articulate their tacit knowledge to the other, then it seems likely that interaction will not be value-creating for the parties involved. The possibilities of transforming tacit into articulated shared knowledge partly depends on the physical and contractual institutional arrangements discussed above, but, once again, there appears to be no one-to-one relationship between institutional arrangements and successful knowledge creation.

The implication that we want to draw from this analysis is that while the specific structure may not matter, the way that it is used does. Both the network and the knowledge approach lead to the same conclusion – that tight linkages, defined by the speed and quality of good flows of information, are more important than the legal structure of relations. If the network arrangements are flexible, and information flows are effective, it is not necessarily a problem that the co-operating elements are in different institutions. If the groups are able to adjust their relations over time as the product, and what is expected from it, changes, they are more likely to maintain an effective value chain whatever their institutional base.

We can see now that the notion of empirical models as a bridge between the positive and normative domains of economics holds in two particular ways. One way is as a knowledge device which spans the two domains. The empirical model embodies the positive scientific object upon which the normative analysis of policy options are based, either directly or via forecasting and simulation outputs. The empirical model therefore plays this dual role of constituting the expertise gained through positive science and enabling normative knowledge to be developed. The other way in which empirical models constitute a bridge is that they provide a clear focus for the people involved – modellers and policy makers – to interact and to share the expertise that each group has. There are, of course, interactions of scientific economics and policy makers without the intermediary of models, but the presence of empirical models allows a specific kind of interaction which involves making explicit and integrating the tacit knowledge of both groups of participants: modellers and policy makers.

Acknowledgements

This chapter draws on the research we undertook in preparing for the Tinbergen Institute's 10th Anniversary Conference and on the discussions that took place there. We thank the Tinbergen Institute and sponsors for their support for the conference and thus this volume. We thank participants at the conference, Charles Baden-Fuller, Sean Holly and Henk van Latesteijn for helpful comments on this chapter.

Notes

1 See also Bodkin *et al.* (1991) for an authoritative history of macroeconometric model-building in the USA and many other countries, but one which has little to say about their policy usage.
2 See also Nelson (1987) for a very broad perspective on the influence of economists on policy-making in the USA, but with almost nothing to say about empirical models.
3 There may also be useful insights from evolutionary theory of the firm [see Nelson and Winter (1982) and Nelson (1995)], but these are more concerned with the process of transmitting competencies through time, an important aspect of the modelling industry, but not the one of most concern to us here.
4 Now that central planning has become even more out of date than just after the War, the Bureau has changed its English name into CPB Netherlands Bureau for Economic Policy Analysis in order to avoid misunderstanding about its task and mission abroad. In the Netherlands its name is still 'Centraal Planbureau'. As its place in the Dutch institutional setting of policy preparation is clear to all insiders, changing its name would be as costly as changing the name of a valuable trademark.
5 This openness of official models is not just to the academic community: the UK Treasury model has been accessible by commercial interests via a consortium arrangement (see Wallis, 1987).
6 For a useful taxonomy of the various types of scenario analyses used, see Wallis (1993).
7 There are huge learning costs (sunk costs) involved to become a professional and experienced modeller, and the skills required for entering the profession are no longer necessarily part of the academic curriculum. Even where the apprenticeship system of normal academic economics includes those studies required for empirical modellers, they typically need further on-the-model experience.
8 The role of models in providing consistent information is also reflected in a description of the difficulties of making forecasts consistent at the international level within the OECD [see Ch. 10 in Llewellyn *et al.* (1985)] and, for a parallel example, see the history of the 'world economic outlooks' at the IMF by Boughton (1997, Chapter 8 in this volume).
9 Here the informal monopoly power of the CPB and the absence of an alternative model due to high learning costs may even be seen as an uncommon example of a technology lock-in.
10 In general there are many unanswered questions about the interaction of applied scientists with their theoretical colleagues. Galison (1997) has adopted the notion of the 'trading zone' from anthropology to help clarify these communications in the case of physics.
11 A parallel example comes from the floating of exchange rates – in December 1983 the floating of the Australian currency meant that 'what had been seen as an exogenous policy instrument became an endogenous variable' [reporting from Grenville, see Wallis (1993), p. 121].
12 Another discussion of the communication problem between scientists and policy makers can be found in Ullmo's discussion of French experience (Ullmo, 1979).

13   Whitley does not give a full account – there is doubtless a further story to be told about internal events at the Bank of England which led to such radical changes.

References

D'Alcantara, G., 1988. 'A comparative analysis of actual Dutch macroeconomic models.' In: Driehuis, W., Fase, M. M. G. and den Hartog, H. (eds.), *Challenges for Macroeconomic Modelling*. North-Holland, Amsterdam, pp. 151–214.

Barten, A. P., 1988. 'The history of Dutch macroeconomic modelling (1936–1986).' In: Driehuis, W., Fase, M. M. G. and den Hartog, H. (eds.), *Challenges for Macroeconomic Modelling*. North-Holland, Amsterdam, pp. 39–88.

Van Bergeijk, P. A. G. and Van Sinderen, J., 1997. Models and macroeconomic policy in The Netherlands. Tinbergen Institute Conference Paper (Chapter 3 in this volume).

Bjerkholt, O., 1982. 'Experiences in using input–output techniques for price calculations.' In: Stäglin, R. (ed.), *International Use of Input–Output Analysis*. Vandenhoeck and Ruprecht, pp. 113–29.

Bjerkholt, O., 1998. 'Interaction between model builders and policy makers in the Norwegian tradition', *Econ. Model.* 15, 317–39 (Chapter 10 in this volume).

Bodkin, R. G., Klein, L. R. and Marwah, K., 1991. *A History of Macroeconometric Model-building*. Edward Elgar, Aldershot.

Van den Bogaard, A., 1998. Configuring the economy: The emergence of a modelling practice in The Netherlands 1920–1955. University of Amsterdam, Thesis.

Boughton, J. M., 1997. Modelling the world economic outlook at the IMF: a historical review. Tinbergen Institute Conference Paper (Chapter 8 in this volume).

Bradley, J., 1997. Policy design and evaluation: EU structural funds and cohesion in the European periphery. Tinbergen Institute Conference Paper (Chapter 9 in this volume).

Bray, J., Hall, S., Kuleshov, A., Nixon, J. and Westaway, P., 1995. 'The interfaces between policy makers, markets and modellers in the design of economic policy: an intermodel comparison', *Econ. J.* 105, 989–1000.

Bryant, R. C., Henderson, D. W., Holtham, G., Hooper, P. and Symansky, S. A. (eds.), 1988. *Empirical Macroeconomics for Interdependent Economies*. Brookings Institution, Washington, D.C.

Bryant, R. C.., Hooper, P. and Mann, C. L. (eds.), 1993. *Evaluating Policy Regimes*. Brookings Institution, Washington, D.C.

Den Butter, F. A. G., 1991. 'Macroeconomic modelling and the policy of restraint in The Netherlands', *Econ. Model.* 8, 16–33.

Den Butter, F. A. G., 1992. 'Scope and limitations of statistical methods for macroeconomic forecasting', *Kwantitatieve Methoden* 13, 5–21.

Centraal Planbureau, 1995. Alternatieve financiering van de sociale zekerheid: Plan van van Elswijk (Alternative financing of social security: the plan by Van Elswijk), CPB Werkdocument No. 79, The Hague.

Church, K. B., Mitchell, P. R., Smith, P. N. and Wallis, K. F., 1995. 'Comparative properties of models of the UK economy', *Natl. Instit. Econ. Rev.*, pp. 59–72.

Coase, R. H., 1937. 'The nature of the firm', *Economica* 4, 386–405.

CPB Netherlands Bureau for Economic Policy Analysis, 1997. Scanning CPB: A view from the inside, Self-assessment report.

Don, F. J. H. and Van den Berg, P. C. J. M., 1990. The Central Planning Bureau of The

Netherlands; Its role in the preparation of economic policy. Mimeo, Central Planning Bureau, The Hague.

Donders, J. and Graafland, J., 1998. 'CPB models and employment policy in the Netherlands, *Econ. Model.* 15, 341–56 (Chapter 2 in this volume).

Donihue, M. R. and Kitchen, J., 1997. The Troika process, economic forecasts and macroeconomic policy in the USA. Tinbergen Institute Conference Paper (Chapter 14 in this volume).

Duguay, P. and Longworth, D., 1998. 'Macroeconomic models and policy-making at the Bank of Canada', *Econ. Model.* 15, 357–75 (Chapter 5 in this volume).

Edison, H. J. and Marquez, J., 1998. US monetary policy and econometric modelling: tales from the FOMC transcripts 1984–1991. *Econ. Model.* 15, 411–28 (Chapter 12 in this volume).

Van Els, P. J. A., 1990. 'Econometric versus quasiempirical models: macroeconomic policy analysis in the Netherlands', *Econ. Model,* 7, 133–47.

Van Els, P. J. A., 1997. Policy-making and model development: the case of the Nederlandsche Bank model MORKMON, Tinbergen Institute Conference Paper (Chapter 6 in this volume).

Van Elswijk, P., 1996. *De markteconomie sociaal ingevuld (Social implementation of the Market Economy).* Van Gorcum, Assen.

Evans, R. J., 1997. Economic models and economic policy: What economic forecasters can do for the government. Tinbergen Institute Conference Paper (Chapter 13 in this volume).

Evans, R. J., 1999. *Macroeconomic Forecasting: A Sociological Appraisal.* Routledge, London.

Fair, R. C. and Shiller, R. J., 1989. 'The informational content of ex ante forecasts', *Rev. Econ. Stat.* 71, 325–31.

Fair, R. C. and Shiller, R. J., 1990. 'Comparing information in forecasts from econometric models', *Amer. Econ. Rev.* 80, 375–89.

Fisher, P. G., Turner, D. S., Wallis, K. F. and Whitley, J. D., 1990. 'Comparative properties of models of the UK economy', *Natl. Instit. Econ. Rev.*, pp. 91–104.

Fisher, P. G. and Wallis, K. F., 1990. 'The historical tracking performance of UK macroeconometric models 1978–85', *Econ. Model.* 7, 179–97.

Faulhaber, G. R. and Baumol, W. J., 1988. 'Economists as innovators: practical products of theoretical research', *J. Econ. Lit.* 26, 577–600.

Galison, P., 1997. *Image and Logic: The Material Culture of Microphysics.* University of Chicago Press, Chicago.

Habermas, J., 1968. *Technik und Wissenschaft als 'Ideologie'.* Suhrkamp Verlag, Frankfort am Main.

Henderson, Y. K., 1991. 'Applications of general equilibrium models to the 1986 tax reform act in the United States', *De Economist* 139, 147–68.

Kærgård, N., 1997. A history of Danish econometrics. Royal Danish Agricultural University, unpublished paper.

Kenway, P., 1994. *From Keynesianism to Monetarism: The Evolution of UK Macroeconometric Models.* Routledge, London.

Latter, A. R., 1979. 'Some issues in economic modelling at the Bank of England.' In: Ormerod, P. (ed.), *Economic Modelling.* Heinemann, London, pp. 25–39.

Llewellyn, J., Potter, S. and Samuelson, L., 1985. *Economic Forecasting and Policy – The International Dimension.* Routledge and Kegan Paul, London.

Martens, A., 1986. 'Round-table discussion: The use of models in a policy environment.' In:

Martos, B., Pau, L. R. and Zierman, M. (eds.), *Dynamic Modelling and Control of National Economies*. Pergamon Press, Oxford, pp. 1–5.

Mayes, D. G. and Razzak, W. A., 1998. 'Transparency and accountability: Empirical models and policy-making at the Reserve Bank of New Zealand', *Econ. Model.* 15, 377–94 (Chapter 7 in this volume).

McNees, S. K., 1990. 'Man vs. model? The role of judgement in forecasting', *N. Engl. Econ. Rev.*, pp. 41–52.

Miles, R. and Snow, C., 1992. 'Causes of failure in network organizations', *California Managem. Rev.*, pp. 53–72.

Morgan, M. S., 1990. *The History of Econometric Ideas*. Cambridge University Press, Cambridge.

Mourik, T. J. and Boeschoten, W. C., 1994. 'A check on the forecast performance of macroeconometric models: a case study for The Netherlands', *Econ Fin. Model.* 1, 139–50.

Nelson, R. H., 1987. 'The economics profession and the making of public policy', *J. Econ. Lit.* 25, 49–91.

Nelson, R. R., 1995. 'Recent evolutionary theorizing about economic change', *J Econ. Lit.* 33, 48–90.

Nelson, R. R. and Winter, S., 1982. *An Evolutionary Theory of Economic Change*. Belknap Press, Cambridge, Mass.

Nonaka, I., 1991. 'The knowledge-creating company', *Harvard Business Rev.*, pp. 96–104.

Polak, J. J., 1998. 'The IMF monetary model at 40, *Econ. Model.* 15, 395–410 (Chapter 4 in this volume).

Polanyi, M., 1958. *Personal Knowledge*. Routledge, London.

Polanyi, M., 1996. *The Tacit Dimension*. Routledge, London.

Review Committee of the CPB, 1997. Scanning CPB; A view from the outside. A review of the research activities and policy analysis undertaken by CPB, Netherlands Bureau for Economic Policy Analysis.

Siebrand, J. C., 1988. 'Macroeconomic modelling for economic policy.' In: Driehuis, W., Fase, M. M. G. and Den Hartog, H. (eds.), *Challenges for Macroeconomic Modelling*. North-Holland, Amsterdam, pp. 99–149.

Siviero, S., Terlizzese, D. and Visco, I., 1997. Are model-based inflation forecasts used in monetary policy-making? A case study. Tinbergen Institute Conference Paper.

Smith, R., 1990. 'The Warwick ESRC Macroeconomic Modelling Bureau: An assessment', *Int. J. Forecast.* 6, 301–9.

Smith, R., 1994. 'The macromodelling industry; structure, conduct and performance.' In: Hall, S. (ed.) *Applied Economic Forecasting Techniques*. Harvester Wheatsheaf, New York/London, pp. 68–88.

Smith, R., 1998. 'Emergent policy-making with macroeconometric models, *Econ. Model.* 15, 429–42 (Chapter 15 in this volume).

Tinbergen, J., 1936. 'Kan hier te lande, al dan niet na overheidsingrijpen, een verbetering van de binnenlandse conjunctuur intreden, ook zonder verbetering van onze exportpositie? In: *Prae-adviezen van de Vereeniging voor de Staathuishoudkunde en de Statistiek*. Martinus Nijhoff,'s-Gravenhage, pp. 62–108.

Tinbergen, J., 1937. *An Econometric Approach to Business Cycle Problems*. Hermann and Cie, Paris.

Tinbergen, J., 1939. *Statistical Testing of Business Cycle Theories, vol. I and vol. II*. League of Nations, Geneva.

Turner, D. S., Wallis, K. F. and Whitley, J. D., 1989. 'Using macroeconometric models to evaluate policy.' In: Britton, A. (ed.), *Policy-making with Macroeconomic Models*. Gower, Aldershot.

Ullmo, Y., 1979. 'Co-operation between decision makers and experts: the example of medium-term planning in France.' In: Janssen, J. M. L., Pau, L. F. and Straszak, A. (eds.), *Models and decision-making in National Economies*. North-Holland, Amsterdam, pp. 15–25.

Wallis, K. F. (ed.), 1984. *Models of the UK Economy: A Review of the ESRC Macroeconomic Modelling Bureau*. Oxford University Press, Oxford.

Wallis, K. F. (ed.), 1987. *Models of the UK Economy: A Fourth Review by the ESRC Macroeconomic Modelling Bureau*. Oxford University Press, Oxford.

Wallis, K. F., 1989. 'Macroeconomic forecasting: a survey', *Econ. J.* 99, 28–61.

Wallis, K. F., 1993. 'On macroeconomic policy and macroeconometric models, *Econ. Rec.* 69, 113–30.

Wallis, K. F. and Whitley, J. D., 1991a. 'Sources of error in forecasts and expectations: U.K. economic models, 1984–8, *J. Forecast.* 10, 231–53.

Wallis, K. F. and Whitley, J. D., 1991b. 'Macro models and macro policy in the 1980s', *Oxford Rev. Econ. Pol.* 7, 118–27.

Westaway, P. F., 1995. 'The role of macroeconomic models in the policy design process', *Natl. Instit. Econ. Rev.* 1995, 53–63.

Whitley, J., 1997. Economic Models: a Flexible Friend for Policy-Makers? Paper for the 10th Anniversary Congress of the Tinbergen Institute, Amsterdam, published as 'Economic models and policy-making' *Bank of England Quart. Bull.*, 1997, May, pp. 163–73.

Wren-Lewis, S., 1997. Conflicts between macroeconomic forecasting and policy analysis. Tinbergen Institute Conference Paper (Chapter 11 in this volume).

Zalm, G., 1998. 'The relevance of economic modelling for policy decisions', *Econ. Model.* 15, 309–16 (Chapter 1 in this volume).

Index

academic economists 173–4,
    295–8
accountability 93–105
ad hoc instrument approach
    154
D'Alcantara, G. 280
Alexander, S. S. 45, 46
Argy, V. 41, 42, 49
ARIMA models 254, 288–9
Armington, P. S. 120
Artis, M. J. 124
Artus, J. R. 120
Aschauer, D. A. 140
Aubry, J. -P. 59
Aukrust, O. 149, 156, 157

Ball, J. 247
Bank of Canada 57–72, 289
    model development 59–60
    PAQM (Policy Analysis
        Quarterly Model) 68–9
    QPM (Quarterly Projection
        Model) 60, 67–71, 98
    RDX2 model 58, 59–61
    RDXF model 61, 65–7, 70,
        304
    research program 63
    SAM (Small Annual Model)
        62, 304
    see also Canada
Bank of England 180, 244,
    245, 250–2, 290,
    299–300, 302–3, 305
    current use of models 252–4
    Monetary Policy Committee
        179, 224–5
    see also United Kingdom
Barrionuevo, J. M. 124
Barro, R. 130
Barry, F. 131, 141
Barten, A. P. 30, 285
Barwise, P. 245
Baumol, W. J. 282
Beld, C. A. van den 12, 13
Berg, P. J. C. M. den 7, 280

Bergeijk, P. A. G. van 17, 29,
    32, 33, 301, 305
Berk, J. M. 82
Beutel, J. 133
Bever, L. de 59
Bikker, J. A. 80, 81, 82
Bjerkholt, O. 156, 157, 246,
    285, 300
Bjerve, P. J. 148, 149, 150, 153
Black, R. 98
Bluebook 189, 191, 299
Boeschoten, W. C. 77, 81, 82
Boissonnault, L. 40
Bollard, E. E. 98
Bolt, W. 82
Bondt, G. J. de 82
Bonhoff, E. J. 16
Bonner model 287
Boreschoten, W. C. 282
Bouey, G. K. 58, 62
Bovenberg, A. L. 22
Bradley, J. 133, 137, 140, 141,
    143, 292
Brainard, W. C. 79
Bray, J. 247
Brayton, F. 188, 196
Britton, Andrew 214, 216,
    219
Broeder, C. den 81
Brookings model 303
Brown, Gordon 224
Bryant, R. 179, 270, 280, 295,
    298
Budd, Alan 209
Budget and Accounting Act
    (1921) 231
budgets
    balance of payments 45–6
    long-term budget model
        238–9
    national budgeting 148,
        149–51
    United States negotiations
        271–2
    see also public finances

Burns, S. T. 175, 249, 250,
    251, 252
Burrell, A. 248, 251, 252
Butler, L. 70
Butter, F. A. G. den 4, 76, 86,
    282, 285

Camdessus, Michel 113
Canada
    industry structure 284
    inflation 58–9, 63
    see also Bank of Canada
Central Economic Commission
    13, 14, 16, 285
Central Planning Bureau see CPB
Christiano, L. J. 82
Church, K. B. 303
Clements, M. P. 172
Clinton Administration 269
Coase, R. H. 282
Coletti, D. 69, 98
Community Support
    Framework (CSF)
    129–44, 293
    budget 136
    Delors-I 130
    Delors-II 130
    evaluation of 133–6, 142–3
    factor productivity
        externalities 139
    HERMES model 137–8
    HERMIN models 138, 142,
        143
    industrial composition
        externalities 139–40
    JOULE energy research
        programme 138
    labour market externalities
        140
    MEANS programme 143
    objectives 132
COMPACT model 179
competition
    in the modelling industry
        29–31, 34–5, 288

competition *continued*
  policies 32–3
  see also industry structure
competitive advantage 134–5
Congdon, Tim 213, 214,
  215–16
Congressional Budget Act
  (1974) 232
Congressional Budget Office
  (CBO) 239, 271–2
consensus building 189–203,
  214–19, 298–300
consultation economies 11
consumer boom 176–7, 208
consumption, intertemporal
  consumption model
  176–7
Cooley, T. F. 82
cost–benefit analysis 281
Council of Economic Advisers
  (CEA) 230, 287
Cozier, B. 67, 70
CPB (Central Planning Bureau)
  6–8, 10–23, 30, 84,
  266, 268, 272, 284–5,
  289–91, 302, 305
  compared to the RDSN 161
  and employment policy
  11–18
  MIMIC model 6, 10, 17,
  18–23, 32
  preparation of economic
  policy 11, 29
  structure of 34–5
Crockett, A. 117
Crow, John W. 65
CS model 12, 14
CSF *see* Community Support
  Framework (CSF)
Currie, D. 175, 214, 216, 217

Dalen, H. P. van 27, 30
Darby, J. 176
Davies, Gavyn 212, 216, 217,
  218, 219, 220
decision models 147, 153, 155
Deleau, M. 181
Delors-I 130
Delors-II 130
Denmark 287
Dennis, R. 103, 104
Deppler, M. C. 121
deregulation 32–3
devaluation theories 211–13
Developing-Country Models
  123
diagnostic budgets 150
Dicks, G. 248, 251, 252
differentiated products 288–90
Domar, Evsey 47
Don, Henk 7, 260, 264–6,
  267–9, 272–4, 277, 280

Donders, J. 5, 7, 28, 32, 161,
  246, 284
Donihue, M. R. 288, 299
Dornbusch, R. 175
Duguay, P. 57, 65, 66, 103,
  188, 287, 297, 304
Dutch Central Bank 30, 35, 76,
  285
  see also MORKMON model
Dutch economy *see* Netherlands

eco-circ system 149
Economic Outlook (OECD)
  114, 124
Economic Report of the President
  236
Economic and Social Research
  Council 171, 173, 245,
  255
Edison, H. 191, 296, 297, 299,
  301
Els, P. J. A. van 29, 30, 77, 78,
  81, 86, 280, 305
Elswijk, P. van 291
Emerson, M. 129, 134, 142
Employment Act (1946) 231
employment policies 5, 9,
  10–23, 263
EMU (European Monetary
  Union) 178–9
energy taxes 5–6, 35
environmental analysis 159
Ericsson, N. R. 103
ERM (Exchange Rate
  Mechanism) 174,
  177–8, 208–9, 211
ESRC *see* Economic and Social
  Research Council
EUROMON model 82, 84
European Monetary Union
  178–9
European System of Central
  Banks (ESCB) 84
European Union *see*
  Community Support
  Framework (CSF)
Evans, L. 98
Evans, R. J. 288, 299
Exchange Rate Mechanism
  (ERM) 174, 177–8,
  208–9, 211
exchange rates 77, 95–6,
  99–101, 174–6
  4–1 rule 250
  Fundamental Equilibrium
  Exchange Rate 178
  and the IMF model 45–6
  Louvre accord 117
  and monetary policy 66
  Multilateral Exchange Rate
  Model (MERM) 120–1
  overshooting 175

Purchasing Power Parity
  177–8
  Uncovered Interest Parity
  175
  expectations 62–3, 81, 103,
  171–2, 175, 298
externalities 138–42

factor productivity externalities
  139
Fair, R. C. 282
Fase, M. M. G. P. 76, 79, 80,
  81, 82, 83
Faulhaber, G. R. 282
feasible instrument approach 154
Federal Open Market
  Committee (FOMC)
  187–8, 189–90, 299
Federal Reserve Act 187–8
Federal Reserve System 188–9
  Multi-Country Model 122
fiscal policy 5–6, 8, 16–17, 47,
  215–17, 230–4, 271–2
  energy taxes 35
  green taxes 5–6
  marginal tax rates 22
  negative income tax 21
  tax allowances 21
Fischer, S. 143
Fisher, P. G. 179, 280, 295,
  302, 303
Fitz Gerald, J. 133, 137, 140
FKSEC model 18, 82
Folkertsma, C. K. 82
FOMC *see* Federal Open
  Market Committee
forecasting 7–8
  confidence intervals 247,
  249
  and conflicts with policy
  analysis 60–1, 169–74,
  179–81, 247–8, 254,
  288–90
  definition of 170
  performance of models
  60–1, 65–6, 70–1,
  82–5, 157, 171, 248
  and policy errors 174–9
  and policy-making 7–8,
  189–90, 193–4
  private sector forecasting
  173
  see also Panel of Independent
  Forecasters
  see also Troika process
  see also World Economic
  Outlook
  4–1 rule 250
FPS (Forecast and Policy
  System) 98
France 287
  modelling industry 274–5

FRB/GLOBAL model 193
Freedman, C. 57, 59, 60
FREIA model 16, 17
Frisch, R. 146, 147, 148, 149,
    153–5, 159, 162, 163,
    285
Full Employment and Balanced
    Growth Act (1978) see
    Humphrey-Hawkins
    Act
Fundamental Equilibrium
    Exchange Rate 178
FYSIOEN model 80

G-5 meetings 113
Garretsen, H. 82
Gelauff, G. M. M. 6, 19, 32
generational accounting model
    82, 269
Gent, C. van 30
Germany 287, 288
Godley, Wynne 212, 213, 214,
    215, 251
gold standard 291
Goldstein, M. 117
Goodhart's Law 249
Gordon, R. J. 7
government expenditure see
    public finances
Graafland, J. 5, 6, 7, 19, 20, 28,
    32, 161, 246, 284
Gradus, R. H. J. M. 32
Great Depression 4
green taxes 5–6, 35
Greenbook 189, 299
Grossman, S. 95
growth
    accounting framework 236
    Solow-type models 236
    theory 130
    trends 47–8
Guthrie, G. 96

Haan, L. de 82
Habermas, J. 290
Haffner, R. C. G. 29, 32
Hansen, G. D. 82
Hansson, B. 103
Haque, N. U. 123
Harrod, Roy 47
Hartog, H. den 13–14
Hasselman, B. H. 16
Healey, D. 249
Hebbink, G. E. 82
Heckman, Jim 276
Heller, R. 42
Heller, Walter 231
Helpman, E. 131
Henderson, Y. K. 280
Hendry, D. 98, 172
HERMES model 137–8
HERMIN models 138, 142, 143

hits model 238
Hodrick-Prescott filters 70, 71
Holland see Netherlands
Houthaker, H. 178
Humphrey-Hawkins Act 232
Hunt, B. 104
Huxford, J. 96

IMF monetary model 39–51
    case for simplicity 40–1
    and exchange rates 45–6
    and inflation 48–51
    and medium-term growth
        47–8
    origins 39–40
    Polak model 303
    uses 41–5
    see also World Economic
        Outlook (WEO)
income inequalities 262
industrial composition
    externalities 139–40
industry structure 28–31,
    172–3, 271–5, 281,
    283–7
inflation 48–51, 116
    in Canada 58–9, 63
    in New Zealand 94–6, 101
    Phillips Curve models 236
    sacrifice ratio 193–4
    Scandinavian model 157
    United States price-stability
        debate 192–6
    zero inflation costs 195
input-output models 147, 153,
    155, 156, 300
INSEE 260, 287
interest rates 65, 95–6,
    99–101
    and the United States
        recession (1990–91)
        196–202
    Overnight Cash Rate (OCR)
        96
International Monetary Fund
    see IMF monetary
    model
    see World Economic
    Outlook
intertemporal consumption
    model 176–7
investment subsidies 17
Ireland, J. 176
Italy 287

JADE model 18
James, H. 120
Jenkins, P. 60
Johansen, L. 155, 158, 160
JOULE energy research
    programme 138

Kamlet, Mark S. 239
Kearney, I. 133, 137, 140
Keijzer, L. M. 81
Kenward, L. 60
Kenway, P. 170, 174, 175, 297
Keynesian models 4, 5, 10
Khan, M. S. 44, 123
Kierzkowsky, H. 59
Kitchen, J. 239, 288, 299
Klamer, A. 27, 30
Klein, L. R. 4, 7, 130, 147, 303
Knoester, A. 33
knowledge management 293–8
Kremers, 32–3
Krugman, P. 130, 131

labour market externalities 140
Lamont, O. 248
Larosière, Jacques de 113
Larsen, K. A. 150, 158
Lawson, N. 245, 249–50, 251,
    252
Laxton, D. 70, 71
LDCMOD 123
leading indicator models 82,
    117–19
Leitch, G. 248
Leontief, W. 153
Levin, A. 196
Lindahl, Erik 149
Liverpool Model 175, 176
Lizondo, J. S. 46
Llewellyn, J. 280
London Business School 173,
    175
long-term budget model 238–9
Longva, S. 156
Longworth, D. 57, 59, 64, 188,
    287, 297, 304
Louvre accord 117
Lubbers, Ruud 260, 261, 262,
    266–7, 270–1, 274,
    275, 276, 277–8
Lucas, R. E. 4, 40, 79, 82, 85,
    120, 121, 174
Lynch, Lisa 260, 262–4,
    269–70, 271–2, 275–6

M1 58–9, 60, 66
M2 66, 193
McCallum, B. T. 95
McDougall, M. 61
McGuirk, A. K. 120
McKibbin, W. 69
McNees, S. K. 240, 282
macro-modelling industry
    structure 26–31, 172–3,
    271–5, 281, 283–7
Magee, S. P. 178
Malinvaud, Edmond 260,
    261–2, 270, 274–5
Mankiw, N. 83, 173

market structure *see* industry
structure
Marquez, J. 296, 297, 299, 301
Marsh, P. 246
Martens, A. 280, 296
Mason, Sir John 251
Masson, P. 62, 122, 178, 179, 181
Maxwell, T. 59
Mayes, D. G. 94, 96, 98, 99, 246, 292, 305
MCI (index of monetary conditions) 66, 99–105
MEANS programme 143
Meese, R. A. 175
Melo, J. de 139
MERM (Multilateral Exchange Rate Model) 120–1
MESEM model 34
Miles, R. 281, 284
MIMIC model 6, 10, 17, 18–23, 32, 268, 277, 300
Minford, Patrick 175, 176, 213–14, 216, 217, 218, 288
MINIMOD 117, 121–2, 304
minimum wage 263–4, 265, 289
Ministry of Economic Affairs *see* Netherlands Ministry of Economic Affairs
Mintzberg, H. 245
MODAG model 158, 160
Model XII 98
Modelling Committee 160
MODIS model 155–8, 160
monetarism 174–6
monetary aggregates 65, 66
M1 58–9, 60, 66
M2 66, 193
Monetary Conditions Indicator (MCI) 66, 99–105
monetary policy 65, 66
in Canada 57–9, 62–3, 65–8
in Netherlands 85–8
in New Zealand 94–6
Taylor's rule models 236
tools 189
United Kingdom 174–6
United States 187–204
Monetary Policy Committee (New Zealand) 97
Monetary Policy Committee (United Kingdom) 179, 224–5
Monnier, E. 143
Montiel, P. J. 44, 46, 123
Morgan, M. S. 260, 278, 280
MORKMON model 76–89
history 77, 79

policy making and development 85–8
explicit linkages 85–7
implicit linkages 88
role and use in policy-making 83–5
stages of development 77–81
Mourik, T. J. 282
Mowrey, David D. 239
MSG model 158–9
Muellbauer, J. 176
Multicountry model (MCM) 190
Multilateral Exchange Rate Model (MERM) 120–1
MULTIMOD 122, 178, 179
Munnell, A. H. 140
Murphy, A. 176
MX3 model 193

Nadal-De Simone, F. 102, 104
national accounting 148–9
national budgeting 148, 149–51
National Institute for Economic and Social Research 173
Neal Resolution 196
Nederlandsche Bank *see* Dutch Central Bank
negative income tax 21
Netherlands 26–36, 267–9, 288, 302
Central Economic Commission 13, 14, 16, 285
Central Economic Plan 11, 284
Central Planning Bureau *see* CPB
competition policy 32–3
consensus building 300
deregulation 32–3
employment policy 10–18
forecasting and policy-making 7–8
industry structure 28–31, 272, 273–4, 284–5
Ministry of Economic Affairs 30, 33–4
Nederlandsche Bank *see* Dutch Central Bank
Plan of Van Elswijk 291
policy analysis and models 6–7
policy-making 265
public finances 31–2
Social Economic Council 268
supply-side economics 4, 31–4
use of economic models 265
value chain 291–2
see also Dutch Central Bank; MORKMON model

Netherlands Ministry of Economic Affairs 30, 33–4
network analysis 281, 283, 284, 290, 292
New Zealand 93–105, 292, 305
FPS (Forecast and Policy System) 98
inflation 94–6, 101
Model XII 98
Monetary Conditions Indicator (MCI) 66, 99–105
Monetary Policy Committee (MPC) 97
monetary policy implementation 94–6
Open Mouth Operations 96
Overnight Cash Rate (OCR) 96
Policy Targets Agreement (PTA) 94
policy-making 93, 97
Reserve Bank Act (1989) 94
NIESR 260
Nieuwenhuis, A. 33
NiGEM model 82
Nonaka, I. 281, 293, 294, 298
Norway 146–63
industry structure 285
industry structure/ organization 285, 302
institutionalization of policy-making 147
Long-Term Programme 151, 158, 159
MODAG model 158, 160
Modelling Committee 160
modelling tradition 153–9
modelling unit choice 151–3
MODIS model 155–8, 160
MSG model 158–9
national accounting 148–9
national budgeting 148, 149–51
Oslo Median Model 155
policy maker/model builder interaction 159–61
RDSN (Research Department of Statistics Norway) 151–3, 156–62, 302
Nyenrode Forum for Economic Research 7

Office of Management and Budget (OMB) 230
oil crises 4, 115
Okun, Arthur 231
on-looker approach 154
Open Mouth Operations 96
optimal control theory 247, 296

optimalization approach 154
O'Reilly, B. 61
Organization for Economic
    Cooperation and
    Development (OECD)
    114, 124
Oslo Median Model 155
Otani, I. 123
overdetermination problem 118
Overnight Cash Rate (OCR) 96
Owen, D. 79

P-star model 193
Panel of Independent
    Forecasters 206–25, 299
    appointment of 208
    classical theories 213–14
    devaluation theories 211–13
    effectiveness of 220–2
    membership 209–10
    recommendations 214–19
    reports 211
PAQM (Policy Analysis
    Quarterly Model) 68–9
Park, Y. C. 123
Passenier, J. 13, 15
PC-Variant 81
pension reform 263
personal knowledge see tacit
    knowledge
Persson, T. 95
Pesaran, M. H. 244, 248
Phillips Curve models 236
Plan of Van Elswijk 291
Polak, J. J. 40, 41, 42, 44, 45,
    49, 296, 303
Polanyi, M. 293
policy analysis
    conflicts with forecasting
    60–1, 169–74, 179–81,
    247–8, 254, 288–90
Policy Targets Agreement
    (PTA) 94
Poloz, S. 64, 65, 69, 83
Porter, M. 27
Portes, R. 29
price-stability debate 192–6
product differentiation 288–90
productivity 237–8, 240
prognostic budgets 150
programmatic budgets 150
Project Link 117
Psacharopoulos, G. 141
public finances 4–5, 31–2
Purchasing Power Parity 177–8

QPM (Quarterly Projection
    Model) 60, 67–71, 98
Quest-model 6

Rational Expectations
    Hypothesis 171–2, 175

see also expectations
Razzak, W. A. 104, 246, 292,
    305
RDSN (Research Department
    of Statistics Norway)
    151–3, 156–62, 302
RDX2 model 58, 59–61
RDXF model 61, 65–7, 70, 304
Reddell, M. 96
regional aid see Community
    Support Framework
    (CSF)
Reifschneider, D. 188
Reserve Bank Act (1989) 94
Reserve Bank of New Zealand
    see New Zealand
Rhomberg, R. R. 42, 120
Ricardian Equivalence 176
Riches, B. 94, 96, 99
Ripley, D. M. 121
RMSM model 47
Robertson, H. 61
Robichek, W. E. 45
Robin Hood policies 21–2, 300
Robinson, S. 139
Roger, S. 104
Rogoff, K. 95, 175
Rooij, M. C. J. van 82
Rose, D. 62, 83
Rutten, F. W. 14, 32

Sachs, J. 69
sacrifice ratio 193–4
Sala-y-Martin, X. 130
SAM (Small Annual Model) 62,
    304
Saulnier, Raymond 231
Scandinavian model 157
Scanning the Future 268
Schadler, S. 48
Schreiner, P. 150, 158
Schuberth, H. 82
Schumpeterian innovation 294
Scotland, F. 60
Selody, J. 62
Sentance, Andrew 212, 217, 219
Sevaldson, P. 156
Shiller, R. J. 282
Shop Hours Act 32
short-run equilibrium values
    (SREQs) 70
Shoven, J. B. 19
Siebrand, J. C. 285
simulations 12, 14–15, 17,
    19–22, 60–4, 66, 81,
    95, 104, 156, 235–9,
    247, 248, 250–1,
    288–90
    Federal Reserve Staff
    scenarios 189–90, 193–4
    World Economic Outlook
    scenarios 115–19, 122–4

see also forecasting and
    conflcts with policy
    analysis
Sinderen, J. van 17, 30, 31, 33,
    301, 305
Siviero, S. 287
Smith, R. 26, 27, 28, 173, 244,
    245, 246, 281, 283, 295,
    297, 302, 304, 305, 306
Smithsonian meeting 120
Snow, C. 281, 284
Social Economic Council 268
social security reform 263
Solow-type models 236
Spencer, G. H. 121
Statistics Norway see RDSN
    (Research Department
    of Statistics Norway)
standard account of model use
    247–8
Stevens Committee 22
Stokman, A. C. J. 82
Stone, R. 4, 149
Stone, W. M. 4
structure conduct performance
    (SCP) 27
structure of the industry 28–31,
    172–3, 271–5, 281,
    283–7
Su, Tsai-Tsu 242
supply-side economics 4, 31–4
Svensson, L. 95
Swank, J. 82
Symansky, S. 178
SYSIFO model 287

Tabellini, G. 95
tacit knowledge 293, 294, 303–4
Tanner, J. E. 248
taxation see fiscal policy
Tetlow, R. 70, 83
Thiessen, G. G. 59
Timmerman, A. 248
Tinbergen, J. 4, 5, 8, 11, 34,
    147, 154, 280, 284,
    285, 289, 291, 303
Tjan, H. S. 13–14
Tkacz, G. 70
Tobin, J. 79
Toirkens, J. 14
Toulemonde, J. 143
transparency 93–105, 292
Troika process 229–41, 299
    history 230–2
    hits model 238
    integrity of forecasts 239–41
    key indicators 234
    long-term budget model
    238–9
    revenue models 239
    structure of 230
    types of models 230, 235–9

Turner, D. 172, 295

Uncovered Interest Parity 175
unemployment 5, 9, 10–23,
  263
United Kingdom 288, 302
  COMPACT model 179
  consumer boom 176–7, 208
  ERM membership 177–8,
    208–9, 211
  financial liberalization 176
  gold standard 291
  industry structure 286–7
  monetarist experiment
    174–6
  PSBR 220–2
  use of economic models 223,
    244–55
  see also Bank of England;
    Panel of Independent
    Forecasters
United States 288
  Bluebook 189, 191, 299
  Budget and Accounting Act
    (1921) 231
  budget negotiations 271–2
  Clinton Administration 269
  Congressional Budget Act
    (1974) 232
  Congressional Budget Office
    (CBO) 239, 271–2
  Council of Economic
    Advisers (CEA) 230, 287
  Economic Report of the
    President 236
  Employment Act (1946) 231
  Federal Open Market
    Committee (FOMC)
    187–8, 189–90, 299
  Federal Reserve Act 187–8
  Federal Reserve System
    188–9

FRB/GLOBAL model 193
Greenbook 189, 299
Humphrey-Hawkins Act
  232
income inequalities 262
industry structure 173, 286
influence of models 191–2
influence of policy makers
  190–1
minimum wage 263–4
monetary policy tools 189
Multicountry model
  (MCM) 190
MX3 model 193
Office of Management and
  Budget (OMB) 230
P-star model 193
pension reform 263
price-stability debate 192–6
productivity 237–8, 240
recession (1990–91)
  196–202
social security reform 263
welfare reform 262–3
see also Troika process

value chain 27, 29, 30, 281–2,
  290–3, 295
VAR models 82, 98, 170,
  288–9
Verbruggen, H. P. 29
Versailles Summit 113
VINTAF model 14–15, 31, 268
Vlaar, P. J. G. 76, 81, 82
Vollaard, B. A. 31
Vries, M. G. de 120

Wage Act (1970) 13
wage controls 12–15
Wallis, K. F. 170, 171, 248,
  280, 295, 298, 300,
  302, 303, 306

Walsh, C. 95
Wassenaar agreement 16
welfare reform 262–3
Westaway, P. F. 280, 296,
  297
Whalley, J. 19
Whitley, J. D. 7, 79, 171, 176,
  177, 179, 180, 188,
  290, 299, 300, 303,
  305
Williamson, J. 178
Winder, C. C. A. 81
Witteveen, H. Johannes 113
Wolfson committee 6
World Economic Outlook
  (WEO) 113–24
  Developing-Country Models
    123
  evolution of 114–18
  forecasting process 118–19
    evaluation of 123–4
  indicators 117–18, 119
  LDCMOD 123
  MINIMOD 117, 121–2,
    304
  Multilateral Exchange
    Rate Model (MERM)
    120–1
  MULTIMOD 122, 178,
    179
  overdetermination problem
    118
  scenarios 115–17
  World Trade Model 121
  see also IMF monetary
    model
Wren-Lewis, S. 26, 174, 181,
  248, 288
Wright, J. 96

Zalm, G. 32, 161, 290
zero inflation costs 195